Developmental Theory and Clinical Process

Developmental Theory
and
Clinical Process

FRED PINE

YALE UNIVERSITY PRESS
New Haven and London

Designed by Margaret E.B. Joyner
and set in Galliard type.
Printed in the United States of America
by Vail-Ballou Press, Binghamton, New York.

Library of Congress Cataloging in Publication Data

Pine, Fred, 1931–
  Developmental theory and clinical process.

  Bibliography: p.
  Includes index.
  1. Psychotherapy. 2. Developmental psychology.
I. Title. [DNLM: 1. Personality Development.
2. Psychotherapy. BF698 P649d]
RC480.5.P54   1985   616.89′14   84-20841
ISBN 0–300–03308–7 (alk. paper)

10 9 8 7 6 5 4 3 2

To Sandra

Contents

Preface

I feel fortunate to have found my way to work that is endlessly fascinating. Both the developmental process and the therapeutic process are full of surprising and unanticipated shifts and turns, of doors that suddenly swing open to reveal unpredicted dilemmas and resources, of moves toward mastery and failure, resolution or arrest, transformation and continuity in perpetually new guises. The processes stimulate thought; the outcomes invite wonderment.

This book contains a series of interrelated essays on these themes. I have come to them via two routes: first, personal involvement in processes of change—in myself, in my family, in my adult students, and in my patients; and second, observational research, most especially in the mid-1960s under the auspices of an NIMH Research Career Development Award that gave me six precious years of study. Looking back over what I have written, I find that thematic continuity is everywhere. An interest in concrete experience stands at the center of the continuity, as does a related preference for experience-near concepts. But there is an evolution also; the move toward experience-near description, blending into theory, has increased over the years in which these essays were written. And recently, in addition, I have found my clinical and developmental writings to be drawing more closely together, the clinical writings increasingly reflective of a developmental point of view. Thus there are both continuity and change in these essays—the book itself showing these two hallmarks of developmental processes.

In a book on development it seems particularly appropriate to acknowledge my debt to those who contributed to my own. Daniel J. Levinson, early on, taught me that the effort to write clearly forces you to think clearly and helped me to become self-critical regarding my writing. George S. Klein and Robert R. Holt were models for tough-minded creative thinking, and I hope I absorbed that from them. Margaret S. Mahler offered me, through example and through opportunity, access to the intersect between clinical and developmental thinking in a working colleagueship that I cherish. And Leo A.

Spiegel taught me in depth about the vicissitudes of the human mind and human development, with me as the case in point.

I have come to appreciate especially the debt I owe to my patients and to my students. For the last sixteen years, especially in my supervisory work with clinical psychology interns, a blend of developmental and clinical thinking took shape for me. As my students told me about their patients, greatly expanding my contact with clinical material, a process took place that I now recognize contributed to *their* development, to their *patients'* development, and to *my own* development. And my own patients, in a more sustained and also more intimate two-sided process, taught me even as I "taught" them, especially by insisting on being heard in all their specificity and manysidedness. That experience has been invaluable to me and has reshaped my thinking.

Some things hold steady in a developmental process, and for that steadiness I wish to thank Lillian Rothenberg. She brought me unchanging reliability and unconditional loyalty and affection during the sixteen years that we worked together and in which time all the material included herein was written. Not only as secretary and typist, but more especially as confidante and as support and ally, she created a facilitating environment where, often, none existed. But for the accidents of personal history she might have been my professional colleague. As is, she is my friend.

The people whose development I have been able to learn from most close-up and over the longest time span have been my now-adult children, Rachael and Daniel. Their interest in my work, as they came of age, has been immeasurably gratifying, and for that I thank them. But I also thank them for, all along, demonstrating to me with their lives how amazing intrapsychic resolution of personal history can be, how sameness and change are always present, how stress and mastery and disruption and renewal tumble forward in a process of personal becoming. It has been a pleasure to be part of it with them.

And through it all, the sustained partnership with my wife, Sandra, both emotionally and intellectually, has been at the center of my life, in appreciation of which I have dedicated this book to her.

PART ONE

OVERVIEW

1

Developmental Theory
and Clinical Process:
An Orientation and a Framework

This book stands at the intersect of developmental and clinical theory. It addresses a number of developmental problems, problems selected because of their significance in the clinical process. It also addresses a number of clinical problems from the perspective of developmental theory. I believe that these two perspectives, the developmental and the clinical, can enrich each other.

A productive tension between clinical and developmental points of view exists as a potential within psychoanalysis. In one polarity, this tension is between clinical work, on the one hand, and child-rearing and observational studies of development, on the other. In a second, related polarity, the tension is between classical psychoanalysis and psychoanalytic psychotherapy, on the one hand, and clinical work with more severely ill individuals and families, on the other. My own training and experience in classical psychoanalysis have been conceptually elegant and powerful; the psychoanalytic world view, as I see it, has been applied in fruitful and convincing ways in the psychoanalyses that I have received and conducted. On the other hand, child-rearing, observational research on development, and clinical work with nonanalytic patients are often characterized by a process of trial and error, only sometimes eventuating in a clear view, and by a relatively atheoretical stance; and yet these are what my everyday life, both personal and professional, has consisted of to a large degree: developmental research, treatment of and supervision of work with patients unsuitable for classical analysis, the rearing of my children, and, not least, work and observation regarding my own development.

Psychoanalysis, both its theory and its practice, has impressed upon me the way a person carries his life within him, recreating and replaying his inner issues in varying surrounds again and again over time. The organizing role of fantasy and of the repetition of relationships from the past, as well as the continued press of individually tailored urges and the defenses, anxiety, guilt, and gratification associated with them, are omnipresent in clinical work and stand out as the stuff of which life is made. I now realize that I have always been more impressed with psychoanalytic technique than with the particular organizing framework and contents (e.g., structural theory, psychosexual theory) that psychoanalysis adduced through that technique. This is heavily affected by personal style, but I believe it also reflects my training in experimental psychology, where the method had primacy over any specific findings. In any event, this is probably in part why I have been receptive to additional contents as they have come along in the literature and through my experience in developmental studies. I see now, also, that I have experienced the more classical *contents* only as samples of the things that could be heard through open-ended listening and as possible ways of organizing these things conceptually. But the *technique* is compelling in and of itself when one has experienced it as analysand and analyst. What is learned from attention to the transference and to resistance, what the patient brings forth given a context of abstinence, neutrality, and relative impersonality on the part of the analyst, and, most importantly, the amazing power of open-ended listening, all leave an indelible stamp upon the mind.

But child-rearing and observational studies of infants and children growing up, while offering continual confirmation of what psychoanalytic theory and technique have taught, also enlarge the developmental picture in ways that can profoundly alter our view of theory and technique. I can summarize these under three headings: early experience, environmental inputs, and quiet pleasure.

Having seen the impact of the first months of life on the infant, and the ways in which this thereafter, in cyclic fashion, affects parent-child relationships and feeds back upon the child, I find it impossible not to think in terms of the events of the months and years until, say, age three as a primary determinant of subsequent psychological functioning. And those early years are not organized solely around "preoedipal" issues in the classic sense (issues pertaining to early psychosexual phases) but around other aims, experiences, and developmental tasks as well. Issues of basic trust (i.e., of primary object attachment and its affective tone and of expectations with regard to gratification of hunger and relief of distress in general), of self-other differentiation, of the beginning of internal self-regulation, of the core relation to one's inner urges as alien and threatening or as acceptable and susceptible to modification, of primary self-feeling (goodness, esteem), and of an appropriate activity-passivity balance all have, I believe, not only their origins, but a substantial degree of their final form established, in this period. It is not that oedipal-level dynamics and pathology are inconsequential, but I doubt that a child gets stuck on the issues of that level (barring gross parental acting out or gross trauma at that age) if things have proceeded in a satisfactory way until that point.

The second lesson of child-rearing and developmental observation is that the significance of inputs from the primary caretakers is enormous for the infant and young child. The pace, reliability, and dosage of gratification and frustration and of stimulation and protection from stimuli, the affective tone of the parental interaction with the child around feeding, toileting, and around the earliest visual, vocal, and motor play, and the parents' expectations and fantasies about their child (consciously or unconsciously communicated to the child)—all have profound shaping effects, defining in a primary way what is taken for granted about the world and the self-to-be of the child. Although he is not infinitely malleable, the child is nonetheless highly susceptible to influence in that early period well before character has formed. It is character that later acts as the filter and mold permitting the person to maintain a sameness in the face of varying stimulation; but character in that sense is not formed yet in this early period. The early influence of the parental inputs is not only impressive in itself but is one of the major things that the child observer, without access to the inner experience of the child, witnesses and can think about; no wonder, then, that this influences his theorizing.

The third lesson of child-rearing and developmental observation concerns the role of quiet pleasure. For the child with optimal developmental opportunities, there are innumerable periods of quiet play, quiet object contact, and quiet bodily experience that provide low-keyed pleasure in unthreatening doses. I believe that this underlies some of what later appears as comfortable self-feeling and object contact, as resourcefulness and the ability to overcome pain, as positive mood—overall, the underpinnings of healthy functioning. These are "background" experiences, so to speak, not of high intensity; but they are omnipresent in the day-to-day life of the child at home. I believe that their contribution to the developmental process has been insufficiently addressed.

These, then, are three lessons learned through developmental observation and child-rearing. The significance of early experience, of environmental inputs, and of quiet pleasure has not been unrecognized by classical psychoanalysis, but it pays them insufficient heed. The reason has to do with the nature of clinical psychoanalysis as an observing instrument. Thus, as for early experience: the highly verbal enterprise that psychoanalysis is has a better fit with those levels of disturbance that emanate from the period when the growing child himself is more solidly verbal. Oedipal-level pathology is from that later period, is more expressible in words, and is reflected in formed fantasies and wishes. Not that all communication in psychoanalysis is in words; acting and affect in the transference clearly go beyond words. And not that early experience and early disturbance have gone unnoticed in analytic theory and work; by no means. But the Oedipus complex is still widely accepted as the core of pathogenesis in "official" circles. As for the role of parental inputs, we know that every analysis searches out an understanding of the unique individual early environment in which the patient-as-child was reared and does not settle for an idea of an "average expectable environment" (Hartmann, 1939). Nonetheless, the impressive degree to which the adult patient shapes his own life—and the fact that we learn it to be a technical error to fail to see any event, no matter how seemingly beyond the patient's control, as a product of the patient's functioning—tilts the balance powerfully toward an intrapsychic rather than an interactive view. A psychoanalytic theory of reality relations has scarcely been developed (cf. Wallerstein, 1973, 1983a). Finally, the role of quiet pleasure may be subsumed under the (rather vague) rubric of developments in the "conflict-free sphere" (Hartmann, 1939); but, nonetheless, it is conflict that rightly becomes the all-absorbing focus of a clinical psychoanalysis. So, while they are represented in the observations and theories of psychoanalysis, I believe that early experience, parental inputs, and quiet pleasures have been relegated to various second places—second to later (oedipal) experience and disturbance, to intrapsychic determinism and repetition, and to a focus on conflict. In part II of this book these three threads from developmental studies appear again and again.

So much for the tensions within the first polarity: classical psychoanalysis on the one hand and child-rearing and observational studies of development on the other. The second polarity referred to above is between classical psychoanalysis and psychoanalytic psychotherapy on the one hand, and clinical work with more disturbed patients on the other. For fifteen years, at the outpatient clinic of a large urban municipal hospital, I supervised work with (generally) nonpsychotic outpatients who were unsophisticated in the ways of psychoanalytic therapy, often not primarily verbal in their ways of meeting the world, and, especially, beyond-the-neurotic in terms of pathology and coming from often destructive familial and social backgrounds. What impressed me about these patients was the role of failed very *early development*, of destructive *parental inputs*, and of the absence of a solid base of *quiet pleasure* in the course of growing up. Because I chose to supervise students seeing patients variously suited or unsuited to analytic therapy, I have had a good deal of contact with such patients. And all this was going on after I received my own psychoanalytic training and while I was working analytically with my own patients.

Over the years, I now realize, I continually made an effort to develop procedures for working with these patients and a simultaneous effort to integrate this work conceptually with the psychoanalytic work, which had a much firmer intellectual base. Both the technical innovations and the conceptual integration gradually came about through increased reliance on psychoanalytic developmental theory, stimulated by my experiences in developmental research and child-rearing. Thus, the centrality of early experience led to a substantive focus on self-other differentiation and the quality of self experience as well as early oral experience, and to a technical examination of safety and support in the therapeutic encounter. The significance of environmental inputs led to a focus on the patients' reality experiences, both as one of the languages in which the therapeutic work was carried out and for the mutative potential of this work (see chap. 12). And the focus on quiet pleasure and the nonconflictual sphere led to an attempt to understand the impact of the steady ongoingness of the patient-therapist encounter, aside from interpretations. All this is discussed in part III in contexts that include psychoanalytic treatment but also go beyond to modifications of that treatment modality.

One other idea that comes from developmental observation and self-observation (as well as clinical work) serves as an ongoing thread for much of what follows—and that is an emphasis on *moments* of experience. For me, this is not strictly parallel to the other three because I also use it as an analytic tool, a way of thinking, and not simply as an outcome of observation. I am referring to the moment-by-moment variation of experience and the way it is patterned, for all of us, in the course of development. Such a concept permits us to think of developmental outcomes as organized in quite different ways and responsive to work in quite different theoretical-experiential "languages." I shall develop this idea especially in chapters 4, 5, and 12.

PSYCHOANALYSIS AS A DEVELOPMENTAL THEORY

In addition to being a clinical theory—a theory of conflict, pathology, and treatment technique—psychoanalysis is a developmental theory; it purports to say how people develop. Consistent with this, it also lays claim to being a general psychology, not only a psychology of psychopathology. Many of the contributions that are today enlivening the field—especially the writings of Mahler (1972; Mahler, Pine, and Bergman, 1975), Kernberg (1976), and Kohut (1971, 1977)—are ultimately developmental theories (although, of these, only Mahler has based her work on developmental observation). These and other writers, in their diverse and sometimes contradictory formulations, are, I believe, each seeing a piece of the "truth"—that is, are describing real developmental and clinical phenomena, though each of these phenomena may be more true of some moments than of others and may come to be more central in the later functioning of some persons than of others. It has also seemed to me that developmentally based impacts (such as education, identification, and confirmation: see chaps. 10 and 12) are powerful and inevitable elements of what is mutative about psychoanalysis, in addition to insight and even in psychoanalytic technique as it is classically practiced. In all this, developmental and classical psychoanalytic formulations co-mingle and mutually enrich one another.

Indeed, psychoanalysis was offered as a developmental theory practically from the beginning, certainly at least from the time of Freud's rejection of the seduction theory as explanation for the prevalence of certain sexual fantasies, in favor of the theory of infantile sexuality. The latter theory itself and also others—regarding, for example, differentiation of the ego and id from an undifferentiated matrix, the mode and timing of the emergence of the superego, the transformation of traumatic to signal anxiety, and the modes of object relationship that are linked to and carried by drive aims—are basically developmental formulations. But the work that began in the late 1930s with Anna Freud's *The Ego and the Mechanisms of Defense* (1936) and flowered in the 1940s (Spitz, 1945, 1946) and since was based more fully on direct contact with children through child analysis and observational research studies. This difference is not absolute. Clearly, Freud, inevitably and unavoidably as a human being and a father, observed children as well and had a childhood of his own. And equally clearly, the psychoanalytically oriented developmental theorists never worked from pure observation alone but always had in mind the organizing principles of thought and the impressions of hierarchies among phenomena that originated in their experience in clinical psychoanalysis.

Freud himself was grappling with what only later came to be thought of as the developmental (in contrast to the genetic) point of view when he wrote:

> But at this point we become aware of a state of things which also confronts us in many other instances in which light has been thrown by psychoanalysis on a mental process. So long as we trace the development from its final outcome backwards, the chain of events appears continuous, and we feel we have gained an insight which is completely satisfactory or even exhaustive. But if we proceed the reverse way, if we start from the premises inferred from the analysis and try to follow these up to the final result, then we no longer get the impression of an inevitable sequence which could not have been otherwise determined. We notice that there might have been another result, and that we might have been just as well able to understand and explain the latter. The synthesis is thus not so satisfactory as the analysis; in other words, from a knowledge of the premises we could not have foretold the nature of the result.
>
> It is very easy to account for this disturbing state of affairs. Even supposing that we have a complete knowledge of the etiological factors that decide a given result, nevertheless what we know about them is only their quality and not their relative strength. Some of them are suppressed by others because they are too weak, and they therefore do not affect the final result. But we never know beforehand which of the determining factors will prove the weaker or the stronger. We only say at the end that those which succeeded must have been the stronger. Hence the chain of causation can always be recognized with certainty if we follow the line of analysis, whereas to predict it along the line of synthesis is impossible. (1920a, pp. 167–68)

This statement seems to me to be almost as true today, after decades of observational, empirical, and clinical work with young children, as it was when Freud wrote it. Prediction is not our forte. There is too much that we never come to understand about a particular individual at a given moment, and too much that we cannot know about life events to follow, to allow us predictive effectiveness. True, of necessity we predict all the time, in child consultations for example, when we recommend waiting before starting treatment, or recommend starting treatment. Such recommendations are based on implicit predictions about what will or will not happen if development is left to proceed on its own. And, of course, there has been very sophisticated writing on prediction in analysis dating back to the late 1950s (J. D. Benjamin, 1959; Escalona and Heider, 1959).

Freud's statement regarding the possibilities of reconstruction as opposed to the difficulties of prediction (or of "analysis" as opposed to "synthesis") is as good as any working definition of the distinction between the genetic and the developmental points of view in psychoanalysis. Genetic exploration in psychoanalysis is principally reconstructive, whereas developmental exploration is generally ongoing, contemporary, formative. The genetic-reconstructive approach is the way the past of the individual is inferred in any specific clinical treatment, but it has also produced a view of development *in general*. This view is the classical psychoanalytic developmental theory: a theory of psychosexual stages, differentiation of the structures of the personality, and the later developmental steps through the latency and adolescent periods. Developmental observation, with a data base different from the genetic-reconstructive mode, has the potential for noting significant areas of human development that may, for whatever reason, not appear so centrally in a classical analysis; it also has the potential for clarifying *how* (in what timetable, by what steps) certain of the phenomena already spoken of in psychoanalytic developmental theory actually happen. An excellent example is the work on the normal separation-individuation process (Mahler et al., 1975) that spelled out the timetable, behavioral detail, and psychological danger-points of a developmental process (differentiation from merger) which analytic writing had long assumed took place (cf. Freud, 1930; Ferenczi, 1913) but for which the details had not been spelled out.

Developmental study, I believe, is crucial for psychoanalysis, both its theory and its practice, for many reasons. But before elaborating them, I should make clear that I am not arguing for developmental study of the preverbal period alone, or for the relevance of such study to child analysis alone. Development proceeds throughout the life cycle, and the observational perspective, different from the clinical perspective, has a place in our learning about all ages; and what is learned from a developmental perspective has a place in the clinical psychoanalysis of adults as well as adolescents and children. For some, I realize, these are self-evident homilies; for others they represent a potential retreat from learning through the "pure gold" (Freud, 1919) of psychoanalysis. Be that as it may, I would like to attempt to describe some of the potential values of developmental study.

1. From the point of view of psychoanalysis as an intellectual discipline, its clinical work and clinically derived formulations deserve to have a "basic science" aspect, a grounding in what is known in cognitive, motivational, and, for present purposes, developmental psychology. Rubinstein (1974), in a related domain, argues that, although psychoanalysis need not become a neurophysiological theory, it at least should not contradict what is known in contemporary neurophysiology. In parallel form, although psychoanalysis need not become solely a developmental psychology, it at least should not contradict what is currently known about development and, indeed, ought to make use of what is known where relevant. In addition, psychoanalysis cannot afford not to be concerned with communication with other scholars. In beginning his work with recorded psychoanalyses in the mid-1960s, Gill (1965) argued that it was necessary to have a data base, for content and process, that could meet the canons of science for adequate intellectual communication with peers outside the psychoanalytic world. I believe that this benefit can also flow when a developmental theory, as psychoanalysis is, is anchored in in-process developmental study.

2. For each of us, life-as-lived is a developmental process. The devel-

opmental issues of our respective ages are what concern us a good deal of the time: finding and developing a satisfactory relation with a mate, advancing in our profession or training for the profession, child-rearing and having children grow up and leave home, aging, illness, and loss—not to mention the more frequently discussed developmental issues of infancy, childhood, and adolescence. Just as the past is recreated in the transference, so too is it brought to bear by each one of us—patient and analyst alike—in our efforts to grapple with the issues of our particular age. To be in touch with a patient requires a sensitivity to the issues of his or her age, an appreciation of their affective significance in ongoing experience, as a base for understanding their problematic tie to old fantasies, deficits, and attempted solutions. And further, close-up knowledge of development anchors us in the actual ongoing phenomena of, say, childhood, or infancy, or young or later adulthood, permitting us to speak to the patient in a language that resonates with internal experience. If, in a clinical psychoanalysis, we are to recognize the indicator value of certain behaviors in terms of their initial time of emergence and what they imply about conflicts that may still be active, and if we are also to guard against simplistic misuse of developmental concepts (see chap. 15), we would do well to have a close-up view of how development takes place.

To illustrate, let me compare the contributions of Mahler (1966; 1972; Mahler et al., 1975) and those of some object relations theorists who work largely with adult analysands. Mahler's unique contribution, tied to her study of infants and mothers over the first three years of life (and beyond), is to show the extension of object-developmental processes over long time spans and to anchor these formulations with behavioral referents from the actual childhood period. This view of the *extended* time period over which self-other differentiation, formation of object representations, and cementing of object relationships takes place is insufficiently represented in some writings on object relations theory that stem from adult clinical work. Mahler's detailing of that extended period not only gives us a developmental theory that is closer to developmental realities but, in terms of child-rearing, enlightens us regarding the period of dangers to and ameliorative opportunities for these developmental processes. And the anchoring of object-developmental processes to *behavioral* referents (peekaboo games, "customs inspection," elated mastery, shadowing, low-keyedness, excited running away and giddy recovery, refueling, coercing the actions of the mother, and so forth) increases our capacity to recognize indicator phenomena in the behavior of our patients and therefore to talk to them in an interpretive language that meshes more closely with their experience.

Developmental study is of further potential clinical relevance in that it offers us a perspective on what we are doing when we are doing psychoanalysis, that is, on how the process works for therapeutic change (cf. Loewald, 1960). In chapters 10 and 12 I take up this discussion and also suggest how, in selected instances, developmental theory may stimulate technical innovations in nonanalytic treatment situations. And last, awareness of the (at times) magnificence of personal mastery during normal development and the (at times) unceasing and unrelieved extent of the operative pathogenic influences may give us a sense of modesty in our clinical work—both in regard to what the patient achieves and in regard to any personal ambition we may have for the patient against the odds of history.

3. In addition to scholarly communication and benefits for the clinical process, observational developmental study offers psychoanalysis new possibilities for discovery. The power of the individual actor upon a stage of his own creation is what impresses in a classical analysis. Listening to the patient in psychoanalysis puts us compellingly into contact with the urges and the affective and ideational derivatives that Freud conceptualized in his astonishingly unifying drive theory. But baby watching, to take the other extreme, where the inside-the-head content is not available to us but where the mother's ministrations (good enough or failed) are, makes the developmental role of object relationship equally compelling. And similarly, observation of children growing up, of their excited new mastery or their affective depletion in the face of lack, defect, or failure of external confirmation makes the central significance of ego function and self experience immediate and real. Certain data are more compelling from one observational perspective, others from others. We can well use any observational perspective available, and the likelihood that the exterior view will be blended with the interior view is greater when the same observers have experience with both.

PSYCHOANALYSIS AS AN INTRAPSYCHIC THEORY

From the beginning psychoanalysis has been essentially a theory of intrapsychic functioning—though of course the expressions of that functioning in behavior and life-as-lived have inevitably been addressed. This intrapsychic orientation of the theory reflects its birth in the psychoanalytic treatment process and ensures its continued linkage to the therapeutics of that process. At the outset (and predominantly still) the intrapsychic theory was organized around sexual, aggressive, and other drives, although the conception of the relevant intrapsychic features has since been expanded to include ego functions and conscience, object relations, and self experience. The significant features of psychoanalysis that produced a drive-oriented intrapsychic theory can be identified as follows:

Dependence upon reconstruction. Drives are omnipresent in clinical psychoanalytic work. Scarcely a thought, an error, an action, a plan appears that does not, if analytic attention is paid to it, seem to show a connection to drive gratification, defense against gratification and the attendant anxiety, or both. Even when action is involved, real events in the real world involving others as well, it is often possible to see the analysand's determinative influence upon these events—acting in such a way as to allow or force them to happen.

Obviously there are events that are clearly beyond the analysand's power to bring about or prevent, but yet the events achieve meaning for the person in terms of the drives then active or activated by the events. With events that are close to us in time we can often see that it is the person's *response* to an event, his *receptivity* to it in terms of his own drive-defense structure that is at work; but we can also see that the event enters the person's life independently and beyond his power to cause or avoid. This is by no means as evident with events from the distant past. There, the external events, the actions of others, may not be recovered in analysis and what does appear is the drive gratification aspect, the drives (far more than everything else among the original causes) being timeless and capable of appearance in the transference.

But that the person's wishes find their way to gratification via events or that memories may be remodeled in the service of gratification and defense does not imply that the drives were influential before the event. One of the most striking things about drive gratification and drive-derived fantasy is how they can become attached to events after the fact. Developmentally, for example, new meanings can be attached to old behaviors at differing stages of development as new wishes become active. Symptoms, so clearly seen to be overdetermined when painstakingly teased apart in analysis, may not have that full range of meanings for the person when they first crystallize. Rather, a symptom, standing out as a focal idiosyncrasy in the person, becomes a candidate for the expression of more, and yet more, wishes, conflicts, and defensive operations as these emerge and become central over developmental time.

Often, in clinical psychoanalytic work, it is sufficient to see the drive processes—in the stages of initial discovery, and then again and again in the period of working through. And it is often clinically irrelevant whether the drive operated as a first cause or found its way into the system only after the fact, giving continuing force to a particular event. But because patient history cannot be fully recovered, and because the clinical work can proceed on the basis of analysis of drives often without regard to when they entered the psychic system, the reconstructive mode of working in psychoanalysis easily gave support to a theory that, formally, put drive development and vicissitude at its center.

Reasoning from pathology. A second source of the centrality given to drive explanation in psychoanalysis is that analysts draw most of their data from pathological instances. This is not to attempt to turn back the clock and argue for the absolute difference of the normal and the pathological. Far from it. But there are relative differences among people, and relative differences among aspects of each person, from which we can learn a good deal. If at one point in the history of discovery it was important to recognize that those differences are "only quantitative," at a later point it may be profitable to attempt to learn the implications of those quantitative differences.

It was part of Freud's genius to leap from what he saw in his patients and in himself to universals in human development. The background knowledge that made this leap more than just a wild one lay in the fact that all persons are born with bodies and born into families—and from these two givens, much else that Freud observed in himself and others could readily be seen to be, if not universal, at least not unique.

But it seems to me to be precisely the difference between relative normality and relative pathology that, in the latter, the infantile drives retain more dominance over subsequent functioning. (I am speaking here of the neuroses and other milder pathologies that are the bread and butter of classical psychoanalytic work. The severer pathologies, of course, are differentiated additionally by their gross ego pathology.) The work of analysis is to free the patient from such domination by the infantile drives: to free him not only to achieve old gratifications in new ways without anxiety but also to be responsive to current conditions, uncontaminated by the past.

Even within any one person in analysis there is bound to be an important difference between those aspects of his functioning that enter prominently into the analysis and those that, going smoothly, enter only peripherally. Or a difference between the moments when the usually smooth aspects of his functioning enter into the analysis and when not. Often in such instances it is precisely the involvement in drives and in conflicts stemming from the infantile period that makes the difference between what enters and what does not enter the analytic process.

Reasoning from the pathology seen over and over again in clinical work, analysts can readily attribute to the drives a central influence in all aspects of the person's current functioning. It seems to me that the drives play a central role developmentally and that, following Waelder's (1936) principle of multiple function, they enter into all subsequent functioning; but nonetheless we do an injustice to the complexity and richness of human development and functioning if we fail to look at the totality of developmental influences and at times to elevate other-than-drive functions to central importance.

The assumption of an "average expectable environment." Wallerstein (1973) suggested that a psychoanalytic theory of reality is an overdue development, necessary to round out the general theory by exploring the reality context in which drive and ego development take place. He suggested that the assumption of an average expectable environment (Hartmann, 1939) was a useful fiction (as was "good-enough mothering": Winnicott, 1960a) that permitted the theoretical study of drive and ego development while, so to speak, holding reality constant, that is, assuming that its variations were sufficiently minor that they could be ignored.

If the clinical psychoanalyst's dependence upon reconstruction and his reasoning from pathology led to an overemphasis on drive in development, here it was an error from the side of the procedures of theory building (taking one variable at a time) that led to such overvaluation. For every clinician knows that in his work with his patients he can assume neither an average expectable environment nor good-enough mothering in his patient's past. Instead he will continually be impressed with the extensive variations in family structure, behavior, and pathology and will aim for an understanding of the "precise individual environment" and not the average expectable one.

As long as our theory building focused on drive development, the omnipresent drives were bound to be given a central role. With the development of a broader ego theory (Freud, 1923; A. Freud, 1936; Hartmann, 1939) important modifications in that role came to be formulated. If we look to variations in the environment, and especially if we look to development in individuals raised in severely depriving, abusing, or otherwise traumatizing environments, we are increasingly impressed with the influences on development that come from the surround. Whether or not persons reared in such environments become candidates for psychoanalysis, the *phenomena* of their development should come into the ken of psychoanalytic theory—or else that theory will be in the anomalous position of claiming to be a general psychology while it fails to examine development in vast numbers of the world's population.

The core psychoanalytic conception of energy. Although reasoning from reconstructive evidence and from pathology, and excluding profound environmental variations, contributed to the development of a central role for drive in psychoanalytic theory, the principal contribution to that role came from the core theory itself as initially developed by Freud. The sole energy source that psychoanalytic theory dealt with in any systematic way was instinctual energy; the principal explanatory concept—whether for the initial motivation or the continuation of behavior—was drive; and a central concept of psychoanalytic technique is the uncovering of unconscious motivation (via its expression in fantasy and/or the transference). With these being among the great and distinctive discoveries or formulations of psychoanalysis, and with the majesty of Freud's genius behind them, it is no wonder that they retained a central position in psychoanalytic explanation.

Holt (1963) gives some of the historical context in which these formulations developed:

> It is easy to see the origin of the economic point of view in metapsychology in the scientific stir caused [in Freud's day] by the concept of energy. Indeed, it became a kind of hallmark of science to use this concept; a truly respectable discipline, such as Freud always wanted psychoanalysis to be, *had* to consider energies. . . . In the summary of Brucke's lectures on physiology which Bernfeld provides, I want to focus attention on one sentence: "The real causes are symbolized in science by the word force" (Bernfeld, 1944, p. 349). Here is the origin of the dynamic point of view in metapsychology, and of the overemphasis in psychoanalysis on dynamics, considerations of forces. . . . If the only true causes of things were forces, then the only true scientific approach was a dynamic one. (pp. 373–74)

Add to this context of the history of ideas the context of the early history of attacks on psychoanalysis and the many revisions of the theory that neglected or threw out the early drive theory (infantile sexuality), and one sees why the drive theory is jealously guarded by psychoanalysts and its critics are viewed with suspicion or worse. But a general psychoanalytic psychology can only be the gainer for considering in full the complex array of influences on development. These do not operate independently of drive, but nor does drive operate independently of them. All operate in a complex network of human functioning where causes and outcomes like chickens and eggs are constantly cycling back upon one another.

Let me turn to a brief conceptual overview for what is to follow in this book. Intrapsychic and drive phenomena remain central; other features of personal functioning—subsumed under "ego" and/or "self" and/or object relations concepts—are also central; inputs from the environment play a major shaping role. Though the latter remain background for the most part in this book, they are nonetheless acknowledged and respected.

A CONCEPTUAL OVERVIEW

All of development—the construction of character, the ultimate form of individual psychopathology, and everything else human—is constructed out of the interaction between the inborn and unfolding givens of a person and the environmental inputs in his or her life. In terms of their relevance for clinical psychoanalysis, that is, in terms of the assumptions one makes about development from that data base, the inborn givens include the individual's capacities for bodily and object-related pleasures at both high intensities and more low-keyed levels; aggressive tendencies and their expression in destructiveness and/or assertiveness; and the ego apparatuses (Hartmann, 1939) of thought, perception, memory, motility, and affect, which form the underpinnings for learning, internal signaling, and adaptation of all kinds. And in terms of their relevance for clinical psychoanalysis, the environmental inputs include primarily the "whos" and "hows" of the primary caretakers. The whos refer, of course, to the presence of mother, father, extended family (grandparents, siblings), other caretakers, and their ages and experience in childrearing. The hows refer to the whole panoply of variables describing their behaviors: their reliability and availability, their tension or ease, their proneness to overstimulate or understimulate, their tendency to praise or blame, to glow or shame, to forbid or entice, the models they provide for identification, their explicit and implicit teaching, and an endless host of others. In addition, the environmental inputs include the adventitious events of an individual's life: illness, loss of parents through death or divorce, physical accidents, degree of wealth and possessions including toys and the experiences (travel, school choice) that money can buy, the home setting (rural, urban, slum), and again an endless host of other factors. And finally, I would note under "environmental" inputs (though they could as well be included under inborn givens) individual defects of learning or physique and individual variations in height, weight, strength, or beauty. From the standpoint of *psychic* life, these are part of the "external" environment that affects individual development directly and through the reactions they elicit.

As noted, it is not surprising that psychoanalysis made no attempt to systematize all this formally, especially the environmental inputs. The array of such inputs is endless, and the contribution of psychoanalysis lay elsewhere. But they are to some degree systematized within individual clinical psychoanalyses around the history of each individual as it is gradually remembered and reconstructed.

Though I have listed ego apparatuses, drive, and environmental inputs separately, they certainly do not operate separately in the process of development. No one area is untouched by the others. What start out as more or less universal needs and urges are shaped by experience to produce highly individualized wishes, tied to fantasies, that characterize each person and his or her personal biological and experiential history (see chap. 6). It may even be that the "inborn" drives achieve their lasting, sustained, and focused status only as an outcome of increases in memory capacity, object constancy, and differentiated perception (cf. McDevitt, 1980). Environmental inputs, in turn, are organized in terms of the urges in each person. Escalona (1968) has pointed out that each input meets a person with specific characteristics and that the outcome is a specific *experience*; it is this experience, not the input or the state in which it is met, that has the developmental effect, that is stored in memory, that shapes what the person carries away. Both Rapaport's (1951) concept of the drive organization of memories and Kernberg's (1976) of self and object representations tied together by affects as the primary units of mental life speak to the organization of the environmental inputs in terms that emanate from the person's history and present state. And the ego apparatuses, too, do not develop in isolation but are affected by significant identifications and by their tie to conflict or to pleasure as well as by their natural maturation and individualized level of capacity.

Thus far psychoanalytic theory, growing from clinical work, has found it useful to conceptualize the organization of experience around at least four features: drive development, ego function, internalized object relations, and, most recently, self organization and experience (see chap. 5). Each of these "four psychologies" is many faceted and, in my view, adds to but does not replace the others. My clinical experience indicates that no one of these four psychologies has absolute hierarchical superiority to any other. There *is* hierarchical organization in every individual, but this is a matter of personal history and not general theory. Each of these areas of development characterizes every person in some way and it is the task of the listening clinician to hear where centrality lies in a particular individual and to conceptualize with the patient, in everyday language, what the inner arrangements are. It follows from this, and from the general developmental point of view, that things can go wrong in any area. Indeed, everything human develops, and anything in human development can go wrong—not only the stepwise progression through the psychosexual phases, the tie to infantile object relations, the organization and affective tone of the self experience, and the function of every aspect of the ego apparatuses or of the development of ego and superego and ego ideal, but any or all of them, in endless combinations, endless hierarchies, in ways quintessentially individual and human.

PLAN OF THE BOOK

After the second chapter in this part, which includes some further introductory thoughts on the impact of developmental research on psychoanalytic practice and theory, the book is organized in two sections.

Part II consists of a methodological note and six chapters on development, all grouped under the general heading "Aspects of Development from a Clinical Perspective." The chapters in no way comprise a general theory of the developmental process. Rather, they represent approaches to *aspects* of development. I could as well have selected other aspects, but in two senses the choice is not at all random. First, each is an illustration of one or more of the "four psychologies" I alluded to above—the psychologies of drive, ego, object relations, and self—or an explication of the idea of the four psychologies itself. And second, they are all representative of a single approach: the attempt to make sense, *developmentally*, of how certain phenomena seen in the *clinical situation* may come about. The chapters therefore represent developmental perspectives on phenomena that are of unquestioned import to the working clinician.

To give a few examples: my discussion of the developmental centrality of "moments" of intense experience (chap. 4) ultimately comes from experience in my personal psychoanalysis and later in my conduct of psychoanalyses, in which I saw again and again that concrete moments of experience, relived in the retelling, were carriers of intense affect, replete with conflict and generative of painful self-knowledge in the way that no discussion of "patterns" or other evasive generalities could be. The clinical observation was available to me and proved fruitful in my attempts to look in close-up and differentiated ways (again in terms of especially significant moments) at the early psychosexual phases of development and to think through their apparent contradictions with one another and with much of the current infant research literature. Or again, my discussion of psychological structure, organizations of psychic content and modes of function that endure over time (chap. 7) initially grew from the powerful impression of the endless complexity of symptoms and character traits, their multiples of multiple functions (Waelder, 1936) so to speak, as these become apparent in clinical psychoanalyses. This proved serviceable in attempting to understand how psychological organization comes about at least in part via the growth of multiple function over time. And a final example, the question of the development of self experience, examined in chapter 9, clearly arose from the flood of writing on the "self" in the current psychoanalytic literature and my attempt to understand phenomena in my patients from that point of view. My interests have started from the clinical and, as will become evident, led me to specific developmental topics, but not to the construction of a general theory.

Part III consists of six chapters grouped under the heading "Aspects of Clinical Process from a Developmental Perspective." The first three of these chapters, closely related to one another, look at the technique and process of psychoanalysis and of dynamic psychotherapy in general (including so-called supportive therapies) from a developmental standpoint. Once again, the roles of very early experience, of environmental inputs, and of quiet pleasure and other "background" phenomena are given attention. The distinction between interpretive and supportive therapies comes out weakened, as both are seen as interpretive therapies, the classical one involving interpretation in the context of abstinence and the ideal "supportive" therapy involving interpretation in the context of support. This formulation, as will be shown, allows both the theoretical and the technical contributions of psychoanalysis to enrich the intellectual wasteland that supportive psychotherapy has traditionally been. The chapters in this section draw on developmental theory to examine what is mutative about psychoanalysis in particular and therapeutic technique in general and what provides the justification for the several languages of explanation: the "four psychologies" once again, plus a language of experience in reality and of its inputs. The remaining three chapters attempt to shed light on the anatomy of various disturbances by approaching them developmentally. Issues of normal development and ways in which it goes wrong form the underpinnings for a differentiated look, first, at disturbances of learning, behavior, and personality organization (borderline conditions) in childhood, and second, at pathology of the separation-individuation process as it appears throughout the life cycle and in varying guises. Here, as well as throughout all that follows, the effort is made to illustrate the mutual enrichment of clinical and developmental theory.

2

The Impact of
Developmental Research on
Psychoanalytic Practice and Theory

Among clinicians who work with children as well as with adults, it has long been felt that experience in child analysis and/or child therapy has an important and productive impact upon their conduct of adult analyses. Although this is a commonly shared view among child clinicians, it is difficult to spell out just where this impact lies. Recently, with the mushrooming of research on early development, a parallel question has arisen: What is the impact, if any, of early developmental research on psychoanalytic theory and practice? In this chapter I shall address this question in several ways, focusing especially on practice. While my main intent is to discuss the impact of early developmental research on practice, it is not possible to disentangle this fully from the effects of child clinical work and of a broad developmental point of view. All will enter into the discussion to some degree, while the last of these, the impact of a broad developmental point of view, will be treated more extensively in the final section of the book.

Let me begin with a review of some of the regions of early developmental research: My list begins with René Spitz, who introduced the mother into psychoanalysis. Although analysts knew that a mother was important, she had not yet found her way, with full scope, into their theories until Spitz (1945, 1946) brought her there. His early hospitalism and group home studies brought issues of attachment and loss, and of adequate stimulation of the infant, to the fore. Though there are reasons to question the inevitability of marasmus and infant death as he observed them, there has been ample subsequent evidence of the close relationship between inadequate stimulation and massive developmental delay—for example, in the systematic study conducted by Provence and Lipton (1962) of infants in institutions. John Bowlby (1969, 1973, 1980), in his ethologically tinged work on attachment, separation, and loss (as well as his 1944 study of the history of early separation in the lives of delinquents-to-be), Martha Wolfenstein (1966, 1969), in her clinical case-study approach to a child's reaction to the death of a parent, and a host of others have continued in this tradition and elaborated upon the theme. The impact of deprivation in major sense-receptor areas, especially vision and audition, with their reverberating impact upon maternal depression withdrawal and upon the whole infant-mother relation (e.g., Omwacke and Solnit, 1961; G. S. Klein, 1962), has been in part a spin-off of this work.

Spitz's (1959) work on the "organizers"—the nonspecific smile, stranger anxiety, and the evolution and position of the "no" response—began to open up a second major research region: the infant's capacities for cognition, communication, and control as they are played out in the mother-infant reciprocal interaction. Stern's (1971, 1977; Beebe and Stern, 1977) truly imaginative studies and methodological innovations regarding mother-infant face-to-face gaze interaction and, more recently, sound-to-sound vocal interaction, Sander's (1977) studies of mother-infant rhythms and attunement, Klaus and Kennell (1976) on early "bonding," and Brazelton's (e.g., Brazelton et al., 1975) infant studies have enlightened us on infant-mother attachment and attunement. At the same time, these studies and the many others on "the competent infant" (Stone, Smith, and Murphy, 1973)—that is, on the perceptual and cognitive capacities of the newborn in the earliest weeks and months—show us the infant as a complex and capable young organism, differentially responsive to stimuli, and thus anchored to reality from the outset.

A third region of research to highlight is infant-mother differentiation. Here, too, Spitz (1957) played a seminal role in his descriptions, inferred from infant observation, of the differentiation of the "not-I" from "I" and, later, of more complex cognitive precipitates of experience, the "other" from the "self." Mahler (1972; Mahler, et al., 1975) is the person most associated with the full explication of this developmental theme in her formulations regarding the symbiotic origins of mother-infant attachment (or, as I would prefer, the symbiotic aspects of that attachment, occurring at affectively significant *moments*), her studies of symbiotic psychoses (1968), and, most important for my topic here, her studies of the separation-individuation phase and process, and the subphases of differentiation, practicing, rapprochement, and object constancy.

A fourth region of research is that embodied in the various works of Stoller (1968) on gender, of Money and Ehrhardt (1972) on genetically aberrant births, of Roiphe and Galenson (1982) on normal and disturbed development in the second year of life, and of others who have contributed to our understanding of the formation of gender identity by the end of the second year, well before the oedipal period. This work has important implications for the development of body-intactness fantasies and of perversion.

No survey of regions of research that have had an impact on psychoanalytic theory and practice can omit reference to the distinctive contributions of Winnicott (1958a, 1965). All the others mentioned above include relatively systematic empirical or more broadly observational research, while Winnicott's work reflects essentially that of an individual who is intimately familiar with mothers and infants, who proceeds by way of an exquisite capacity for inference—or an exquisite imagination, if you prefer—who feels his way into the infant and the mother and tells us what it's like inside, how things get formed, what they mean to one another, and the like, and whose clinical psychoanalytic reports are at one with, permeated by, his developmental concepts. Influenced by M. Klein (1921–45) and her emphasis on the earliest months of mother-infant experience, he abandoned her reconstructive approach and concepts distant from anything knowable about infant mental life, replacing them with concepts tied to inferrable infant-mother experiences drawn from their actual actions and interactions.

There are undoubtedly other regions of research that come to mind when considering the impact of early developmental research on psychoanalytic theory and practice, but these serve as a starting point. Now to the real question: What can be said about their impact, especially on practice?

As noted above, infant researchers, as well as analysts whose work includes the treatment of children, often feel that those infant/child experiences pervasively affect their clinical work with adults. Yet, they are typically vague when they try to state just how, just what this effect is. Still, there must be something. When I raise this ambiguity with students whom I supervise in adult work, they almost unfailingly tell me that the developmental orientation clearly shows in my supervision (in contrast to their other supervision), but they, too, cannot put their finger on just how. So what is this phenomenon that is both there and not there? What follows is clearly one person's viewpoint; any effect so intangible and difficult to express must be in substantial part a matter of personal style. One thing I can assert, though: Any or all of the effects of child developmental research upon practice are only *potential*. There is no doubt that large numbers of practitioners are unaffected by them at all.

Let me group the effects into five categories:

1. *A climate of thinking.* Not all early developmental research has point-for-point correspondence with variations in technique. In fact the largest impact is, rather, in the establishment of a whole climate of thinking, in the sense that Freud's original contribution created a whole "climate of opinion" among educated persons. This entails a set of *receptivities* to various modes of understanding clinical phenomena. First, there is a receptivity to concepts close to that of *mothering*, such as Winnicott's (1963a) "holding" environment and Kohut's (1971) "mirroring," and more broadly to concepts of mutual interaction and shaping within a family surround. This is so because, as discussed in chapter 1, infant observation teaches us the power of caretakers. From the couch, we know only of the patient's thoughts; caretakers (and the "other" altogether) appear only as thoughts, memories, fantasies. But in infant observation, lacking access to the infant's inner life, what we see is infant and caretaker interaction and their progressive shaping of each other. And that shaping is impressive in degree. So we are receptive to concepts implying the role of the other, the mother, the primary caretaker—and for that matter, of fathering too.

Second, there is a receptivity to concepts of *deficit*. Seeing development as a process of construction, and aware of the multitudinous ways in which the construction can go awry (in the taming of motility, the organization of memory, the modulation and differentiation of affect, the socialization of thought, the interiorization of defense, and the organization of character, among others), we take deficit concepts (in interconnection with conflict concepts) as natural, not at all foreign. These dual receptivities—to the role of the other and the role of deficit—affect clinical work, I believe, largely through matters of phrasing, tone, and tact. The result is not radically different from classical technique but is rather subsumed within it. It is often present only subtly and "indigenously," and that is why it is hard to point out the effects precisely.

Finally, there is a receptivity to *diverse* modes of formulating developmental and clinical phenomena—in terms, say, of drive, ego function, object relations, and self experience (see chaps. 5 and 12). It was Freud's genius to synthesize the cacophony of clinical phenomena that he and every analyst hear into his organizing concepts regarding psychosexual phases and their unfolding, interaction, and penetration into every aspect of adult function. But observation of the growing infant and child shows that synthesis to be too exclusionary, subsuming too much under it. For the child, I believe, experience is differentially organized at different moments—now around drive, now around ego function, now around object connection, now around self; and these organizations are affectively significant and deserve to be represented in our clinical thinking. Observations of infants and children tend to promote receptivity to these varied concepts because they have a natural fit with the observed experiences of the child. This will then inevitably affect what the analyst's free-floating attention lights upon in the patient's material and how he subsequently conceptualizes it. Although the analyst works with "evenly hovering attention," a prepared mind has much in it to hover *over*, and it is principally what is in the prepared mind that will subsequently serve as the organizing framework of an individual session.

2. *A language of communication.* Early developmental research affects the practice of psychoanalysis in the language that the analyst (*at times*) uses in speaking to the patient, or, more precisely, in the phenomena to which that language refers. Knowing the significance of early gaze and vocal/nonverbal interaction between mother and infant, aware of phenomena like the "practicing" of motor-independence activities, of shadowing, low-keyedness, and coercion—all drawn from Mahler's (Mahler et al., 1975) work—and feeling convinced of the power of early infant-mother bonding and of the gap left when early attachment has been interrupted or underdeveloped, the analyst can at times speak to the patient in a language closer to his or her early experience, hence more evocatively in terms of the recovering of memories and more empathically in terms of understanding inner experience. The other side of this coin is that the analyst can be attuned to current behaviors of the patient that hark back to these early phenomena and thus can get cues to where the patient is at. Just as it is true that we want to be sensitive to triangular conflicts as guideposts to the oedipal period, so is it true that we

want to be sensitive to, for example, shadowing and coercion as guideposts to unresolved issues of the rapprochement period.

These points apply not only to the findings of early developmental research but to the analyst's familiarity with the childhood period in general—with phenomena of the nursery, the family dining table, the classroom, the playground. For a language close to the patient's concrete experience is evocative in the way that visual images of a dream are suggestive for associative content, in the way that return to the site of an old experience leads to a rich recall of the past, in the way that the taste of a madeleine released a flood of childhood memories in Marcel Proust (1918).

Beyond the specifics of infancy and childhood that the developmentally experienced analyst may bring with him to adult analyses is a broader view of life itself as a developmental process. Blos (1962), for example, exemplifies this in his writing on adolescence, especially on the developmentally significant integrative work of the late adolescent period. I recall having commented to a colleague that a certain oddity in another colleague was a real achievement, not a failure, albeit a negative achievement. My friend looked puzzled and then lit up with recognition: "Oh," he said, "you mean it's *character*!" And, as I thought about it, that *is* what I meant. But the differing way of thinking is not inconsequential, because the developmental view (seeing it as "a negative achievement") readily becomes a language to which patients can respond with recognition; "character" remains to find a language in terms of clinical process. A developmental view of the life process leads to the recognition that every age has its issues—whether it be the feeding and toilet training of infancy, the learning and peer-relatedness of childhood, the independence and sexuality of adolescence, the mating, child-rearing, and work of adulthood, or the decline and losses of old age. Attunement to these issues (just as to, say, rapprochement or oedipal issues) addresses the patient where his life's action currently is. I am not suggesting a psychoanalysis of current events, but I am suggesting that, as in the transference, old conflicts and defensive styles are reexpressed in the way people deal with their current life issues, and familiarity with both the legacy of the past and the nature of current issues at every life phase enriches an anyalsis.

3. *Modifications for psychoanalytic psychotherapy.* In this area, for the sake of brevity and for illustrative purposes, I will draw only upon some of my own work. It is not an area of psychoanalysis proper, especially when we consider psychoanalytically oriented *supportive* therapy, but it deserves mention nonetheless. The work I refer to evolved from my supervision of interns and residents who work with child and adult patients, many of them ranging between mildly and grossly unsuited for what usually goes under the name "psychoanalytic psychotherapy." In an effort to make that work ethically tolerable, clinically satisfying, and intellectually stimulating for myself and my students, I have often found myself bringing alternative approaches (such as focused therapy, brief therapy, family and individual therapy combinations) to bear on it. The alternative approach that seems to have been most fruitful is the one that relates developmental thinking to these difficult-to-impossible

therapeutic endeavors. In chapter 10, I try to spell out some of the ways in which psychoanalysis, as it is ordinarily carried out, includes a development-facilitating *ground* (in addition to an interpretative *figure*); but especially, I try to apply conceptions of how development ordinarily takes place to clinical situations of *failed* development, in an active attempt to facilitate belated development in the areas of failure. Additionally (see chap. 11), I have tried to apply some conceptions regarding child-rearing, specifically regarding growth in what I call the area of optimal strain, to interpretive psychotherapy with fragile or otherwise unreceptive patients. That work involves a view of the parental role in not allowing things to be either too easy or too difficult for the growing child, a view that optimal growth comes at various junctures with optimal strain. The technical interventions I propose are aimed at giving fragile, panic-prone and flight-prone patients active support in the here and now of the patient-therapist interaction so as to enable the patient to work with interpretive content. The intent, to increase the defense and object-relational support structure while increasing the anxiety level (through the introduction of sometimes painful interpretive content), is to support the patient's tolerance for strain at a higher level of demand. This is based not on the "good-enough mothering" or "primary maternal preoccupation" of the infancy period but on what I regard as significant parenting functions later on in development, those involved in providing a setting of optimal strain to facilitate but not overwhelm growth possibilities.

4. *Applications in early interventions.* This, too, is not psychoanalysis proper but it should be mentioned, even if only briefly.

By detailing the markers and time span of separation-individuation, early gender formation, the earliest infant-mother gaze, affect, and rhythm at-tunements, early developmental researchers have enabled us to intervene in more knowledgeable, precise, and less diffusely "kindly" ways in faulted early developmental situations. Thus, in a paper on "Ego Disturbances," Redl (1951) writes: "This short paper . . . sets itself a limited task: to lure the practitioner into becoming much more impressed with the need to be very specific in the use of the term 'ego disturbance' and to stimulate the clinician to seek a much wider repertoire of techniques whenever he is confronted with the task of 'ego support' " (p. 273). He then illustrates specific areas of deficient functioning that may require specific kinds of intervention. Harrison and McDermott (1972), who reprinted this paper in their volume on child-hood psychopathology, introduce it with the following editorial comment: "Teasing out the precise aspect of ego function requiring specific differential therapeutic attention in lieu of global support for a vaguely defined 'weak ego' transforms an impossible task into a [merely] difficult one" (p. 532).

Infant researchers have similarly provided the knowledge and some tools for making the task of early intervention only a "difficult one." Thus, Mahler's (Mahler et al., 1975) description of the slow course of the child's emergence from symbiosis through a long separation-individuation process alerts us to the extended time span during which appropriate interventions can be made in faultily proceeding developmental situations and gives us subphase-specific behavioral markers (stranger anxiety, facial exploration, and so forth) that aid in the evaluation of how the process is going for the child. Beebe and Sloate (1982) have applied specifics of their knowledge stemming from work on infant-mother interaction to the treatment of a seriously disturbed infant-mother pair, with some success.

5. *Negative effects.* This is an aspect of early developmental research that *is* directly related to psychoanalysis in impact—unfortunately, probably substantial in scope. I refer to the misapplication and/or overreliance on concepts drawn from such work. My own unhappy experiences with this have been centered mostly in the area of separation-individuation, not surprisingly, because I have often been asked to chair conferences on patients where separation-individuation pathology was said to be central and I would find myself (depending on the context) educatively or embarrassedly or impatiently trying to explain what in my view separation-individuation pathology is and is not (chap. 15). New concepts, unfortunately, are half-ignored and half-overextended. The overextension and misapplication of Mahler's concepts have been very apparent. But I believe this is also true of "holding" and "mirroring" concepts. It is not that they have no place, but they have been overextended, at the price of simplistic thinking, sometimes simplistic technique, and often simply intellectual error.

So much for the regions of early developmental research and some of their effects on clinical practice. I have said that some of these effects are only potential (that is, many practitioners are unaffected by them) and others are negative. Let me add that the aim of early developmental research is *not* to "get the facts," as though knowledge of the "facts" could or should replace the emphasis on analysis of *psychic* reality in later clinical work (Schafer, 1983a). Only in the region of early intervention does this getting-the-facts have a possible immediate applicability. In ordinary clinical work it is, of course, the "facts" as subjectively experienced, remembered, and transformed that remains the only appropriate focus, and the one that permits work within the patient's subjective reality.

Let me now turn to the third area for discussion: the need for modesty in attributing effects on practice to infant development research.

The truly amazing thing about psychoanalysis, both its practice and its general theory, is how much has been learned or inferred about development from clinical work itself—from the analysis of transference, acting out, and other repetitions, from attention to memories, and from reconstruction. I am referring not only to Freud's (1905) creative synthesis of free associations, and knowledge of perversion and of foreplay, into his conception of psychosexual stages. For Freud, and others after him, also recognized phenomena of merger, symbiosis, and differentiation: the "oceanic feeling" (1930) and Ferenczi's (1913) work on stages in the development of the sense of reality immediately come to mind. And although Freud (1915) recognized the significance of the object, in his theory at least, primarily as the end-point in the search for gratification, his clinical work, most especially that of transference, implicitly held a concept of object representations and of repetition of old object relationships. Melanie Klein (1921–45), in her portrayal of early drive processes in object-incorporative and object-expulsive terms, and Fairbairn (1941) after her, in his emphasis on the object-seeking (not only pleasure-seeking) nature of drives, clearly brought the object, the primary caretaker, into the developmental theory of psychoanalysis. And although issues of self-esteem were dealt with primarily in terms of the theory of libidinal drives (e.g., castration and phallic pride) or of ego ideal, and although the "self" was often ambiguously blended with the "ego," concepts of self and self-esteem were clearly present and utilized.

In fact, one can look at the effects of infant research in reverse: the effect of psychoanalytic theory and practice on early developmental research. Many or most of the significant contributors to those areas of infant research that have impacted upon psychoanalysis have been shaped first by clinical practice and psychoanalytic theory, which have influenced what they looked for, what they saw, and how they formulated it.

One must also recognize that good clinical practice has probably always been ahead of clinical or general theory. Thus, although we have no general theory of reality relations and the role of the family surround (cf. Wallerstein, 1973), analysts work with their patients not in relation to their "average expectable environment" (Hartmann, 1939) but to their unique individual one. And though object loss as an actuality did not begin to reach its full significance until after Spitz's (1945) (and related) work, the role of separations around vacations, the "Monday crust," and other interruptions was part of the day-to-day work of every clinical psychoanalysis. And, I suspect, a softening of the analytic stance with more seriously ill and depressed patients was widespread: an automatic establishment of a more "holding," more empathic environment, the recognition of deficit states regarding ego function and faulted early dyadic experiences. *Psychoanalytic theory* may have been strongest in the domain of the neuroses; but the humanity and interpersonal attunement and broad knowledge of their own and others' struggles in the course of development led at least many practicing *psychoanalysts* to work in ways, and with mental contents, that we can now formulate more clearly in part because of research on early development.

As I have said, although I suspect that good clinical practice early on worked with what *later* could be conceived of as the impact of early developmental research—a receptivity to the role of caretakers, to phenomena of deficit, and to diverse (drive, ego, object, self) ways of formulating things as well as a sensitivity to the actual phenomena of infant and child life as they echo in the analysis—a theory was not always available to formalize these ways of working. Many social-psychological features of the world of analysis slowed the development of such a theory. These include the awesome power of Freud as mentor and of one's own analyst similarly; the need for referrals, which lead to caution in what one presents about one's work to the world; the ease with which the motives of revisionists can be interpreted in this field (i.e., the resort to ad hominem argument) and the "timelessness of teaching," that is, the tendency to teach what we were taught rather than what we ourselves have come to think or do. But the advent of child analysis and then of early developmental research, providing a new data base and anchored in the data-gathering frame of reference of the larger science outside the analytic community, helped to change this in some ways, so that variations of developmental theory and to a lesser extent of technique began to find formal places for themselves.

The present is certainly a time of ferment in psychoanalytic theory. The thrust given to an object relations theory by Sandler and Rosenblatt's (1962) work on "the concept of a representational world" and by aspects of Mahler's (Mahler et al., 1975) and Kernberg's (1976) developmental formulations, and the thrust given to formulations centered on a "self" embodied in aspects of Schafer's (1976) and George Klein's (1976) work as well as, quite differently, Kohut's (1977) work, add to our earlier drive and ego psychologies to give a multi-faceted theory that permits rich new possibilities for encompassing the vicissitudes of the developmental process and the exigencies of clinical work. Although as I have said regarding the impact of developmental research on clinical practice, point-for-point correspondence of developmental research and new directions in theory cannot be supported, the cultural climate (of which developmental research is a significant part) sets the tone for new ventures in thought that culminate in new directions in theory.

Other things play a role, too, in the evolution of ideas. Original minds sensitized by personal history to additional aspects of clinical and developmental reality come along. The natural disinclination of creative people to settle for what has been handed down, their inclination instead to have a new say, also adds to our ways of seeing things. The "widening scope" (Stone, 1954) of psychoanalysis, as practitioners see a broader set of pathologies and attempt to spread the psychoanalytic contribution to formerly excluded patient groups, provides a new clinical data base that leads to the evolution and enhancement of theory. But among these background factors in the evolution of psychoanalytic theory, early developmental research certainly holds a prominent place. The encounter with the cognitive capacities of the newborn, with the mutually interactive infant-caretaker role, and with the time, timing, and observable events of specific pieces of the developmental process cannot help but provide a soil for the development of a theory, broadened in some aspects, perhaps overstated in others, at varying distances from actual clinical work, and yet ultimately contributory to a general psychoanalytic developmental psychology.

PART TWO

ASPECTS OF DEVELOPMENT
FROM A CLINICAL PERSPECTIVE

3

A Note on Method

Webster's Dictionary (1971) defines "essay" in two principal ways: "an analytic or interpretive literary composition usually dealing with its subject from a limited or personal point of view"; and an "attempt; an initial tentative effort." The chapters in this part should be seen as essays in both senses.

Although they are *informed* essays, I cannot point to a solid evidential base for them. They reflect a point of view, a way of thinking. A great deal of psychoanalytic writing is really in the form of essays, however presented. Even clinical case reports, subject to shaping influences both in the conduct of treatment and in the writeup of the work, are not exceptions to this. I believe this is inevitable. The attempt to describe the development and functioning of the human mind in psychological terms is not yet an objective scientific endeavor. But I believe that thoughtful, reasoned, internally consistent, experience-near writings can order the phenomena of mind for us at least tentatively in ways that can be useful both clinically and in stimulating further thinking.

Material drawn from a clinical psychoanalysis may lead us to convincing formulations regarding functioning and history in the individual instance; though these in turn can be suggestive for more general formulations, they are certainly not decisive. And systematic experimental studies of development do not fill the gap; in general these are (and must be—by the limits of experimentation) aimed at discrete areas of function and lack the holistic view that I undertake here. Finally, although some in-depth longitudinal studies do permit formulations of the kind that I undertake here (e.g., Mahler et al., 1975), they simply do not exist for most areas of development and, indeed, are themselves subject to the essayist's art or error. So, given these realities,

A portion of this chapter is based upon material originally published under the title "In the beginning: Contributions to a psychoanalytic developmental psychology" in the *International Review of Psychoanalysis*, 8:15–33, 1981.

one can wait or one can try; I tried. In this double sense, then, these chapters are essays: they are statements from "a limited and personal point of view" and they are "attempts." While I draw upon what I have experienced and learned from clinical work, observational studies, child-rearing, and self-observation, these chapters are certainly not summaries of "data." Equally certainly they do not represent deductions from a general theory, although they are informed by psychoanalytic theory throughout. Predominantly, they are exercises in thought.

The mode of thinking represented in the style and conceptual intent of what follows is experience-near, developmentally descriptive, and, to the limits of my ability, highly differentiated. Clearly, all of these represent choices. That it is *experience-near* is a choice based on the belief that a study of development, even a clinically and theoretically inspired one such as this is, can and should seem reasonable and real, close to point-at-able phenomena. By and large, I attempt to avoid using metapsychological concepts unless I can define them in experience-near terms. I am not taking a stand against metapsychology; I simply do not find it useful or necessary in the enterprise undertaken here. That the way of thinking is developmentally *descriptive* is problematic at times because this entails shortfalls in theoretical explanation throughout. I cannot propose an array of basic concepts and their hierarchical relationships, such as may be found in a fully developed theory. Rather, I worked from the view that description should come before explanation and, beyond that, that the flow back and forth between the two domains should and can be an easy one. And finally, that the way of thinking about development is *highly differentiated* reflects the actualities of the developmental process. Though organizing concepts are surely necessary to orient us among multitudes of data, the fact of development, like the fact of a clinical psychoanalysis, is discrete, differentiated, never-ending in its complexity. In a psychoanalysis, major interpretations, which come only periodically, organize large amounts of the clinical phenomena in sometimes astonishingly rich ways. The same can be true of developmental formulations, where the movement between differentiation and synthesis can enrich our understanding.

Developmental formulations oriented toward psychoanalytic concepts but based on observational studies are subject to the criticism that they are drawn from material lacking in access to subjective experience. This criticism is especially apt and powerful when it comes to formulations regarding the preverbal period, where such access is absent not only in fact but in principle. How can we proceed in drawing inferences regarding the period of infancy in particular? Do we have to abandon the whole project? Clearly the project has not been abandoned, and for good reason. Working clinicians—and it is working clinicians who have made the major contributions to psychoanalytic developmental theory—are again and again drawn to formulate developmental hypotheses in order to make sense of content, process, and organization issues in their patients.

So how should we proceed with inferences? The following holds for most hypothesis formation in psychoanalytic developmental theory: we learn what we can of inner life by self-observation and by verbal reports from others (usually patients); we trace these data back in individual history as far as memory allows; and then, beyond that point, we make inferences. The inferences should have two overriding characteristics: first, they should have a certain "psycho-logic," that is, they should fit with and not violate what we believe we know of human functioning; and second, they should be based on observations which, from the outside, appear to bear on the phenomena that we later know from the inside (through self-observation and patient report). Thus, Freud (1900), in discussing dreams of flying, questioned how such dreams (well before airplane flight was common) could be accompanied by actual sensations of flying. His answer: every infant has experiences of being swooped up into the parental arms—hence, of "flying." The source of the later reported interior sensation (of flying) is explained by inference from something that seems to be related to it from an exterior view. In our (Mahler et al., 1975) research on symbiosis and awareness of separateness, we worked similarly: knowing that both these cognitive-affective states exist in the older child and in the adult, and not assuming them to be inborn, we looked at early mother-infant interaction to see what inferences we could make regarding the ways in which ideas of merging and ideas of separateness come into being. Specifically, we looked for behaviors that, in *exterior view*, were suggestive regarding the development of *internal* ideas of merging and separateness. Like all inferences, such an inference clearly is not proof against error; however, it should be seen that it does have a logic and a rationale.

Peterfreund (1978), in "Some Critical Comments on Psychoanalytic Conceptualizations of Infancy," criticizes psychoanalytic notions of an "undifferentiated phase" as well as the language used to describe the infant in general. I shall use several of his points as means of entry into a discussion of inference regarding infancy and early childhood. He concludes: "I believe that meaningful psychoanalytic theories of infancy will not emerge from the current metapsychology but from different frames of reference—neurophysiological, biological, genetic, evolutionary, informational—all of which are basically consistent with one another" (p. 440). And at the outset he states that psychoanalytic conceptualizations of infancy go awry largely because of "two fundamental conceptual fallacies especially characteristic of psychoanalytic thought: the adultomorphization of infancy, and the tendency to characterize early states of normal development in terms of hypotheses about later states of psychopathology" (p. 427). Although I believe that there is considerable justice in Peterfreund's critique, I view it as a challenge to be met rather than as a basis for discarding a psychoanalytic developmental psychology. The challenge is to see whether thoughts drawn from adult experience and from psychopathology can be useful in our attempt to understand infant experience and, more generally, to see whether a phenomenologically recognizable and conceptually fruitful approach to infancy can be set forth using a familiar language of psychoanalytic psychology without abandoning that language for neurophysiology, genetics, information theory, and the like.

Since there is clearly no self-evident value in retaining a traditional psy-

choanalytic language, the justification for making the effort to do so should
be made explicit. First and foremost, I do it because I think it can be done
and because that language deserves to exist in parallel with any other languages of description and explanation. Second, it is to use a language that
will permit us as working clinicians to relate our experiences, won in work
with patients, to normal developmental theory. And third, the retention of
a psychoanalytic developmental language is based upon the assumption that
infancy is continuous with childhood and adulthood and that the use of a
common descriptive language will help highlight those continuities. This is
not to suggest that there may not be discontinuities as well or that other
theoretical languages may not enhance our understanding; but it is intended
to reemphasize the obvious fact of developmental continuity. We are all one
species, and each of us is one person from birth to death.

I believe that the potential gains from using a language that brings out
continuities between infancy and normal adult life or between inferred infant
experience and psychopathological states are threefold. First, since we cannot
know the inner experience of infants firsthand or by direct report but can
know this for the childhood and adult periods, the assumption of developmental continuity alerts us to look for *possible beginnings* in infancy of states
and experiences that we know to exist later on. Granted that adultomorphization may result from such thinking; but so, too, may developmental understanding. This is a potential gain in our understanding of *earlier* phenomena
by drawing on *later* ones. The reverse also holds: potential gains may be
made in understanding *later* phenomena by drawing on *earlier* ones. That is,
because we generally hold a developmental concept of pathology in our
clinical work, and because one of our common ways of "explaining" a particular psychopathological product is to trace it back to its earlier and earlier
presumed beginnings, a conception of those beginnings in earliest infancy
can potentially enhance our understanding of the origins and development
of psychopathology. Granted this can lead to circular reasoning, but it can
also lead to useful hypotheses. And finally, a conception of infancy and early
childhood in psychological terms, a conception that helps us to understand
the infant's experience and how early events take place, may provide us with
advantages in clinical technique. Thus, it may enable us to speak to patients
in a language phenomenologically closer to inner experience. Also, it may
lead us to a conception of how events that did not take place earlier should
normally have taken place (e.g., defense formation, object constancy), and
this may at times provide hypotheses regarding specific technical interventions
(see chaps. 10 and 11). These are all *potential* values in a language of developmental continuity. They can be fulfilled, missed, or corrupted, depending
upon the success of the enterprise. It seems to me that the risks are well
worth taking and that the enterprise should be cautious, experience-near, and
not inconsistent with empirical data.

In elaborating his criticism that psychoanalytic theorists tend to understand infants (both their pathology and their normal development) in mis-
placed adultomorphic terms, Peterfreund (1978) gives the example of Mahler's

(1966) comment on the "omnipotence" of the infant or of the omnipotence within the "dual-unit" (the merged image of mother and child in the child's mind). He takes such concepts to task as unproductively adultomorphic. (Indeed, I believe that they can also be productively adultomorphic.) He writes:

> To spell out the situation a bit, since the term "infantile omnipotence" pervades psychoanalytic literature, an infant may scream and make what *adults* consider to be impossible demands. But we must recognize that the infant knows no other way, in contrast to adults who have other capabilities. The infant's apparently "omnipotent" behavior has a totally different significance from that of an adult who acts similarly. (p. 436).

Of course that is true. But the relevant developmental concept of infantile omnipotence has nothing whatsoever to do with making "impossible demands." Instead, it has to do with internal experiences, inferred on the basis of observation and what we know of later experience. The attack under the banner of adultomorphism does not hold up, and I can use a response to it as an illustration of reasoning in this area.

As with "merger" experiences, we know that experiences of the "omnipotence of thought" (Freud, 1913a), in the sense that the thought equals (brings about, causes) the deed, are present in adult functioning. Though perhaps clearest in some obsessional neurotics, it is also present in all of us at times in certain intense relationships (child/parent, spouse/spouse, analysand/analyst) where the expectation is that one's unspoken thought should be known to and acted upon by the other. Where might such an idea come from? An answer is suggested through an external look at the infant's experience, coupled with the understanding that the infant does not have an adequate conception of causality. We make the inference that the infant's experience of need, regularly followed by the arrival of comfort (sometimes even before he cries), leads to an inner experience of "omnipotence." "My thought, my need, my wish, brings relief" (that is, not "my mother's actions" but "my need"). We believe that such experiences underlie the later experience of omnipotence of thought. Omnipotence is, then, not the attribution of adult-like "impossible demands" to the infant but an attempt to infer the way events in the infant may be experienced. And it is attributed not arbitrarily but in an attempt to make sense of the development of such magical thinking in the adult. The child's painful loss of omnipotence, which Mahler (1966) writes of, has its source in the growth of self-other differentiation *and* more realistic notions of causality.

It seems clear that such reasoning about development could be wrong, but it is not unreasonable. The effort to understand early development proceeds in two complementary directions. In one, an attempt is made to understand the historical basis for a phenomenon that we discover in some adults in psychoanalysis ("my thought should be your command") by looking (again from the outside) at certain behaviors and events in infancy that appear to be related to it, and we then propose that these are possible developmental forerunners. In the complementary direction, we develop hypotheses about possible inner states of the infant drawn through apparent parallels to reportable adult subjective states. Neither of these modes of thinking is anywhere near foolproof. But if the tasks of developing hypotheses about infant inner states and about infant forerunners of adult experience are not to be summarily discarded, it seems to me that these are reasonable ways to proceed. As long as such hypotheses are recognized as hypotheses, as long as they do no violence to other known facts, and as long as they are formulated with caution and precision, it seems to me that they reflect a productive use of "adultomorphic" thinking about infancy. The use that I shall make later of concepts like "structure" (chap. 7) and "self" (chap. 9), as well as my emphasis on the significance of "moments" (chap. 4), also reflects this attempt to move productively back and forth between phenomena of adult psychoanalysis and (inferred) phenomena of infancy in order to develop formulations about each.

Problems of inference to subjective states exist for observational studies of the postinfancy (i.e., verbal) period as well, as do problems linked to the fact that we cannot understand developmental significance solely from the present import of events but also have to understand it through subsequent outcome. But here, even more readily than in formulations regarding infancy, observers who are steeped in the triple vantage points of clinical psychoanalysis, self-observation and memory, and observational research will of necessity bring all these to bear in the attempt to understand any given phenomenon. That such attempts may be for good or ill goes without saying. Ideas from one of the domains may be used too readily to color and distort understanding in another. But potentially, and ideally, enrichment of formulation can also come via the triple vantage point. Theoretical formulations regarding development, in such instances, move from the external to the internal, from the observed to the inferred, with a grounding in subjective experience, with knowledge of the ways in which events and newly emerging functions become absorbed into ongoing modes of a person's functioning— all coming from experience in clinical psychoanalysis and self-analysis.

In any event, although the inference process represented here is certainly subject to criticism, we cannot, I believe, simply replace it by inference drawn from reconstruction in psychoanalysis. Nor will experimental research easily fill in the gap. Each has its contribution to make. I do not believe that psychoanalytic data are necessarily "pure gold" (Freud, 1919); this is often a fiction. We know well that personal (countertransference) issues can lead to profound distortions in our understanding of the data of a psychoanalytic session, and so, too, can firmly held theoretical predilections. The data are soft and easily molded. Properly conducted, with allowance for time, waiting, and rethinking, the clinical psychoanalytic process has built-in correctives for such distortions. But there is nonetheless no doubt that psychoanalytic data are subtly and profoundly malleable. In an exhaustive examination of interpretation, which steadily bears upon psychoanalytic evidence, Spence (1982) convincingly details the pervasive opportunities for omission, selection, and distortion throughout. This is not to say that our concepts regarding the overall body of psychoanalytic data are not compelling and useful but that in *individual instances* we cannot take the reported phenomena automatically as solid evidence.

We can all adduce examples—impressive, amazing sometimes—of the way in which diverse contents of a psychoanalytic session can come together with a convincing parsimony and conceptual elegance. In some published papers "beautiful examples" of sessions reflect such "good analytic hours" (Kris, 1956a). But there is a deceptiveness here if we imply (and students, unfortunately, often think we do) that this is what sessions are regularly like. Uncertainty, openendedness, puzzlement are equally often the order of the day. No single mode of observation, psychoanalytic or otherwise, has a corner on the market of potentially fruitful insights.

In the chapters that follow in this part, an attempt is made to describe development in experience-near, in-process terms—at times, I recognize, more successfully than others. The objective is to take clinically relevant concepts and to understand how development happens in relation to the phenomena to which they refer. While I hold as background what I am familiar with from observational developmental studies, psychoanalytic process, child-rearing, and my own interior world, the end result is essentially a product of the thinking and reasoning that selects among and organizes the material of these several domains in ways that are meant to fit with recognizable experience as well as general theory. I shall first discuss "moments" (and "backgrounds") of experience as a step toward more differentiated thinking, and then shall go on to discuss issues in the areas of the "four psychologies" of drive, ego, object relations, and self.

4

Moments and Backgrounds
in the Developmental Process

Gradually, throughout this book, I intend to put forth a moderately expanded view of developmental and clinical concepts that, for me, are consistent with psychoanalytic theory. The developmental concepts address what might be thought of as different motivational, or behavior-inducing, systems in the child, or as different developmental lines (A. Freud, 1963). The clinical concepts run parallel to these because the adult patient on the couch was once the child who had these experiences and carries them within in developed and altered form.

To encompass this expanded view, I shall emphasize moments of experience—both in the developing child and in the clinical situation—moments in which experience of quite different kinds is laid down in memory or repeated in treatment. The argument for this emphasis on moments is presented in this chapter, contrasting moments of high affective intensity to other "background" phenomena (which are themselves other "moments"). In the following chapter I shall use these ideas to work toward a more integrated view of the several conceptual languages of psychoanalysis in relation to developmental and clinical process.

INTRODUCTORY REMARKS

A close look at the earliest phases of infant life, and at the "phase" concept itself, has the potential for supporting more differentiated thinking about human development. A focus on "moments" in particular permits the reconciliation of psychoanalytic formulations with those of other research that reveal additional and contradictory aspects of infant function. The flood of recent research on "the competent infant" (Stone et al., 1973)—that is, re-

This chapter is based upon a portion of "In the beginning: Contributions to a psychoanalytic developmental psychology," *International Review of Psychoanalysis*, 8:15–33, 1981.

search on the perceptual, cognitive, and relational "competencies" already present in the earliest days and months of postuterine life—demands some revision in the psychoanalytic concepts of oral, or symbiotic, or undifferentiated phases. I do not believe that these concepts need be abandoned— only modified; and recognition of the moment-by-moment variation in the infant's functioning will provide a tool for that modification. Since (it will be argued) the phenomena relevant to the psychosexual and object-relational phase concepts are momentary in nature, there are many moments left in the infant's day in which the competencies may be found—without any necessary contradictions in our view of what the infant is like. I shall develop this emphasis on moments below, in relation to phases; it will later (chaps. 5 and 12) turn out to have clinical usefulness as well.

MOMENTS AND BACKGROUNDS IN THE DEVELOPMENTAL PROCESS

Through the telescope of psychoanalytic treatment (A. Freud, 1951), the distant look backward through reconstruction of the past, depth of field is ordinarily lost, as it is in the optical instrument as well. Events are foreshortened or, at least, duration is difficult to estimate. Were the (adult) patient's childhood oedipal anxieties at crisis intensity for several days, several weeks, several months? Did the period of anal retention and mother-child battle over it last for months? Years? Was the infant's emergence from symbiosis a developmental event of brief or extended duration? Ordinarily, reconstruction does not permit us to say.

The reconstructive telescope creates other (historical) perceptual distortions as well—most significantly in its tendency to focus on highly valent, high-intensity experiences—on figure rather than ground. Not only because such experiences are likely to have more residua in the pathology, showing up in bits of memories, moments of acting out, transference repetition, but also because by their very nature they are more articulated experiences, focal and highly valent events and mental states are more likely to be refound through reconstruction. Background factors, part of the quiet flow of the child's life, are less likely to be thus re-found.

Yet, to understand development and to take a differentiated look at the period of infancy, the duration of events (moments vs. continuities) and their degree of intensity or articulation (figure vs. ground) are of crucial significance.

Moments. Let us first look at the idea of moments of experience, and start (somewhat indirectly) by asking: What phase is the child in during the second year of life? The anal phase? The separation-individuation phase (Mahler, 1963)? The phase of formation of basic gender identity (Stoller, 1968; Money and Ehrhardt, 1972)? All of them? How many phases can a child be in at one time? The answer is that the child can be in a great many so-called phases simultaneously because the phase concept does not speak to the totality of his experience at any one age—even though the concept is often used carelessly as though it does just that. Rather, I believe, the phase concept is more appropriately used to refer to a period of peak intensity and peak developmental significance of certain (whatever) phenomena, without prejudgment of their duration. If the phase concept refers to moments, albeit significant moments, of the person's experience, then there is room for many such moments in the day and therefore for the coexistence in time of many so-called phases.

But such moments are, in fact, what I believe the phase concept must refer to. The child in the anal phase is not living an all-anal life. Motor development, play, cognition and the understanding of reality, residual oral phenomena, and precursor conscience phenomena are all parts of the life of the many-sided one- to two-year-old. But anal phenomena, events having to do with the production and/or withholding of feces, with the mother's caretaking/cleaning of the child's body, with early efforts at toilet training and its associated smiles and grimaces as rewards and punishments, and with the mental phenomena accompanying all of these, come to be increasingly *central moments* in the child's day—central in that they are associated with high-intensity bodily sensation (around defecation and body cleaning) and high-intensity object relations (around toilet training and, again, cleaning). As such they have a psychological significance far beyond what can be measured by their temporal duration. The affective intensity (pleasurable, painful, and a mixture of the two) associated with such moments of anal centrality give those moments great importance. There are additional ways also to look at their importance. Thus, Rapaport's (1951) concept of the "drive organization of memories" alerts us to the fact that, early on, memories and percepts get organized around such high-intensity moments. And Greenacre's (1958) discussion of how developmentally co-occurring events can put their stamp on one another is also relevant. Indeed, her example deals precisely with the way in which anal-zone issues affect attitudes around the (simultaneously occurring) development of speech—with the withholding or "foul" expulsion of speech; the use of words to attack, smear, or give a "gift"; the concept of "verbal diarrhea" and parallel "verbal constipation." Such concepts help us to understand the mechanisms through which high-intensity "anal moments" have an impact far out of proportion to their temporal duration.

The fact that these moments are likely to occur most frequently in the second and third years constitutes the justification for calling this period "the anal phase." But the term can lead to confusion because, as already stated, that time period simultaneously encompasses the separation-individuation phase and probably untold others as well. More accurate than the term "anal phase" would be something like "the period of critical formative events in the anal line of development." Such a phrase does not seem to exclude the idea that the second and third years may simultaneously be the critical formative period in numerous other lines of development as well.

I have dwelt on the anal phase at some length because I believe that it includes phenomena that we know reasonably well and therefore can serve as a clarifying example, and also because the ideas that I have tried to formulate are applicable to all phases and, most notably for the purposes of this book, to early infancy as well. Thus the normal symbiotic phase (Mahler, 1963) is not "all symbiosis" for the infant; nor is the normal autistic phase all nona-wareness of the surround. In the light of data from experimental research on infancy regarding cognitive development (Stone et al., 1973) and mother–infant attunement (Sander, 1977), the concept of normal symbiosis can be meaningfully applied only to high-intensity, affectively significant *moments* of the infant's day. Thus, the postnursing moments of falling asleep at the mother's breast or in her arms against her body, especially since they follow and powerfully contrast with moments of distress and confusion during crying and hunger, are moments, like the moments of anal centrality, that are likely to be psychological highpoints of the infant's day and thus to become organizing nodes for other experiences. These moments (which look from the *outside* as though they could be accompanied by merging, melting, bound-aryless experiences in the infant) are among the justifications for referring to this period as the normal symbiotic phase—or, better, as the period of form-ative impact of experiences of boundarylessness.

To look at the neonate in a conceptually differentiated way, we have to look again in terms of moments. Just as the several blind men who each touched a different part of the elephant described it in differing ways, so too would the sighted observers who see the infant only at particular moments describe it in different ways: as a red-faced, bawling protoplasmic mass; as a soft, limp, sleeping one; as an organism organized around vigorous sucking activity and food intake; as a quiescent organism capable of sustained gaze. Wolff's (1959) round-the-clock observations of infants, for example, led him to describe a period of "alert inactivity" (awake, not vigorously crying in hunger, not drowsing off into sleep) during which the infant is capable of sustained gaze and visual tracking of moving objects. This period, a period of the neonate's perhaps most advanced cognitive or precognitive activity, can be seen for only a few moments during the first twenty-four hours, with a gradual but progressive increase in the time spent in alert inactivity over the next few days. States of distress, of gaze focus, of sleep, and others all belong to each and every infant.

To describe the infant as "undifferentiated," as though that captured the developmental psychological significance of all the varied aspects of its day, is clearly a vast oversimplification. Instead, we might have to think in some such way as the following: that visual fixation during alert inactivity is the starting point of wakefulness, reality attunement, and perceptual-cognitive activity; that distress and crying are the starting point for all frustration and negative affect with flight reactions, defense activity, and affective expression; and that nursing and falling asleep at the breast mark the beginnings of directed (individually preferred) drive gratification and object relationship.

Before turning to conceptual domains in which these views are particularly helpful (normal autism and symbiosis, for example), I should like to discuss another aspect of early development that permits further differentiation of our view of infant experience and that, once again, is better seen through the microscope of observation than the telescope of psychoanalytic reconstruction. I refer to what I described earlier as "ground" in contrast to "figure," that is, to quiet, low-keyed, and continuing background factors in the infant's experience. These, too, are moments, but moments of very different affective intensity, yet with their own formative impact upon the developing child.

Backgrounds. To my mind the most exquisite attempts at description of such background factors are Winnicott's, expressed in his many writings on the infant–mother relationship and captured overall in one of his book titles: *The Maturational Processes and the Facilitating Environment* (1965). In trying to show how the environment facilitates development, he builds on the idea that contrasts, interruptions in continuity, make for awareness, and the reverse for nonawareness (background quality). By analogy, a person floating in water that is exactly at body temperature would lose many of the usual cues (muscle tone and temperature variation) for awareness of the body; the contrast of body and surround would be minimized. Winnicott writes of a similar perfect fit in mother–infant relations, producing a similar state of nonawareness in the infant:

> If the mother provides a good enough adaptation to need, the infant's own line of life is disturbed very little by reactions to impingement. . . . Maternal *failures* produce phases of reactions to impingement and these reactions interrupt the "going on being" of the infant. An excess of this reacting produces not frustration but a threat of annihilation. . . . In other words, the basis for ego establishment is the sufficiency of "going on being," uncut by reactions to impingement. (1956, p. 303; emphasis added)

Winnicott here tries to capture the sense of uninterrupted continuity of existence ("going on being"), core to the later experience of self, at its point of (imagined) origin. When needs are perfectly met, experience flows. Interruptions in such perfect meeting of needs break the continuity of experience but, if they are timed and dosaged correctly, lead to other aspects of ego organization. Here, in the same paper, is Winnicott's way of emphasizing the *background* nature of the facilitating environment (the mother's caretaking):

> What the mother does well *is not in any way apprehended* by the infant at this stage. . . . In the language of these considerations, the early building up of the ego is therefore *silent.* . . . According to this thesis a good enough environmental provision in the earliest phase enables the infant to begin to exist, to have experience, to build a personal ego, to ride instincts, and to meet with all the difficulties inherent in life. (p. 304; emphasis added)

And with slightly different emphasis elsewhere:

> It is axiomatic in these matters of maternal care of the holding variety that when things go well the infant has no means of knowing what is being properly provided and what is being prevented [i.e., what stimuli the mother is warding off]. On the other hand it is when things do not go well that the infant becomes aware, not of the failure of maternal care, but of the results, whatever they may be, of that failure; that is to say, the infant becomes aware of reacting to some impingement. As a result of success in maternal care there is built

up in the infant a continuity of being which is the basis of ego-strength; whereas the result of each failure in maternal care is that the continuity of being is interrupted by reactions to the consequences of that failure, with resultant ego-weakening. (1960b, p. 52)

The quiet continuity of experience, when needs are met reasonably well and therefore do not become imperious and disruptive, when the facilitating environment is "silently" (from the infant's point of view) doing its job, is what I refer to as a "background" experience and is what Winnicott here asserts is critical for early ego development. Later (chap. 6), when I discuss the so-called undifferentiated phase from the point of view of regulation of the infant-mother exchange (Sander, 1977), it will be clear that early object relationships must have their origins in these quiet background moments as well as in the high-intensity interchanges.

A second example comes from White's (1963) work on "independent ego energies." Drawing on a review of research on curiosity, exploratory behavior, and play in animals and children, White advances the hypothesis that there are independent ego energies ("independent" in that they are not derived by neutralization from drive energies) that are available to the organism from the start of life and are connected with the functioning of the motor, perceptual, and cognitive apparatuses. He uses this concept to advance the idea that the child develops "feelings of efficacy" (the ability to do things, to have an impact, to *matter*), growing into a more general feeling of *competence*, as he or she exercises motor and cognitive capacities in exploration and play. Attunement to reality and enhancement of self-esteem are among the significant developmental achievements that are carried by such activities and their accompanying feeling tone.

White in this area, like Winnicott in his, emphasizes what I am calling the "background" quality of these exploration/play activities and their accompanying affective states. In contrast, when bodily needs or intense psychological/affective states are aroused, they take center stage. The exploratory and play activities, for all their contribution to development, go on only in quiet times, in the infant's "spare time." In White's words:

> Earlier in the essay effectance was described as an energy that operates freely in the infant during the spare time that is not occupied by aroused instinctual urges or by sleep. When instinctual drives are aroused, the activity of the nervous system—the "ego apparatus"—is directed toward instinctual aims. Only when drives are quiet does the system operate in the pure service of feelings of efficacy, and with the breadth and nonspecificity that is most conducive to the growth of varied competencies. In the newborn infant there is very little of this spare time, though exploratory activity can be detected virtually from the start. By the end of the first year, however, playtime may amount to as much as six hours of the child's day, manipulation occupies great stretches of his time, and exploration has become a very obvious part of his behavior. (p. 85)

White's point is that a lot is happening developmentally when the infant is "just" filling his "spare time" with play.[1]

Taking his argument one step further, White suggests that a certain portion of the pathology in pathological development should be attributed, not alone to defects in early drive regulation and object relation, but to the interferences of those two with the child's capacity to engage in quiet play and therefore with the fulfillment of the developmental functions of exploration and play. "When deprivation and anxiety are very severe, so that the infant when awake is constantly yearning for instinctual gratification and security, exploratory play, *the spare-time activity between periods of crisis* [ground vs. figure], may simply be swamped and crowded out" (p. 190; emphasis added). How might such a "crowding out" exert developmental effects? White's ideas suggest, for example, that the natural attunement of the perceptual apparatus to the "world out there" provides a basis for our thinking of reality appraisal and secondary process functioning not simply as detour activity en route to drive gratification (Freud, 1900). Quite the contrary; this attunement is a *stabilizer* of interest in reality apart from cyclic drive activation and serves significant developmental functions from the very beginning of life.

In contrast to White's emphasis on what I am calling the background activity of exploration and play in the *absence of drive activity* and Winnicott's emphasis on the background continuity of being when maternal activity *prevents drive arousal from disrupting that state*, I have tried to describe *drive-related* pleasures that also have a background quality and may have facilitative effects on development as well. My material is derived from a longitudinal study of normal children aged four to eight, with retrospective interview material as well, and is part of an effort to describe the developmental line of pleasure-in-looking as it began to take shape for me in that study.

In anticipation of that material (chap. 7), picture the young child spending most of the day with his mother and other members of his family. Numerous gratifications are very much part of everyday life. He is frequently ministered to, touched, lifted, handled; he sees his mother, father, and siblings eating, talking, washing, dressing; he takes in his family with his eyes; their bodily functions are part of the routine of his life; they defecate, urinate, bathe, and clean up; he notices their odors as well as their looks. All his sense organs take in the familiar stimuli. And this is all around him: no special behavior on his part is necessary to experience it. Contrast this to a later period, when these everyday gratifications usually become less available. Concern for privacy limits the child's experience. With the development of conscience, the fantasies attached to these gratifications make them sources of conflict to the child.

In the early period, many of the pleasures are quiet pleasures; they are a

---

1. Psychoanalysts should not be content to argue against White's ideas on the ground that play serves functions in drive gratification and object relation. More than others, we should know that one function of a behavior does not exclude others, and the multiple functions even of infant play have been well detailed (Drucker, 1975).

background to the child's life. Except for hunger and feeding, they are neither as focal nor as cyclic as, for example, adult sexual activity. Gratification is not usually intense enough to lead to intense excitation. One pleasure can replace another at this stage; to some extent they are functionally equivalent. Such diffuse and omnipresent gratifications seem to me to play important roles in paving the way for the final forms, much later on, of structuralized modes of gratification, sublimation, and aim inhibition. These segments of early infantile experience, not readily seen through the reconstructive telescope, nonetheless have a significant and specialized role to play in the evolution of the gratification system.

The random, goalless (background) quality of such pleasures may be not only one reason why such pleasures are not *satisfied*, as Brunswick (1940) says, but also a reason why sometimes they are not later *repressed*. Recently, in a seminar on child development where we were trying to recapture, through personal memory, what child life was like, one participant came up with the following: "I remember what it was like coming home after being away at school all day. I remember [with the comfort of familiarity] the smell of the house and knowing that food would be there." Smells and food. Derivatives, and not such distant ones, of early bodily zonal and object-relational central events. And yet nonspecific, of low intensity, divorced from direct infantile object contact or modes of gratification—and lasting, not repressed, but lasting as part of the low-keyed background of childhood life, giving it its touch of pleasure.

I have given three examples of background phenomena and their indispensable functions in the facilitation of development: one drawn from Winnicott and the mother-infant relationship, one from White on the infant's activity in exploration and play, and one on low-keyed continuing gratification close to early bodily experience. Spiegel's (1959) discussion of the development of the sense of self has a related emphasis on the significance of figure-ground relationships. Not all background phenomena are beneficial, of course—consider Kris's (1956b) concept of *strain* (as opposed to shock) trauma or the chronic patterns of distorted communication in some schizophrenic families that contribute to endogenous, taken-for-granted thought disorder. I have tried to select background phenomena in normal, perhaps optimal, development; hence their beneficial aspect here. Recognition of the significance or, even more, of the *existence* of these background states in infancy should highlight the usefulness of thinking of the high-intensity experiences as momentary in nature—intense moments set against quieter background moments.

Let me now apply some of these ideas to the concepts of the normal autistic and normal symbiotic phase by way of illustration.

ON A "NORMAL AUTISTIC" AND "NORMAL SYMBIOTIC" PHASE

On the basis of her work on symbiotic psychosis (Mahler, 1968) and her observational work with normal infants, Mahler found it useful to introduce the terms "normal autism" and "normal symbiosis" to describe the earliest periods of infancy, the forerunners of the separation-individuation phase. These terms are meant to highlight contrasts and continuities with the separation-individuation phase, clarifying what its psychological tasks will be. Thus, objectlessness (normal autism) and lack of differentiation from a significant object (normal symbiosis) set the tasks of the separation-individuation process: development of relatedness to a significant other, with the achievement and maintenance of awareness of self-other differentiation. Although the theoretical reasoning is clear and has an internal logic, the specific selection of terms and their fit with the phenomena of infancy have been criticized as being somewhat troubled. I shall attempt to review both the criticism and the phase concepts here, in ways consistent with the approach taken so far in this chapter.

Both Lester (1977) and Peterfreund (1978) have taken to task the terms "normal autism" and "normal symbiosis" on the ground that their derivation from pathology has led to conceptual unclarity. I shall again draw largely from Peterfreund's critique, selecting only those of his arguments that permit me to clarify some misconceptions and to re-state ideas regarding earliest infancy in ways that I believe do not violate the inferential and empirical standards he calls to our attention.

Peterfreund writes:

> There may be some superficial resemblances between a given normal infantile state and a later psychopathological state, but one must seriously question the wisdom of giving these states similar names and describing them in similar ways. Superficial resemblances do not justify an equation of states, and, in this connection, I believe that the ideas of fixation and regression must be used with great caution. A man who has suffered a cerebrovascular accident and is therefore unable to speak may be said to be suffering from aphasia. But he is not in the same state as an infant of two months who cannot speak. To characterize a normal two-month old infant as in a "normal aphasic" state of development would be grossly misleading; and it would be equally fallacious to describe the man who suffered the cerebrovascular accident as having "regressed" to an earlier state of "normal aphasia." (p. 439)

I agree fully regarding "normal aphasia," but I do not believe that the argument applies to the terms "normal autism" and "normal symbiosis." The difference has to do with developmental continuity. No one assumes that the nonspeaking period of infancy is causally and developmentally linked to later aphasia due to a cerebrovascular accident. But, *rightly or wrongly*, just such an assumption has at times been made with regard to normal and pathological autism and normal and pathological symbiosis. The question of the *correctness* of these assumptions about continuity and causality should be kept separate from their *rationale*.

For the specific rationale of these terms, one has to look at them one at a time in terms of the history of work with infantile psychoses. Thus, Mahler's early (1958) work on symbiotic psychotic children had led her to understand aspects of their functioning in terms of their notions of merger with the mother and their panic over awareness of separateness. Study of normal infants presented her with the sight of experiences (e.g., falling asleep at the mother's breast) that looked (from the *outside*) as though they might be accompanied by subjective experiences akin to merger and "oneness"—hence a "normal symbiotic phase." This is a form of inference about infancy that I discussed, and tried to defend, in the previous chapter. Later I shall suggest that the intensity and consequences of such *moments* of merger justify the concept of a normal symbiotic phase and, similarly, that the intensity of these moments and of moments of the loss of such merger go a long way toward justifying our thinking in terms of a causal relation between events of this phase and the onset of symbiotic psychosis.

The rationale for the use of the term "normal autism" is similar, though its usefulness may be more disputable. Two points contribute to the rationale, the first historical, the second clinical: Freud (1920b) had written of the protective shield against stimuli and of a period of primary narcissism (1914a), both speaking to the relative imperviousness and lack of attunement of the infant to a world "out there." And Kanner's early views (1942) (later modified) on the *psychogenic* causation of infantile autism (the aloof mother's failure to respond to the infant, which leaves the infant locked in his inner world) provided a model for thinking of early fixation of the to-be-autistic patient in the earliest period of nonresponsiveness — thus, developmental continuity. This, then, is the historical and conceptual rationale for the idea of a "normal autistic phase." Later, I shall suggest that the term is at best relative and merely descriptive and perhaps even quite far from the mark. Further, I shall argue that the idea of intense moments of "autism" (formative, with developmentally "causal" power), parallel to intense symbiotic moments, probably does not apply.

In the broad view, these rationales for the use of the terms "normal autism" and "normal symbiosis" are consistent with two modes of thinking characteristic of psychoanalytic theorizing in general: (1) to look for early normal periods of development that provide the *anlage* for, that give shape to, later forms of pathology, based on the assumption that these later forms must have had an earlier edition; and (2) to reason that the severer the pathology, the earlier the "early edition"—that is the point of "fixation." Issue can be taken with these two modes of reasoning, but their clinical-developmental applicability in at least some areas seems sound.

Let me now try to describe and re-state some ideas about a normal autistic and normal symbiotic phase in ways consistent with what has been presented so far: that is, by taking a differentiated view of moments of experience, drawing on observation and logical psychological reasoning, attempting not to do violence to empirical data, and utilizing experience-near rather than relatively abstract concepts.

The normal autistic phase. Aside from its historical derivation largely from pathology (Kanner's work), to what might the term "normal autism" refer? Stated most baldly, and emphasizing only what we can be most sure of, we can say that the newborn sleeps a lot. A very small part of his day is spent in wakefulness, and at that, much of the awake period is spent crying (until feeding or other comfort arrives), and there is every reason to believe that crying is not a state in which optimal cognitive functioning (discrimination of and specific reactivity to the perceptual world) takes place. Beyond this, we are not on sure ground about such things as the degree of receptivity to stimuli (the "stimulus barrier"), the working of the distal receptors, and the built-in organization of the perceptual world. But we do know that the infant spends most of his day sleeping, waking principally when hungry, and slipping into sleep again as he is sated. Physiological rather than psychological processes may be dominant, and the function of this period is perhaps best seen in physiological terms: the infant protected against extremes of stimulation, in a situation approximating the prenatal state, with continued physiological growth and the development of extra uterine homeostasis. But this is certainly not all-or-none; it does not mean there can be no responsiveness to external stimuli. Beginning with the early studies by Wolff (1959) and Fantz (1961), among others, such responsivity in the newborn has been clearly demonstrated, Wolff (as noted earlier) additionally describing the fleeting states of "alert inactivity" in which it is most likely to occur. And Sander (1977) has described the evidence for subtle interactive attunements involved in the regulation of the infant's exchange with its mother.

Peterfreund is critical of the following statement by Mahler and Furer (1972): "In this phase [normal autism], which extends from birth until the second month of life, the infant makes no discernible distinction between inner and outer stimuli, nor does he seem to recognize any distinction between himself and inanimate surroundings" (p. 213). Instead, Peterfreund suggests (and I agree):

> The simple observable fact that a hungry infant reacts to and nurses from the breast and not from a stick of wood or from its own finger negates any idea of an undifferentiated phase in which the infant cannot distinguish inner and outer stimuli or distinguish between himself and inanimate objects. The infant's nursing behavior indicates that some rudimentary distinctions are being made which, when more fully developed, will eventually be classified by adults and called "inside" and "outside" as well as "animate" and "inanimate." It is reasonable to suggest that such rudimentary distinctions, based on elementary classifying systems, are active at birth, built into the organism as a result of evolutionary development, and transmitted by the genetic code. (p. 433)

Still, this does not damn the idea for which the "normal autistic phase" concept is reaching. The concept provides a *contrast point* for a later period when the infant's investment in the mothering one is clearly *relatively more* in evidence. As such, the concept may have value at least for the description of relative variations along developmental lines, provided that it is not used in an undifferentiated way. Additionally, I believe that the Mahler and Furer remark can be productively re-stated not in terms of the absence of any discernible differences among stimuli, but in terms of the absence of *organizing concepts* that *make sense* of those differences. This is especially important with regard to the normal symbiotic phase, discussed in detail below.

Yet there are serious problems with the concept. Lester's (1977) critique utilizes a quotation from Escalona (1953) to suggest a possible phenomenology very different from what the term "autism" seems to imply:

> At first, the world is a succession of different sensations and feeling states. What varies is the quality, distribution and intensity of sensations.... Even if the baby turns his head toward the nipple and grasps it, his sensation is that the nipple comes or is; no other state with which to contrast this exists. Light and darkness; harshness and softness; cold and warmth; sleep and waking; the contours of mother's face... being grasped and released; being moved and moving; the sight of moving people, curtains, blankets, toys; all these recede and approach and comprise the totality of experience in whatever constellation they occur at each split second in time. With recurrence, there develop islands of consistency. (p. 25)

This is very different from "autism."

Should we retain the concept of a normal autistic phase? There seem to me to be nothing but uncertainties surrounding an answer. The concept probably captures something that marks a *relative* difference from what comes later (and, as such, suggests one starting point of development), but it also fails to represent the developmental implications of phenomena captured in the quotations above from both Peterfreund and Escalona. What of the arguments from the side of pathology, the idea that there is a developmental continuity between this early phase and infantile autism? Here, the data are not all in. Kanner's modification of his earlier views was only partial (see Kanner and Lesser, 1958, regarding psychogenic and/or biological causation), and recent work by Massie (1975) leans toward the side of early psychogenic factors (maternal behavior) that "leave" the child in his "autistic" shell. Although I myself am by no means convinced on that score, I believe that the possibilities cannot yet be excluded. And finally, what of the "moments" notion? The idea that the significant, developmentally formative, and affectively intense *moments* of this phase are the "autistic" ones seems to me unlikely; the withdrawn sleep state is perhaps of greater physiological than psychological significance. And yet, if we are to take work like Massie's seriously, we have to consider that the withdrawal moments *may* be the significant ones for the to-be-autistic child. In a related vein, Beebe and Stern's (1977) work on gaze avoidance shows the finely attuned capacity for such behavior in the first year of life and strongly suggests its adaptive/defensive utility.

The usefulness of the concept of normal autism is unclear. However, it is my opinion that Mahler's other contributions regarding symbiosis (and, later, separation-individuation) do not stand or fall with the fate of the normal-autism concept, which is distinctly of secondary import in her work. The more significant concept is normal symbiosis.

The normal symbiotic phase. In her description of the changing totality of the infant's experience (quoted above), Escalona (1953) ends by saying that "with recurrence, there develop islands of consistency." Some of these "islands," perhaps the main ones, involve aspects of the relation to the mother.

I should like now to turn to that, around the formulation of a normal symbiotic phase.

Several sources alert us as clinicians and theorists to the presence of
subjective experiences of merging, of boundarylessness, in human functioning. Panic regarding loss of self and delusional living out of fantasies of unity
(see chap. 15); reports from less ill patients (and nonpatients) of transient
states, perhaps when falling asleep, feverish, or orgastically aroused; experiences in alcoholic or drugged states; and wishful aspirations in various (especially Eastern) religions regarding oneness with the universe, as well as in
states of being in love—all these at times speak to aspects of "merging" with
another or with the inanimate. Where do these experiences come from? Here
is an instance where adult pathology and normal adult experiences lead us
to look back to childhood and earlier for events which, from the outside,
seem as though they might have produced subjective experiences that are
formative for those later experiences.[2]

Looking at the hungry infant nursing at the mother's breast and then
falling asleep at (or "into") the breast, recalling parallel experiences of falling
"into" sleep and into one's soft surround (lover or pillow) in our own experience, becoming aware that cognitive functioning is least articulated at
such moments, one can infer that these may be the prototypic moments for
the experience of "merger." Perhaps other moments, perhaps many others,
of holding, of mutual eye gazing, of echoing "cooing" voices of mother and
infant in unison, produce similar experiences. And these moments, most
especially the moments of sleepy-gratification-following-hunger, appear to
be the kinds of "moments" I described earlier: affectively supercharged, becoming central to the organization of an array of percepts and memories,
formative in their effect far out of proportion to their mere temporal duration.[3] And the contrasting moments of intense negative arousal in the absence
of comforting or gratification, moments ordinarily followed (and altered) by
the "merger" moments (and thus associatively linked to them), may heighten
the significance of the gratification moments (and, ultimately, increase the
primitive longing for those moments). None of this should be taken to
suggest that the two- to seven-month-old is "all symbiotic," all "merged." In
moments of ease, in the "spare time" between periods of imperious drive
arousal that White (1963) speaks of, times when quiet play is going on, the
infant is in quite a different state; we need not assume that he is "differen-

2. Although I shall stay with now familiar terminology and refer to such experiences as
"symbiotic," I am well aware that this is by no means identical to the biological concept of
symbiosis involving the relation between two organisms, each indispensable to the biological
life of the other. Neither in infancy (where it is an idea in one person's mind), nor in some
cases of *folie à deux* (Anthony, 1971) (where it may be a shared fantasy but not a biological
fact) is the actuality of mutual physical dependence for the continuance of the biological life of
two partners involved.

3. Research on mother-infant bonding (Klaus et al., 1972), while not by any means based
on merger experiences, nonetheless speaks to the power of certain kinds of mother-infant experiences (here, flesh-to-flesh contact in the earliest postnatal days)—a power to influence relatedness
even over the long term.

tiated" or "object related" at these other times, only that the merger experiences are not central then. The "symbiotic phase," like the "anal phase" discussed earlier, is best understood in terms of supercharged formative moments rather than in terms of any single totality of experience.

In discussing the normal symbiotic phase, Mahler (1966) also speaks of the "omnipotence" of the infant or of the omnipotence within the "dual-unit" (the merged mother-child experience in the *child's* mind). As discussed in chapter 3, Peterfreund (1978) takes such concepts to task as unproductively adultomorphic. As I have said, the relevant developmental concept of infantile omnipotence has nothing to do with making "impossible demands" as Peterfreund claims, but instead concerns inferred internal experiences of high intensity concerning achieved satisfactions (see chap. 3). The child's painful loss of omnipotence that Mahler (1966) also writes of comes about inevitably through the growth of self-other differentiation and of more realistic notions of causality.

We believe that these experiences of omnipotence and loss of omnipotence, part and parcel of the early significant relation to the mother, add to the supercharged quality of the symbiotic phase *moments*. Together, I suggest, the moments of merger and omnipotence justify the concept of a "symbiotic" phase; and the excessive (pathological) centrality of the moments of merger for some infants, plus the painful loss of merger and omnipotence for all, help to explain the panics and/or longings regarding loss of boundaries that are seen in later pathology.

The normal symbiotic phase can be discussed not only in terms of moments but also as a "deficit state." "Deficit" must clearly be in quotation marks because, as Peterfreund points out, the infant is what it is and is in "deficit" only by contrast to an adult. But the comparative approach is useful for expository purposes, and I shall pursue it briefly.

When we discuss the child in the normal symbiotic phase, we need not assume that he makes absolutely no distinctions among stimuli emanating from himself and his mother (and from inanimate objects, for that matter). Presumably a light is experienced differently from a sensation of hunger, and the mother's face (visual) differently from the child's own hand (perhaps visual and kinesthetic). But the important point is that there is no reason to believe that the child has organizing concepts that subsume the diverse stimuli that we, as adults, know to be "mother" and the other diverse stimuli that we know to be "child." "Mother" is, for the infant, a collection of stimuli—body warmth at one time, a red dress at another, a smiling face, a frown, the back of the head, a sound of footsteps, or a voice. Need we assume that the child knows that the smiling face "is" the same person as the frowning one, or as the voice from another room? In our work, we made no assumptions about such concepts (mother, self) as being inborn; we knew they existed later, and so we tried to study how and when they developed. The phase that we call "differentiation" (Mahler et al., 1975) is the phase in which we felt that the *external* evidence was suggestive regarding the development of such concepts.

As for the point where the child does not yet have organizing concepts, where mother and self are collections of stimuli rather than organized and constant wholes, it is just such a state that provides the rationale for concepts long offered by psychoanalytic theorists (starting with Freud's [1915] "purified pleasure ego") that suggest that early experience is organized into "the good experience" and "the bad experience," that is, along affective-experiential rather than cognitive-conceptual lines. The absence of clear cognitive concepts of mother and self provides the setting in which the moments of merger can more readily become the basis for the organization of experience. Or, at the other pole, the later development of reliable and differentiated concepts of mother and self, a development that is anchored in perceptual reality, counterbalances fleeting merger experiences and provides the setting in which the illusion of oneness is gradually given up, as external perception and higher level cognitive organization supply a powerful counterweight to affective experience and wish.

I believe the symbiotic-phase concept, as described herein, to be a significant one both developmentally and clinically. Seen as organized around affectively significant moments, it loses none of the clinical utility it has when seen as a totality of the infant's experience but is now not in conflict with the findings of developmental research on the competencies of the infant in that same time period.

I have been arguing for the utility of recognizing that infant experience varies from moment to moment. I do not mean this literally, of course; "moments," as I am describing them, can also be somewhat extended in time. But the value of the moments conception is that it permits us to see, in these differing moments, the possible origins of the innumerable phenomena that contribute to shaping all of us in the course of development. Here my focus has been relatively narrow, to make the point of view clear. In the next chapter, however, I shall substantially expand the use of the moments concept as a vehicle for the integration of conceptual variation at the level of the developing person.

My focus in this chapter has been on affectively intense moments that (I propose) lie at the heart of the early psychosexual and symbiotic phases. These are set against more quiet backgrounds, themselves "moments," which have their own developmental contribution to make. Overall this conception permits more differentiated description of infancy and of the origins of normal development and psychopathology.

Specifically, I have proposed redefining a phase as a period of critical formative events in any specific line of development, ordinarily organized around phase-specific, affectively central (whether intense or low-keyed) moments. The theoretical gain of recognition of the momentary nature of these affectively significant experiences (whether orality, anality, symbiosis, or whatever) is that it permits reconciliation of psychoanalytic observations and formulations with those of other research which reveal additional and seemingly contradictory aspects of infant function at other moments of the infant's day. Throughout, I have attempted to give an experience-near description of infant development, one not inconsistent with data from naturalistic and experimental research. The ideas advanced were applied to the normal autistic and normal symbiotic phase concepts (with a reappraisal of their nature) and in the next chapter will be applied more widely.

5

The Psychologies of Drive,
Ego, Object Relations, and Self

My aim in this chapter is to present an experience-near developmental framework that is capable of containing and integrating the various developmental theories that psychoanalysis has thus far produced. These are referred to by our concepts of drive, ego, internalized object relations, and self. The attempted framework for an integration is, however, at the level of the developing individual, not at the level of general theory. In pursuing this integrative task, I shall draw heavily on the concept of "moments" set forth in the previous chapter and on Waelder's (1936) concept of multiple function. The material I work with will be, and is intended to be, thoroughly familiar to those versed in psychoanalysis and its current literature. Indeed, as I try to show, it is inevitable that our theories grapple with this very familiar material. My aim, as above, is to provide a framework for understanding how all this familiar material can find its place and fit together in the development of the individual, and thus in our theories.

The expansion of psychoanalytic theory over the years has led to increased awareness of a widened array of phenomena in the patients with whom we work. Thus, there is not simply a widening scope of patients worked with in psychoanalysis (Stone, 1954) but also a widened scope of phenomena that we can become aware of in *each* patient. Naturally, some of these phenomena are more central than others in any patient, and overall they are hierarchically arranged in quite different ways in each patient.

For me, the broadened scope of both the clinical and the developmental theories of psychoanalysis is consistent with the view that everything in the person develops and that development can go wrong at any point and in any locus. Additionally, it follows that there is no single center to what goes wrong—neither oedipal stage pathology, nor merger and differentiation, nor self experience, nor any other. Even further, I believe, in consequence of the

First presented in April 1983 as the Honorary Brian E. Tomlinson lecture at New York University.

54

diversity of pathology, that there is no single route to its alteration. None-theless, current psychoanalytic theories give us the scope to conceptualize this diversity in many ways. Thus, the pathology we see can usually be organized conceptually around urges and the conflict attendant upon them (drive psychology), around defense organization, adaptation, and reality test-ing (ego psychology), around the unceasing repetition of old relationships and the experiences in them (object relations psychology), around aspects of boundaries, self experience, and esteem (self psychology), and around endless combinations and arrangements of all of these.

Later in this chapter I shall touch upon aspects of the clinical situation in relation to these ideas, but most of that clinical discussion is reserved for later chapters, especially chapter 12. Here I wish to focus principally on developmental formulations. Such formulations can start from developmental research or from the clinical situation. In the latter instance we see clinical phenomena and ask how might they have come about? What kind of de-velopmental path would account for them? To answer such questions, we can scan what we know of development—from observational research, child-rearing, and self examination; this chapter is in that mode. In it, I shall detour through a developmental path only to arrive back at reasonably familiar clinical ideas. The aim, once again, is to provide a developmental substrate for the broad set of clinical theories with which psychoanalysis is now engaged.

From a current perspective, the growth of both the developmental and the clinical theories of psychoanalysis can be seen as having taken place in three great waves: drive psychology, ego psychology, and object relations theory (cf. Settlage, 1980). I shall discuss these at both a general conceptual level and at the level of ongoing human experience, especially focusing on expe-riences in the growing child's life. At a conceptual level, the evolution of self psychology is subsumed, to a degree, under the evolution of object relations theory, representations of the self developing in counterpoint to the object (Spitz, 1957), and formulations regarding the self having evolved in a similar counterpoint. But at the level of the growing child's life I shall often refer to object and self experiences separately since their highpoints are often quite distinct.

The discussion is centered on the idea that every individual develops his own personal and internal drive psychology, ego psychology, object relations "theory," and self psychology. The "personal psychologies" (in contrast to the theoretical ones) are formed in differentially significant moments of ex-perience that have quite different shape and that are laid down as affectively charged active memory organizations of varied quality—now in terms of an experience of urge, now of achievement, coping, or mastery, now of object connection, now of self experience. These inevitably grow, for good or for ill, successfully or faultedly, out of unavoidable experiences of childhood, given the inherent characteristics of human thought and feeling, and are part of every individual. In the course of development these differential experiences are repeated again and again in different contexts and with differing outcomes, gradually becoming interconnected with one another, so that eventually every psychic act potentially relates to all these subjective experiences and comes to have multiple functions in relation to them. Thus, the *phenomena* to which the ideas of each of the three great historical waves refer have central affective significance in the lives of growing individuals and therefore must be addressed in developmental theory whatever the present status of any particular *theoretical* formulation.

The same holds true for clinical process, where the phenomena addressed by the three great waves will inevitably have some (generally significant) place, again whatever the status of particular theories. Clearly, the patient who free associates on the couch was once the child who went through certain formative experiences, shaped in terms that we refer to as drive, ego, object, and self. Though of differing centrality and existing in differing hierarchical arrangements, each of them will surface within every analysis and can be productively addressed. I will not be supporting a random eclecticism of technique, but I will be arguing for a broadened range of conceptual organizations for the interpretation of clinical content. I do not believe that this content is currently ignored; but I wish to provide a conceptual developmental framework for the work that is ordinarily done.

THE THREE GREAT WAVES

To a considerable degree, the evolution of ideas in the three great waves—drive psychology, ego psychology, and object relations theory—is based on new modes or domains of observation: the use of free association and the couch, the turn to child analysis and then to infant and child observation, and the "widening scope" of patients worked with in analysis later on (Stone, 1954). These developments, plus new observations within the standard clinical psychoanalytic situation, led to new formulations. But additionally, the roles of individual contributors, perhaps specifically attuned to one or another aspect of human function because of their personal life histories, cannot be ignored.

The first wave, drive psychology, was initiated by Freud's abandonment of the seduction theory (1897) and his articulation of the theory of infantile sexuality (1905) and led to the early mushrooming of writings on drives, their manifold transformations, and their role in psychopathology. It is certainly no accident that the first great formulations of psychoanalysis were those having to do with instinctual drives. Freud came of age scientifically in a time of Newtonian, physicalistic science (Holt, 1972), a world of force and counterforce, within which his ideas regarding instinct and repressive barriers, cathexes and countercathexes, readily fit. Further, Freud was born into the world of middle-class Middle Europe in the repressive, antisexual culture of the mid- and late nineteenth century. The personal organizing issues for him (as discovered in his self-analysis) and for his patients, those that took center stage when the free-associative process was first undertaken, were those of sexuality (especially) and, more broadly, of urge, of social and internalized taboo, and hence of conflict, defense, anxiety, guilt, defensive failure, and symptom formation. But additionally, Freud was born into a more or less intact family with reasonably reliable (even if conflicted) relationships; hence the kinds of inner formations and life experiences that we might today conceptualize in terms of deficit in ego function or early failures of object contact and core identification were not centrally part of his personal experience and psychopathology. Furthermore, his progressive clarification of patient suitability for both the rigors and potentials of psychoanalytic treatment led him to exclude those with defective ego function (e.g., those whose intrapsychic defenses and observer capacity could not be called upon reliably to work with the anxieties triggered by the psychoanalytic process or those for whom free association tended to lead to excessive loosening of thought organization) or those with faulted early object experience (e.g., where a transference neurosis could not develop or where the patient could not stand the isolation and abstinence of the analytic posture and conduct on the couch). These exclusions restricted his access to these forms of pathology and the demands they would make upon developmental and clinical theory.

In the history of the development of ideas, these limitations of focus have to be viewed as fortunate for the development of psychoanalysis as theory. No science and no scientist can study "the whole problem" in any area at once. Only by narrowing focus (and ordinarily, as well, by having conceptual organizers for the narrowed area under study) does a science progress. And Freud's early discoveries in drive psychology proved stimulating enough to further the growth of psychoanalysis as theory and treatment method for its first three to four decades. The formulations regarding instincts and their vicissitudes (1915), the earliest formulations regarding character largely in terms of the widening and defended-against life of the drives (Freud, 1908; Abraham, 1921, 1924), a view of defense early on in terms of the vicissitudes of drive (1915) and ultimately in terms of conflict with drive, the understanding of what is resisted by the resistance, repeated in the transference, and of those fixated and pent-up forces that power the analytic work itself, a developmental theory formulated around psychosexual stages and the forms of the tie to the object that are consequent upon movement through those stages—all these testify to the seminal nature of Freud's earliest drive-based psychology. The potential in this area of theory formation was enough to absorb the creative energy of the first generation of analysts for years.

But clinical observations and the requirements of theoretical clarity did not allow things to rest at this point. In retrospect it can be seen that even the early drive psychology was not articulated without a conception of what later came to be called the ego and of its specific functions. Certainly Freud needed a conception of defense (repression) from the outset. And his theory of dreams (1900) could not help but deal with the nature of the *thought* process and its role as a detour route to satisfaction, the rise to *perceptual* intensity of the dream, the *inhibition of motility* during sleep—all aspects of human function that later achieved a central role in psychoanalytic theory under the term "ego apparatuses," inborn and a potential base for ego development (Freud, 1937a; Hartmann, 1939), the guarantors of autonomy from the drives (Rapaport, 1957), and having pervasive developmental and functional ties to those drives.

These were some of the early seeds of an ego psychology. Later developments pushed the theory along in that same direction. Many clinical observations contributed: (1) adaptation was an observable fact of life, and the capacity of individuals to deal with adversity and to make something creative and constructive out of conflict could not go unnoticed by the analysts who were working close up with these individuals; (2) psychoanalytic treatment could rest with *analysis* (Freud, 1919) because the work of synthesis and integration, notwithstanding the place of working through (Freud, 1914b), seemed to be a native feature of human function; (3) character, forged out of drives and their transformation (Freud, 1908; Abraham, 1921, 1924), turned out to be a major adaptive (vis-à-vis the outside) and regulating (vis-à-vis the inside) achievement in personal organization and development and not only a vicissitude of drive; and (4) the observation that anxiety seemed to *precede* (and hence signal) defense rather than to *follow* repression (as a transformation of libido into anxiety) (Freud, 1926) led to a conception of a much more powerful ego that could, via the anxiety signal, call the pleasure-pain principle into play against the drives in a situation of conflict.

The work of the early child analysts and child observers, especially A. Freud (1926, 1936), also contributed to the press toward an ego psychology, because childhood is, par excellence, a time of the rapid development of new modes of mastery, of (under fortunate circumstances) creative resolutions of conflict, of the development of skills and interests that themselves foster adaptation, conflict resolution, and self-esteem. No child observer or therapist can fail to be impressed with the side of the person that manages, copes, or even simply muddles through: the "ego." And drive theory, the unconscious, and later (Freud, 1923) the theory of the id itself created a need for an ego theory. For if the id does not learn, if the unconscious is timeless, how can human adaptation and mastery be derived solely from them? Some conception of an inborn learning-and-adaptation structure (i.e., the ego apparatuses) or a process by which drive energies could be transformed in their function (i.e., neutralized [Hartmann, 1955; Kris, 1955]) was needed to account for the clear observables of human development *off* the couch—in life.

And so Freud developed a formal theory of the ego as one of the tripartite systems of the mind (1923), expanded it (Freud, 1926) in a reformulation that led to a "strong" ego concept (not merely one that rode the "horse"— reality, drive, conscience— in the direction it wanted to go but one that could steer it) and was followed in this area by others who made major systematic contributions (A. Freud, 1936; Hartmann, 1939). The result is a theory of the ego, its development, and its functions; a conception of autonomy, adaptation, and the conflict-free sphere; as well as a conception (even if not fully articulated) of the characteristics of ego function requisite in a patient who undertakes an analysis. And so the second wave, ego psychology, reached its crest.

The third great wave, object relations theory, is still propelling us and so is more difficult to see in perspective. However, the movement toward an intrapsychic (rather than interpersonal) object relations theory and for its essential unity with drive psychology—both conditions ensuring its tie to the mainstream of psychoanalysis—was implicit in the writings of Melanie Klein and of Fairbairn, probably the two contributors whose work set the direction toward the development of an object relations theory. Klein (1921–45) spoke of early *drive* processes (libidinal and destructive) in terms of the incorporation and expulsion of good and bad *objects*, thus cementing the tie (or actually creating a certain equivalence) of drive and object. And Fairbairn (1941), coining the term "object relations theory" and emphasizing the object-seeking (rather than pleasure-seeking) nature of the libidinal drives, also cemented the conceptual tie of drive and object. Though Freud (1915), too, had spoken of the object in terms that tied it to drive—the object being that through which satisfaction is achieved—Fairbairn's shift in emphasis and in the concept of the object was significant. The focus moves away from object as secondary to satisfaction and toward the primacy of object seeking in itself. The concept of the object changes along with this, for it is not simply nipple, or thumb, or teddy bear, or a certain activity (i.e., anything that serves to satisfy drive) that is conceived of as object but rather the whole significant primary caretaker (at the outset), and later others.

But it remained for a new mode of observation to become significant—in this case direct infant and child observation—for object relations theory to achieve its greatest impetus. Thus, Winnicott's whole body of work (1958a, 1965) provides a bridge between Klein's and Fairbairn's work and later contributions. Based as it is on close-up observation of mothers and infants and on his unique attempt to imagine his way into their experience, and formulated largely in object-relational terms (bridging the interpersonal and the intrapsychic, the between-persons and the within-minds), Winnicott's work can be seen as an attempt to bring Klein's reconstructive concepts down to earth, anchoring them in possible (even though still only imagined/inferred) actual mother-infant experiences. From this point of view, Melanie Klein's error lay not in turning to inferred/imagined phenomena of the earliest months but in dragging oedipal and superego concepts along as she did so rather than abandoning them for that period. Winnicott did this, for that age, speaking of destructive and incorporative processes in terms closer to the observables and inferables of the mother-infant dyad.

Once the turn to child observation took place, the focus on object relations was inevitable. The psychoanalytic situation, especially with the neurotic patient, is one that readily supports the view that the patient's life is largely of his own making. Barring the prototypic situation of a safe falling off a roof onto a person's head as he walks down the street, a patient's "fate," including "accidents," and certainly his ongoing inner experiences and object relations, seem to entail endless experiences of, or repetitions of, what he brings along with him in life. A focus on wish, fantasy, and character rather than on what others do to the patient leads to the most effective psychoanalytic work. What we "see" is the powerful impact of wish and fantasy; we only "hear about" the role of other persons. But in child (especially infant) observations exactly the reverse obtains. The powerful shaping influence of the primary caretaker, the opportunities, deprivations, satisfactions, and models she (and others) provide, is what even the psychoanalytic observer sees most readily; in contrast, the child's inner life is essentially unavailable to us, except via inference. The growing child-observational tradition among analysts thus gives support to theoretical formulations around the primacy of the object in development. Bowlby's (1969, 1973, 1980) work as well, influenced also by ethological research, falls into this broad tradition and has culminated in his emphasis on the object-related concepts of attachment and separation.

Two areas of clinical work, at varying distances from the mainstream of psychoanalysis, also led to formulations emphasizing the role of the other in the development of the individual. In each, new clinical observations, stemming essentially from the difficulty in understanding the development of psychopathology primarily from a drive-defense standpoint, led to these object-related formulations. First, clinicians who had substantial contact with schizophrenics (Sullivan, 1953; Fromm-Reichmann, 1950) developed interpersonal theories that, while by no means equivalent to what has come to be called object relations theory within psychoanalysis, nonetheless pointed the way to the significance of the *other*. That the interpersonal view arose at least in part out of work with schizophrenics reflects the by now widely held view that the earliest object relationships were somehow faulty for these individuals. Freud's consideration of the "narcissistic neuroses" in which transference would not be formed reflects his observation that something is basically wrong in their connectedness to others. As the data base (here schizophrenia vs. neurosis) varies, so too do the explanatory formulations (exactly as child observation and psychoanalytic treatment produce different data and therefore somewhat varying formulations). The second clinical development, more recent and arguably closer to the mainstream, is in Kohut's (1971, 1977) work, where, again, encounters with a clinical population somewhat different from the classical neurotic patients led to formulations centering on a "self" and to a developmental theory heavily weighting the confirming/mirroring/rewarding inputs of the *other*.

For Freud (1915), the position of the object was defined as the end point in the search for gratification. The very term "object" (rather than "person") clearly reflects that the "thing" through which gratification is achieved *could* be a person but could also be a part of a person (thumb, breast) or an inanimate object (blanket, bottle, or, as in fetishism, an item of clothing). By and large, this is not the case for object relations theory. The object is a person or his/her representation, with varying degrees of veridicality based upon distortion by drive and defensive processes. So "object relations theory" has come to refer to internal mental representations of self and other (Sandler and Rosenblatt, 1962) in varying experienced and ideal forms, bound together by affects (Kernberg, 1976), memories, and behavioral expectancies, and having a determinative influence upon current functioning. It seems to me that the developmental formulations regarding progressive differentiation of self from other (Spitz, 1957; Mahler et al., 1975) and the varying affective tones of the self experience (Winnicott, 1965; Mahler, 1966; Kohut, 1977) also stem ultimately from an object relations view—self and other developing in counterpoint. What defines contemporary object relations theory is not simply the primacy of object relatedness, as proposed initially by Fairbairn (1941)—for drive satisfaction and object rapidly become interwoven and as circular as chicken and egg—but a view of mental life that is organized around self and object representations and their relations and repetitions in addition to an organization of mental life around drive, defense, and conflict.

Thus, subsuming self psychology under object relations theories for the moment, we now have three interrelated sets of theoretical constructs: drive psychology, ego psychology, and object relations theory. Each new wave has brought with it competitive conceptual battles: first the concern lest a focus on the ego lead to a turn away from Freud's rich discoveries regarding the drives, and currently, the dual conceptual battles between formulations in terms of conflict and in terms of deficit (the latter born in faulty early object experiences), and between formulations regarding the "superordinate" status of a "self" (Kohut, 1977) and the classical emphasis on drives and their history of conflict. Yet, there is no doubt that many a theorist and many a working clinician experiences these expansions in theory as together producing rich new possibilities for encompassing the vicissitudes of the developmental process and the exigencies of clinical work. The three waves have emerged as new forms of observation (the couch and free association, infant and child observation) or new clinical observations within psychoanalysis or observation of new areas of pathology (psychoses, narcissistic pathology) have stimulated revision and extension of concepts. Turning now from general theory to descriptions of development and more experience-near concepts, I shall try to show how the phenomena addressed by these diverse areas of theory development are experientially integrated in the life of the developing individual.

DRIVE, EGO, OBJECT, AND SELF IN THE LIFE
OF THE DEVELOPING CHILD

Development, like all of life, consists of an endless sequence of moments, at least some of which have a primary inner experiential organization that we (from the outside) try to capture with one or another of our concepts of drive, ego, object, and self. But regardless of *our* concepts, these diverse moments of experience lead to the formation of a personal drive psychology, ego psychology, object relations psychology, and self psychology in every individual's internal world. Some of these moments of experience, from the outset, echo in more than one of these four spheres; in any event, as behavior sequences become more complex and intertwined and are repeated in new contexts with new outcomes, most psychic experiences come to have functions in relation to several or all of the four. Multiple function gradually becomes the rule. In this section, I shall emphasize *moments* of experience as a reconciler of the competing demands of drive-, ego-, and object-theoretical formulations and *multiple function* (Waelder, 1936) as a conceptual tool for the integration of those demands. Wallerstein's (1981, 1983b) view of self psychology and drive psychology as different developmental *lines* is an alternate approach to reconciliation.

Moments of Experience in Development

In the previous chapter I argued that the phase concept does not properly refer to the totality of a child's experience but rather to certain affectively central *moments* of the child's day (say, defecation and diapering, regarding anality, or nursing and falling asleep at the breast, regarding symbiosis). From this standpoint, there is time in the infant's day for the psychological work of the issues of various "phases" to be active. I suggested that a more accurate way to refer to what we now call a "phase" would be as a period of critical formative events in the anal (or oral, or symbiotic, or separation-individuation, or gender identity, or oedipal) line of development. And these critical formative events are often short-lived, occurring around moments of intense internal need and satisfaction or frustration, for example. Emphasis on moments of experience permits us to see that there is plenty of time in the infant's and child's day (innumerable moments) for experience to be centered upon and organized around different phenomena, including phenomena that we refer to under the rubrics drive, ego, object, self.

In the previous chapter I also contrasted certain "background" phenomena to the high-intensity moments. These background phenomena are more ongoing and low-keyed than the affectively intense moments but themselves have significant roles in the formation of, for example, experiences of self continuity (Winnicott, 1956), competence and self-esteem (White, 1963), and self and object concepts and relationships (see chap. 9). In larger view, what I have described as "backgrounds" are yet other "moments" of the child's day—moments, once again, where experience is organized in discrete ways with formative potential for one or another line of development. Thus, not all the significant moments need be of high intensity. Quiet moments, repeated again and again, can also play a significant role in development. In parallel terms, Winnicott's (1963b) discussion of the infant's "two mothers," the "object mother" who is the recipient of the infant's id tensions and the "environment mother" who protects, manages, and more quietly satisfies, is a way of referring to divergent infant-mother experiences that occur at different moments in time with different formative effects for different aspects of the person.

The application of all this to my present argument is straightforward. A look at the ongoing behavioral realities of the growing child's life immediately reveals phenomena variously linked to one or another (or more) of the domains that we conceptualize in terms of drive psychology, ego psychology, object relations theory, or self psychology.

Thus, the regularly recurring moments of need tension—of hunger and satisfaction, of bowel pressure, release, and the bodily stimulation of being cleaned, of the special excitements for a young child who "has" his father or mother all to himself and of the mental representations and elaborations of all these—lead to the development of a personal and internal (not a universal and theoretical) "drive psychology" for every child. And this personal drive psychology will be characterized by configurations of satisfaction and frustration that are unique in their form, reliability, associated tensions and conflicts, displacement and elaboration in fantasy, repression or aim inhibition or sublimation, and the like.

In the area of a personal "ego psychology," significant formative moments again abound in the life of every developing child. Each achievement in the development and unfolding of the apparatuses is such a moment: eye-hand coordination, pulling oneself to a stand, crawling, walking; the development of the reflexive cry into a purposeful communicative call, the emergence of speech-like rhythmic vocalization, later of "mama," of "no," and of verbalization; and the development of memory, of concept formation, and of thought more broadly. All these contribute to the child's personal intrapsychic "ego psychology" both in the joys of their first emergence and in the reliability of their ultimate automatization—or, contrariwise, in the pain of their failure or distortion, with secondary negative consequences for self-esteem, adaptation, and fantasy formation. Similarly, each new capacity for autonomous function, whether wrested from or ceded by caretakers, the autonomy of movement, of "no," of bodily self-care and self-feeding, and on through development, adds to this personal ego psychology. This is especially significant in the development of intrapsychic defense (chap. 7 and 8), when the child comes to regulate his own psychic homeostasis without leaning on the mother for such regulation—when the absent mother can be replaced by a substitute or by her image, when anxiety can be mastered in play, or when any of the array of defenses becomes part of the child's automatic repertoire. All these are significant for the chid's personal "ego psychology" in their development or failure of development, in their delays or precocities, in their pleasurable reception and confirmation by caretakers or their nonconfirmation and undercutting, and in their varying degrees of involvement in conflict such that the achievements themselves are part of the developing psychopathology.

Finally, in the region of the child's personal intrapsychic "object relations/ self psychologies": from early on, the child has experiences with the mother that take place outside the setting of intense need tension. These include what Winnicott (1956) refers to as the infant's "going on being," when the mother protects him against intrusions from inner and outer stimuli (the relation of the child to the "environment mother" [Winnicott, 1963b], who "manages" rather than the "object mother," who receives the id tensions). Similarly, the child has experiences of his own efficacy (White, 1963; Broucek, 1979; chap. 9), contributing to the experience of self, when he plays and has an *effect* on the environment, acting as a cause, one who makes events happen. These experiences, too, occur largely when imperious drive urges are quiet; in fact, excesses of those imperious urges because of chronic nonsatisfaction and resultant chronic tension wash out these quiet moments of play, preventing their occurrence (White, 1963). Such moments of object relatedness, not around drive, and of exploratory play, outside the periods of drive urgency, are among the beginning points for early object relation and self formation (Winnicott, 1956; Broucek, 1977, 1979; chap. 9). They add to those other moments of object relatedness of which Freud (1915) wrote, where the "object" (person, thumb, bottle, or whatever) exists as the thing through which drive gratification is achieved. The domain of the child's personal and intrapsychic "object relations psychology" includes the joys and disappointments of the early confirming or disconfirming object-related experiences (Kohut, 1971, 1977) and the internalizations from them (Tolpin, 1971) as well as the drive-based conflicted and intense engagements with the object that are laid down as self/affect/object memories (Kernberg, 1976). And the domain of the child's personal "self psychology" similarly spans the quiet moments in which aspects of the self experience may be born (Winnicott, 1956) and later experiences where progressive "ownership" of the drives may (or may not) be achieved.

In sum, important aspects of the early experience of every child, whether developing optimally or poorly, are inevitably organized around what we address, in theoretical terms, with our concepts of drive, ego, object, and self. Affectively significant moments of experience in each of these areas abound during the course of development and lay down memory and fantasy organizations of considerable power. These organizations become nodal points for the subsequent organization of experiences of all kinds. Stated in another way, the growing child's experience compels us to have theories of drive development, of ego functioning, and of object and self relations and representations if we are to have a general psychoanalytic psychology of development. This does not mean, of course, that we need to be committed to any *particular* theory in any one of these areas but only that theory has to address each of them if it is to represent the child's experience adequately. Later I shall argue that clinical theory and technique must address each of these domains as well.

MULTIPLE FUNCTION AND DEVELOPMENT

In giving the examples, above, regarding specific developments in the child's personal and internal drive, ego, object, and self psychologies, I tried to select instances that represented developments in one or another of those areas in relatively focal ways. But in fact, most developmental experiences come to connect with *all* these "personal psychologies" of the child. Certainly by late in the second year, if not earlier, developmental complexity has reached a level in which interconnection of intrapsychic experience becomes the rule and it is impossible, except artificially for the sake of exposition, to tease out single threads of development that clearly represent one domain or another. We come to the time when every psychic act has to be conceptualized in terms of multiple function (Waelder, 1936). Just as an emphasis on moments of experience, varying in their prime content, impact, and subsequent organization, permits reconciliation of the competing demands of drive, ego, and object relations theories upon the child's developmental time, so the concept of multiple function permits integration of the place of these theoretical points of view in the developmental actualities of the child's life—that is, they become integrated in the person, whatever theory has to say.

When Waelder first presented his ideas regarding multiple function, he argued that every psychic act has functions in relation to drive gratification, conscience, adaptation to reality, and repetition. I have no problem with the first three. But what of repetition? In Freud's (1920b) original writings on the subject, the idea of repetition is presented at two quite different conceptual levels. The first, the view that repetition involves a specific mode of mastery of trauma (of excessive stimulation), as in the case of the child's throwing away the wooden spool in a "gone" and return repetition of the mother's going away or in the larger case of the traumatic neuroses of war, is a clinical formulation based upon inferences regarding stimulus overload and processes of stimulus reduction; from this standpoint the tendency toward repetition, although highly significant, need not be seen as a continuously acting principle (and therefore not necessarily involved in every psychic act) but only as a specific mode of mastery under special circumstances. The second level at which Freud presented the repetition compulsion, as a derivative of the death instinct and the tendency of all living matter to return to quiescence (entropy), is a highly abstract biophysical speculation, quite distant from clinical phenomena. Though this concept provides a basis for conceiving of repetition as a continuously acting principle, one that may on that count be represented in every psychic act, it is formulated at an entirely different level of abstraction from drive gratification, conscience, and adaptation to reality and is therefore out of synchrony with them in terms of relevance to the phenomena of development and clinical practice.

Later writings, after Freud, seem to me to provide a better basis for understanding the place of repetition in human life (aside from its role in mastery of excessive stimulus inputs). The concept of a "representational world" (Sandler and Rosenblatt, 1962), an inner affective-cognitive template that is slowly built up in each of us based upon recorded experience as it is transformed (distorted) by wish and fear, provides a basis for thinking of the tendency to repeat as a continuously acting principle and one that is relevant at the same clinical level of conceptualization as drive gratification, conscience, and adaptation to reality. Kernberg's (1976) conception that mental life is constructed out of self and object images bound together by an affect continues this line of thinking. From these points of view, each person can be thought of as an actor upon an inner stage (Sandler and Rosenblatt, 1962) —a stage of memory and internalized object relations—with a set of internal dramatis personae all with established parts in the play, and with the person himself having one or more of the established roles, all carried over internally from the past and codetermining current behavior. Again from this point of view, one can define pathology in terms of the degree to which behavior is determined by these images, roles, and expectancies from the past rather than by current realities. And still again from this point of view, repetition can be seen as a clinically relevant, continuously active principle having an impact on all behaviors; there is always a tendency to reenact old modes of being and relating, to live out old fantasies, whether out of attachment and gratification or out of trauma and mastery or (more likely) *both*. In fact, an application of the concept of strain trauma (Kris, 1956b) to the old childhood relationships may offer a bridge between the observation that repetition takes place in relation to these relationships and Freud's view of the place of repetition in relation to mastery of trauma.

Returning to the use that I wish to make of Waelder's concept of multiple function, I would restate that all behaviors come to have functions in relation to drive gratification, conscience, adaptation to reality, and repetition of old internalized object relationships. I would add, partly in the light of Kohut's (1971, 1977) work and partly because of the pervasiveness of at least some of the clinical phenomena to which he has re-called our attention, that all behaviors also come to have functions in the maintenance of self-esteem. Whether the struggle to maintain self-esteem stems from biologically based self-preservative instincts (self, here, in the bodily sense) or from that propensity (at the human level) for any inner experiential ("self") organization to maintain itself, I am not sure; but certainly the maintenance of self-esteem is seen clinically as a constant undercurrent in much or all of our functioning.

Thus Waelder's concept (as extended here) runs parallel to the three broad theoretical positions under discussion. Drive psychology is obviously represented in the drive-gratification function of behavior; ego psychology is represented in those functions having to do with adaptation to reality; drive and ego psychology together link to those functions having to do with the demands of conscience; and object relations theory is represented in those functions of "every psychic act" having to do with the repetition of old internalized object relationships and with the maintenance of self-esteem. And while I have highlighted specific childhood experiences that may lie at the core of a person's evolving personal and internal drive, ego, object, and self psychologies, Waelder's concept provides the pathway to an understanding of how these various "personal psychologies" come to be represented in, or to put their stamp upon, all behavior in an integrated way. Behavior comes to have multiple functions, functions in each of the several domains that theory has addressed.[1]

I have stated that psychic acts "come to have" various (and multiple) functions. The phrase "come to have" is meant to highlight my view that

---

1. The concept need not be applied mechanically. Waelder himself, in a later work (1960), suggested that not all psychic acts are equally successful in serving functions in each of the several areas.

new behaviors do not spring forth full grown with all their multiple functions intact, like Athena from Zeus's brow, but that multiple function itself is a developmental achievement (chap. 7). As for some relatively clear instances at a conceptual rather than life-as-lived level, behaviors will not have functions vis-à-vis adaptation to reality until a conception of reality develops, or vis-à-vis the demands of conscience until superego formation begins. This is important because considering multiple function itself as a developmental achievement takes the magic out of the concept; multiple function is not, like Athena, fully formed at birth. In the long course of development, continually recurring behaviors can accumulate additional functions as they are repeated in different contexts, with different courses and outcomes over time. Differences in the drive state or ego state of the moment, or in the inner representations that are active, or in the actual responses of the other, will all influence and add to the memories that are laid down and, in turn, to the subsequent "purposes" (functions) of the behavior.

For example, the situation of the hungry infant, waking, crying, sucking to satiation, and falling asleep at the breast, is central to the formation of the personal and unique drive psychology of the individual. The patterning of drive and its satisfaction begins to be molded at these moments through particular associated bodily/sensual experiences (touching, rocking, warmth) and through the pace and reliability of, or the intrusions upon, this satisfaction. But later, and certainly well within the infant's first year, with the infant more wakeful after feeding or capable of quiet delay before feeding as well as of self-initiated pauses within the feeding, the nursing moment also comes to be a time of hand exploration of the mother's face, of mutually responsive cooing, of smiling, with all the implications these have for the development of the child's personal ego psychology, use and control of motor and vocal behavior, exploration, social adaptation, and defense (delay) itself. Similarly, and probably from the instant of the first mother-infant contact, vague self/object/affect experiences begin to be laid down, the core of the personal and internal object relations psychology. Or let us take the emergence of the "no" gesture and word (Spitz, 1957) as a core of a personal ego psychology, promoting control and mastery. Inevitably it impacts upon the object, whose altered responses (empathic or intrusive), together with the inner state of the infant at the time, will alter the object representations that are laid down and that become part of the individual's personal and internal object relations psychology as well. And, for example, the control the "no" gives to the timing and to the selectivity-of-object of drive gratification ("no, not now"; "no, this—not that") reshapes the personal drive psychology. Or, in the domain of initial object relations moments, the times of quiet mother-infant play, outside the press of need tension, are simultaneously formative for benign and loving object images and for the exercise of ego skills; these moments later (some might say early on as well) become involved in wish, fantasy, conflict—the world of more intense drive gratification.

I began this chapter by describing how, in part through variations in the site and mode of observation, psychoanalysis moved to encompass first a drive psychology, then an ego psychology, and currently a psychology of object relations and the self. I then attempted to show how these several domains of theory are needed in order to encompass the array of significant formative experiences in the life of the growing person; if we had not found our way to these theories, so to speak, it would be necessary to invent them. Life demands it. Numerous events in the life of every child (and adult as well) involve affectively significant moments that are experienced primarily in terms of drive gratification, ego function, object relations, or self. These are laid down as memories and perhaps as active organizations (tension states, wishes, tendencies toward repetition) to which other experiences are subsequently assimilated (Piaget, 1952a). Additionally, as development proceeds and the chance arrangements surrounding any act proliferate in unending variations, these and all behaviors come to have multiple functions or, stated otherwise, to be accommodated (ibid, 1952a) to these new experiences and to change their inner shape accordingly. The intent of this emphasis on moments of significant experience is not to stress the purity of those moments as formative for one or another of the several domains I have been discussing—that is mainly an expository device — but to show that the several theories compete only at the level of conceptual framework and not in terms of phenomena of the child's life; in that life, there is plenty of time for experiences shaped in diverse ways. And the intent of my emphasis on multiple function is not to stress the absoluteness of that achievement—as though each and every behavior in fact did serve every function described—but to emphasize that the concept of multiple function and, especially, of its development over time permits us to see how specific behaviors accrue new functions and how all behaviors become interrelated over time, binding together, within each individual, his personal and internal drive, ego, object, and self psychologies in the form that eventually we come to see in the analytic patient on the couch.

THE PERSPECTIVE FROM THE ANALYST'S CHAIR

As stated earlier, it is evident that the patient who free associates on the couch was once the child who went through the formative experiences I have been describing. How do these experiences appear from the perspective of the analyst in relation to the adult patient in analysis?

Before proceeding with this question, and because I have been expansionist in my view of the regions in which relevant psychic phenomena lie, I want to state clearly that I am not arguing for a random eclecticism at the level of theory or for acceptance of any *particular* theory—whether it be Fairbairn's (1941) object relations theory, or Kohut's (1977) self psychology, or even, for that matter, Freud's drive psychology or Hartmann's (1939) ego psychology. Instead, I have been arguing that the diverse *phenomena* that the various theories address are part of every person's life. They will also, therefore, be part of every patient's analysis. This is not to say that each domain will be equally relevant for every patient, but only that the analyst will gain from having in mind a diverse array of concepts that will permit him to hear the patient's material in variously organized ways. We listen with "evenly suspended attention" (Freud, 1912), but this means only that we do not prejudge the content; rather, we allow it to achieve whatever shape it achieves in any particular hour. We may be a blank screen for the patient's transferences, but our minds are not blank. A truly (conceptually) blank mind will hear nothing in an analytic patient's associations; and a mind with a single set of organizing concepts will hear material only in ways susceptible to being organized by those concepts. It seems to me that we now have a broad array of concepts and, while they make things more complex, they also reflect the actualities of development more fully and therefore we and our patients are the gainers for it.

Moments and multiple function, concepts that I have used to organize my discussion of development, are certainly relevant to the clinical situation as well. Every analyst learns that it is in moments of experience, looked at close up, in depth, that the most significant analytic work gets accomplished. While patients tell "stories" and discover "patterns," it is in the richness and anguish of in-depth recounting of particular moments of experience (what is happening right now, or as the patient brushed by the analyst coming through the door, or last night in bed with a spouse, or while seeing your child depart for school) that affectively significant and personally convincing work gets done. But this mirrors the developmental process. Intense moments serve as organizers of experience. In development, this intensity is the source of ongoing impact; in analysis, it is the source of discovery and conviction. But additionally, these moments, in analysis as in development, are organized in very different ways—sometimes around significant experiences of urge, or mastery, or object connection, or self-esteem, for example; and each is repeated many times. Naturally, certain themes govern each particular patient's functioning, but nonetheless, no one is unilinear, and we do best not to worry when differing clinical moments do not fall into identical conceptual molds.

And as for multiple function in clinical work: whatever the developmental origins of a specific item of behavior, whichever way it was primarily organized intrapsychically in terms of the several domains discussed, when it appears in analysis in the adult it is inevitably part of a complex web of meanings that unfolds bit by bit. And this, I suggest, is the end product of a slow accumulation of meanings over developmental time. It is every analyst's experience that most of what is presented by the patient is interpreted now from this standpoint, now from that, until its full array of functions is unearthed. I do not mean to suggest that this is a self-consciously systematic enterprise or that it should be; instead, it slowly happens that way to varying degrees. Thus, a person's use of his intellect may be understood at one time in terms of its defensive use against drives, at another as a valuable ally in the analytic work, and at yet others as an instrument for self-castigation in the service of conscience, as a basis for living out an old relationship to the parent/analyst through the mind's work, and as an effort to shore up a fading sense of self-esteem. It is unlikely that these will be equally important in any one patient, though it is quite possible that all will arise, and it is virtually certain that one or more will be central in patients where intellectuality is important. Part of what we subsume under working through includes interpretation from the standpoint of the manysidedness of multiple function.

To highlight the degree to which new environmental inputs all through life can be diversely organized at different moments and in terms of the full range of potential psychic functions, we need only look at patients' responses to interpretation itself. For a patient's receipt of an interpretation is itself a psychic act having potentially multiple functions. Thus a patient may "hear" an interpretation in any or all of the following ways at different moments: as a gratification or deprivation (from the standpoint of drive); as a condemnation or permission (from the standpoint of conscience); as an access to a new view of reality or as a stimulus to cling to one's old defenses (from the standpoint of adaptation); as a repeated or a reparative object relation experience (from the standpoint of internalized object relationships); and as a humiliation or as a sign of special attention (from the standpoint of self-esteem).

In relation to clinical work, I am not suggesting that we work with specific models of the mind (Gedo and Goldberg, 1976; Gedo, 1979); my conception of our work is much more fluid than that, allowing for steady shifts in the frame of interpretation. Nor am I suggesting that were we ready to formulate our understanding in terms now of drive, now of object, and so on, that we would then have a full theory of technique prescribing mutative interventions for every form of pathology. And I am certainly not proposing that we already have such a set of techniques for each occasion. But recognition of the several potential shapes of the clinical content is a step in that direction. Although the history of the development of ideas is not as simple as this, Freud's use of interpretation, to raise to consciousness what can be seen as "outdated" for the adult, so that unconscious fantasy determinants of behavior can be revised, is appropriate to aspects of the work with drive conflict; and Kohut's emphasis on empathy and on allowing an idealization in the transference, for example, can be seen as an attempt to develop clinical techniques to deal with a form of pathology now defined in terms of the self. I have found it useful (indeed, powerful) to interpret not only from the point of view of drive/defense/superego conflict but, additionally, from the point of view of the patient's tendency to act as a character in his own internal play (Sandler and Rosenblatt, 1962), repeating old roles again and again. But the question of precisely which techniques can heal a defective ego or "fragmented" self (Kohut, 1977) is still largely open. However, so too are many such questions in relation to drive (e.g., masochism) and unconscious guilt (Spiegel, 1979). Nonetheless, the conceptual capacity we now have to organize the material in multiple ways, now this way and now that for one patient, more this way than that in different patients, gives us greater clinical power for work in the region of the widening scope of analysis (Stone, 1954).

In their 1959 paper, Rapaport and Gill proposed that a full accounting for any psychic event requires that it be described from five metapsychological points of view: economic, dynamic, structural, adaptive, and genetic. Whatever the fate of aspects of psychoanalytic metapsychology, I am proposing that, at a developmental and clinical level, behavior can be described in terms of five functional points of view: drive gratification, adaptation to reality, the demands of conscience, repetition of old internalized object relationships, and issues of self cohesion and esteem. These are variously hierarchically arranged in each individual, with one or another having centrality at different times in an analysis or, overall, with one or another being the central thread for any particular analysis.

Given the expansion of conceptual frameworks characterizing present day psychoanalysis, it becomes incumbent upon us to define what properly fits under the umbrella concept "psychoanalysis." What makes something *psychoanalytic* theory rather than developmental or clinical theory more broadly? In relation to technique and treatment, Freud (1914c) spoke of transference and resistance as the defining features of psychoanalysis. Thus he did not focus on specific contents but rather on certain processes that occur in the work. For psychoanalysis as a theory no such direct statement has been made. Perhaps early on one might have thought in terms of Freud's drive theory (1905) and his structural model (1923) as the defining features. But these turn out to be too specific, I believe, too content based. In the light of the developmental and clinical relevance of drive, ego, object, and self psychologies, often going off in their own directions, what, if anything, binds this together as "psychoanalysis"?

I believe two major organizing points of view tie together (though they do not fully unify) the numerous threads that go under the name of psychoanalytic theory. Ultimately both have to do with a view of the mind, in all its complexity, in its inclusion of unconscious mental function, and as the site wherein history is carried and current life is determined. The first is the interconnected triad of *psychic determinism, unconscious mental functioning,* and (for want of a better term) the *primary process*—or that aspect of thinking that works with symbol and metaphor, with "irrational" connections, and does not heed the rules of reality. I say these are interconnected because only through a recognition of the workings of the unconscious mind and the primary process can we see our way into the core concept of psychic determinism (Freud, 1900). The second, more relevant to the inconsistencies engendered by the diverse contents offered by the three great theoretical waves, comes closer to a content-based definition but is still far from simply that. Rather, I suggest it is a focus on *intrapsychic life*, especially as shaped by *early, bodily based,* and *object-related* experiences, and organized in *interrelated* (both *multiply functional* and *conflictual*) ways. The bodily based experiences of drive and gratification, of apparatus and function, are among the contents thus organized, as are the object-related experiences involved in drive gratification, enhancement of the self experience, and shaping of the representational world. As concepts mushroom, the core definition of what is a psychoanalytic theory broadens, or perhaps loosens; but I believe the two features noted above to be two broad underlying commonalities.

Psychoanalytic theory and its theory of technique are currently undergoing considerable expansion and controversy. I have tried to show that the expansion mirrors phenomena of development and of clinical process. Although the developmental phenomena as we know them can hardly be brought to bear to test the adequacy of any specific theory in these several domains, they do compel us to work with the several theoretical approaches and suggest potential pathways, at the level of concrete experience, for their integration. And while the range of clinical phenomena as we know them is not fully responsive to individually tailored modes of technical intervention, at least we have a diversity of languages with which to speak to patients in ways potentially closer to their own internal experience.

SUMMARY

My aim in this chapter has been to present an experience-near developmental framework that is capable of containing and integrating the various developmental theories that psychoanalysis has thus far produced. Such a framework should also provide a developmental substrate for the several clinical theories with which psychoanalysis is now engaged. In pursuing these aims, I advanced several arguments: (1) that the phenomena that provide the bases for drive, ego, object relations, and self theories are inherent in the life of the developing individual; (2) that there is time for all of them, for they take but moments, quiet moments or affectively intense moments, but moments repeated again and again with formative effect; (3) that in the repetitions of these moments the phenomena experienced in them gradually become integrated with one another and accrue multiple functions; and (4) that, in this manner, each individual develops his personal (intrapsychic) drive, ego, object relations, and self psychology. These appear with varying centrality and in varying hierarchical arrangements in the adult-as-patient. If the clinician retains his basic tool of receptive listening, all the while having a broad range of organizing schema in the back of his mind, the potential match to patient experience will be greater.

6

Developmental Considerations regarding Ego and Drive

In the four remaining chapters in this part, I shall discuss selected issues within each of the several "psychologies." The specific issues discussed are intended only to exemplify the contribution of a developmental approach to questions stimulated by phenomena of the clinical situation. In this chapter I comment on the relationships between what we conceptualize as "ego" and "drive." Chapter 7 considers the structuralization of drive-defense relationships; chapter 8 takes up the subject of libidinal object constancy; and chapter 9 explores aspects of the self experience. Many other issues could of course have been singled out for discussion.

EGO AND DRIVE: FUNCTIONAL AND INTERACTIVE LINKS

In recent years, psychoanalysts have not infrequently expressed an interest in cognition, perception, and learning, often in particular an interest in the work of Piaget or others concerned with the development of cognitive processes. Whence this interest? Classically, psychoanalysis has made unique contributions to the study of the development and characteristics of drive, affect, conflict, and fantasy. It has been the fields of psychology and education, the one more theoretically and the other in more applied ways, that have focused centrally on cognition, perception, and learning. And yet the two areas have come together with considerable mutual gain. In this section, and in schematic form, I shall try to illustrate the distinctive contributions that psychoanalysis can make to an understanding of development in the cognitive sphere, attempting in so doing to clarify aspects of psychoanalytic developmental theory itself.

Based upon material previously published under the titles: "The development of ego apparatus and drive" (*Contemporary Psychoanalysis*, 19:238–247, 1983) and "In the beginning: Contributions to a psychoanalytic developmental psychology" (*International Review of Psychoanalysis*, 8:15–33, 1981).

Psychologists and educators have generated an enormous research literature on thinking, learning, memory, and perception. This research is in part
descriptive (answering the question: What are thought and learning like?)
and in part developmental (How do they change over time?); it is in part
theoretical (addressing issues, for example, of the essential characteristics of
learning) and in part applied (addressing issues, for example, of how our
understanding can help us in education). It dates broadly from early intro-
spectionist studies of thinking, from controversies over Gestalt versus ele-
mentaristic views of perception, and from exploration of the varieties of
conditioning and of insight and their roles in human learning. But most
importantly for the point I wish to make here, this research literature, and
the aspects of human functioning to which it refers, stands quite stably on
its own two feet. Conditioning takes place with or without psychoanalysis
and its insights; the development of concepts of conservation and causality,
as Piaget (1930, 1952b) has shown, follow their due course; and learning
adheres to reasonably well established principles—of the value of spaced
learning, of primacy effects, of reminiscence phenomena, and the like. Empirical research in these areas has taught us many of their principal features.

But beginning with the development of psychoanalytic ego psychology—
perhaps starting from Freud's monograph on *Inhibitions, Symptoms, and Anxiety* (1926), with its concept of a stronger ego that was not simply buffeted
by drive, conscience, and external reality, and then flowering with Anna Freud's
The Ego and the Mechanisms of Defense (1936), with its respect for the surface
of human functioning as well as its depth—conceptual bridges were built
between drive psychology and processes of learning, thinking, memory, and
perception. A concern with adaptation and with defense brought to more
rational processes of learning and thought a degree of significance that did
not match that of unconscious fantasy and powerful affects but has proved
indispensable to an understanding of how fantasy and affects are transformed
and controlled.

Hartmann's work (1939, 1964) in particular legitimized a psychoanalytic
interest in perception, thought, and memory—in what he termed the ego
apparatuses. Let me summarize some of his concepts briefly, apply them schematically to my topic, and then go on to discuss a few aspects of psychoanalysis, on the one hand, and the development of cognition and perception,
on the other—aspects that stand out more clearly when the two areas are
viewed in relation to each other.

THE CONCEPT OF EGO APPARATUS

Early psychoanalytic theory had a conceptual problem. Although clinical
experience attested to the constructive forces in development and the adaptive
capacities of man, early psychoanalytic concepts in general failed to account
for these adaptive capacities. They said in effect, "In the beginning [of de-
velopment] there was id." But the id was conceived of as timeless, unchanging—thus incapable of learning. Yet learning was a fact of life. A concept of

a stronger ego, there from the start (in some form) and capable of bringing about adaptation and change, was needed. The theories of sublimation and neutralization (Hartmann, 1955; Kris, 1955) were one solution to the problem; they spoke to the transformation of drives and/or energies into forms subserving defense, adaptation, and socially valued creation. Freud's (1926) second theory of anxiety was another solution to the problem. By acknowledging the ego's capacity to signal danger, it also gave recognition to the way in which the pleasure principle can be called into operation—on the side of defense, and against the danger—thus adding great power to the working armamentarium of the ego.

I shall not pursue these two points here but instead shall focus on the third solution to the problem, the concept of ego apparatuses, which is central to my present concern. Hartmann obviously did not discover these apparatuses, although, in a sense, he discovered them *for* psychoanalysis. By giving the name "ego apparatuses" to those biological givens that serve to make perception, thinking, memory, and the like possible, he recognized their value as *tools* that subserve what we call ego development. That is, they make it possible to take in information from the surround, to record it somehow in the brain, and to elicit and resuse it later on, in short, to learn from experience. Thus, the apparatuses of learning and thinking and the others can be functional for those developments (of delay, defense, reality testing) that psychoanalytic developmental theory *is* concerned with. Here, then, is one large area of linkage between psychoanalysis and cognition-perception—not in the form of a substantive contribution from psychoanalysis to an understanding of cognitive development, but an explication of the *functional* role of cognition for *all* areas of personality development.

PRIMARY AND SECONDARY AUTONOMIES AND THEIR RELATIVITY

Hartmann (1950) suggested that the ego apparatuses have an initial (a primary) autonomy from drives. That is, they do their work (of perception, remembering) quite apart from hunger, other bodily states, and the psychological ramifications of these bodily states. But this autonomy is only relative, not absolute; any and all aspects of human functioning are susceptible to involvement in conflict. Some, more complex, features of human functioning (such as interests and occupations, or even character traits), born in the developmental mix of drive gratification, anxiety, and defense, can *later* become relatively independent of conflict, achieving a secondary autonomy.

These concepts point to a second large area where psychoanalytic contributions shed light on cognitive and related functions. I shall refer to this as the *interactional* issue. The functional issue, discussed a moment ago, asks: How do the ego apparatuses, including cognition and perception, aid in the development of other aspects of the person? The interactional issue asks: What are the consequences for cognition, perception, and the like of the fact that the development of these apparatuses goes on in a person who also has powerful urges and affects, as well as complex object relationships? Both questions bridge the traditional areas of psychoanalytic discovery and the traditional foci of study in psychology and education.

Before turning to more concrete illustrations of how these bridge-building issues express themselves, I must mention one area in which Freud made a monumental substantive contribution to our understanding of cognitive development, indeed of cognitive functioning throughout the life cycle. This is of course Freud's (1900) formulation of the primary process in mental life: that form of thinking most familiar to us from dream life, quite another side of the cognitive picture from the one usually addressed by educators and researchers on learning, memory, and the like. I mention it here not only to give psychoanalysis its due but because it underlies much of what I want to discuss. It is because the human thought process does not merely follow the straight and narrow (though it can do just this) that it can come to have a multiplicity of functions in the course of development and to be linked to a wide array of intrapsychic conflicts. That the human thought process is capable of (or susceptible to) displacement of ideas, symbolization, and associative processes along idiosyncratic and unconscious pathways is a key, as Freud has shown, not only to dreams but to wit, creativity, neurotic symptom formation—indeed, to all aspects of human functioning.

ILLUSTRATIONS

Let me return now to illustrations of what I have termed the functional issue: the role played in development by the fact that we have inborn (and unfolding) capacities to perceive, to remember, and to think.

To begin with *separation-individuation and libidinal object constancy*: We do not assume that the infant is born with preformed differentiated concepts of self and other. They have to be developed. The separation-individuation process (Mahler et al., 1975) details that aspect of object relationship having to do with the development of these differentiated concepts. Complementing classical psychoanalytic theory, which shows how object ties develop around the sources of drive gratification, theoretical formulations regarding the separation-individuation process detail how the very concept of self and object develops out of cognitive, perceptual, and affective experiences. Suffice it to say here that these differentiated concepts of self and other grow from repeated *perceptual* experiences (especially visual, tactile, and kinesthetic) that are laid down as *memory* traces and that are eventually synthesized into whole concepts through the gestalt pattern-forming tendencies of the *perceptual* apparatus and the synthesizing tendencies of *memory* and *thought*. The affective significance of these events is responsible both for powering their development and for inducing conflict and disturbance within them (Mahler et al., 1975; see also chap. 8).

Not only do the workings of the apparatuses of cognition and perception mediate the development of differentiated concepts of self and other but, in consequence, as Mahler (1952, 1966) has shown, a heavy emotional price is paid—that of awareness of separateness. But then the *memory apparatus* is highly functional in the young child's efforts to deal with that very experience of separateness. The development of the memory image of the absent love object is beautifully designed, so to speak, to resolve the child's polar wishes for autonomy, on the one hand, and closeness to mother, on the other. By carrying her image within him, the child can have his mother with him, with no sacrifice of his autonomy; he need not stay physically near her to have her image inside. To take this process just one step further, here again a feature of the thought process serves to bring about an essential human *emotional* phenomenon. For the memory of the absent object is, in varying circumstances, not only a comfort but a burden. If people were forever for us "out of sight, out of mind"—that is, if there were no object constancy— then we would not experience longing for specific love objects (cf. Spiegel, 1966). Instead we might move promiscuously from relationship to relationship as need-gratifying opportunities presented themselves. If this were the case, all human social organization would be different from what it now is.

In short, the integral functional relationships between our thought processes and our affects and urges shape our distinctively human characteristics. Our drives must take the expressive shape made possible by the stimulus-receiving, recording, re-eliciting, and representational qualities of our cognitive apparatus.

Second now, to illustrate the functional issue in relation to the development of *delay, signal anxiety, and defense.* The human infant is born helpless, defenseless in the face of mounting tensions, until mother arrives or apathy or sleep sets in. Somehow, from this state of potentially boundless tension, a higher order anxiety will evolve in the course of development—optimally, an anxiety that serves as a signal triggering psychological defenses, which limit the tension-producing powers of the occasion. How does this development take place? I believe it is something like the following, once again with the cognitive apparatus turning out to be highly functional for other aspects of psychological development.

The infant who has been reliably gratified when hungry, for example, can gradually come to greet a new occasion of hunger differently from one who has not been so gratified. The *memory* of repeated pairings of hunger and satisfaction sets up an *anticipation* that satisfaction will again be forthcoming, an anticipation that we call basic trust. In that moment of *delay*, when the anticipation of gratification (or the recognition of danger and the memory of its prior resolution) slows the rate of tension-development, higher order adaptive behavior (calling mother) or, later, intrapsychic defenses (withdrawal of interest from the psychological danger situation, averting one's thoughts, stifling the affect) come into play. *This* occurs rather than having the first sign of anxiety, in snowballing fashion, stimulate the memory of previous panic, thus leading rapidly to an escalation of the anxiety once again to panic proportions.

In short, it is the memory apparatus, based on previous learnings, that makes possible that pause in the face of a psychological danger situation in which new developmental solutions may emerge.

This brief presentation is intended only to highlight the crucial functional role of the cognitive apparatus. I have tried to illustrate, with these examples, how our inherently human tools of perception, learning, and thought are functionally indispensable for the transformation and modulation of phenomena from the affect/impulse sphere.

I would like now to illustrate the other bridging concept, which I have referred to as interactional—that is, the consequence for cognition and the like of the fact that it is going on in a person who also has powerful urges and affects—but this time with clinical examples.

An energizing effect. The daughter of two highly intelligent parents, with a father who was distinctly making use of his intellect in his profession and a mother who distinctly was *not* making use of her intellect in her business, was born with a bodily defect that was of realistic concern to the family. She was brought to me at age seven when a change of residence triggered nightmares in the child. Quite apart from the presenting problem, I had occasion to learn a good deal about the functioning of her intellect. Highly intelligent, the child used her intellect extensively. She learned well in school, talked profusely and cleverly, argued her cause vigorously, had intellect at the center of her defensive functioning, and had interests (hobbies) that had major cognitive components. More interesting from the standpoint of this chapter is how (by inference) her intellect became that way. And here the energizing aspect of intrapsychic conflict and object relations shows its role. She was enormously curious and astonishingly knowledgeable in areas linked to her defect. The link was clear, though she herself was never explicitly, undisguisedly curious about the defect itself. Furthermore, her intellect played an important role in the family triangle, seeming to represent both her identification and her object relationship with her father. The identification was self-evident in the modeling of her style after his, and the object relation was clear from his pleasure-filled response to her intellect as his favored mode of interaction with her—the more so since he was unable to find this satisfaction with his wife. Overall, while this child's intellect showed signs of obsessional overdevelopment, its positive aspects, stimulated by her fantasies regarding her defect and by the family patterns of relationships, were clear.

A distorting effect of drives and object relationships upon cognitive functioning. An article by Newman, Dember, and Krug (1973) entitled "He Can but He Won't" reports a study of highly intelligent underachievers. All these children showed high promise early on regarding their intellectual functioning. They all spoke early and well and were shining lights of success in their familial world. But as they reached school, each failed in one form or another to master intellectual work. What had happened? The authors show us in convincing detail how intellect had been caught up in their narcissism as an extension of maternal narcissism. The early intellectuality had become so much the basis of self-esteem, of feelings of worth if not of perfection, and of narcissistic union with mother that the children could neither risk nor manage the encounter with real schoolwork, which always held the possibility of failure and was in any case external to the narcissistic duo. Thus, intellect, at first stimulated, was *distorted* by its tie to infantile narcissism and infantile object relationships. It came to serve them rather than its true function of learning.

An inhibiting effect. Clinical examples of the inhibiting effect of the interaction between drives/affects/fantasies, on the one hand, and an aspect of cognition, on the other, abound. To give just one, in a case of elective mutism in a young boy, the inhibited cognitive function was speech. School success and learning suffered secondarily since he would not speak in school. At age eight, entering therapy, this boy was, not surprisingly, mute in this situation as well. The symptom (though by no means all the boy's troubles) was resolved rather rapidly. In therapy, the child was not only electively mute but also nearly immobile. A turning point in our understanding came one day when the therapist noticed that the boy had an erection as he left the office. In rapid order thereafter, we learned that the patient feared moving in the therapy hour because he feared displaying his erection and that not speaking was essentially the same issue displaced upward. That is, speaking out equaled sticking out, and underlying the fear of penile display was the wish for that very display. Thus, the cognitive (actually cognitive-motor) function of speech, and school learning secondarily, had been inhibited through its relation to exhibitionistic urges. (The symptom was, of course overdetermined, and we learned much more about it; but what I have given is enough to illustrate the inhibition.)

So much for these few brief examples.

Let us now turn to related issues, this time casting a somewhat wider net, by reexamining the concept of an undifferentiated phase. My aim is both to attain a more differentiated conception of the earliest period of life and to explore, at least conceptually, the origins of drive, ego, object relations, and self phenomena.

WHAT IS UNDIFFERENTIATED IN THE UNDIFFERENTIATED PHASE?

Peterfreund (1978) writes: "In general, psychoanalytic theoreticians of infancy are preoccupied with the origin of the ego. The newborn is said to have no ego and to be unable to take in the external world. Early infancy is spoken of as a state of 'undifferentiation' or 'non-differentiation,' meaning that the infant makes no discernible distinction between inner and outer stimuli and is unable to distinguish between himself and inanimate surroundings" (p. 427). But, he adds later, "Everything now known about infancy— from behavioral and biological studies—argues against any conception of an undifferentiated phase in which the infant supposedly cannot distinguish inner and outer stimuli or distinguish between himself and inanimate objects, and against any idea that in the human infant the function of and the equipment for self-preservation are atrophied. These typical psychoanalytic characterizations of infancy simply do not fit the observable facts—not those observable to unsophisticated observers, and certainly not those observed by sophisticated workers" (p. 433). Among the latter, Peterfreund points to the work of Emde et al. (1976), as well as of Wolff (1959) and Fantz (1961).

I am in essential agreement with Peterfreund's argument. Let me use it as a justification for a differentiated look at the "undifferentiated phase" concept. I have noted previously that early psychoanalysis had the conceptual problem of how to account for change, learning, and development, given the concept of the id as timeless and unchanging. As part of his effort to resolve this problem, Hartmann pointed to the importance of biological givens that serve to make perception, thinking, and memory possible. But he offered this formulation within the context of the larger formulation of an undifferentiated phase. Cautiously, or so it seems to me, he suggested that "in some cases it will be advisable to assume that both the instinctual drive processes and the ego mechanisms arise from a common root prior to the differentiation of the ego and the id" (1939, p. 102). Thus, the seeds of both are there at the outset but not yet "the ego mechanisms" and "the instinctual drive processes" as we come to see them later on. The problem of how the ego can be born out of an infertile (unchanging) parent—the id—has been conceptually bypassed.

Still, Hartmann wrote at what was an undifferentiated phase in our understanding of infancy, and so it remains for us not to be stymied by the lack of differentiation in the undifferentiated phase concept *itself*. More recent infant research and conceptual clarification allow a more refined statement today. Consistent with this, let me pose the following question: To what aspects of the infant's functioning can the terms "undifferentiated" and "differentiated" be applied? I pose the question in this way because differentiation is neither either-or nor once-and-for-all. That is, the infant need not be seen as either differentiated or not differentiated but, perhaps, as differentiated in some but not other aspects of its functioning. Similarly, the degree of differentiation, even in any one area, may vary from moment to moment.

Peterfreund (1978) argues that the very use of the term "undifferentiated" is adultomorphic; that point is of course well taken. The infant is what it is and functions at its degree of differentiation; it is undifferentiated only by adult standards. So let me clarify my use of the term. It is not the *infant* that is undifferentiated; rather, those aspects of the person that *we* later subsume under the concepts "ego" and "id" (or other concepts) may (or may not) be undifferentiated. The term is not pejorative but is merely a conceptual tool.

So what *is* undifferentiated in the undifferentiated phase? Are ego and id undifferentiated? Self and other? Primary process and secondary process? Anxiety and pleasure? Libido and aggression?

As for ego and id, we can say nothing about their differentiation at birth. These are theoretical abstractions and no more. But if we turn to the ego apparatuses (that is, the inborn givens for perception, memory, learning, and so forth) and the biological drives (most imperiously, hunger, at the start), there is a good deal we can say. It is clear that the visual apparatus for example, and hunger are not "undifferentiated" at birth. One can hardly even say that they are "differentiated," though that comes closer; in fact they are different segments of the organism waiting their day, so to speak, to achieve psycho-logical relevance. And a substantial part of their later psychological relevance is achieved through the *integration* of the apparatuses with the tension states (drives); it is their progressive interrelation of function, rather than their differentiation from an undifferentiated matrix, that is the central develop-mental line.

Thus we start with biological givens, the "apparatuses." These have com-plex developmental histories in their own right. but psychoanalysts have been interested in the distinctive problem of the organization of these apparatuses in relation to the drives. This relation can be stated schematically as follows: affect signals the presence of a drive state, and the individual uses his per-ception and his store of memories, all organized by thought, to find a means to gratification; he then goes into action to achieve it. Thereafter affect again signals the termination of the drive state. At this point, the apparatuses of affect, perception, memory, thought, and motility have become functional for meeting the needs of the person. In general we can say that the inborn apparatuses achieve their psychological relevance when they become func-tional for drive gratification, object relation, and adaptation. When the per-ceptual apparatus has developed to the point where the child can use perception to locate the nipple or bottle, the perceptual function has come into being. When the memory and recognition of mother's footsteps as she comes to nurse permit the child to look toward the doorway, all the while delaying crying although he is hungry, the more complex function of anticipation has come into being through development of more discrete functions.

Many of these developments take place quite early, or may even be there from the start. Thus, Sander (1977), who has studied the regulation of the infant-mother exchange network in the earliest days of life and finds subtle but important contributions to this exchange from the side of the infant, suggests that we cannot think simply of apparatuses waiting to be "used" as "tools" of the "ego" but instead must think of them as serviceable from the start in the regulation of events in the infant-caretaker communication system.

In summary, it seems reasonable to say that the ego apparatuses achieve functional relevance by being tied to psychological aims regarding drive and object relation. But so too does development of drives come to be connected with apparatuses and integrated with them. The physiological tension states presumably achieve psychological status in part through memories of images (of gratification or distress) associated with the tension states. Furthermore, the drives achieve more regularized and individually characteristic modes of discharge when mediated by the apparatuses, when learning, anticipation, intentionality, perception, and the like govern the pathway, the choice of object, the pace, and the delay of gratification in any particular instance. Very early, then, it is the linkage of modes of drive gratification to ego functions that gives them mental representation as well as organized, repeated, pre-ferred—in short, structuralized—form.

It is clearly insufficient to describe this developing two-way network of inborn apparatus and biological need simply by referring to an undifferentiated phase; as noted earier, progressive interrelation of function, rather than differentiation from an undifferentiated matrix, is the central developmental line.

In what sense are self and other undifferentiated or differentiated in the beginnings of life? At least two separate problems are subsumed in this question, the first having to do with the *concept* of self and other, the second with the relationship of self *to* other. As I discussed in chapter 4, research on the separation-individuation process (Mahler et al., 1975) has led us to believe that *concepts* of self and other—concepts that are superordinate to the many discrete perceptual and cognitive "bits" of what will later be "self" and "other," and that organize them into at least partially unified categories—are undifferentiated at the start or, more precisely, that they are actually not there at the start. In contrast, as I have noted, affectively significant moments with a quality of "merger" occur in this early period with lasting developmental impact.

As for the *relation* of self to other at the start, the situation is quite different. Summing up his work on the regulation of exchange between infant and caretaker, Sander (1977) writes: "Current research in early infancy is beginning to provide provocative evidence that human existence normally begins in the context of a highly organized relational system from the outset. This relational system interfaces two live, actively self-regulating, highly complex, living (and adapting) components—the infant and the caretaker, each already running, so to speak" (p. 15). Work by Stern (1971) and Beebe and Stern (1977) shows equally complex regulations of gaze behavior later in the first year, including both contact and avoidance between infant and caretaker. It is not clear to me that this is best described as differentiated behavior, but it is clear that it is not well captured by the term "*un*differentiated."

What of primary and secondary processes? Are they undifferentiated at the start of life? Again, the term "undifferentiated" (or "differentiated," for that matter) is insufficient to capture the phenomenon. If we regard displaceability as the distinguishing feature of primary process, fixity may be similarly viewed as the hallmark of secondary process—that is, a world of stable meanings. From this standpoint, the *focused* tracking reported by Wolff (1959) and the perceptual *preferences* reported by Fantz (1961) and others in the earliest days of life suggest the presence of at least the roots of secondary process even on day 1. Experimental psychological research on perception, memory, and thought provides a vast corpus of study on the development from these simple beginnings to the complex achievement of adult "secondary process" thought.

On the other hand, Holt (1967) has forcefully argued for a developmental conception of primary process as well. While suggesting that the *in*capacity for delay (one of the defining attributes of primary process) need not be thought of as requiring a period of development to be attained, he nonetheless argues for a structural conception of primary process based on the regularities in that mode of thought—defined operationally by its translatability and hence absence of randomness. In that conception, primary process, too, is seen as an organized mode of thinking that is developed. With these ideas and the results of infant research in mind, it may be most fruitful for us to think of the task of development not as the differentiation of primary and secondary process out of an undifferentiated matrix or as the differentiation of secondary out of primary process but as the *elaboration* of each, over time, out of their simple origins.

How do the terms "undifferentiated" and "differentiated" apply in the realm of the affective life of the newborn—say, with regard to anxiety (or unpleasure) and pleasure? Certainly there is no reason to believe that something like signal anxiety is present in differentiated form at the start since it requires considerable learning, automatic anticipation, and a developed memory system. But, in general, it is in the nature of affects, being quantitative, that they can rise or diminish and that one affect can gradually blend into another. Observation of infants readily reveals, as their perhaps most obvious feature, at times gradual and at times more rapid state and mood variations. Although these seem differentiable (to the observer) at the extremes, and presumably are experienced differentially by the infant, there is a vast middle ground where differentiation is not at all clear. Interestingly, affects are not all that reliably differentiated—by the observer or by the subject—later in life either, with pleasurable excitement bordering on anxiety, depression blending into anger, fear surrounding eager anticipation, and the like. Elsewhere (Pine, 1979) I have discussed in greater detail the gradual differentiation of affects, in parallel to the attainment of diverse developmental achievements (see also Schmale, 1964).

Finally, as regards libido and aggression in relation to the question of differentiation versus undifferentiation, we are once again dealing with theoretical abstractions. The concepts are far from precise and are highly inferential, and it is difficult to approach them directly. Nonetheless, let me make a few comments, taking off from Freud's (1915) early ideas regarding the "purified pleasure ego" and from recent clinical interest in the phenomenon of "splitting" (Kernberg, 1967).

We know as a matter of objective reality that some pleasant and some unpleasant experiences originate in one's own body (e.g., satiation and warmth, pain and cold) and some originate in another (e.g., the mother's loving smile, her rocking, or feeding in contrast to her anger, rough handling, or misreading of infant cues). But, as I have already stated, there is no basis for assuming that the infant is born with concepts of self and other that can subsume these contradictory (good and bad) experiences attached to what *we* know to be self and other. Some infant observers and observers of wishful, pathological, and normal adult states have speculated that the infant's world, to the degree that sensory experience and memory permit differentiation at all, is more likely to be divided (for moments at least, and at the extremes) into "good experiences" and "bad experiences," with no accompanying differentiation of the source of the good or bad in self or other. Affects rather than concepts serve to organize experience. From this standpoint, the task of development is for the growing infant to learn to divide the world "objectively" into self and other (both containing "good" and "bad" parts), even if, subjectively, the pleasure-unpleasure experience remains a significant dimension.

Freud's conception of the purified pleasure ego goes a step beyond inferences about direct experience to inferences regarding primitive mechanisms; he suggested that the infant not only experiences pleasure as belonging to the self (the "pleasure ego") but rejects the unpleasure experience as not belonging to the self (hence the *purified* pleasure ego). Kernberg, in discussing "splitting," similarly indicates that some later pathology is organized around actively keeping the love and the hate apart, a defense that functions to preserve the representation of the love object from the destructive forces of hate but simultaneously permits the luxuriant growth of hate, unmodified by (because split off from) love. Developmentalists (McDevitt, 1975; and see chap. 8) have written in a similar vein, commenting on the young child's task of fusing the loving and hating feelings. The course of development of the pleasure-filled and distress-filled experiences is complex, probably (like that of affects) differentiated at the extremes but blending at other times. One can think of splitting as "enforced differentiation" of these experiences and of the fusion of love and hate as healthy "dedifferentiation" (or, perhaps more accurately, as "synthesis"). In any event, the developmental task involves some form of unification of the loving and hating experiences.

To sum up, I have used the concepts of undifferentiation and differentiation as tools for the analysis of infant mental life. To do this required inference from infant research data and naturalistic observation, and inference "backward" from adult experience. I have extended the discussion of undifferentiation beyond Hartmann's original use of it for ego and id, and have included ego-id, self-other, the thought processes (primary process and secondary process), affects (pleasure-unpleasure), and the concepts of libido and aggression. Though clearly remaining inferential, it seems to me that the application of the concepts of undifferentiation and differentiation to diverse *areas* and varying *moments* of the infant's experience permits a reasonably articulated—that is, *conceptually differentiated*—view of the infant.

7

Structuralization of Drive-Defense Relationships

Continuing with the themes of differentiation and interconnection discussed in the previous chapter, I should like additionally to return to the concept of multiple function (chap. 5), using all these ideas in relation to the psychologies of drive and ego. The concepts of multiple function and of structure together provide a means of dealing with the development of order and permanence in psychic life. Such order and permanence—rigidities and endless repetitions, hidden in the morass of day-to-day variation in the patient's free associations—are the stuff of clinical work; the fact that change in this "permanence" does not come easily is a given in that work. Here, I will apply this chapter's main theme—*that the growth of order and permanence comes through the achievement of multiple function*—in an examination of the development of relationships between urges and the defenses against them.

MULTIPLE FUNCTION AND THE CONCEPT OF STRUCTURE

Waelder (1936), in his classic paper on multiple function, suggests that any specific psychic act is an attempted solution to problems of the ego vis-à-vis the drives, the superego, external reality, and the compulsion to repeat. In chapter 5, I have suggested a modification of Waelder's formulation, specifying the repetition of internalized object relations and adding a fifth necessary "solution": the maintenance of self-esteem. Every psychic act potentially solves several problems, thus having multiple functions. This complements the idea that every psychic act results from diverse forces in the person, thus having multiple determinants. I would suggest that any psychic act that is determined

Based upon material originally published under the titles: "On the structuralization of drive-defense relationships" (*Psychoanalytic Quarterly*, 39:17–37, 1970) and "On the separation process: Universal trends and individual differences" (In *Separation-Individuation*, ed. J. B. McDevitt and C. F. Settlage [International Universities Press, 1971]).

by so diverse a set of requirements and successfully resolves them is likely to have a degree of permanence; it will appear again in similar circumstances.

As Waelder himself (1960) points out, we need not suppose that all psychic acts are equally successful in resolving psychic problems: they are only attempts. Some acts—practiced, altered, and perfected over time—are likely to have more functions and to be more permanent. Symptoms, repeated masturbation fantasies (Arlow, 1953), certain actions (Stein, 1967), interests, and occupational choices, as well as certain established everyday modes of gratification achieved in the course of development, are likely to be in this class.

What is "successfully" functional in psychic life is measured against intrapsychic criteria, ultimately the experience of pleasure or anxiety and other unpleasant affects. These affects guide our behavior as, usually without awareness, we select and retain modes of thinking and acting that maximize pleasure and minimize anxiety. This does not imply that pure, immediate pleasure is the sole aim of human behavior; psychoanalysis is a thoroughly *modified* hedonistic theory. The concepts of sublimation, delay, reversal, tolerance of anxiety, aim inhibition, and masochism, for example, deal with modifications of the pure-pleasure aim.

How "permanent" will successfully functional behavior become? Only partially. The accumulation of memories, including memories of the past acts that led to pleasure or anxiety, always adds new determinants to future acts. And we constantly perfect, through alteration and emphasis, and without conscious intent, our ways of resolving the multiple problems we face. "Each attempted solution of a problem must be conjointly determined, modified, and arranged through the existence and the working of the other, until it can serve, even if imperfectly, as an attempted solution for all these problems" (Waelder, 1936, pp. 51–52). Maturation—of the pleasure organization, the capacity actively to affect the environment, the cognitive apparatus—also constantly introduces new factors. Thus, the permanence of any "solution" in mental life is limited.

What about the "similar circumstances" in which successful multiply functional behavior reappears? There are no identities in human life; any repeated situation impinges on a somewhat new person, new at least by virtue of his or her having experienced it before. Indeed, we are here concerned not with bits of behavior that recur in identical form in identical situations but with complex arrays of behavior, organized in relation to one another and to a *range* of circumstances. Some aspects of this psychic network may be active at one time, others at another, always achieving a momentary optimal balance among pleasure, anxiety, and the diverse requirements of the moment.

Let me say a word also on the concept of structure. Its essential importance in psychoanalysis derives from the fact that the theory requires concepts capable of dealing with permanence and order. In classical psychoanalytic theory, the maturation of the drives and ego apparatuses (Hartmann, 1939) and the cyclic and peremptory character of the drives (Rapaport, 1960a) allow us to account for changes in individual functioning that occur from year to year as well as from moment to moment. If we are to understand character and defense and the laying down of relatively permanent memories we must have a theory that can encompass order and permanence within the constant flux of development.

The concept of multiple function is one avenue to an understanding of permanence in psychic life. So too is the concept of structure, as Nagera's (1967) review makes clear. Holt says, "The central defining feature of a structure is its *organization*: it is an arrangement of parts in a pattern, which does not necessarily have to have any simple kind of ordering, and does not necessarily endure for long, though we are usually most interested in the structures that persist for a matter of months or years" (1967, p. 350n). In some instances, at least, the concepts of structure and multiple function are related. A multiply functional psychic act from one point of view is a structuralized arrangement from another. A particular psychic act may be viewed as functioning to solve a number of "problems" (deriving from wishes, anxieties, environmental opportunities), or the several environmental opportunities and internal intentions may be conceived of as organized in relation to one another around particular culminating behaviors.

In psychoanalytic writings, the term "structure" is used to describe phenomena on a continuum of complexity and scope (cf. Nagera, 1967). Gill (1963, p. 8n) refers to "macrostructures" and "microstructures." Thus, a "structure" may be simple (a memory trace, for example, or a single idea); more complex (e.g., a defense mechanism); or a highly complex organization of the psyche (id, ego, and superego). More complex structures are sets of relationships, organizations. Beres (1965), for example, describes the ego as a set of functions ordinarily organized in a particular relationship to one another and arrayed on one side of a conflict. While simpler structures such as memory traces or some defenses often appear to be unvarying acquisitions or achievements of the psychic apparatus that can be drawn upon again and again as differing occasions demand, they too exist in a relational context. In this chapter I discuss this relational aspect of structures.

Structuralized relationships do not consist of automatic unvarying sequences. The more or less permanent structure is really a set of possible responses, each one potentially involved in a given situation; the specific final response is dependent upon quantitative and contextual factors. A particular gratification may be pursued vigorously until it rises above a specific intensity; at that point, and only then, an anxiety signal may trigger flight or intrapsychic defense. Or the gratification may be pursued only in one situation and not in another. Or it may be pursued in one way in one context and in another way in another. Such a set of structuralized relationships achieves the maintenance of some optimal level of pleasure or comfort given the current situational and intrapsychic realities. Some specific behavior may be multiply functional in solving the problems of drive, anxiety, guilt, and adaptation at a given moment, but the range of potential behavior "choices" widens during development. This widening occurs because the memory store of experiences and outcomes increases and because maturation increases the capacity for new behaviors. This widening range of "choice," though not necessarily conscious, is the development of what Waelder referred to as the aims the "ego assigns to itself" (1936, pp. 48, 49) with regard to the other psychic agencies. It is, in short, the growth of ego activity.

Modes of gratification are also structuralized. Often the opposite is emphasized: it is said, for example, that drives "press for discharge" and the controlling structures make delay possible and maintain constancy (Rapaport, 1960b). To emphasize that drives aim toward satisfaction, however, is not to say that the satisfaction does not take place in structuralized ways. In recent years a number of writers (Gill, 1963; Schur, 1966; Holt, 1967) have examined the structural elements of the "id" and the primary process. From an observational viewpoint, it is clear that an individual satisfies his wishes in uniquely individual ways; he shows preference, he excludes certain kinds of gratification, he has a specific style. In short, he has a regular and patterned mode of gratification. D. Shapiro (1965) shows how even in the so-called impulsive character, we are not simply seeing pure breakthroughs of drives. Modes of gratification are not, after infancy, random, replaceable one for another, or otherwise inconsistent with the total character of the individual. They show variations within a range of tolerable and pleasurable qualities and quantities, but an overall regularity of mode of gratification is readily discerned in the individual instance.

In chapter 6, I discussed at a general level some of the interrelations among the tension states (drives) and the built-in capacities (ego apparatuses) of the organism. Broadly, I suggested there that the capacities for perception, learning, memory, thinking, motor behavior, and affect achieve their psychological relevance through becoming tied to (functional for) the need-gratifying and object-relational aims of the person. Conversely, I suggested that the core aims and urges of the person reach their final psychological shape only when mediated by the apparatuses—when learning, anticipation, intentionality, perception, and the like govern the pathway, the object, the pace, and the delay of gratification in any particular instance. Holding these schematic statements of interrelationship in mind as general background, let us turn to more specific examples of the *development* of structuralized relationships between urges and the defenses against them. I shall be using the terms drive, urge, aim, and wish more or less interchangeably since my objective is not to address classical drive theory but instead to discuss motive at an observable and/or phenomenological level.[1]

EXAMPLES FROM THE DEVELOPMENT OF DRIVES

The general developmental process moves from less to more internal differentiation and integration of the personality. More precisely, in the area of

1. In the remainder of this chapter, I will be drawing my illustrative material from the data of a longitudinal study of preschool and early school-age boys that I carried out some years ago.

drive-defense relationships this development proceeds from diffuse pleasure and/or distress, to focal gratification, focal anxiety, and thence to structuralized gratification and defense.

By the term "diffuse," as applied to either pleasure or distress, I refer to an early stage in which the instigators of affect are, from the infant's point of view, random, changeable, not subject to his control, and have at best nebulous cognitive representation. Principles of pleasure-unpleasure may guide behavior, but we cannot speak of multiple function in Waelder's sense of the term since psychic acts do not have reference to the superego and conception of reality, which are not yet developed.

By the term "focal gratification" I refer to the beginnings of specificity in the source of pleasure. Specificity results partly from growth of the cognitive apparatus, and hence from development of the "wish" in Freud's sense (1900, p. 566), but probably it also results from physiological development of the erotogenic regions of the body. With the specific wish comes a more articulated "task" for later structuralized and multiply functional behavior to encompass; this task is the gratification of that wish. Focal gratification means two things. First, a particular gratification is not readily replaceable by some other pleasure but is an end in itself. Thus, the sexuality of the infant is polymorphous, apart from certain phase-specific central gratifications, but preferred modes of sexual gratification, normal or pathological, in the adult are specific. Second, the specific gratification is an organizer of experience (cf. Spitz, 1959) and not merely an element in it. An example is the part played by clothing as one element in a woman's attractiveness to the normal male and its central position in the view of, say, a shoe fetishist.

By "focal anxiety" I mean the linkage of an unpleasant affective state with a specific cognitive content. At times the child may be fully aware of the external or internal source of his anxiety, so that he can label it and anticipate it. For example, the young child learns that a particular state of affective distress is associated with his mother's absence and he attempts to keep her near. However, since it seems likely that defense can develop almost simultaneously with anxiety, the child may in some instances never become fully aware that an unpleasant affective state occurs under certain precise circumstances. In any event, even what is conscious at some point can certainly later become unavailable to consciousness as a result of defensive processes. The essential point, however, is that when gratification of a drive leads to anxiety a new task is posed for subsequent psychic acts. This is true whether the anxiety arises from fear of retaliation from the outside, from fear of the strength of the impulses (A. Freud, 1936), or, later, from internalized proscriptions. The task is to achieve drive gratification while also dealing with anxiety in some manner.

The term "structuralized," as applied to behavior serving either gratification or defense, refers to two characteristics of the behavior: (1) it is repeated, predictable, and regularized, and (2) it is actively produced, intended, by the child. The infant's gratifications arrive for him through his mother's activity. However, he very soon learns that he himself can make such gratifications come to him through crying and calling his mother. Henceforth he is ever more active in achieving gratifications by his own efforts. Similarly, the crying and thrashing that bring relief to the infant with his mother's arrival are not at first intended by him for that purpose but must soon become thus intended, a change that grows by degrees into the defensive and adaptive processes that the child himself initiates and that are universally found even in early childhood. Thus structuralization is indicated by the fact that the child actively produces a particular repeated form of behavior. This behavior is the result of an inner arrangement of forces that has arrived at a certain stability; it need not be created anew each time a particular demand arises. The implication that the child is able to construct or "structure" a particular environment for himself by this point in his development is also correct, within limits. Again, the essential point is that such structuralized behavior represents a solution to the multiple demands acting within the psyche and, in the ideal and perhaps most stabilized instances, results in some act or acts that best meet all these demands.

The following illustrations (using scopophilic and anal impulses) will focus on a stepwise progression from (1) a time when the psychic acts are not structuralized and multiple function (with reference to drives, reality, and superego) cannot be said to exist, to (2) the development of focal gratification and anxiety with their more specific wishes, demands of reality, and demands of conscience in conflict with one another, and finally to (3) the development of structuralized drive-defense relationships and multiply functional behaviors that serve as a solution to the multiple demands upon the psyche at any given moment. I do not mean to imply, in what follows, that scopophilia and anality should be conceived of as equivalent drives; quite the reverse. At least in the infant, the visual apparatus may be better conceived of in terms of ego apparatuses (Hartmann, 1939) powered by independent ego energies (White, 1963), as an apparatus of the organism that is especially susceptible to recruitment to drive aims. However, I do assume that both scopophilic and anal impulses become important nodal points for the development of structuralized relationships.

SCOPOPHILIA

The child's pleasure in looking develops from diffuse pleasure to focal gratification, focal anxiety, and thence to structuralized gratification and defense. Certainly, looking is one of the more striking early activities of the infant. In states of alert inactivity (Wolff, 1959) the newborn takes in the world through his eyes, much as he does through his mouth (Erikson, 1950). As the infant develops, he follows moving objects, his head and eyes turn in the direction of a sound or toward the door through which mother usually comes. Just what connection there is between looking and pleasurable affect is unclear, but it is evident that looking at mother, eye to eye, is, like fingering her face, a typical accompaniment of nursing. And looking, with attention caught by something, can be associated with a temporary inhibition of crying or other signs of upset even in the first weeks and increasingly thereafter.

But looking is only one of many pleasures for the young infant and toddler in his home, with his mother and other members of his family. He is frequently ministered to, touched, lifted, handled; he sees his mother, father, and siblings eating talking, washing, dressing. He takes in his family with his eyes; their bodily functions are part of the routine of his life; they defecate, urinate, bathe, and clean up; he notices their odors as well as their looks. All his sense organs take in the familiar stimuli. And this is all around him; no special behavior on his part is necessary to experience it.[2] Contrast this to a later period, when these everday gratifications usually become less available. Concern for privacy limits the child's experience. With the development of conscience, the fantasies attached to these gratifications make them sources of conflict to the child.

In the early period, many of the pleasures, including looking, are quiet pleasures; they are a background to the child's life. Except for hunger and feeding, they are neither as focal nor as cyclic as, for example, adult sexual activity. Gratification is not usually intense enough to lead to strong excitation, although some experiences with looking (for example, primal-scene exposure) are exceptions. One pleasure can replace another at this stage; to some extent gratifications are functionally equivalent. Quiet and taken-for-granted satisfaction can be obtained through seeing mother or other means. Ruth Mack Brunswick says, "Pleasure is obtained from innumerable sources: the child's appetite for it is random and without a particular goal, one reason perhaps why that appetite remains unsatiated" (1940, p. 305). It is in this sense that early looking is a diffuse source of pleasure. Although there is no focal excitation in these situations, there is every reason to believe that such incidents are part of the quiet familiar pleasures of the child's life, incidents in which the child's use of mother as an object for his pleasure does not yet cause conflict but cements his relation to her.

Let us consider the emergence of focal pleasure in looking, a pleasure that later becomes a source of anxiety, which in turn triggers the development of defenses that eventually become more structuralized, with or without continuing opportunities for gratification. Several steps in this process were observed in our study of a group of normal boys aged four through eight. Not all these steps may take place in all children, nor do we know exactly in what order or when they occur or how much they overlap. However, age four seems to be an excellent time to observe the development of the sensually linked urge to look. It is a time when rapid changes are taking place, and we saw wide individual variations in the particular developmental point achieved.

Somewhere around this age, then, a variety of things begin to happen.

2. So many are the pathological influences in the lives of some children who arrive for treatment that we often wonder why they are not even more disturbed than they are. One answer may lie in these numerous, often unnoticed everyday gratifications through familiar stimuli that are almost unavoidably part of the early life of the child.

(1) The pleasure in looking at mother becomes an outstanding ("focal") one. It is no longer just part of a totality of small, familiar gratifications; it stands out. Presumably it is no longer readily replaceable by other pleasures. Mothers often respond to this stage in the child's development by feeling that the time has come to be more cautious about the child's seeing them undressed. (2) In several children we thought we saw a forestage of anxiety. At this point there appears to be something "special" about seeing mother undressed. Seeing her seems no longer just part of the backgrund of life at home; it is no longer taken for granted. And yet the situation does not seem entirely pleasurable for the child, nor does his reaction convey anxiety very clearly. Rather, he appears to have made those cognitive and perceptual differentiations that make mother's nakedness stand out as a very specific environmental presentation; he seems to feel that something is not quite right, but a specific conflict involving defense against looking has not yet crystallized. The child may show surprise, exaggerated excitement, or giggling when seeing mother. (3) We see beginnings of internalized defensive processes, where some intrapsychic alteration of the impulse to look takes place. These defenses seem to be not yet consistent in the four-year-olds: they may be here today, gone tomorrow, and back the next day; or they may be present in one situation and not in another.

What initiates these developments in relation to looking? And what further factors influence its course? Very early in life looking is a pleasure taken for granted with little or no focal excitation; later, after the development of focal excitation, there is defense against these urges. The initial change from background pleasure to focal pleasure in looking is likely to be the result of more or less universal maturational and developmental events: the diminished significance of earlier oral and anal pleasures; awareness of sex differences, concern about them, and anxiety-instigated desires to look; the biological linkage of looking and genital excitation. Casual, everyday seductions by the mother of her now "manly" young child also contribute.[3] And the change from focal pleasure to anxiety and defense is undoubtedly stimulated by the fears and prohibitions of the oedipal period, including superego development.

Let us consider a possible variation in the normal progression of development suggested by the data from our four-year-olds. In looking at the mother or other females, the child discovers the anatomical differences between the sexes. Even before he experiences anxiety in connection with the sexual aim of looking at mother (because of the quality of the excitation, the fantasies attached to it, and the fear of punishment), looking at her when she is undressed can be stressful to the male child because of what he sees—

---

3. It may be that focal excitation in looking appears before the phallic phase as well; consider how the adult's mouth waters at the sight of food. Nonetheless, it seems to me that the excitation in looking at the phallic level, at least in boys, is the most fully developed form whereas the others are only forerunners. If the earlier forms are highly developed in particular individuals, one would expect them to have some shaping influence on phallic-level scopophilia. On the other hand, individuals also vary in the degree to which scopophilic impulses are displaced or regressively reattached to prephallic objects as a result of conflict at the more advanced level.

that there are human beings who have no penis. Somewhere in the oedipal period and on into latency, the pleasure and genital excitement connected with looking at mother, along with the other oedipal fantasies and impulses of which it is part, lead to the fear of punishment by castration and are, in one way or another, partially renounced. At that time, the earlier sight of the female genital makes the fear of castration seem realistic. But seeing the penisless body can lead directly to anxiety at an earlier period because of fear of what is strange and fear of body injury (cf. Roiphe and Galenson, 1982). These may exist before the fear of castration as punishment for sexual wishes, although the degree and specificity of the anxiety are radically altered when conflict over the drive is added to the attitudes already present. In very young children for whom this sight is extremely distressful because of circumstances in their earlier development, we may guess that sight of the female genital will have not only retrospective significance when castration fears over oedipal fantasies arise but also a prospective effect on the shaping of the Oedipus complex and on the further course of the development of looking.[4]

I have so far discussed emergence of focal excitation, and later of anxiety, out of early, quiet background pleasure in looking; we have noted some suggestions of internalized defense as well in our four-year-olds. By age eight (and no doubt somewhat earlier, but we did not have those data), a certain end point in development had been reached. At this stage, by and large, the child's mode of contact with the visually arousing stimulus (in our data, the sight of the naked or partially undressed female) is an achievement in the sense that it is to a large degree the child's creation and is repeated with variations without having to be created anew each time. It is also multiply functional in the sense that it balances for him his impulses and his defenses in the setting of a particular family pattern. We infer that structuralization in the sense defined earlier has occurred.

At this point, gratification in seeing mother is not only very specific and focal but also structuralized. What does this mean? Consider a child who intrudes on his naked mother, touches her, and says, "Oh boy, what fat!" Other evidence from our observation of this child makes it evident that he relies heavily on "cute" verbalization in a large number of situations, and that he is relying on "cuteness" on this occasion too. The boy began to speak early and was the center of family attention; then and now, his mother responds to him principally when he makes "cute" remarks. His comment here has a defensive function in that it makes the situation playful, but it is also seductive. Furthermore, it is consistent with a long-developing way of behaving. Another eight-year-old boy, whose general inhibition often makes

4. Ordinarily this further development includes a strong investment in looking because of the sexual pleasure as well as the information necessary for adaptation that it brings. It also includes inhibition of aim of the sexual component, such as interest in female clothing, and sublimation, such as a general interest in art. Clinically it may be possible to distinguish impairments of the adaptive functions of looking that are rooted primarily in the wish to look at the incestuous object from those that are rooted relatively more in the fear of discovering the female genital.

it hard to "read" his feelings, regularly intrudes on his mother when she is in the bathroom, but he "looks through her" as though he does not notice her; here, as elsewhere, he shows "no reaction." Each child establishes contact with his naked mother in regularly repeated and historically characteristic ways. In this sense, then, the mode of gratification is structuralized. It is part of a complex organization that includes the child's characteristic modes of defense, overt behavior, and relations to reality. It represents a resolution of multiple requirements and is therefore highly resistant to change under ordinary circumstances.

In summary, the child's scopophilic impulses grow out of a taken-for-granted array of everyday gratifications including looking; a focal sexual pleasure in looking develops later. Then anxiety specifically connected with looking appears, until finally the child develops structuralized modes of gratification and defense that, ideally, permit a modified form of gratification without concomitant anxiety. Individuals differ in their movement in this progression. They differ in the effect (upon the development of the urge to look) of the sight of the anatomical difference between the sexes; in the pace of movement from one step to the next; and also in the degree to which the structuralized outcome is ineffective, as indicated in part by the amount of diffuse discharge and the affective state accompanying it.

ANALITY

For anal impulses, the developmental steps are the same: from diffuse excitation to focal gratification, focal anxiety, and thence to structuralized gratification and defense.

We can probably assume that defecation produces a state of diffuse excitation in the infant; there is a generalized flood of stimulation, evident in widespread tension throughout the body. The experience appears to include distress and relief, in sequence, and perhaps also specific anal-erotic sensations. Although there are brief moments during the infant's day when defecation is actually taking place and when functioning of his bowels is his central experience, at other times bowel function has no special importance; it is not an organizer of experience of other events of his day. The toddler may defecate in his diaper and then run around playing, presumably enjoying play while at the same time experiencing the warmth and touch of the fecal matter against his buttocks; the fecal pleasure is but one element in the total experience.

Sometime during the second year of life the gratification associated with defecation usually becomes much more focal. There are several reasons: maturation and actions taken by the mother jointly lead to some abandonment of oral gratifications; moreover, maturation of the nervous system permits greater control over the anal sphincter so that what has probably been an experience of passivity in defecation can now be experienced more actively and less stressfully; and there is a general cathexis of the musculature by the toddler, probably extending to the anal sphincter as well. Also, mother and others attend to the child's bowel functioning as attempts are begun to train him, and the child becomes increasingly aware of the stimulation provided when he is cleaned. At this time bowel activity comes to have more of an organizing role in his experience; it becomes a focus of his relation to mother and a prized pleasure that he is not easily willing to renounce.

Where is the child at age four in the developmental progression for anal impulses? The following is based on inferences from data showing how the child reacts to external stimuli that arouse such impulses and interests. The children we studied at age four usually showed anxiety and some preliminary defensive reactions. Overall, these developments for anal impulses were further along at age four than for scopophilic impulses and yet were markedly different from what was evident in the eight-year-olds.

What can be said about the nature and source of focal anxiety? Certainly the fear of loss of love stimulates the child's attempt to "civilize" his bowel functioning and become trained. Defecation is, moreover, essentially a solitary activity; the child is left alone with powerful internal excitations without the possibility of mother's giving him immediate support. This can trigger anxiety. And the child imitates the attitudes of his parents and older siblings. Yet these reasons do not seem sufficient to account for the consistent and widespread defenses against anal impulses that we usually see in the adult. And in fact the anxiety of the four-year-olds seems to disturb them less than that of the eights disturb them; it is not so fully internalized, and the children remain closer to gratification without defensive compromises. The link of anal activity to the fantasies of the oedipal period, as well as the defenses against these and the formation of the superego, probably account for the difference between our four- and eight-year-olds.

Confronted with the arousal of anal impulses, the reaction of eight-year-olds is an achievement comparable to their reaction to scopophilic stimuli: the behavior pattern is to a large degree the child's creation and is repeated by him, with variations, without having to be created anew each time. It is also multiply functional in the sense that it balances his impulses and defenses in the setting of particular family patterns. We infer, once again, that structuralization has occurred. In the ideal case, this serves to resolve the multiple demands upon the person in relation to anal impulses; it does so through multiply functional acts that organize relations among the demands of drives, defenses, reality, and conscience.

Thus, we saw one child who continually talked about bathroom odors, ostensibly trying to avoid them but always keeping his mind on them while he kept his sense organs away from them. His mother participated in these conversations. Another child vigorously sprayed the bathroom whenever there was an odor, in the process creating a far stronger odor from the spray can, but one that he could experience without conflict. And his mother provided the spray. These examples show how repeatable, individually characteristic modes of behavior are evolved that strike some balance among gratification of drive, defense, and the opportunities and proscriptions of the particular home.

AN EXAMPLE FROM THE DEVELOPMENT OF CHILD-
MOTHER ATTACHMENT

The history of the child's relation to and separation from the mother follows
a course from (1) diffuse pleasure, distress, and delineation of body boundaries
to (2) more differentiated gratification, anxiety, and object concept, and thence
to (3) object relationship and structuralized defense and gratification.

Much of what is postulated under this developmental line is familiar. We
assume that, in the world of the newborn, inner and outer, self and other,
are not consistently distinguished. Seen from the outside, the newborn seems
to move from a state of relative ease and well-being to intense distress, to
eager intake of milk with blissful satisfaction, subsidence of distress, and a
return to ease and well-being. In hunger, the distress soon becomes a generalized discomfort that pervades the whole body, with crying and thrashing
about. With nursing, the whole body relaxes. For the newborn, the more
intense affective states (during hunger and hungry intake) are likely to pre-
clude use of his minimal capacity for cognitive-perceptual activity. At times
of high arousal, the infant is unlikely to have a very differentiated picture of
the source of his distress or comfort. White (1963) describes the way in
which intense drive activation will overrun apparatus functioning, including
cognition. It is the generalized distress and relief, and the probable absence
of a clear idea of their source, that characterize the diffuse pleasure and distress
of the newborn. Coupled with these is the presumed absence of a consistent
and clear concept of where self ends and other begins.

During the course of the first year, two overlapping and parallel developments take place, the second demanding a higher level of cognitive development than the first. In the first, the child gradually develops a primitive
idea that states of well-being are associated with the presence of an external
object, the mothering person. At this stage, to some degree, any external
object that brings about the state of well-being is satisfactory. The infant
associates the need-satisfying object with states of well-being, shows positive
responses in the presence of the object, and, at times, anticipatory discomfort
("crankiness") as the object begins to leave. Later in the first year a second
step takes place: a firmer, specific attachment to a single object, the primary
mothering person, develops. At this point, the child's states of well-being
and discomfort center more fully on the presence or absence of that specific
person. Stranger anxiety and separation anxiety at this period indicate that
the child has developed some concept of a separate and differentiated self,
mother, and "other."

It is this frequently described pair of overlapping and parallel developments that represents the movement to more differentiated gratification and
anxiety in connection with the mother. The two seem to devleop simultaneously. As the child's pleasurable experiences come to be more specifically
attached to the presence of, first, a general need-satisfying object, and, second,
to a constant object, the mother, so too does anxiety (affective distress) in
the absence of that object develop. The terms "focal anxiety" and "focal

gratification" perhaps best capture the quality of what has been achieved: a differentiated awareness of the link between a specific stimulus (presence or absence of mother) and a central significant affect. This focalization of anxiety and of gratification, however, neither lessens the anxiety nor makes it possible for the infant to ensure the gratification. Rather, it represents only the achievement of those differentiated perceptions and anticipations that will later form the base of more active modes of coping with the anxiety and guaranteeing the gratification. At this stage, then, the infant, experiencing anxiety with his differentiated awareness of separation from mother and wishing for specific gratifications from her, has not the resources actively to avoid the one or to ensure the other. These are the achievements of the third stage.

Although I said earlier that the specific source of focal anxiety is not always clearly conscious (e.g., in relation to drives and the fantasies attached to them), in the case of anxiety associated with separation from the mother there is no question that the source of the anxiety is at times clearly in consciousness, and that this remains true for long periods in many children. It seems likely that focalized anxiety requires for its existence certain cognitive achievements (that is, the child, via memory, anticipation, and perception, must have learned to recognize the mother's comings and goings and to recognize when such situations are about to occur again and must have stored up memories of distress and of action tendencies relevant to it). In addition, one may speculate that such cognitive developments receive an added impetus from this anxiety—when the child, under the pressure of anxiety that is not too debilitating, actively scans his environment and uses whatever resources he has to find, re-find, or avoid losing the absent or soon-to-be-absent mother.

I also said earlier that "focal gratification" refers to the observations that (1) the particular gratification is not readily replaceable by some other pleasure but is an end in itself, and (2) the specific gratification is an organizer of experience (Spitz, 1959) and not merely an element in it. In the case of the focal gratifications associated with the connection to mother these two characteristics are particularly clear. It is precisely the point of the child's development beyond the purely need-satisfying type of object relationship that the mother is not readily replaceable by others and that gratification depends on her presence. In terms of the mother's being an organizer of pleasurable experiences and not merely an element in them, the point is equally clear. A child in the second year of life, busily at play and seeming to be absorbed with inanimate objects and with his own motor activities and vocalizations, may immediately lose all pleasure in these activities when mother leaves the room. Mahler (1965) clearly decribes this in the rapprochement subphase of the separation-individuation process; pleasures are not sustained autonomously but require the general organizing presence of the mother.

By the end of the first year, most children have advanced beyond the point where no specific focal link between a cognitive experience (the presence or absence of the mother) and an affective state has been made. The differentiated focal pleasure and focal anxiety have come into being as a result of the cognitive and emotional developments of the first year, which include the growing awareness of separateness from mother. The next step to be achieved is structuralized defense against anxiety over separation from mother and structuralized gratification in her presence. These two in part define the object relationship of child to mother. The object relationship—which includes, in the child's mind, his specific potential actions in relation to, specific memory images of, and various reliable expectations of behavior from mother— in effect is the form in which the former mother-child unity is reestablished at a higher developmental level.

In all human development, organizations of behavior reflect not simply mindless growth of complexity but serve a dynamic function in reconciling diverse aims. The structuralized behavior serving either gratification or defense in relation to contact with and separation from mother is brought about by the child with regularity because (in the ideal case) it deals with anxiety, maintains autonomy and adequate relations to reality, and simultaneously provides gratification. Such behavior is constructed and perfected over time through the interconnection of highly charged affective states with the apparatuses of the organism (memory, affect control, thought, mobility) and represents a solution, balancing diverse demands and opportunities within the child and his surround.

With regard to separation, the main forces that have to be balanced are the child's anxiety about the mother's separations, his wishes for continued gratification, and his knowledge of the fact of repeated (even if brief) separations. We have seen a number of different solutions to this among the children we have worked with. However, for most individual children a point comes in development when a particular solution begins to be used with regularity. These are achievements of the child, having been perfected over a course of time until this optimal (even if poor) solution was arrived at. One eight-year-old child, for example, whenever his mother was going out at night, would ask where she was going, when she would be home, who would be the baby-sitter, and whether he could stay up a little later than usual and have an extra piece of cake. Thus he made it possible to retain a specific picture of the mother in her surroundings when she was gone (by having found out where she was going) and to anticipate and feel assured of a specific point of her return. He was also able to ensure having substitute gratifications in her absence. Provided that these conditions were met, the child did not experience anxiety when the mother went out.

Let us consider two other children, quite different in their reactions to the parents going out at night. One, aged four, as soon as he saw mother's "good" dress laid out on the bed, immediately realized what was ahead for the evening, went into his room, and fell into a deep sleep. The other, aged eight, made a point of remaining awake the entire time his parents were gone and then greeted them upon their return. He would stay up until midnight and then would ask whether they had brought something for him. The solutions of these two children, though descriptively opposites, and though both chidren experienced a good deal of anxiety, were equally structuralized. Both children produced these solutions regularly, having evolved them over time. The focal anxiety was dealt with via its connections to the defense capacities of the child, his capacity to influence (or not influence) his environment, and any available opportunities for continued gratification.

It should be clear from these examples that a structuralized defense against the anxiety of separation from mother, like structuralized behavior in any other area, need not be a healthy solution. It is simply characterized by its regularity of appearance and by the fact that, within the limits of the child's capacities and with respect to his particular anxieties and wished-for gratifications, it marks the best possible reconciliation of these diverse requirements at a given point in time.

What about the pleasures in contact with mother? In what sense are they also structuralized? Ordinarily, the structure in modes of gratification with mother is not strikingly evident because the gratifications are so pervasive. They remain part of the quiet pleasure of taken-for-granted home life well into the latency period. But these gratifications certainly are structuralized; the child actively brings them about in special ways that he prefers, and they are central features of his day. One child stays near mother as he plays; another requests that she sit with him at bedtime; still another likes to cuddle in her lap during stories; and so on. The central significance of these gratifications most always becomes clear when their loss is threatened—when the mother is going away, when the child is displaced by a sibling, or when he is expected to renounce them as part of growing up.

Even early on, the child's modes of obtaining gratification from contact with the mother cannot vary with complete freedom. This is in part because the preferred gratifications of a child serve, for him, to retain what is known and comforting by the very fact of being familiar and repeated, to fulfill specific fantasies built around particular pleasures, while simultaneously protecting against too great an intrusion upon his autonomy. A behavior reconciling such diverse aims is not readily replaced. But as the child grows up, a new demand and limitation are increasingly placed upon the allowable and preferred forms of gratification with mother. This is the demand for defense stemming from the fact that the mother becomes increasingly the object of a wide range of impulses. Thus the child's contact with mother is obviously not only a source of gratification but in itself leads to anxiety and defense. The child cannot simply continue receiving gratifications from his mother that are direct continuations of his earliest ones. The contact with mother itself is a compromise formation built out of the child's principal impulses, the anxiety and defense connected with them, and the particular forms of gratification that can be retained. The situations in which a child finds gratification in contact with his mother are structured by the child in the sense that the behavior pattern is to a large degree of his creation, is repeated by him, and balances for him his impulses and his defenses in the setting of a specific family pattern. The behavior is achieved in ways actively produced by him and consistent with defensive procedures regularly relied upon by him.

In summary, the child follows a developmental progression in which affect, both pleasurable and unpleasurable, becomes increasingly differentiated and focalized while the diffuse infant-mother body boundaries give way to awareness of separateness. This period of focal separation anxiety, and even of focal gratification, is inherently unstable. Affect is at a high level, and the child can neither actively avoid separations nor guarantee the longed-for gratifications. Stability is the achievement of a third stage, when a reliable and remembered object relationship serves to replace the earlier symbiosis and to fill the gap of the separateness the child feels between himself and his mother. At this time also the child's capacities for affect control and acting upon his environment, on the basis of remembered and perceived cues, are brought to bear upon his strong affective experiences, so that there is a greater capacity to deal with anxiety and actively to attain pleasure. Behavior through which these things can be brought about serves multiple functions for the child and is organized in relation to the diverse requirements of drive, defense, conscience, and reality. In this sense it is structuralized and, if successful in meeting these diverse requirements, is likely to have considerable stability.

As the cognitive apparatus matures, as more refined intentionality, modulation of affect, control over motility, and appraisal of reality are attained by the child, the timing and the form of drive gratification change; from these changes come permanence and order in his psychic life. These new relations among drives, ego functions, external reality, and conscience can be viewed as the development of structuralization or of multiple function, each of them helping to account for order and permanence. The formation of a relatively permanent set of relationships among these diverse requirements of the person is what we refer to as structuralization. The development of psychic acts that function to resolve these multiple demands is the development of multiple function; when optimally successful, such acts have a fair degree of permanence. A psychic act that successfully satisfies these diverse functions, and that additionally serves as a significant repetition of the past, may have greater durability than one that does not.

I have illustrated the development of structuralized and multiply functional psychic acts through description of steps in the development of scopophilic and anal impulses as well as the attachment of the child to its mother. There is an early stage of diffuse pleasure or general excitation that can be described neither as structuralized (it is not psychologically organized or semipermanent) nor as including multiply functional psychic acts in the sense that Waelder intended the term (the psychic apparatus cannot yet act on considerations of reality and of conscience). In later stages, when focal gratification and focal anxiety appear, not only do more specific wishes and more specific demands of reality and conscience appear, but there is conflict between them.

Ideally the developmental sequence I have discussed ends in a solution to the diverse demands through a structuralized relationship between drive and defense that permits retention of some opportunities for gratification.

With this achievement psychic harmony is attained, as we see it in persons of all ages in the many everyday acts syntonic with the ego and surroundings that also gratify wishes. These gratifications occur at peace with conscience and the social milieu. Such small pleasurable acts provide the background gratifications of everyday life that express on a small scale settled and lasting adjustments between drives and defenses. These may include those few examples of lasting pleasures described above as well as a wide range of other toned-down pleasures: chewing gum, swatting flies, smoking cigarettes, throwing darts, taking pictures. Psychic disharmony, conflict, may result when the gratification enjoyed becomes, for one reason or another, more highly invested, or when the fantasies associated with it come closer to awareness, or when for many possible reasons guilt or anxiety makes a new solution necessary.

I suggest that specific defensive postures that include opportunities for gratification in ways syntonic with the individual's conscience and with his social milieu can have a high degree of permanence. They may continue until maturational forces create a new imbalance in the relation of wish to defense, or until radical alterations in the milieu provoke more expressive or repressive handling of the wish, or until there is a softening or hardening of conscience in the course of development. In childhood such maturational forces are at their height, as are also the changes in the child's milieu as he encounters people who vary in their tolerance of his means of seeking gratification. And so in childhood, relations between urge and defense, though they may be structuralized for a time, are likely to undergo frequent and major changes.

From the clinical point of view, the multiply functional behaviors I have described, which are "adaptive" in the inner psychological world in which affect signals how successfully one is managing, may be adaptive *or* pathological in the external world of functioning and relatedness. Thus, from this point of view, pathology may be seen as the failure successfully to achieve multiple function (e.g., gratification may be fully renounced or self-esteem may be sacrificed or conscience offended) or as the settling in of rigid behaviors that are successful in some internal sense (multiple function is achieved) but at a major price for other aspects of relatedness or adaptation. In either case, the adult patient in treatment will find these partially or more rigidly structuralized behaviors to be a focus of the clinical work.

8

Libidinal Object Constancy

The discussion of the structuralization of the child-mother relationship with which chapter 7 concludes leads naturally to another side of that relationship that is built up intrapsychically: libidinal object constancy. Conceptually, libidinal object constancy has a place in the "personal psychology" of self (as a significant stabilizer of autonomous functions) as well as of internalized object relations (which it represents in part). Yet the achievement of libidinal object constancy also reflects a significant step in ego synthesis that has implications for major drive-modulating functions.

Psychoanalytic work assumes the patient's achievement of a core capacity for object relatedness, whatever the conflicts and distortions in that relatedness. But object relatedness has another aspect—which is often subtler, not always apparent at the outset of treatment, and may require special forms of intervention later on (cf. Fleming, 1975). That aspect is what we refer to as libidinal object constancy: the capacity to form and have available internally carried images, remembrances, and sets of expectancies regarding relatedness, even in the absence of the object.

Since the capacity to hold on to the object has generally been attained in patients seen in psychoanalysis, its presence, mode of development, and functions can often be taken for granted or, from a developmental-theoretical standpoint, ignored. In fact we know little about how failures to attain such object constancy come about, what it is that makes a person unable to "record" in memory and to make functional use of early object connectedness in the present. The "badness" of the early object relatedness per se does not provide the key, for we know that even horrendous early parent-child interactions can be internalized, incessantly repeated, and used as a basis for ongoing functioning in the present.

Originally published in *Psychoanalysis and Contemporary Science* (3:307–313, 1974), New York: International Universities Press.

In an attempt to clarify developmental aspects of the attainment of libidinal object constancy and thus contribute to the clinical utility of the concept,
I shall here address two interconnected problems: *timing* of the development
of libidinal object constancy, and the *functional significance* of that achievement. My main point is that it is possible to develop certain aspects of libidinal
object constancy long before an individual has the ability to make full use of
them.

The term "object constancy," introduced in the psychoanalytic literature
by Hartmann (1952), is a variant of Piaget's (1937) earlier term "object
permanence." Hartmann's term has become the usual one in psychoanalytic
writings and for that reason I shall use it here when referring to the *libidinal*
object. We do not assume that the newborn comes equipped with object
representations or that such representations are permanently established after
the first encounter with the object. Piaget studied the stages in the development of the representations of physical objects, for example, toys. Psychoanalysts have been interested in the development of constancy in the
representations of the libidinal object—the stages in and timing of the infant's
development of a permanent representation of the mother.

It seems to me that too narrow a focus on the time of the achievement
of libidinal object constancy (often a search for the specific month) deflects
attention from the issue of the functional significance of that achievement.
Fraiberg (1969) and McDevitt (1975) have pointed out that the question
of "when" hinges on the definition of object constancy: whether it is seen as
the specific attachment to the mother, the recognition of her, the later capacity
to evoke some image of her in her absence, or the ability to use this image—
whatever form it may have—in the full functional way that develops still
later. McDevitt has given additional substance to this point by showing which
of these aspects of libidinal object constancy become relevant at different
ages. Even if we decide when the infant can evoke the image of an absent
physical object (approximately 18 months, according to Piaget's studies), we
should expect variations in this time if it is the *mother* who is the "absent
object," if she is away for a longer or a shorter time, or if the child is in a
state of high arousal, tension, longing, or craving. For the high drive state
which, by definition, is part and parcel of the attachment to the libidinal
object is likely to produce conditions for the representation of the object (or
the loss or destruction of that representation, or the inability to make use of
it) that are very different from those holding for a less salient and more
transiently sought physical object.[1]

Let me expand on this point. In a series of precise and masterfully analytic
experiments, Piaget demonstrated that it is not until about eighteen to twenty
months that the infant has a full representation of the object as existing in
space in its own right and separate from his actions upon it. The object is,
at this point, still a practical one for the infant, of interest primarily for what

---

1. See Décarie (1965) for a thorough and thoughtful review of Piaget's work and the
psychoanalytic usage of this concept up to that time.

he can do with it. Later the concept of the object comes to have other facets as well for the child (see Kaplan, 1972).

In connection with the psychoanalytic concept of libidinal object constancy, as in all aspects of the infant's relation to the mother, we must also speak of a developmental process—a process that begins well before the age at which Piaget's studies place physical object permanence and continues long after that. It cannot be located at this or that developmental point (as is also the case of physical object permanence); libidinal object constancy undergoes developmental change, as does everything in human growth. Well before the age of eighteen to twenty months, the infant shows a specific and differential response to the mother; but, as Piaget has shown, recognition per se does not guarantee that a concept of the object's permanence (or a permanent concept of the object) has developed. Even earlier, the infant (through his own action—crying) behaves as though he has a concept of the mother in her absence, a mother who can be summoned back; but, again, Piaget has shown that the concept of the permanence of the object, *separate from the action of the infant* and existing in its own right, comes later than these action-reappearance sequences. We can say only that *something* begins to exist in the infant as early as the middle of the first year of life—a "something" that is the forerunner of the later concept of the permanent object. What that "something" is we cannot say for certain. However, we should not rule out the possibility that some aspects of the representation of the libidinal object develop more rapidly than does the representation of the physical object;[2] the heightened learning and recording of memories that may take place under conditions of optimal arousal (i.e., a state of need that does not reach traumatic dimensions) and under conditions of repeated encounter seem likely to solidify some aspects of the internal representation of the libidinal object well before eighteen to twenty months.

Factors in the post-eighteen-to-twenty-month period must also be taken into account in a comparison of physical object permanence and libidinal object constancy. The libidinal object is subject to extremes of longing and rage, and the representation of that object may be wishfully or defensively distorted or protected (see McDevitt, 1975). This is not true of the physical objects Piaget studied—and indeed, if it were, they would be libidinal objects in our sense. Thus we cannot even assume that once permanence of the physical object has been attained, constancy of the libidinal object has also been attained. We can say only that the cognitive potential is there. The presence of intense libidinal and aggressive ties to the object may thus make for *more rapid* but *less fixed* attainment of a permanent cognitive/affective representation of it in all its aspects.

Piaget has given us an approximate baseline time for the achievement of libidinal object constancy. But we might better pursue the question of its

---

2. Bell (1970) showed that "person permanence" developed before "object permanence" when the mother-infant relationship was harmonious, with the reverse sequence when it was disharmonious.

functional significance. Not solely in terms of "when," however. When is the Oedipus complex resolved? We have to ask, rather: By whom? In which aspects? How firmly? So, too, with the achievement of the full functional significance of the capacity to hold on to some image of the specific and highly cathected mother; the questions have to be more refined. Or take the development of the capacity to anticipate. When the infant, well within the first half year, can stop crying and wait, apparently at the sound of his mother's distant voice or approaching footsteps, we can say that at least the beginnings of the anticipatory function are present. But some people are forever unable to make full use of this function. Developmental achievement clearly is in some aspects a matter or organismic potentiality but in other aspects a matter of individual history.

What is the functional significance of the achievement of object constancy? And when and how fully are those functions attained? McDevitt (1975) has discussed at least two aspects of these questions.

1. McDevitt describes a child who, in her ninth month, repeatedly looks to the door through which her mother has gone. Her behavior suggests that she already has some capacity to sustain an inner "something" like a memory of the absent mother, but her distress as she looks reminds us that she cannot yet reliably use that inner something for comfort. To be able to achieve comfort from the internal object representation instead of from the actual love object in the flesh is an immense developmental gain. It not ony protects the child from absolute dependence upon the physical presense of the mother— which cannot be sustained in any event—but it does this with no loss of the child's developing autonomy, rather, indeed, a potential gain. By carrying an image—not only a "picture" but a set of expectations of her behavior, an expectable relationship—inside, the child is free to rove autonomously, not dependent upon the mother's physical presence to stabilize his functioning. The internal object representation permits a greater closeness than the reality object can reliably provide, with no sacrifice of the autonomy the child has already achieved through his developing locomotor independence and capacity to delay gratification. By the end of the third year, most children achieve this capacity to take comfort from the internal libidinal object representation to a considerable degree. But this does not settle the developmental issue. People vary all through life in their relative dependence upon immediate contact with the reality object for comfort and pleasure; they vary also in their capacity to take comfort from the internal memory or image of the love object.

2. In dealing with a second aspect of the functional significance of the achievement of object constancy, McDevitt draws on phenomena that Mahler (1972) has described as characterizing the third subphase of separation-individuation, rapprochement, and that present specific developmental difficulties for the child's use of his capacity to evoke the image of the absent mother. These phenomena have to do with rage toward the mother that is not easily integrated with affectionate feelings and with the resultant interference with the child's use of the image of the mother for comfort even

though it can presumably be evoked. Mahler suggests that the awareness of separateness at this stage (in contrast to real physical separation) leads to a loss of the child's experience of sharing in the mother's omnipotence, to opposing tendencies toward shadowing (trailing after mother) and independence, and at times to keeping the image of the "good" and the "bad" mother separate ("splitting") as a way of preserving the loving and beloved image in the face of the anger and disappointment consequent upon the awareness of separateness and loss (see also Kernberg, 1967). McDevitt suggests that rage can disrupt the development of libidinal object constancy: "The mental representation of the mother is so buffeted by violent and angry feelings that the stability of this image, at least from the libidinal as distinguished from the cognitive side, is disrupted" (1975, p. 731). Mahler et al. (1975) suggest that object constancy can usefully be conceptualized as including the capacity not only to evoke the image of the absent mother and use it for support but to unite all aspects of the mother, the good and the bad, in one concept.

This latter achievement, too, has immense developmental significance. It serves to temper rage and disappointment by connecting them with memories of the loving as well as the frustrating actions of mother. The unification of the multiple aspects of the mother in a single broader representation that can hold together even when the child is frustrated or angry is more or less achieved by most children by the age of three or so. But development is infinitely variable, and we all have encountered people who never fully achieve this unification—who lose all sense of the love in the object when they are disappointed or enraged or, contrariwise, who again and again succumb to illusory expectations of receiving the love of the object, unable to hold in mind the memories of disappointment and hurt.

At least one additional function—beyond the reconciliation of closeness and autonomy, and beyond the tempering of extremes of disappointment and wishful longing—is served by the development of the sustained internal image of the mother or other love object. Because it *is* internal, it can be shaped, gradually and over time, to represent both wish and reality in ways that other images and ideas are shaped to the person but that external reality cannot as easily be. The internal object can be better or worse than the object in the flesh. Excluding some memories, some aspects of the object's functioning in reality, allows the internal concept of the object to heal, to perform in ways that the real object does not or did not. Here, I do not believe we can speak of degrees to which different persons succeed in shaping the inner image of the object to their own needs; such internal representations are inevitably so shaped. The long-term developmental issues are, rather, inherent in this shaping process itself—with changes in the quality of the inner image over time. At one time what is central and necessary is the loving presence of the internal image; at another time, its prohibitive aspects and support of internal controls; at yet another time, its praising aspects and aid in the regulation of self-esteem. Here the internal image of the object shades into the introjected parent with all its functions throughout the life cycle.

Thus, the internal representation of the libidinal object, once attained, does not remain static any more than does anything else in human development. It is reshaped and extended not only with the growing cognitive capacities of the developing person but also with his encounter with and resolution of the emotional issues of each new stage. Thus, for example, the new view of the parent consequent upon the period of oedipal resolution and school entry, and the further new view at adolescence and even when one reaches parenthood in one's own right, cannot but alter the internal object representation as well. What distinguishes flexible adult functioning is the capacity to evoke, as appropriate, one or another aspect of the object representation, aspects that exist in a hierarchical arrangement shaped to individual need.

I am well aware that I am suggesting a significant extension of the scope of object constancy, but I believe that this extension is necessary in order to make its broader psychological significance clear. The image of the libidinal object becomes an important internal regulator of longing and rage, gives the freedom to be autonomous while closeness is retained, and later is also a regulator of self-esteem. It is the product of the total experience of the infant organism in the earliest months and years, which includes cognitive as well as emotional development, and it later becomes a major tool of those aspects of the person's functioning that we ascribe to the ego.

9

Formation, Expansion, and
Vulnerability of the Self Experience

In one of the earlier psychoanalytic papers on the self, Spiegel (1959) pointed out that "self-feeling is an ultimate, not further describable, clinical fact, but the self is not a clinical fact in the same sense that self-feeling is. It is a conceptualization or construct which we invoke to clarify clinical phenomena" (p. 87). Several other authors have explored the concept of self as well as self-feeling (e.g., Sandler and Rosenblatt, 1962; Jacobson, 1964; Lichtenstein, 1965, G. S. Klein, 1976). My focus will be entirely on self-feeling; I shall discuss the experience of self—its contents and *how* they get to be experienced as part of "*my* self."

Dealing with processes (how experiences get into the self), not only with content, and with the preverbal period at least in part, I shall of necessity be inferential in my approach, but I shall try to draw a picture that is at least consistent with what we have come to understand through clinical psychoanalysis and through child observation.

For the most part, I shall be discussing that area of experience of which the person feels a sense of ownership, responsibility, and/or familiarity—the "I" or the "me" as the source of an urge, an effector of action, or a center of experience—in contrast to the "it" which is experienced as acting upon me (whether from inside or outside) or the potential "me" experience that is nonetheless disowned or unrecognized. Among the latter, experiences that take the form of "I wasn't myself" or "I don't know what came over me" or "I can't believe I'm doing this" highlight the experienced discontinuity between actions or feelings and the ongoing, familiar, and "owned" self-experience.

While the material to be discussed could be stated in terms of conflict, structuralization, internalization, and narcissism, I shall use experience-near

Originally published as "The experience of self" in the *Psychoanalytic Study of the Child* (37:143–167, 1982), New Haven: Yale University Press.

terms in order to describe phenomena relevant for any theory of the self. Among these phenomena, those from very early experience, from moments of quiet play, relatedness, and just "being," and those evolving from inputs from the surround (all discussed in chap. 1) have a special place.

FORERUNNERS

As development proceeds, a number of attributes that take shape in the earliest weeks and months become so taken for granted as part of inner experience that later they may hardly be noticed, much less verbalized. These become part of familiar inner experience not by incorporation into an already focused sense of "I" (which they predate) but by being part and parcel of the earliest formation of experience, so that the world seems no other way. I recall hearing as a child (and I have no idea if this is true) of a person born with a clicking sound in his ear who took it for granted that the world simply included that sound and did not discover until adolescence that it was not a universal. There are parallel psychological experiences, of such early origin that they simply *are* the way the inner world is for the child. I have called these "forerunners," but I do not mean to suggest that they are forerunners to the construction of some *concept* of self—some "I" based on self-other differentiation, the constancy of self-awareness, or the like. Rather, they are parts of the *experience* of self that take shape even before awareness of self becomes stabilized (generally assumed to be in the second year; see, for example, Mahler et al., 1975). When self-awareness comes into being, it does not come unencumbered. Much that was previously experienced is brought along as baggage, giving "*a* self" immediate form as "*my* self." When a person first is aware of an "I," it immediately has a distinctive experiential shape based on his or her personal history.

I shall discuss several early-developing attributes and their sources. Although they overlap, I shall nonetheless describe them one by one, as : ease/ continuity, satisfaction/joy, activity/effectiveness, and worthwhileness. Clearly, these are developmental ideals, actualized only if all goes well, and certainly varying in degree. At the opposite poles we may see reflections of disturbed development in these areas in patients who struggle to convey to us chronic states of malaise that are difficult to articulate. These attributes (at either pole or in between) can be seen as primitive character traits (or at least *characteristic* traits), not based on conflict and compromise formation but formed through earliest experiences; naturally, later conflict and compromise can be superimposed upon them. While I shall try to describe substantive areas of early experience, my intent, in each instance, is to suggest that these formative experiences occur so early that they become taken for granted as the way the (inner) world simply *is*.

Ease/continuity. We become aware of the ease and continuity of the ongoing experience of ourselves by their absence, at times when they are interrupted. While many aspects of inner conflict or external stimulation that contribute to such interruptions are familiar to us from clinical work, the

question of the original sources of this ease and continuity, and of its interruptions, remains open. Winnicott (1958b) has addressed these issues in his
work on the capacity to be alone, but I wish to focus on work in which he
attempts to describe even earlier experiences.

Winnicott (1956, 1960b) attempts to capture in words some of the infant's earliest experiences that underlie the subsequent development of ego
functions and of the self-experience. He writes of the "going on being" of
the infant at times when the mother shields him from intrusive and disruptive
stimuli and effectively protects an ongoing quiescent state:[1]

> If the mother provides a good enough adaptation to need, the infant's own
> line of life is disturbed very little by reactions to impingement.... Maternal
> failures produce phases of reaction to impingement and these reactions in-
> terrupt the "going on being" of the infant.... the basis for ego establishment
> is the sufficiency of "going on being," uncut by reactions to impingement.
> ... According to this thesis a good enough environmental provision in the
> earliest phase enables the infant to begin to exist, to have experience, to build
> a personal ego, to ride instincts, and to meet with all the difficulties inherent
> in life. (1956, pp. 303–04)

"As a result of success in maternal care there is built up in the infant a
continuity of being which is the basis of ego-strength" (1960b, p. 52).

The presumed underpinnings of the stable self-experience are these quiet,
unintruded-upon states of being that Winnicott has attempted to convey.
Protected against intrusion (of excessive hunger or external stimuli) by the
mother's ministrations, the infant simply *is*, has an ongoing experience of
ease and continuity. These are the first formative experiences of a self, and
it is therefore not surprising that one of their distinguishing features is that
they are non-self-conscious. Although they provide the first continuity of
experience of the kind that will later be carried inside as self experience, they
occur long before the sense of ownership can be identified as such by the
infant. These experiences are passive in the sense that they are not something
that the infant shapes, but rather something that happens (or not) to the
infant as a result of maternal actions.

Thus, ironically, the first (presumed) (pre) self experiences are brought
about by an external agent; this is the inverse of another irony that Winnicott
discusses, that the first *inner* experience, drive pressure (or need), is experienced as an "it" that *happens* rather than as an "I" that *wants*. The processes
by which drives become part of the self are complex and require psychological
work on the part of the growing child. I shall return to this in a later section.

Satisfaction/joy. The term "joy" is here used with reference to phenomena
that Kohut (1977) presumably attempted to capture in his work. With regard
to satisfaction, let me draw upon what I described in chapter 7 under the
rubric of the child's "diffuse" (low-keyed, nonspecific) gratification. There I

---

1. I have discussed this aspect of Winnicott's work as well as White's work (1963) in a
different context in chapter 4.

presented it in the context of a discussion of the research from which these ideas emanated, but for present purposes I simply want to call attention to the range of bodily based satisfactions that are omnipresent in the everyday life of the infant and preschool child, at home, with its mother and other family members. Touching, rocking, seeing, smelling, sucking are everywhere. All sense organs participate in the intimacies of these bodily exchanges; they are part of the routine of everyday life. No special behavior on the child's part is required to bring them about; they are all around him.

These are low-keyed pleasures. When any one of them becomes focal and is accompanied by high affective intensity in the course of development, it will almost certainly be accompanied by fantasy development and by problematic response from caretakers—in short, become embroiled in conflict. And then conflict, too, becomes part of the ongoing self experience. But early on, the experiences can add a sense of quiet bodily and receptor pleasure to the ongoing self experience. This is the other side of the coin of those early experiences that are involved in the predisposition to anxiety (Greenacre, 1941).

What Kohut (1977) refers to as the sense of "joy" is akin to the satisfaction just described but is much more intense and grows in part from those moments of mother-child reciprocal interaction, or of the mother's lovingly mirroring her infant's sounds and actions, which produce strong and focal positive affect—ranging from a smile to giddy excitement—in the infant. Such experiences are inherent in the "good" experience of early infancy. Together, these forms of gratification that come from the body (in the setting of the familiar surround of ongoing family life) and those that come from the more focal and intense moments of mother-infant reciprocal interaction can potentially add a sense of pleasure to the ongoing self experience. Not so incidentally, a successful and gratifying imitative-interactive ("mirroring") experience is likely to set up a circular reaction in which the infant produces rewarded behavior again and again and thus contributes to a tendency toward activity, as Kohut emphasizes.

Activity/effectiveness. Some early-developing sense of activity, of one's capacity to *do*, to have an *effect*, occurs in most of us; but this is something that must develop. Its absence can be sorely limiting and contribute to what appears clinically as *apparent* resistance to change; I am thinking of one aspect of those frequently seen situations where insight does not lead to change, which Freud (1926, 1937a) thought of in terms of a "stickiness" of impulse gratification or "resistances of the id" (cf. Stewart, 1963). In some of these instances, I believe, the individual may never have come to experience himself fully as a successful maker or doer, as an active force in means-ends relationships, and so the very idea of initiating change is unavailable.

The drives may be seen as the primary source of the sense of activity, but there are problems with this formulation because of their possible "external" quality (Winnicott, 1960a); I shall take this up later. Certainly the infant's cry that brings the mother can be experienced as the first activity, especially after its automatic aspect has turned into purposeful behavior. But there is another important contributor to a primary sense of self-as-active—that is, early infantile play (White, 1963). Play, outside the sphere of conflict, can contribute a quality that is later included in the self experience precisely because it is nonconflictual, low-keyed, "self"-initiated; and that quality can be an active one—the self as *producer* of events.

If maturation proceeds with normal supports and stimulus inputs, early infantile play can contribute to the sense of self-as-actor, as initiator-of-action, in an automatic way that just "happens." In the first half year, the infant already plays, that is, engages in behavior that seems neither to emanate from distress nor to culminate in gratification of bodily based urges. Quite the reverse, this play comes at quiet times, when the infant is awake and not compelled to cry or suck by hunger or other distress. At such times, the infant produces gurgling sounds (vocal play), makes sights appear and disappear by movements of the head, produces tactile sensations by touching and pushing soft toys and rattles, creates sights and sounds (soon after) when the hands can be brought together at the midline, in sight of the eye, touching and pushing crib toys, and more.

In this constantly recurring activity, (again, non-*self*-conscious, presumably, at the beginning) the infant is slowly becoming aware of himself as one who makes things happen, an actor upon the world. I describe such play activity (coming *from* the infant, through the exercise of his normal capacities, and not only in the space between mother and infant that Winnicott (1971a) describes) as just "happening" rather than as psychic work because it emerges automatically, given a normally supportive and stimulating environment. Yet, like the "going on being," this "making things happen" can be seen as one of the earliest formative bases of a self experience. Robert White has developed these ideas most fully in relation to psychoanalytic developmental theory in his monograph on *Ego and Reality in Psychoanalytic Theory* (1963) and elsewhere. His thesis is that self-esteem flows not only from narcissism or praise but also from effectiveness, the capacity to make things happen.

Worthwhileness (self-esteem). After presenting an account of the child's exploration and play, White (1963) turns to a discussion of self-esteem, arguing that esteem accrues from external response to the child's real accomplishments as well as through the act of accomplishment in itself. He writes:

> This account of self-esteem, which locates its inner source in efficacy and the sense of competence, is not intended to crowd out the esteem income that may or may not be provided by others. This is a very real factor, but we must remember that supplies of esteem are not bestowed whimsically; they have some relation to what the person has done. Esteem is constantly involved in a transactional process in which effort expended and encouragement received work in a complementary fashion. (p. 193)

I would like to underline this but also add to it by emphasizing other experiences of "good-enough" infancy. If the early experiences that Winnicott describes of the child's "going on being," those that I have described regarding early diffuse preconflictual pleasure, and those that Kohut (1971, 1977) described in terms of developmentally required parental "mirroring"—if these occur, they are likely to produce a feeling of well-being, from which a sense of worthwhileness and ultimately self-esteem flow. These experiences, along with the child's experience of having an effect in early play, lay the foundations of a nondefensive, and realistic, sense of self-worth, although compensatory, defensive, and magical elements also are components of self-esteem.

Naturally, experiences of loss, pain, nonsatisfaction, and (later) conflict are also included in the self experience, partly as a result of the inevitable (and developmentally required) failures of the mother-infant pair to maintain full comfort in the infant. But I have been describing developmental ideals—the positive sources of early self experience *if all goes well*. And I have emphasized that they are so much part of the early formation of experience that they are taken for granted and immediately give personalized shape to the sense of "I" when self-awareness stabilizes later on. If a particular growing infant misses these early foundations of self experience (the continuity of being when the mother's ministrations protect the infant from excessive intrusion of inner or outer stimuli; the bodily and relationally derived gratifications that can fill the infant with a range of affects from quiet satisfaction to joy; the developing sense of self-as-actor when the periods of quiet exploratory play are fully established; and the sense of worthwhileness that, I believe, originally flows from all of these), can the self experience ever after, no matter what experience follows, no matter what therapeutic interventions we undertake, be full and comfortable? I doubt it.

THE CRYSTALLIZATION OF THE SELF AND ITS CONSEQUENCES

The "location" and "duration" of self experience are affected by the crystallization of self-awareness. This crystallization makes possible a progressively clearer sense of ownership as "mine" (location); furthermore such experience can also be retained over long stretches of time (duration), which has especially important implications for the vulnerability of the self.

In research described elsewhere (Mahler et al., 1975), we attempted to study early developmental sequences that lead to an emerging self-awareness, self-other differentiation, and self and object constancy. We made no assumptions regarding the presence of these interrelated phenomena at birth, assumed from observation that they were present from at least early childhood in settings of reasonably normal development, and attempted to look at events of the first two or three years that might permit inferences regarding their time and mode of emergence. This effort led to the formulation and detailed delineation of the subphases of separation-individuation (Mahler, 1972; Mahler et al., 1975). In brief, we could see that several events, largely in the second year of life, reflect and make possible a more crystallized self-awareness. The onset of upright locomotion in the "practicing" period leads to near-incessant self-propelled motility in the setting of intensely felt exuberance, and this motility and affect together define the self as an entity in space; increasing self-other differentiation is accompanied by a progressive capacity to respond to one's name and to personal pronouns (I-you) and later to use names and pronouns actively; the memory system and the nature and style of object relations become progressively more organized, evolving into a characteristic mode that becomes both a definer and a content of the self; and the establishment of object constancy (Hartmann, 1952; chap. 8), and presumably of self constancy in relation to and contrast with the object, lends a permanence to the world of inner experience.

What consequences do these developments have for self experience? The temporal dimension, holding experience as "my own" over time, is crucial. In order to bring this point out more clearly, I shall take a brief detour to describe recent work on aggression in early childhood. Utilizing data from our observational study, McDevitt (1980) finds that aggressive reactions to frustration or stress are common in the first months of life and in the differentiation and practicing subphases but that these reactions are short-lived, terminating at the termination of distress. In contrast, in the rapprochement subphase (15 to 24 months), a period of increased awareness of the permanence of the object and of the object as a specific source of frustration, anger reactions can be retained over long periods of time. McDevitt suggests that the two are linked, the increased specificity and permanence of the object world permitting lasting reaction tendencies toward that world.

Applying these ideas to my topic, I suggest that with self-awareness, the feeling of the self as the center of experience can become an ongoing one. Naturally this is not an all-or-none phenomenon, and something like it was probably there before, but I am speaking about a direction of development with increasing articulation and continuity. Experiences that are familiar are "mine," are part of me, have a consistency with the ongoing experience of self (Bergman, 1980). "Ownership" of experience, rather than experience coming and going in a random world, seems to be the direction of growth from the earliest months into the second year of life, crystallizing as self-awareness crystallizes.

But awareness of self also entails the possibility of vulnerability. Epigrammatically, what does not exist cannot be injured; what does, can. Both Mahler (1968) and Kohut (1971, 1977) postulate special vulnerabilities of the newborn self. How would this work? Karel Capek expresses it in metaphor in his play *The Insect Comedy* (1922), in which a series of parables on the lives of insects reveals the human situation to us. One continually reappears as a leitmotif: a chrysalis again and again calls out, with a sense of excitement and anticipation, and with the implicit expectation that the world shares that excitement, "World, I am about to be born!" And finally it is born, flutters joyously around the stage, flies too close to a candle flame, and dies a moment later. Death can follow when birth comes. With this perspective in mind, I turn to a review of the death (or vulnerability) of the self in the work of Mahler and Kohut.

Mahler (1952, 1968) suggests that the emergence of self-awareness, the infant's coming to realize that he is not part of the mother, sharing in her power and safety, is accompanied by a self experience of smallness, loss of fantasied omnipotence, and, in general, a saddened mood. In extreme instances, there is disorganizing panic culminating in regressive abandonment of self-awareness (in the syndrome of symbiotic psychosis). The point is that the change in the self experience consequent upon the progressive clarification of self-other differentiation and self-awareness has, even in optimal development, a shadowy underside of sadness and loss, with more pathological components in some specific instances.

Kohut (1971, 1977), on the other hand, focuses on the child's need for a mirroring-confirming response from the caretaker. In a schematic sense, the child (through one or another behavior) is saying proudly and excitedly, "I'm me! Look what I can do! Look what I am! Look!" And the parental (failed) response is some form of "Shut up and don't bother me." This is undeniably one aspect of the psychopathology of everyday child-rearing. A common and painful sight on any street, in any playground or supermarket, indeed in the homes of our friends or ourselves, is the failure of that confirming response: the child's joyfully bringing an achievement to the caretaker only to be met with rebuff, depression, inattention, self-preoccupation, or destructive undercutting of the achievement. And I see every reason to expect that when such failure to respond is chronic, the outcome will be as Kohut describes it—a blunting of the self experience, of initiative, and of autonomous functioning. Indeed, as I have already said, the self experience is organized in good measure around the capacity to *do*, to have an *effect*. Failures of parental response and their destructive impact upon the child are clearly observable. That they have not earlier been formalized in the developmental theory of psychoanalysis reflects the essential data base of that theory: the patient's associations and fantasies, which are generally more cautiously structured by us in terms of intrapsychic life (which we "see" before our eyes and ears) rather than interpersonal events (which we only hear about).

Such nonconfirming responses may of course occur from the beginning of life, and not only after self-awareness has emerged. Thus, in a powerful film of an experiment conducted during an infant's first half year of life, Brazelton (1976) demonstrates the debilitating impact upon the infant of the caretaker's failure to meet the infant's expectancies for a certain kind of reciprocal-mirroring behavior (see also Brazelton et al., 1975). In the film, we see an infant at about six months propped in a chair as his parent walks in. The infant's face breaks into a gleeful smile, his arms flap excitedly, and his eyes follow the movements of the approaching parent. But the parent, on instruction, keeps a poker face and sits facing the infant, completely immobile. Within a few seconds, the infant's behavior begins to deteriorate. First he shows seeming puzzlement and he pauses; the exhilaration disappears and active behavior comes to a standstill; and very soon body tone collapses, the infant slumps and sags, and appears to be, for all we can tell, in a depressed state. The effect on the observer is powerful, affectively and conceptually, the latter because it leaves no doubt that infant development takes place in a reciprocal interactive system.

I propose the hypothesis that the failed parental response to the child's initiatives *after* the achievement of more articulated self-awareness can have new levels of destructiveness. Thus, in line with McDevitt's observations of how the child late in the second year can hold aggression over time and direct it at an object that has attained permanence, the child whose initiatives are not responded to has at that time the capacity to hold, to own, those slights and to carry away a more sustained and self-referential sense of failure, hopelessness, or emptiness. Issues of reversibility of pathology and of critical periods are perhaps linked to developmental turning points of this sort.

I have proposed thus far that certain early developing qualities (continuity, satisfaction, effectiveness, worthwhileness—and their opposites) are so much part of the early formation of the very experience of the world that they are taken for granted and become long-lasting individual characteristics. At the time of crystallization of self-consciousness, of an "I" experience, these characteristics automatically come to define the quality of that experience so that *a* self becomes *my* self. At this point of crystallization, the child's capacity to "own" experience, to feel the self as the experiencing center of the world, also comes into being. At the same time, pathological experience can be owned, held over time, so that the emergence of a distinct self is closely correlated to its vulnerability.

EARLY CONFLICT-PRONE EXPERIENCES
AND THE BOUNDARIES OF THE SELF

One of the ways in which patients differ from one another is in the degree to which they can recognize and experience various mental contents as egosyntonic rather than disown them. These conflict-prone contents, as I shall call them, include a variety of impulses, affects, thoughts, and fantasies specific for each individual. How is it that some patients can own these experiences, while others disown them (e.g., through repression, splitting, or rejection of what arrives in consciousness in spite of oneself)? Conceptually, one can think of this question in terms of the borders of the self, its "breadth": what is included in and excluded from the self experience. Earlier, I discussed relatively benign, even favorable, components of the self experience (which are problematic when development does *not* go well); here I turn to the integration of inherently difficult feelings and thoughts into the self experience (which are ordinarily problematic in their very existence).

I begin once again with Winnicott (1960a):

> It must be emphasized that in referring to the meeting of infant needs I am not referring to the satisfaction of instincts. In the area that I am examining the instincts are not yet clearly defined as internal to the infant. The instincts can be as much external as can a clap of thunder or a hit. [That the "external" can become "internal" is suggested by Winnicott as he goes on.]...The infant's ego is building up strength and in consequence is getting towards a state in which id-demands will be felt as part of the self, and not as environmental. When this development occurs, then id-satisfaction becomes a very

important strengthener of the ego, or of the True Self; but id-excitement can be traumatic when the ego is not yet able to include them, and not yet able to contain the risk involved and the frustrations experienced up to the point when id-satisfaction becomes fact. (p. 141)

I believe Winnicott's comment about the infant's learning to "ride instincts," quoted earlier, refers to the same phenomenon: "id-demands" can be felt as part of the self when the child "risks" their excitement while awaiting satisfaction. In contrast, I have described some low-intensity gratifications that may be included in the self experience without disrupting it, even early on; these are "tame" pleasures. Winnicott is referring to a more active process: the taming of drives. Another point in development when the individual must accomplish active work in order to include powerful drives in the self experience is at puberty, when new sexual urges impinge upon the character structure formed during the school-age years (Bernfeld, 1938). Anna Freud (1936) discusses how, in one form of pathological adaptation to adolescence, these urges are excluded from the self experience as the adolescent holds on to preadolescent forms of adaptation.

How does the originally "external" drive become "internal"? How does it come to be experienced as "me" or "mine" rather than "it"? Winnicott's (1958b) answer is: When the drive occurs in the context of the supporting, facilitating, environment, "id-relationships strengthen the ego when they occur in a framework of ego-relatedness" (p. 34), and ego-relatedness is the "type of relationship that exists between an infant and the ego-supportive mother" (p. 36). There is certainly circularity in this formulation, but one can break out of the circle by looking at the specific mechanisms that are at work. I shall describe three of them to suggest ways in which phenomena, disruptive and outside the self experience, can be altered and eased so that they can be included in that experience.

Holding. Winnicott (1965) writes of the holding, the facilitating, environment. The caretaker who is reliably there for the infant and child at the time of need accomplishes several things: she ensures reliable gratification, so that the child need not experience a sense of threat, possibly culminating in panic, at the first sign of need-tension. When the need arises and is accompanied by the expectation of gratification (rather than the anticipation solely of mounting need), we have the first *delay*, and delay is the situation in which higher order defenses can gradually develop. The mother who is there to gratify the child's need makes the need and its gratification part of the child's relationship to her, thus holding the child under the umbrella of her safety and protecting him from being alone with his need. In addition, the mother's holding of the child's negative affects, her surviving his destructiveness (Winnicott, 1963b), and the child's experience of low-intensity, nontraumatic negative states in the mother's safe presence must also facilitate the gradual inclusion of such states in the child's self experience. How successfully hatred/anger/rage or depression/sadness/longing or sexuality in all its diverse aspects comes to be experienced as part of the "me" defines the "breadth" of the borders of the self experience as I am using that term.

Repetition. Repetition of events that are too powerful to enter the self experience readily, that instead "happen" to me as their passive container, can occur in at least two ways, each of which can foster a taming of the experience and its gradual integration as something owned as mine. First, there is repetition as an effort to gain mastery (Freud, 1920b). Thus, in a study of the early development of anal and scopophilic impulses (see chap. 7), it seemed to me that young children repeatedly enter into highly arousing situations related to those impulses, not solely in order to obtain pleasure but in a driven replay of an overstimulating situation—an attempt that can best be conceptualized as an effort to gain mastery through repetition. And just as repetition serves mastery in the domain of supposed "pleasure," of impulse gratification, so too it serves more broadly in development. Thus, Loevinger (1966) and G.S. Klein (1976), following her, speak of "reversal of voice," the turn from passive to active in development. Active repetition of an event, in which the person is the actor again and again, can slowly bring the event into the arena of ownership, something I produce, at my timetable, in my way, with results that gradually come to be predictable and familiar (Loewald, 1971).

There is also a form of repetition in which the person is not the initiator, the actor. This form is inevitable and automatically produces familiarity and sometimes the taming of experience. I have in mind such cyclic experiences as hunger, bowel pressure, genital arousal, and rage, which simply come upon one out of the biology of the organism or inborn reaction tendencies to inescapable events. These, too, come to be more familiar, predictable, known by virtue of their very repetition, through which learning takes place: learning of early warning signs, of the course of the experience, of outcome. And this learning, adding a cognitive (and controlling) aspect to the experience, slowly permits the then less overwhelming and less surprising experience to become familiar, to be owned.

Appeal. In the course of development a large array of inner phenomena is in an unsettled state at any given time. They include wishes and preferred modes of gratification, preferred fantasies about oneself, preferred modes of relatedness to others, and defenses against any or all of them. The unsettled state is due to shifts in what is externally defined as permissible as development proceeds, or in what is internally tolerable, dependent upon the anxiety, guilt, or conflict associated with these phenomena. Into this situation comes a steady flow of environmental "offerings"—things perceived, experienced—and some of these "fit" with the person's inner life: that is, provide solutions in the form of a pleasure gain, a reduction of negative affect, a solidification of defense, the living out of a fantasy, or the like. We say of such things that "they appeal to me," and, in favorable circumstances, they can be pursued so that they become parts of our lives.

Examples are numerous. An adolescent who had long-standing learning difficulties based on perceptual problems affecting the organization of the visual field was given a camera as a gift, fell in love with the picture-taking experience (which affords a form of control of the visual field), and subsequently became a professional photographer. A child who recently had attained long-delayed bowel control was given finger paints (but not so soon after the attainment of control as to be a threatening seduction to mess again), and using them became a favorite activity for months. An adolescent struggling with his newfound sexuality became an avid member of a teen group, which afforded him an opportunity both to express and to control his sexuality and to displace it from the home. An addict-to-be, plagued by feelings of emptiness, anxiety, and generalized malaise, had a drug experience which temporarily relieved this state; it "appealed" to him—that is, he was "hooked."

The implications of such experiences are twofold. First, they remind us that not all symptoms, defenses, or interests, not all sublimations and displacements, need be created from scratch by the individual. Rather, the individual's inner unrest provides the soil in which one or another environmental offering will find a fertile ground. Second, and central to my point, such experiences and the new modes of functioning they foster provide a way in which unsettled and unsettling inner experiences can be transformed in part into modes of activity or thinking that come to feel familiar, owned, self-directed, and self-consistent.

LATER MODES IN THE EXPANSION OF THE SELF

Throughout life the individual performs psychological work, as a result of which new thoughts and behavioral modes are brought into the domain of the self experience. I shall single out adolescent sexuality, parenthood, and work to illustrate this process. In each, a psychological event comes into the life of a person, often is experienced as somewhat foreign, only to end up (optimally) as centrally located in the self experience.

Adolescent sexuality. During the school years, prior to puberty, the child ordinarily achieves a certain stabilization of functioning. In what Bornstein (1951) refers to as the second period of latency, character development reflects this stabilization of individual style. Then the changing biology of the organism at puberty introduces strong sexual drives. Sexuality is a newcomer at first, an intruder, whether welcome or not, and not yet part of the familiar self experience. Adolescence has, in fact, been defined as the period of psychological adaptation to the biological changes of puberty (Bernfeld, 1938). Blos (1962) has described the progressive restabilization of the adolescent as he or she adapts to the intrusive, conflict-laden, new sexuality with its rearousal of infantile sexual fantasies. He discusses the way in which these conflicts lose their disturbing quality as they become "characterologically stabilized." From another standpoint, Blos comes to "the conclusion that infantile conflicts are not removed at the close of adolescence, but they are rendered specific, they become ego syntonic—that is, they become integrated within the realm of the ego as life tasks" (p. 134).

Spiegel's (1959) discussion of the "pooling" of unfamiliar experiences with old and familiar ones until the former too become a more familiar part of self-feeling is an earlier attempt, in process terms, to describe these same phenomena. Indeed, one of his prime examples is the way in which newly experienced adolescent sexual impulses are gradually, through repetition, integrated into the self-feeling. His discussion is also significant for my earlier remarks on the role of repetition in leading to the taming and assimilation of conflict-prone affects, impulses, and fantasies.

The term "metabolization" from biology captures the process. Nutriments are ingested and metabolized, thereby becoming usable by, and capable of being incorporated into, the physical organism. Psychological "foreign bodies" too can thus be metabolized, worked over, "characterologically stabilized" until they become familiar, part of the experiential self. Sexuality early in adolescence is disruptive and is almost "watched" by the adolescent as it "happens," but later on it is taken for granted, owned, as part of one's own being.

Parenting reveals similar phenomena in relation to a very different "intruder." In a study of parental responses to the birth of a first child, R. Pine (1978) gives numerous variations on the theme of parents' sense of a division between their "own" needs and those of "the baby." Actions with regard to the infant are not yet fully part of the self. She writes:

> What does it mean to "become" something? [Here, a parent.] It seems that change must occur in a person's internal self-image and identity, in a person's behavior and in the way other people view that person. It is almost certain that if one were to ask a mother or father several hours after delivery if [he or she] felt like a full-fledged parent, [the] answer [would be] "no." In fact, as this study will show, if they are asked the same question several months after delivery, most of them would still answer in the negative.... There are many implications of the fact that mothers and fathers with their first child have not fully incorporated parenting into their self-images and into the ranges of behaviors congruent with their sense of self at the time the child enters their lives. (p. 24)

The young parent often struggles to preserve an area of "self" against the demands of the baby-intruder, or guiltily struggles against that split. Yet, at the opposite developmental pole, when the adult offspring leaves the home, the parent is often left to re-find and re-mold a sense of self deprived (to a degree) of the caretaking function. What has happened in between? Some developmental processes have fostered a movement from parenting as an assumed role to parenting as a central part of the self experience.

Work. In teaching graduate students in psychology or psychiatric residents, one often becomes aware of the need of beginning professionals to preserve an area of "self" distinct from their work. They often try not to let their "work" intrude into their "lives." Yet, among older colleagues, this split generally is absent; one's work and one's life are intertwined. While the young often see this as work swallowing up one's self, I believe that the opposite is equally often the case: one's self subsumes one's work. And I see no reason to believe that this does not happen in any field of work.

In each of these areas—adolescent sexuality, parenting, work—at least two interdependent processes take place, marking the movement toward inclusion of the phenomena in the self experience. One is characterological shaping (Blos, 1962): the ways in which we think about, feel about, and perform actions in relation to the new phenomena come to be expressions of our general mode of functioning—done in this way, not that way; in short, in *my* way—and thereby move from the domain of assumed role to the domain of familiarity. The other is the slow accretion of *multiple functions* (Waelder, 1936) by the new behaviors. As I have tried to show (chaps. 5 and 7), multiple function does not spring forth fully grown with every new behavior but is gradually achieved as new behaviors (here, sexuality, parenting, work) are shaped to our particular modes of gratification, defense, expression of conscience, and adaptation, in this way coming to serve these functions. Together this characterological shaping of the new events and the achievement of their serving multiple functions make up the metabolization of new behaviors that can then be experienced as part of the self. Together they move behaviors from the domain of the new and "tacked-on" to the domain of the familiar and indispensable; they come to be experienced as part of an expanded "self"—now including (for example) self-as-sexual, self-as-parent, and self-as-worker, all intertwined.

This chapter has focused on the *experience* of self, on the *development* of that experience, and especially on *how* things come to be included in the self experience. Broadly, I treated of those psychological phenomena that feel familiar, "owned," stemming from an "I" that does or feels or thinks rather than an "it" that happens to me. I have discussed four domains: (1) early experiences that (ideally) contribute a sense of continuity, satisfaction, activity, and worthwhileness even prior to a crystallized awareness of self; experiences which are so much part and parcel of the way the world is first formed mentally for the infant that he takes them for granted and which, when self-awareness, "*a* self," emerges later on, immediately give it individualized shape as "*my* self." Without such early experiences in a more or less optimal form, I suggested, the potential for the good self experience is limited ever after; (2) a time of crystallization of self-awareness, probably culminating in the second year of life, during which experience comes to be phenomenologically "located" in the self as the center of experience and can, with the development of self and object constancy, be held in mind over longer periods; these changes may have particular consequences for pathogenic experiences, which at that point also can be held over time and located in the self, making this an especially critical period in the development of self pathology, affecting the experience of differentiated boundaries and of personal worth; (3) the work of achieving ownership of conflict-prone experiences (involving impulses, affects, and fantasies), which is accomplished slowly over time; it is facilitated by the *holding* role of the caretaker (which makes those experiences more tolerable), active and/or unavoidable repetition (which contributes to an increased sense of familiarity and of personal activity), and the *appeal* value of environmental offerings (which provides pathways to displacement, sublimation, and adaptation); repression, splitting, and other forms of disowning would be the alternatives in areas where such processes have not been successful; and (4) the characterological shaping and accretion of multiple functions by such late-developing phenomena as adolescent sexuality, parenting, and work, whereby they too come to be experienced as familiar and indispensable—that is, "metabolized" into the self experience. The way in which such new experiences are individually shaped by a person during psychoanalysis provides another here-and-now expression (like the transference, though less intensely) of the impact of the past on the present.

The approach has been developmental, both descriptive and inferential. I believe it is best to make it explicit that significant evaluative and ideal considerations are present in psychoanalytic theory and practice concerning these phenomena. We generally regard a self experience with a maximal range of *contents* to be preferable psychologically, such that the broad array of a person's thoughts and feelings can be held as "my own" rather than disowned. Indeed, psychoanalytic treatment can be viewed as a process essentially geared to the pursuit of this ideal. At the other extreme, we would regard as pathological, overinclusiveness of the self experience, such as aspects of omnipotence and grandiosity can entail, involving irrational feelings of power, responsibility, or guilt about events beyond the domain of the actual self-as-actor. Similarly, we ordinarily regard a broad range of *qualities* of the self experience to be preferable, with generally positive tone, but nonetheless with a substantial range of moods and self appraisals, dependent upon inner and external reality conditions. Again at the other extreme, we would raise clinical questions about chronic excesses in either direction in mood or self-esteem, whether high or low.

The centrality of the clinical task of helping the patient to accept ownership of, responsibility for, the many disowned parts of himself is recognized in all analytic work. Loewald (1971) gave it particular attention in suggesting that the work of repetition in the analytic process, changing the passive to the active experience, must move the patient toward such ownership. And Schafer (1976, 1978) has argued for the central position of the person as actor. His is both a theoretical-philosophical stance in regard to a view of persons rather than mechanisms and a technical stance in thinking about (though not necessarily in talking to) patients. I have approached the same issue developmentally.

The developmental problems presented in this part, as noted earlier, are only illustrative of specific developmental issues in one or more of the psychologies of drive, ego, object relations, and self, and illustrative of a developmental approach to problems that ultimately have significance in the clinical situation. In the next part, I shall reverse my perspective, more fully attending to direct clinical issues, but bringing the developmental point of view to bear upon them.

PART THREE

ASPECTS OF CLINICAL PROCESS
FROM A DEVELOPMENTAL
PERSPECTIVE

A. DEVELOPMENT AND CLINICAL TECHNIQUE

Psychoanalysis, and psychotherapy more broadly, are themselves developmental processes. All change that grows from life experience, human interrelatedness, and the exercise of human capacities is developmental, including the change that takes place in the special circumstances of the treatment situation.

But beyond that, a developmental perspective can shed light on the therapeutic process and influence its course. An understanding of the mutative factors in treatment is enhanced through this perspective, and alterations in treatment may grow from more active use of some of these factors. Additionally, a close-up picture of the child's life can change the way in which the content (not only the process) of a treatment is conceptualized.

10

Therapeutic Change:
A Parent-Child Model

Freud's early faith in the value of catharsis (Breuer and Freud, 1893) as a mechanism of therapeutic change gave way to emphasis on insight and working through (Freud, 1914b), processes requiring considerable cognitive effort, the achievement of affective conviction, and repeated relearning, reconviction, and testing out over time. Although these processes are in the foreground of those through which change is achieved in psychoanalysis, other processes are also present in the background. Interestingly, when we turn beyond classical psychoanalytic treatment to work with more seriously ill patients with deficient ego functioning, many of those background factors come into the foreground as instrumentalities of change.

Drawing from a parent-child model, I shall here address issues in the facilitation of development as they apply to an understanding of therapeutic change.[1] All the ideas to be advanced here grow out of experiences in developmental studies and in work with severely disturbed patients. All the

Originally published under the title "On therapeutic change" in *Psychoanalysis and Contemporary Science* (5:537–569, 1976), New York: International Universities Press.
    1. Although some analytic writers have discussed treatment from points of view related to the one to be pursued here (cf. Winnicott, 1955; Alexander, 1956; Mahler and Furer, 1960; Blanck and Blanck, 1974; Silverman, 1978), by and large these issues have not been treated extensively in the more classically oriented psychoanalytic literature. The interpersonal theorists (Sullivan, 1940, 1953; Fromm-Reichmann, 1950, 1959) often come closer; but I shall, in contrast to them, try to relate my discussion to the distinctively intrapsychic-historical viewpoint of psychoanalysis. Strupp's (1973) paper on the relative roles of nonspecific interpersonal factors and specific technical factors in bringing about therapeutic change contains a thought-provoking analysis of issues quite similar to the ones to be treated here; however, the whole thrust of his paper, the way the ideas are put together, is radically different from my own emphasis. And finally, Loewald's (1960) paper on the integrative value of the patient's object relationship to the analyst and of the analytic process itself, though couched in more theoretical terms, is a precursor to the present paper. Like Loewald, I am attempting to understand some of the "silent" features of analytic technique as it currently exists. Unlike Loewald, however, I shall also raise specific issues of technique, and ways of thinking about the development of technique, for supportive and child therapies—in this case by drawing on developmental considerations.

mechanisms for bringing about change that I discuss can come under the heading of "good parenting"—that is, they parallel what good parents *are* or *do* for the child. But this umbrella concept may obscure rather than clarify what I wish to say. For the analyst/therapist is not a parent to his patients, and I am not proposing that he behave like one; nor (except literally, in child treatment) is the patient a child, and I am certainly not proposing that he be treated like one. Instead, I shall propose that aspects of the therapeutic process can be understood by drawing on our knowledge of the facilitative role of the parent in the development of the child.

Considerations regarding the facilitation of growth, including elements of identification and of safety in a relationship, are relevant to the classical process of psychoanalysis as well as to other therapies, and so it is interesting to consider why psychoanalysis has been relatively remiss in formalizing them. Historical reasons are not hard to find. Freud's and Breuer's early discovery of transference, and Breuer's experience of it as a danger (Jones, 1953), led to a tendency to keep the patient-analyst relationship "pure." Further, the traditional criticism of psychoanalysis as nothing but "suggestion" has led theorists to lean over backward in an attempt to deny the real power of the analyst in the patient's life. Additionally, clinical experience with short-lived transference cures supports skepticism about the power of the relationship alone, without insight, to lead to lasting change. Perhaps most pervasive in its impact has been the drive bias of psychoanalytic theory. In early psychoanalytic theory, object relationships were seen largely as carried by drive; the "object" was indeed defined by its end-point position in the search for gratification. Only more recently has the independent, facilitative, and indispensable role in the growth process of the primary (mothering) object been given systematic theoretical attention (Mahler et al., 1975; Winnicott, 1965).

I have said that the technical issues I shall be discussing can be compared to what good parents "are or do for the child." For clarity in exposition, I shall retain this distinction between the passive ("are") and the active ("do") throughout. By "passive" I refer to modes of impact upon the patient that are inevitably consequent upon the therapist's mere *presence*—his reliability and consistent commitment to what is beneficial for the patient. I focus on these modes of impact in an attempt to understand relatively "silent" aspects of the effect of all therapies, including psychoanalysis. By "active," I refer to specific technical *interventions* that a therapist undertakes, tailored to a particular patient at a particular time. A focus on these interventions and their rationale may enable us to generate hypotheses regarding further interventions in work with ego-deficient patients.

THE PRESENCE OF THE THERAPIST

Psychological treatment can be viewed as the relation of one person to another where a part of the task is to enable the patient to take in and make his own what is "given" by the therapist. I am well aware that there is more to the process, but, for heuristic purposes, let us adopt this point of view for the moment. It is a formulation that provides a natural link to the historical issue of parenting, in which the establishment of a relationship and the influence of the parent and her or his input to the child are at the center of the process. In psychological treatments, as in parent-child relations, the ways in which the other becomes significant for the self (the problem of object relations) and the ways in which what is in the other becomes part of the "me" (the problem of internalization) are at the core. The further question, in what areas and under what conditions developmental processes that have not taken place earlier can take place later on, is of obvious significance for parenting and for psychological treatments as well. This is a question that touches on the reversibility of pathology, on critical periods, and on "silent" effects of therapy; it underlies much of the clinical discussion to follow.

Psychoanalysis quite rightly views treatment rather differently from the way just stated. Much of the clinical theory of psychoanalysis sees pathology in a way that tends to make the technical treatment goals of insight and working through appear eminently rational, indeed expressly tailored to the nature of the problem. Valid though this may be, it obscures other, equally valid points. In general, when problems and solutions are defined within the terms and framework of a specific theory, the theory tends to be self-validating, and this is true of psychoanalysis no less than of other theories. Let me clarify this point.

The clinical theory of psychoanalysis has had much to say about interruptions of the ongoing developmental process resulting from, for example, fixation or regression in the libidinal sphere; developmental failures in the ego sphere, including reliance on primitive and maladaptive defenses; trauma that leads to unending repetition of the past; and excessive cathexis of primitive parental images which ensures that all later object relationships will be colored by issues of omnipotence and powerlessness, irrational authority and weakness, idealization and disillusionment.

The implicit rationale of psychoanalytic technique has been derived from a conception of the pathogenic consequences of such interruptions. Thus, whether the aim of analysis is expressed in topographic terms (to make the unconscious conscious), in structural terms ("where id was there shall ego be": Freud, 1933, p. 80), or in genetic terms (the uncovering and reconstruction of the past), the essential objective has been to bring residues of the past into awareness so as to reduce their pathological sequelae. As early as 1900, in *The Interpretation of Dreams*, Freud wrote that "as a result of the unpleasure principle, the [primary process] is totally incapable of bringing anything disagreeable into the context of its thoughts" (p. 600). Instead, such "disagreeable" content is subject to processes of displacement and condensation that eventuate in dreams, slips, jokes, symptoms, and aspects of pathological character traits. Treatment attempts to allow the "disagreeable" content into consciousness, so that it can be dealt with in new ways.

Hypotheses regarding technique and its mode of impact can also be derived from a psychoanalytic theory of normal development, not only from the clinical theory of its interruptions. What we know about how development takes place can be profitably related to the distinctive psychoanalytic point of view, a view that brings focus to a wide range of clinical psychopathological and normal developmental issues. Many of these ideas refer to the facilitation of normal development. Such concepts as "good-enough mothering" (Winnicott, 1960a) and the establishment of basic trust or "confident expectation" (Benedek, 1938) via the mother-child relationship are relevant here; Mahler's (1965) emphasis on the development of the child's ego functions in the matrix of the mother-child relationship is also to the point. All these concepts point to the role of the actual parent, and later internal representations, in the development of the child.

PSYCHOANALYTIC THERAPY

In the literature on classical psychoanalysis, the patient-analyst object relationship has been discussed in terms of the therapeutic alliance; but such discussion leans more toward the role of this alliance in enabling the work of analysis (conceived of as insight and working through) rather than toward its intrinsic role in bringing about change. However, most people who have undergone psychoanalysis feel that they have learned and gained from the contact with their analyst, from the kind of person he or she is and the way the analyst functions—quite aside from the insights gained in the analysis. I say "the kind of person the analyst *is*" rather than "seems to be" to emphasize, in Greenson's (1967) terms, the *reality* aspects of the relationship. I am not here speaking of major transference-based perceptions or even of what Alexander (1956) calls the "corrective emotional experience." Instead, I refer to part-identification with aspects of the analyst's style, values, or way of thinking, pervasively evident to the analysand during the analytic process; specific, though incidental, educative moments; moments of the analyst's confirmation of the analysand's subjective reality; and beyond these the important context of safety in the analysis, to which I shall return below. None of this alters the centrality of the role of insight and working through in the analytic process; nor does it advocate or require any extra-analytic "friendliness" in the patient-analyst relationship. Identification and the impact of the object relationship occur inevitably in the analytic process as it is classically carried on because processes in the patient are receptive to them, indeed create them.

It is my impression that all this is self-evident to analysts *during the time* they are patients, although, ironically, they often lose the perception of this about their own patients when they are sitting behind the couch. I think there are at least two reasons for this. First is the analyst's theoretical and personal preference for seeing insight as the effective agent for change; although I share this theoretical leaning, I see no reason why it should keep us from also seeing other aspects of the process. The second reason for analysts' being less clear about, for example, identificatory and educative aspects of the process when they are therapists rather than patients is that many of these processes go on silently—they do not enter the sphere of conflict or of verbalization. They are experienced more or less silently by the patient, often with a feeling of their great impact, but they are often not reported to the analyst. The relative neglect of such phenomena says more about the belief systems of analysts than about the truths of analysis.

Just as so-called supportive therapies are likely to include "interpretive" aspects, as I shall discuss below, so insight treatment inevitably includes aspects that stem from the patient-analyst relationship itself, and these are one source of patient change. When Alexander developed such observations into his concept of "corrective emotional experience," he aroused considerable opposition. This was in part because of the overtones of manipulation and playacting in his recommendation that the therapist "can also consciously and planfully replace [his own personality reactions] with attitudes which are favorable in promoting what is the essence of the whole therapeutic process— the corrective emotional experience" (1956, p. 100). Interestingly, though, an earlier idea of Alexander's does not imply role playing. In 1948 he wrote: "Emotional and intellectual support is to some degree present in all forms of treatment. It results from the therapeutic situation itself, independently of the special techniques employed, provided the therapist instills confidence in his patient and listens with benevolent understanding to his patient's complaints" (p. 274). This is what I refer to as the effect of the "mere presence" of the therapist.

The ideas that I shall present are not new; here I wish only to draw them together in the context of certain inevitable learnings that take place in the analytic situation, focusing on those that have their undoubted origins in the universal parent-child relationship. There are certain modes of impact of one person upon another that are, I believe, active throughout the life cycle; as such, they are present in the early parent-child relationship and also in the analytic situation. I shall mention three that are closely related. First, the patient makes certain *identifications* with aspects of the analyst's functioning; that is, what was experienced as other comes to be part of the self (Schafer, 1968). These identifications may be with a tone of voice, a form of humor, an attitude of calm under adversity, a habit of questioning "why" about oneself, a style of expression, an interest or avocation. These "silently" become part of the patient's functioning. Sometimes the patient is aware of their origin with an accompanying inner sense of relatedness and sometimes not; sometimes they are lasting and sometimes short-lived. Second, the *educative role* of the analyst, although far more significant in child analysis, does not disappear in adult work if for no other reason than that the patient will not let it disappear. The role of authority in education is ever of significance, and information received from the awesome authority of the analyst has a high likelihood of being taken in. This applies not only to the dynamically linked information of the insight process but also to attitudes about behavioral options, modes of functioning in the real world, that now and then are intentionally or unintentionally embedded in interpretive comments— or that are found there by the patient hungry for them. And third, the analyst seems not only to clarify but to *confirm the inner reality* of the patient. For all patients at times, the analyst's statement or restatement of what the patient already knows or has said confirms it, gives it the impact, again, of the awesome authority of the analyst. These are all functions inevitably served by the parent for the child and are processes of interpersonal impact that have no "critical period" of effect—that is, they are active throughout life in relationships that have an authority differential between the participants, whether parent and child or analyst and patient.

The role of speech is a key aspect of the analytic process wherein an inevitable shaping role is played by the analyst for the patient, a broad aspect that draws from each of the three features described above. The medium of psychoanalysis conveys a powerful message to the patient, training him in the use of words, in certain habits of thought, in modes of delay and the control of action (cf. Loewenstein, 1956; T. Shapiro, 1970). Ironically, that this is sometimes less true with certain patients than we would wish is testament to the lasting power of identifications with the old parental styles, now also built into the structural and psychodynamic arrangements within the particular patient.

A second feature of analysis that I should like to discuss is what I call the analytic "context of safety." Another of Alexander's statements that aroused opposition was his comment that the fact of a difference between the analyst and the parent is the "essential therapeutic agent" (1956, p. 41) in analysis. There is an ambiguity here. "Essential" may mean "more important than insight," but it need not. It can also mean "basic to the rest"—that is, setting the conditions under which all the rest, including insight, can take place. It is obvious that in order for a patient to gain from analysis it is essential that he come to his sessions, but this does not mean that coming to sessions is the "essential therapeutic agent." But as regards the nature of the analytic relationship, it is not at all banal to define "essential" in this way. For the nature of that relationship provides a context of safety in which growth can take place. The analyst *is* different from the parent, without manipulation or playacting. And that *is* essential to all the rest.

Children can develop, and so can adults, more successfully if there is a reasonable stability to their environment, so that they can develop a reasonable trust in it; if the environment enriches, makes demands, and spurs them on, so much the better. The analytic situation provides all this. It is within this context that the work of insight regarding urges, affects, fantasies, and conflicts can go on.[2]

It is easy not to notice this. Especially when it is working smoothly, it is "invisible." Perhaps because Sullivan worked with psychotic patients he early

---

2. Numerous writers have contributed to this area. Bowlby (1969) gives primacy to the attachment of the child to the mother—as a given, not by association with oral needs. Mahler (1965) discusses the child's growth in the matrix of the mother-child relationship. White (1963) argues that exploration, the development of competence, the use of the ego's "independent energies," take place given reasonable safety in the child's life. In the face of internal drive tension, these ego energies are washed over; the drive pressures are more imperious, demanding first attention. In general, "good enough mothering" (Winnicott, 1960a) allows development to proceed.

noted the absence of these core object attachments and turned to the technical importance of interpersonal relationships. But Freud's patients (and most patients considered suitable for analysis) had a reasonable stability in their core attachments from infancy and early childhood. Given a basic inner context of object relatedness and some degree of trust, center stage is readily seized by the drive-linked fantasies and conflicts. But work with a ghetto population, disorganized families, or institutionalized infants (Provence and Lipton, 1962) makes it clear that when that early context of safety is absent, *it* is the crucial factor in lack of developmental progress and takes center stage in therapeutic work.

The point is that the analytic setting, like the average expectable environment (Hartmann, 1939) with good enough mothering, provides a context of safety in which the rest (the child's growth, on the one hand, or the analysand's communication, developing insight, and trying out of change, on the other) can take place. Like Lewin's "dream screen" (1946), the breast on which the dream is projected, but here in a broader context of basic attachment, the analysis, like the child's growth, is enacted upon the solid stage of safety in a relationship. Without this stage, which we too easily take for granted (when it is there), the action would not take place.

Child Psychotherapy

Let us look briefly at child therapy from a similar standpoint. In the psychological treatment of a young and growing child, especially a treatment that continues over a fairly long period, the child begins to endow the therapist with functions more typically reserved for the parent. This does not involve the therapist's behaving in parentlike ways; rather, it involves the uses the child makes of the therapist. Beyond this, the therapeutic "context of safety" has a special place in child therapy as well as the general role already discussed.

Childhood is a time of the relatively rapid emergence of new intrapsychic and behavioral modes of function. These developing capacities (ego functions, sublimations, modes of object relationship and adaptation), whatever their built-in maturational components, grow in the matrix of the mother-child relationship. This, it seems to me, has at least a fourfold implication: (1) new capacities are modeled after those of the mother (or father); (2) they may be used (practiced, developed, perfected) in the relationship to her/him; (3) when used elsewhere, they may be shared with her/him in the kind of verbal exchange whereby the child brings them to the home, gathering permission and support for his new achievements outside the home and making them part of his relations to his parents; and (4) they come to serve functions, often multiple functions, in the context of the relationships to the parents as well as intrapsychically, and thus become part of the more permanent psychic repertoire. My general point is, however, that for the growing child in long-term therapy, all this inevitably takes place in the relationship with the therapist as well as in the one with the parent.

Beyond this specific position of the child therapist in the development of the child (which coexists peacefully with the therapist's interpretive role) is the specific facilitation of the emergence of new functions provided by the context of safety of the treatment relationship. The degree to which the mother-child relationship is benign or malignant determines the degree to which progressive new capacities, on the one hand, or survival techniques, on the other, will emerge from the child's potential repertoire. Work with severely disturbed children from multiproblem families with considerable social as well as psychological pathology makes clear the many survival mechanisms that *can* emerge from the child in his efforts to cope with overwhelming stress (cf. Malone, 1966). In childhood, with its rapid development of new modes of function, the therapeutic context of safety permits not only exploration and the risks of change but also the emergence of more benign, healthy, adaptive modes at each developmental step.

One other feature of child therapy, though not so closely tied to issues of internalization and object relationship as those already discussed, nonetheless sets the therapist in a position of inevitable overlap with the parental function as regards the growth process. The child's psychological equilibrium is regularly disrupted as a consequence of new environmental demands from without and new needs and capacities within. The therapist is thus working with a system in disequilibrium. And, while at times it may be hard to keep pace with the growth process, to attune ourselves to emerging changes, it is nonetheless true that there is a distinct advantage to working with systems in disequilibrium. Too fixed, too satisfied, too defended a system is less amenable to change. Crisis theorists (Lindemann, 1956; Caplan, 1960) have shown that a person in crisis is susceptible not only to the breakdown of his traditional mode of functioning but also to being influenced toward new, more constructive reequilibration. Blos (1962) makes a similar point about the constructive potentials of the growth crisis of adolescence. The long-term therapist of the growing child, like the "long-term parent," is inevitably present and therefore in a position to deal with those periods of disequilibrium *during* the disequilibrium.

SUPPORTIVE PSYCHOTHERAPY

When we consider therapeutic change in supportive therapies, the parent-child model is particularly relevant, for the presence of an interested therapist almost automatically "supports" the brittle or severely ill patient's *ties to human objects* and capacities for the *maintenance of defense*, as do the presence and interest of the parent earlier. Rapaport (1957) has drawn upon Piaget's (1952a) concept of "nutriment" in arguing that certain psychological structures require a continued input of stimuli for their maintenance. These proposals were originally applied by Rapaport to studies of stimulus deprivation in an attempt to explain the alteration of function that emerged in those conditions. For the isolated and brittle patient, the therapist's presence provides the nutriment for the continuance of an object tie and the maintenance of defense.

The conditions under which the need for stimulus input of this kind can gradually be replaced by internalization have yet to be determined. However, a detour into the child's early history suggests some relevant developmental considerations and points to the clarifying role of events that take place between child and caretaker.

The young infant is fully dependent upon the physical presence of its mother for its survival. This soon expands beyond the need for physical care to the need for her presence to provide a feeling of safety and satisfaction. "Separation anxiety" and "stranger anxiety" are concepts that speak to the other side of that comfort. But the actual presence of the mother is not forever required. Eventually the child develops "libidinal object constancy," an internal representation of the mother that he can use (for comfort, for control) in the way he can use the actual mother (chap. 8). This is achieved gradually and never totally, but most of us achieve it to a fair degree. Thus, developmentally, ongoing interaction with the real external object is replaced to a degree, and in some ways, by internalization. So too, optimally, in supportive therapy, although how and under what conditions remain unclear.

The same is true of defense. Conceiving defense broadly as the control of impulse and/or of unpleasant affect, we are reminded that the mothering one is an "auxiliary ego" for the infant—an external source of those defense functions that will later spring from inner sources. In my research on normal development (Pine, 1971) I was struck by the usefulness of the concept of "anaclitic defense" (cf. Spitz, 1946)—defense in which the child stills anxiety by making actual contact with the actual mother—a phenomenon especially found (not surprisingly) in relation to anxiety over separation. But this, too, is later replaced (more or less, and by most of us) by internal defense processes.

A critical question for supportive therapy is: How does the need for continued stimulus input (the therapist's presence as nutriment) change over to internalization, in which the patient can sustain object relationships and his inner defense processes relatively autonomously? Though the answer is not readily at hand, we should recall that it is also by no means entirely clear precisely when an interpretation in insight therapy will be taken in by the patient in a way that can produce constructive and inner-determined modification of function. Issues of internalization are relevant there too. The "brilliant" and awesome interpretation in a first session or the controlling and powerful interpretation of an overbearing analyst may be internalized quite differently from the insight that develops slowly, with the patient's participation, in the context of an ongoing therapeutic alliance. But once we raise questions regarding internalization, whether of interpretation or of object representations or defense processes, the parent-child relationship, the initial source of such events, becomes relevant as a source of understanding.

To sum up: I have been discussing aspects of technique and of therapeutic change from the point of view of a psychoanalytic developmental theory. In particular, I have tried to show the relevance, for a rationale of therapeutic change, of a psychoanalytic theory of *facilitation* of development to complement the more usual clinical theory of *interruption* of development. I have focused principally on clinical phenomena (in classical psychoanalysis, in child therapy, and in supportive therapy) that can be understood in terms of the object relationship to the analyst/therapist, identifications and other internalizations with or from him, and the general therapeutic context of safety that permits all of the rest of treatment (both exploration and development or change) to go on. I have pointed especially to developmental phenomena that do not pass a critical period after which they are inoperative but which, at least to some degree and in some areas, operate lifelong. As such, they are in the foreground of some therapies, though in the background of all.

These various points of contact between technique and the parent-child relation go only so far, and no further, in enlightening us regarding technique. My aim has been to expand (not replace) our rationale of technique and therapeutic change, and to raise questions regarding the areas and times in the life cycle when processes central to early development (especially internalization and developmental facilitation) are still operative and therefore relevant for therapy as well. Until this point, I have been focusing on the "mere presence" of the therapist with this twofold aim in mind. I turn now to the "actions" of the therapist with similar aims. I shall focus principally on child therapy and so-called supportive therapies in the hope of contributing to our thinking about the opportunities for reversing developmental failure.

THE "ACTIONS" OF THE THERAPIST

In a 1951 paper on ego disturbances, Fritz Redl wrote: "This short paper . . . sets itself a limited task: to lure the practitioner into becoming much more impressed with the need to be very specific in the use of the term 'ego disturbance' and to stimulate the clinician to seek a much wider repertoire of techniques whenever he is confronted with the task of 'ego support' " (p. 273). He then goes on to illustrate *specific* areas of deficient functioning that may require *specific* kinds of intervention. In their introductory comments to this article, reprinted in their volume on *Childhood Psychopathology*, Harrison and McDermott wrote: "Teasing out the precise aspect of ego function requiring specific differential therapeutic attention in lieu of global support for a vaguely defined 'weak ego' transforms an impossible task into a difficult one" (1972, p. 532). My route to this work has been similar and my intent comparable. Confronted by "impossible" therapeutic situations, I have tried to think about them in ways that would transform them into something merely "difficult."

Technical variations of the kind that grow out of Redl's work with delinquent adolescents, like some of those with severely disturbed patients in my own work, may or may not warrant being called by Eissler's term "parameters" (1953). Eissler referred to variant techniques within the context of an essentially classical psychoanalytic therapy, variant techniques themselves subject to later analysis. But sometimes the variant may be larger than what is classical, so to speak, and then we should speak of alternative therapeutic modalities rather than parameters as such. I mean to address the whole range here, with greater and lesser variations from "classical" technique.

One is more impressed with the need for technical variations in work, like Redl's, with nonanalyzable patients, and the examples I shall draw upon stem from such work. In my own experience, there have been three routes to such variations. In each, work with "impossible" clinical situations became merely "difficult" as I drew on developmental theory to catalyze technical variations and new thought. First was my experience for many years in supervising and teaching work with difficult, multiproblem, intrapsychically chaotic, socioeconomically distressed, and environmentally overstimulated children and their families in a municipal hospital clinic. The work brought frustration and pain and hardly much reward; I found that the only feasible approach was to meet the work as an intellectual challenge, to draw stimulation and satisfaction from the attempt to let experience, theory, and at times novel techniques guide me, a process that often had a feedback to better therapeutic outcome as well. Second was my experience over the years with some of my own patients whose chronic and severe deficiencies of ego functioning were slow to alter. In response, within the context of reasonably orthodox therapeutic procedures, I found myself making technical variations focused on specific aspects of the pathology. And third has been my involvement in varying ways with Margaret Mahler, Manuel Furer, and Anni Bergman, whose work with symbiotic psychotic children (Mahler and Furer, 1960; Mahler, 1968; Bergman, 1971; Bergman and Furer, 1974) includes comparable efforts to deal with "impossible" pathology by creating variations in technique within the context of sophisticated psychoanalytically guided treatment.

An aside may be in order to clarify the personal ideology underlying this work: It seems to me that a therapist who is "psychoanalytically oriented" is so oriented in whatever he or she does, although just *what* he does (especially beyond the range of the "average expectable analyzable patient") should vary with the patient's psychic structure. Technical variations, too, even major ones, can be "psychoanalytically oriented." Although "psychoanalytically oriented psychotherapy" is often used as synonymous with "insight therapy," this is actually a usurpation of the former term. The usage seems to imply that insight therapy has learned from the vast contributions of psychoanalysis while supportive therapy, for example, has not been thus "oriented." It is as though the latter is a mindless wasteland, not guided by a theory of human functioning. Psychoanalysis has status, and naming has power; and the contrasting names of psychoanalytically oriented (insight) therapy versus supportive therapy have been self-fulfilling to a degree, so that theoretical considerations have been applied to the work of supportive therapy much more slowly.

I propose instead two parallel terms: psychoanalytically oriented *insight* therapy and psychoanalytically oriented *supportive* therapy. Both therapies may of course also be "psychodynamically oriented" or "family oriented" or "behaviorally oriented" or whatever—but they remain parallel. For if we genuinely operate with a theory of human development, structure, and change, such as psychoanalysis (among others) provides, then all our thinking, no matter what the problem or who the patient, is influenced by that theory. It is true that insight therapy, far more than supportive therapy, draws upon psychoanalytic *technique*, but they can be equally oriented by psychoanalytic *theory* more generally—in particular, by its conceptions of development and change, on the one hand, and of psychic structure, and human thought, affect, and drive processes, on the other. In what follows I have tried to draw upon psychoanalytic *developmental* theory to elucidate aspects of technique in supportive therapy and in work with ego-deficient patients. In the next chapter I draw on the theory of technique as well.

The clinical illustrations presented below are intended as examples not so much of new approaches as of the application of psychoanalytically enriched parent-child considerations to the creation of developmentally forwarding strategies for use with particular patients at particular points in their therapy. The examples are certainly not new *methods* of therapy. They are merely clinical moments, technical bits, which took place between therapist and patient in the context of complex, multifaceted, therapeutic relationships that included considerable interpretive work of a reasonably familiar kind as well as the moments of variation.

Indeed, no therapy is ever totally "supportive" in the sense that no exploratory and interpretive work whatsoever goes on. And, conversely, there is no such thing as "pure" insight therapy in which the mere presence of another, the analyst, does not lead to the "supportive" stabilization of defense and of object relationships or in which the analytic context of safety does not provide the setting for risking change. I believe that supportive and insight therapies are not counter*posed* in some *opposition* to one another but counter*poised*, in some *balance* with one another. In any event, the "supportive" therapies I have in mind are complex affairs, intellectually taxing, including flexibility and variation in techniques, and also including many moments of interpretive work. In describing them, I shall try to show how the particular technical *acts* of the therapist or the *form* of his or her presence had therapeutic impact, and I shall relate them to developmental, parent-child issues.

Let me begin with a fairly simple and not unusual clinical vignette, which represents my first awakening to these phenomena. Some years ago, I was seeing a sixteen-year-old boy in psychotherapy who had been brought after having drawn a much younger boy into performing fellatio on him. As I got to know him, it became clear that in that incident and elsewhere he acted on impulse, without plan or anticipation of consequence, in an almost haphazard way, without the impulse itself appearing to have a very powerful impelling force (cf. D. Shapiro, 1965). Just as his planfulness was deficient, so too was his whole cognitive and affective life rather vacant and undifferentiated. Reared by a depressed mother, abandoned by his father, this was the developmental outcome, although the specific formative steps were not known to me.

In the second year of therapy, the following incident took place: Robert was telling me about a high school dance he had attended. "All the other guys were dancing with girls except me.... But I wasn't angry." Should I point out the denial of anger? My past contact with him amply justified that interpretation; in his life he never had "gotten," and once again at the dance he wasn't "getting"; he was chronically angry. For some reason not known to me then or now, I chose not to. Instead I said: "Perhaps, as you say, you weren't angry. Perhaps you were envious; perhaps you were wishing that you could be dancing too." He lit up, and that moment between us became important for both of us. It was the start of my "teaching" him, not only to help him develop and use differentiated affects, but to help him develop other ego functions as well (anticipation and planning, verbalization, judgment) to fill the vacant and undifferentiated psyche with the tools of ego function.

For me, that moment in 1957 was the start of this chapter—a long-range effect. For Robert, the effect was more immediate. When I introduced him to his envy in that situation I believe I did several things: I showed him that a certain unarticulated inner sensation, vaguely and confusedly experienced, was indeed an identifiable affective state, known to others and therefore socially shared and somewhat more acceptable; I helped prevent a process (signaled by the "I wasn't angry") whereby all his feelings would typically get caught up in the flow of his anger, thereby losing their specificity and their differentiated signal value for him; and I believe that, through words, through the naming of emotional states (Katan, 1961; cf. T. Shapiro, 1974), I aided the control function: words providing a moment of recognition and delay in which discomfort over a feeling might have a chance of being handled in ways other than through denial or immediate discharge through action.

At a level a bit more removed from the concrete clinical data, just what had happened? Following Anna Freud's (1926) comments about psychoanalytic work with children, I believe that I had shifted for the moment from an interpretive mode to something that was an amalgam of an educative and an interpretive one. Though Katan's (1961) paper had not yet been written, its later publication helped me to understand that the naming of feeling has an important role to play in normal development as well. And in her paper, it is clear that that function is ordinarily carried out by the empathic parent. In this instance, I believe, the developmental function served by the naming of feelings helped this adolescent in much the same way as it helps a growing child; its "critical period" of effect, so to speak, had not passed. Some learnings can be taken in from the "benevolent parent" at any point in the life cycle.

Let me give another example. This one is more recent and, in contrast to the work with Robert, involved a more explicit and conscious attempt to draw on developmental formulations to deal with a specific deficit in ego function that was making therapeutic advance impossible. The clinical situation was one of failure in the development of the signal function of anxiety.

How does signal anxiety ordinarily develop? Presumably, the infant, experiencing distress, has repeated experiences of gratification (or termination of distress). At some point, the distress begins to be associated with these previous experiences of relief; memory thus comes into play, and there is a capacity to anticipate relief once again. In these moments of delay, where distress is held in abeyance (because of the anticipation of relief) and therefore does not escalate, it seems to me probable that the opportunity for higher order defenses (at first simply the "defense" of calling mother) can develop. In contrast, for the child for whom relief is not forthcoming, the beginning of distress is a "signal" only of the previously unrelieved distress, a memory that accelerates the escalation to panic next time around.

Emmy was a child who could neither use the affect signal to call inner defenses into play nor rely on her capacity to terminate distress. At age nine, there was a clear deficiency in the process: anxiety signal → defense → control of anxiety. She was almost totally unable to tolerate affective discomfort. A spark of anxiety would rapidly escalate to a conflagration of panic—indicative of a borderline ego organization (Rosenfeld and Sprince, 1963). That is, anxiety did not function as a signal that brought an array of defenses to the fore; all it signified was that panic was on the way. How then to talk? Any but bland or neutral words set off screaming or physical flight from the office, in a reaction that I was convinced was well beyond her capacity to control. Months went by in quiet play, but the talk situation did not change. As in a phobia, so too with the panic: the potential affect storm was such that the danger situation was avoided at all costs and steps toward new understanding or mastery could not be made.

It seemed to me that aid in the form of a break in the cycle anxiety → panic → flight had to come from the outside, just as it does in the course of development when the parent's ministrations still the child's anxiety and substitute for the inner defenses that are not yet functional. What was done, in steps and in varying combinations, at times by written note and at times by speech, was to tell Emmy such things as the following: "In about a minute" (or "after the game of checkers"), "I'm going to ask you a question" (to alert her anticipatory function); and perhaps adding: "I'll only ask one question and then I'll stop and we'll play again" (to let her see a *terminus* of the threat and to let her see that the therapist would aid in bringing it to a halt); or later: "After the game, I want to talk for about five minutes" (perhaps laying down a watch where she could see it), "but if it's too hard, just say 'no more' and we'll stop" (to give her some active control over the danger). Overall, the aim was to titrate the stimulus load for the patient and to help her achieve a more active anticipatory capacity to combat her more usual passive experience in the face of affect storms. Emmy became much more able to talk in these bits, although they represented only a small part of the work.

This entire process is not unlike the situation in which a therapist indicates to an impulsive adolescent or adult patient that "after this session, because of what we talked about, you may have the urge to . . ." —saying this as a way of helping the patient with defective control functions to anticipate and control an impulse. This was, by the way, another important part of the work with Robert—the therapist's warning filling in for the historically unsaid and (in any event) uninternalized parental "Don't." In addition to aiding the anticipatory function, such a warning provides a model for the causal thinking (feelings lead to actions, actions have consequences, thought can lead to controls) that is often absent in such patients (D. Shapiro, 1965). How fully *this* can be internalized by older patients in the course of treatment, when it has not been accomplished earlier, is less clear to me; but my impression is that it is only minimally possible.

Let me give a third example drawn from child therapy before turning to adult "supportive" work. The capacity to hold "disagreeable" contents in consciousness is a developmental achievement of enormous consequence; in admittedly simplistic terms, it permits us to think adaptively about such contents and forestalls their (potential) proliferating effect outside awareness and/or the need for the maintenance of repressive defenses against them. With adult patients we have learned that such unconscious fantasies have already had a widespread effect, and we approach them by *listening*, by letting the patient tell us, so that gradually we are able to understand the fantasies in many of their ramifications.

But some parents of young children do not do it that way. A parent may say: "I know you're angry at me, and I'm angry at you, but you still have to do what I told you to." Or another says: "Boys have penises and girls have vaginas, and they are different." Or another says: "We adopted you because we saw you and we knew we would love you." Simple statements all, but unmentionable by certain *other* parents. I suspect that such differences from the outside foster or counteract tendencies inside the child that ultimately define what is thinkable and what unthinkable (or unmentionable) for a particular child.

The therapist of the child can stand in either place: as an analytic therapist with a "wait and learn" attitude toward relatively unavailable content or as a parent-educator who explains about certain difficult-to-think-about matters in order to foster the growth process. The former approach leads to rich and complex understanding; but it is our familiar analytic procedure and, since I have nothing new to add to it, I will not discuss it further here. I would like to give a clinical example of the more active, parent-like intervention, with its general developmental and precise clinical rationale in this case.

Susanna came to therapy at age eight, bright, winning, but with an abstracted, faraway air. She was referred by her school, which reported that her faraway quality seriously interfered with her peer relationships and that she periodically engaged in a form of aggressive activity, quite out of character for her, which gave them much concern. The activity, seemingly coming out of the blue and having a driven, repetitive quality, involved her plowing aggressively, at full steam, through a crowd of her schoolmates, bowling them over, knocking them aside. In the history taking, one fact stood out: although this child had a relatively accident- and illness-free development, she had been hit by a truck at age eighteen months and injured so severely that parents and physicians alike viewed it as miraculous that she had survived, and without any physical sequelae. While the accident was not available to Susanna's memory, she was well aware of the (accurate) family view of the miraculousness of her survival.

Her psychotherapy could not help but to focus on this accident because of what she brought to the sessions. Almost every session would begin with some kind of behavioral enactment, often in an abstracted or somehow off-center way, of the accident. It quickly became apparent that her plowing through her schoolmates, trucklike, knocking them over, was yet another enactment of the same thing. In the office she would, for example, drop to the floor suddenly, as though dead, or beep (like a truck horn) at the most unanticipated moments.

In the course of the therapeutic work, there was occasion again and again to link them to the accident. Susanna responded at first with curiosity, then with recognition. Though after a while she became rather fed up with talk of the accident, she continued her enactments; and though she became an-noyed at these "translations" of them, she continued to hear them. In view of the extent to which this material dominated the therapy, it was impressive how little was learned about its connection to her wishes, object relationships, and character structure; mainly I saw repetition in fantasy: the point-by-point correspondence of the enactments with the accident (though there were variations on the theme that revealed the developing magical notions of mastery especially). Susanna functioned remarkably well in her life; the trau-matic residue of the accident seemed to have been quite compartmentalized, appearing with a faraway quality in her various play enactments, but not touching many other areas. Blos (1962), in discussing late adolescent de-velopment, speaks of a kind of ideal outcome where derivatives of early trauma are remade into constructive life tasks (for example, a sickly Teddy Roosevelt who becomes an outdoorsman and soldier). For Susanna, the residue of the trauma seemed cut off from much of the rest of her life—not affecting many areas but also kept unmodified by subsequent experience.

The therapeutic work was governed by the effort to help Susanna "talk out" ideas relating to the accident, apart from whether ramifications of the accident in her fantasy life were ever expressed. (This was not a preformed approach; it grew in response to the material that she did, and *did not*, bring into the sessions.) Much as the proverbial postsurgery patient wants to "show you my operation" and talk about it, and much as some sensitive parents may encourage talking and retalking about traumatic incidents as a way of working through the stimulation that could not be mastered all at once, so too with Susanna. The result was striking. The two school-linked presenting problems dropped away, and Susanna developed new age-appropriate inter-ests (bicycle riding and skating) that, in the clinical material, were clearly the heirs of the old odd enactments of the truck accident (moving vehicles). By their pleasure and age appropriateness and by the fact that the old enactments dropped away when these new interests arrived, they seemed to signal that the developmental process had been freed (Winnicott, 1971b) and that the old trauma had entered the mainstream of her functioning in a way that could power constructive activities rather than in the old compartmentalized way.

In these three brief case reports, I have tried to illustrate fairly small sections of complex and multifaceted therapies, sections that I believe can be illuminated by an examination of their relation to aspects of the functioning of the "good parent." I turn now to a somewhat more extended report of the treatment of a young woman in a therapy that could variously be considered insight oriented or supportive. It is the latter aspect that I wish to focus upon. Though not created out of theory, the therapeutic power of this supportive aspect became comprehensible to me by being examined in terms of a developmentally oriented dynamic theory.

I first met Carrie when she was sixteen, a complex, bright, sensitive, but chaotic and impulse-ridden adolescent who was capable of genuine loyalty, concern for others, and receptiveness in an object relationship but virtually incapable of preventing herself from rushing into action to escape even the least amount of affective discomfort. Brought up in Ireland by a borderline foster mother (who foster-cared numerous children) and with the periodic presence of a man whom she believed to be her true father (and who later disappeared), during her early teens, before she emigrated to the United States, she was given the hurtful information that the man was not her true father and that her natural mother was a prostitute who had "given her away."

After she emigrated to the United States, Carrie had periodic brushes of difficulty with her school and other community agencies as well as with her foster mother, and she eventually was referred for psychotherapy to a neighborhood settlement house clinic. I saw her once, then twice a week for about two and a half years before the therapy terminated abruptly, to resume some years later in a very different form. In that first period of therapy, the work was rich but erratic. When working well, she would, with a mix of stammering and hesitant yet passionate and strong expression, work on aspects of her pained relationships to her various parents and even, at times, on her defensive style of flight, action, and chaos that overrode painful affect. But she would often miss her sessions,, sometimes for weeks at a time, and sustained work on some issue in the therapy over several sessions was rare.

The interruption in the therapy came about as follows: her attachment to her male therapist had all along been difficult for her to manage, and interpretive work did no more than forestall the next anxiety-ridden flight from her strong feelings. In particular, both her transference longing for the therapist-as-good-mother and her erotic fantasies about the therapist-as-oedipal-father precipitated flight from the therapeutic relationship. The flight led her into relationships first with a man who was clearly a substitute for the therapist (a destructive and inappropriate relationship that she was able to give up upon interpretation and major control imposed by the therapist) and later with a young man close to her own age, who was not at all an inappropriate partner.

Into that relationship, however, the pathology of both her foster mother and his mother came like an invasion. First his mother, then hers, made clear their interest in having "the children" sleep together premaritally under their watchful and delighted eyes. Carrie thought, indeed *knew*, that this whole thing was bizarre, but she was caught in the web of her attachment to the young man, her sexual excitement, her entanglement with her foster mother, and her flight from the therapist and could not easily extricate herself. But then she did. The young couple (then aged 18) left both mothers to live together. Carrie left therapy, and I did not hear from her again for a few years. So ended the first phase.

After a few years without contact, I received a phone call from her. This call set the pattern for our contacts over the next eight years. She would call, say she wanted to see me, set an appointment, and fail to show up. This occurred about once a year. After the first few episodes, I began to talk to her over the phone about her obvious wish and fear regarding seeing me; after a while, I urged that she consider seeing someone else, perhaps a female therapist. She refused, even though she quite clearly recognized her inability to get herself to see me. During those phone calls I learned that she had had out-of-wedlock twins in the interim and had continued the chaotic, action-oriented, trouble-prone style of her life.

Then came a series of calls that eventuated in our resuming contact, a severe depression, and a brief period of disorganization. A crisis had erupted over her children: their father was making a move to take them out of the country with him. Beyond that, Carrie was torn between her awareness that she could not take care of the children (because of her need for action to escape unpleasant feelings, and hence a need to get out of the home, generally at unpredictable times, and away from them) and, on the other hand, her enormous guilt over subjecting them to the same cycle of abandonment and loss that she had experienced. At that period she did come to see me a few times, and we talked on the phone often; I helped her to accept her inability to care for the twins at that time, to allow a relative to care for them, to visit and not abandon them, and to tolerate (by anticipation) her guilt. The immediate crisis past, again began phone calls and broken appointments.

At that point, I established a new arrangement. I would hold an hour each week for her. It was "her hour," whether she used it or not. I was always there. She understood that, because she so often failed to show up, I would hold this hour not in my private office, where I saw regularly scheduled patients, but at my hospital office, where I could always use the time at my desk if she did not come. There was never any fee. She understood that I might schedule cancelable appointments in her hour but never permanent ones. She would be spared the embarrassment, and I the annoyance, of broken appointments. We kept this arrangement for seven years. Carrie periodically called *during* her hour about the possibility of coming to her next scheduled hour. She called about six to ten times a year and came two or three times a year; but we often discussed real issues at least for a while on the phone. Whenever I was going to be away during her hour, I always dropped her a note in advance so that she would not call or arrive to find me absent. And with this arrangement, Carrie settled down. She held a job for over two years for the first time; her panics became more manageable; she stopped skirting the edge of asocial trouble; and she visited her children, for whom she cares deeply. She was well aware that her life was far from perfect, but she was functioning with more stability than I had ever seen in her. Gradually my contact with her faded.

What happened in this work? I would like to describe what I attempted to do when I *did* see her and what I believe happened when I *did not* see her but when "her hour" was nonetheless reliably there.

In the (occasional) sessions there were two main areas of work. First, I tried to help her identify her feelings and to anticipate her action tendencies, to "lend" her control and the tools for control, much as I have described in some of the other brief case reports. Central to this work were genuine insight and uncovering focused on her inability to tolerate painful feeling and linked to her painful imagined memory of "my mother giving me away, selling me, like a piece of meat." The agony and tears of this and other remembrances produced an instantaneous and driven need to "appear happy" by an array of actions and giddy affect. And second, we worked on the interrelated issues of guilt over her children, the realities of her own capacities for care, and the guilt-depression storms that lay in the wake of this.

But that work is the regular stuff of psychotherapy, here half "supportive" and half "insight oriented," the two in a comfortable relationship in one unified "therapy." More germane to this chapter was the rest of the work: the sessions that were there for her, used or not. It was my impression that the unconditional availability of the hour (and of the place where and the person with whom it would take place) gave her a home base. It anchored her. This young woman, whose past was uncertain to her, had one place where she knew she could always "go home again." I use these words deliberately. The developing child, in early steps away from the mother, in adolescent ventures with friends, and in later more or less independent adult existence, "knows" that he or she has a parental home to go back to, and this, whatever the ambivalence, I believe makes separation more possible. Its loss with the death of the parents and the loss of the parental home, the home of one's childhood, is felt as an acute reality loss.

Beyond this, I believe that the conditions of our arrangement gave Carrie *control* over her approach and distancing in relation to the therapist (something that is desirable but not always achieved by the child in relation to the parent)—whether this was linked at any one moment to the oral longings or the sexual attraction in that approach-distancing conflict. With such control, approach would not be required, and distancing would not lead to loss. Developmentally, the parent who can be reliably there, yet not intrusive, cedes the child a like control.

In one of our last phone conversations, Carrie told me she felt she was finally growing up. Although she had not seen me for months, she had kept in touch by phone and was feeling close to me. As we were saying goodbye, she thanked me "for being around," by which I believe she was expressing her own recognition of the importance of a home base.

In this chapter I have attempted to illustrate (1) aspects of classical and supportive therapies in which an understanding of how change comes about can be enriched by considerations stemming from the parent-child relationship, and (2) technical variations in work with ego-deficient patients that can be generated by parallel considerations. The intent has been to supplement our understanding by focusing on phenomena that are in the background of classical analysis (where insight and working through remain in the foreground) but come into the foreground in work with ego-deficient patients.[3]

From a developmental perspective, all the questions underlying the ideas put forth here have to do with object relations and internalization, with what one person does or provides for another, and how what is done or provided by the other can facilitate change or be taken in by another. The degree to which, and the areas in which, a "critical periods" phenomenon characterizes human functioning are by no means clear. We have no definite clear knowledge about whether and in what areas developmental processes that have been missed at their proper time for synthesis forever remain unavailable. This is the problem of reversibility of pathology couched in developmental language. Human developmental phenomena are endlessly complex, and it seems likely that we are dealing with problems not of an either-or nature but where many partial or faulted or unstable developments remain as potentials even when initial learning and development have not taken place.

To take a simple instance, the educative function of the naming of feelings seems to last, and to be usable by patients, at any point in the life cycle, whether or not there is individual historical precedent for it; it has no single critical period after which it is functionless. But even far severer and more complex disturbances are sometimes able to be "redone" when later experiences provide part of what has been missed. Thus, the astonishingly deprived and developmentally stunted infants in institutions described by Provence and Lipton (1962) make remarkable (though incomplete) recoveries when they enter good foster homes. And some of the symbiotic psychotic children described by Mahler and her colleagues (Mahler, 1968; Mahler and Furer, 1960; Bergman and Furer, 1974) are able to make at least some use of a corrective symbiotic experience even at a developmentally delayed point in their life cycle.

I am not arguing for more therapeutic optimism. My own experience with patients with severely stunted development by no means justifies such a stand. I am suggesting only that (1) attention to the developmental, parent-child issues in all treatment can enrich our understanding of how change takes place; (2) attention to what parents are or do for their children may

3. It is an interesting aside to consider the verbal process of classical psychoanalysis from a developmental standpoint as well. For patients who have achieved early self differentiation and object attachment and in whom internal processes of defense and cognitive function are reasonably well elaborated, it may be precisely the speech-and-explanation modality that accords with their developmental receptivity and needs. For such patients speech maintains an optimal contact-and-distance from the analyst (see Stone, 1961) and permits the articulation and integration of vague impulse-affect states (see Loewald, 1960).

yield hypotheses regarding technical variations in work with patients with relatively intractable ego pathology; and (3) attention to the conditions and areas in which learning and internalization that normally occur earlier can *still* occur later will help us to develop further theoretical understanding regarding human development while we simultaneously learn about therapeutic technique.

In the next chapter I shall expand these ideas in a specific technical direction, focusing on the use of the supportive surround, the growth-facilitating environment, in the psychotherapy of more fragile patients.

11

The Interpretive Moment

My aim in this chapter is to present a style of interpretation, along with certain supportive props, for occasional use with fragile patients who are ordinarily unable to work in an insight-oriented interpretive mode. It grows from my efforts over the years to bring a psychoanalytic orientation to bear on the realities of therapeutic work with the seriously disturbed patients whose treatment I often supervise at a large urban hospital outpatient clinic. I have found it ethically more comfortable in such work not to search for the so-called good patient for insight therapy but instead to see whether "good" variations on technique might be developed for less-than-optimal therapeutic situations. This chapter reports on a limited area of success in that search. In developing my theme I shall attempt to describe aspects of the interpersonal and intrapsychic psychology of (what I shall call) "the interpretive moment" in order to develop a rationale for consciously and intentionally varying that psychology and to provide a gateway into a discussion of insight and supportive therapies.

The ideas presented here follow from those discussed in chapter 10 and are further expanded in the next chapter, in relation to the mutative factors in psychotherapy. They relate to a conception of the parental role in supportively protecting the child from excess stimulation while at the same time encouraging growth and change. Again, I question the traditional distinction between insight therapy and supportive therapy, proposing instead that a more useful distinction, one enriching the potential of so-called supportive therapy, is between *interpretation given in the context of abstinence* (i.e., classical psychoanalysis) and *interpretation given in the context of support*.

Interpretation is generally regarded as the central mutative agent in psychoanalytic work—whether it is interpretation that ties together past, present,

Reprinted with revisions with permission from the *Bulletin of the Menninger Clinic*, 48(1):54–71, copyright 1984, The Menninger Foundation.

and transference, or in the "here and now" of the transference (Gill, 1979), or those specialized interpretations that we call "constructions" (Freud, 1937b). Though the mechanism of action of interpretation is debatable, each of the many arguments is based on recurring observation of the potential power of such action. Thus, interpretation may have its effect by increasing the dominion of the ego and subjecting unconscious content to more rational thought processes (Freud, 1933), or by permitting old, poorly resolved fears and fantasies to achieve a new organization with the patient's current capacity for mental function, this organization in the context of the implicit parent/child-like setting of the analyst-patient relationship (Loewald, 1960; see chap. 10), or by lessening the condemnations of conscience by the very fact that the interpreting analyst is not judgmental as he speaks of (and permits the patient to speak of) wishes and fears that are ordinarily taboo to the patient (Strachey, 1934). Not that interpretation lacks shortcomings. No one sitting behind an analytic couch for years can fail to be aware of them, and numerous concepts have been advanced over the years to account for them—from inexact interpretation (Glover, 1931) and poor timing (Freud, 1913b) on the part of the analyst to unconscious guilt making for a need to stay ill, the compulsion to repeat, or "the resistance of the unconscious" (Freud, 1926) on the part of the patient. But all these are problems within a characterological setting in which interpretation is nonetheless conceived of as the central and most efficacious form of therapeutic intervention.

What is that setting? Having in mind the contrasts that I shall turn to below, I note that it includes (besides some minimum of intelligence, motivation, and suffering) the presence of at least (1) some array of reasonably reliable intrapsychic defenses so that the patient can protect himself against affect flooding and the experience of disorganization; (2) some capacity to hold the idea that the therapist, while pointing out unpleasant inner or life-history reality, is not doing so in order to condemn, humiliate, provoke, or ultimately abandon the patient; and (3) some broad presence of an inner psychological organization that can receive the interpretation offered—some soil on which it can fall and take root.

In some patients, however, it cannot be assumed that all (or any) of these requirements are consistently present (even though they may be at moments). What follows describes an attempt to work with such patients (at times) interpretively, in a distinctive manner. This did not grow from a conscious effort to "apply" interpretive procedures but grew over the years in a trial-and-error way, through many attempts to work with these patients, until I began to notice that in small ways the procedures to be described were effective.

The patients, children or adults, are generally characterized by a fragility of defense, a tendency toward panic, anxiety, depression, rage, or other affects that are experienced as overwhelming, moderate disorganization at least at times, and perhaps flight from treatment in the face of these. These features, rather than a specific diagnosis, are what characterize them; diagnostically, they vary across the range of severe character disorders, impulsive personalities, depression, and reintegrated postpsychotic states. They were not overtly psychotic or grossly disorganized at the time of the work, and though they were not always able to hold onto the idea of the goodness of the object, they did—often out of desperation—want help and could make a basic attachment of considerable force. This overall setting nonetheless made for difficulties in using interpretive approaches because of the patient's panic-driven flight from or rejection of them and/or the therapist's fear of upsetting the patient's shaky balance.

Although the work did not develop in this way historically, for the sake of exposition I shall approach it from the point of view of the psychology of the interpretive moment: what is going on in the patient that leads the analyst to judge that the moment is right for interpretation and what goes on in the patient when the interpretation is given.

For the patient ordinarily considered analyzable, the "right" moment for interpretation is often characterized by a certain affectivity, a surfacing and aliveness of conflict, that heightens the likelihood that the analyst's words will have impact, triggering further affect and productive thought processes. But in more fragile patients, this very affectivity creates a psychological situation of risk and potential disorganization. For them, the moment of potential influenceability is simultaneously a moment of vulnerability. Is there a way out of this dilemma?

As for what goes on in the patient after the interpretation is given, any patient can respond to an interpretation not only, say, with confirming associations or total rejection but also, say, as though it were a seduction or a condemnation. Waelder (1936) pointed out that every psychic act has multiple functions in relation to drive gratification, the demands of conscience, adaptation to reality, and repetition. And I want to highlight the fact that a patient's *receipt* of an interpretation *is itself a psychic act having multiple functions*. Today, as discussed in chapter 5, we might modify Waelder's work by noting that these functions include not only drive gratification, the demands of conscience, and adaptation to reality (as he saw them), but also repetition specifically of old internalized object relationships (Sandler and Rosenblatt, 1962; Kernberg, 1976) and the maintenance of self-cohesion and self-esteem (Kohut, 1971, 1977). Thus a patient may "hear" an interpretation as a gratification or deprivation (from the standpoint of drive); as a condemnation or permission (from the standpoint of conscience); as an access to a new view of reality or as a stimulus to cling to his old defenses (from the standpoint of adaptation); as a repeated or reparative object-relation experience (from the standpoint of internalized object relationships); and/or as a humiliation or a sign of special attention (from the standpoint of self-esteem).

In work with fragile patients, I have found it of considerable clinical value to present the interpretation in such a way as to increase the probability that it will be received with functions relevant to good object relationships, benign aspects of the superego, and support for flexible defenses. As for the dilemma described above—that the moment of influenceability in the fragile patient is simultaneously a moment of vulnerability—it is my impression that interpretations formulated in this way (i.e., supporting positive functions) provide a way out of the dilemma. By actively supporting the patient's best possible level of functioning, they minimize the vulnerability and make interpretive intervention possible.

In the following descriptions I shall present four overlapping ways of speaking to fragile patients, ways that are carriers of interpretive content but make it more possible for the patient to receive and to work with the content offered. I refer to "interpretive content" rather than interpretation because the whole speech act by which the content is carried is radically different from the classical mode, yet there is no question that difficult content is introduced for the patient to work with.

SOME CLINICAL INTERVENTIONS

A fragile patient reveals just as much comprehensible content as does a better organized patient and often more. The question is whether and how this can or should be imparted to him. All the following interventions are based on the assumption that something is understood by the therapist and that clinical considerations indicate that the time is right for imparting it. The question is *how*. In each of the following cases I attempt, first, to understand aspects of the interpersonal and intrapsychic psychology of the moment of interpretation and then vary the mode of intervention in ways that seem suitable for the patient. The variations are based on efforts to minimize the shock power of the interventions and/or to emphasize the therapist's benevolent presence. The specifics and the rationales are given below using, as a vehicle for discussion, a contrast with the rationale of classical technique. Because I find that suggestions in this area are so readily overextended or misunderstood, I offer two important cautions first: (1) these are only *moments* in a treatment that, like any other, is based primarily on quiet listening; and (2) they are not accompanied by any advice-giving or active "doing-for" the patient. The *style* of intervention is gentle and supportive, but its *aim* is to make difficult interpretive work possible and thus to permit the therapeutic process to move ahead in small ways.

1. *Close off the implicit expectation of patient responsibility for associative response to the interpretation.* In classical psychoanalysis, an interpretation is ordinarily given in such a way that something is left open-ended. A demand is left floating in the air (through vocal tone or sentence structure) that leaves the patient room to react to what has been said; indeed, the whole prior analysis has set up the expectation of such response. Along these lines, a prime indicator of confirmation of an interpretation is generally considered to be the new material—memories or other spontaneous thoughts—that it elicits. It is my impression that this open-ended expectation of response, at least as much as the interpretive content itself, can trigger panic and flight (or rage or depression and flight) in fragile patients. Their experience of interpretation is that they have been given new and frightening information and are left alone with it, facing a void, not sure what it "means" (in terms of

their own badness, dangerousness, babyishness), where it will lead, what they are to do with it, whether they should act on it, and what attitude the therapist has toward it.

Let us consider a woman who, reared by her mother and maternal grand-mother, has always idealized them and her whole childhood. Various defenses against her awareness of her anger have been interpreted, and memories suggestive of quite painful early caretaking events have emerged (though almost as "asides"). In a session where she is not feeling well taken care of by the therapist, her anger mounts, although the patient does not seem to be aware of its link to her feeling of not being taken care of. The therapist might say: "I wonder if the anger you are feeling has something to do with your idea that I can't really understand you, and whether those feelings also came when you felt uncared for by your mother and grandmother as a child." The next move is the patient's. (Implicitly: "Take what I said and do some-thing with it.")

But with this particular patient we knew what she does with it. She panics, feels guilt-ridden, and stays away from subsequent sessions. When we take into account that there have been moments of real eruptive violence on her part in the past and some confusion of reality in relation to anger, we might well hesitate to make such an interpretation. Yet the patient is here in our office, the material is active, it *is* the material of the session, and it is linked to the patient's decision to seek help in the first place. Do we "support" the patient? How? Do we look the other way and ignore the material? As I have implied, I have found that the interpretation can sometimes be conveyed if (among other things) it is made clear that the patient has no immediate "next move" to make. The patient is not left alone with the interpretation—alone to face the thoughts it stimulates or to wonder what the therapist thinks about her anger, or whether she is "supposed" to act on it, or feel guilty about it, or what. Thus, this patient might be told: "Do you see what's happening, Ms. X? You're getting angry again, and I don't think you really know why. But I believe it's because you felt I wasn't taking proper care of you [and the therapist's tone is explanatory, sympathetic—not awesome, not the voice of the holder of secret knowledge]. That's probably coming up now because of those memories you told me about your mother and grandmother not taking care of you as well as you like to believe. You know, children get angry when that happens, and you must have too. But you want so much to believe they were perfect that every time you get anywhere near your angry feelings you get frightened and stay away from therapy. But that's just what our work is about. Look. You *were* angry. It *does* frighten you. We are going to discover that together again and again. And we will work on it together as time goes on, and you'll be able to see how it affects you even now." In some ways, the therapist's intervention here is like that of a traditional family doctor: "Here's the diagnosis and treatment plan; cooperate with me and we'll get you back on your feet again."

There is more to this interpretation than just not leaving the patient alone with the responsibility of thinking about the content. Any interpretation is likely to be multiply functional, and I am not aiming here to extract a pure type. The therapist promises to be there with the patient, not in outside life but in therapeutic *work*; the therapist's acceptance of the aggressive content is made clear—not only is he nonjudgmental but in fact he views the anger as inevitable and entirely to be expected; and—what I consider to be the central point—the patient is not implicitly asked to associate to the content right at the moment, in the heat of conflict. Of equal importance are two observations that I have made repeatedly: (1) after a while, when the material is more familiar and does not take the patient by surprise, he *can* permit himself spontaneous thoughts in relation to it at the moment it comes up; and (2) by taking some pressure off, the suggestion that the material can be worked on later often enables the patient to work on it *now*.

The patient described, given a statement along the lines outlined above, was able to move along in the work one small step. There is no magic here. Interpretive interventions of this sort are not the whole of any treatment, but neither are they one-shot affairs. Like any other intervention, they are repeated again and again when the session content and the patient's state seem to demand it.

2. *Strike while the iron is cold.* Timing is significant in relation to any interpretation. Among other considerations, timing involves giving interpretations when the conflictual issues are active, bubbling over in some way—"hot." Usually this means at least that they are active in the here and now of the transference and that the patient is suffering some affective discomfort that, whether or not he knows it, is linked to these conflictual issues. But this factor is precisely the problem with fragile and panic-prone patients. Their history with anxiety (or rage or depression) is that it tends to mushroom, to swamp them; and any interpretive inputs by the therapist run the risk of tipping the balance toward that full and painful affective reaction rather than giving the patient, as intended, an understanding of what is going on inside him so that he is better able to come to terms with it.

Sometimes the therapist may decide that the patient simply cannot deal with interpretation at the "hot" moment. On a number of such occasions I have found it useful to do the interpretive work in a later session, when the conflict is not active, when "the iron is cold." The form of the interpretation would then be: "Do you remember last week when you were so upset about [and a reminder is given]? I think that perhaps you were feeling [and an interpretation is given]." Or, "I've been trying to understand what happened a few days ago when we were talking about [again, a reminder] and you began to feel really troubled. Maybe what happened was [and again, an interpretation]."

The therapeutic aim is to make the interpretation *usable* by the patient. For this, there has to be an adequate control structure to receive it. In these fragile patients, the control structure is usually more functional when it is removed in time from the heat of the conflict. Although some intact individuals may generally be at their adaptive best under pressure, this is not the case, by definition, with fragile patients. It is certainly true that in neurotic patients, especially obsessional ones, interpretations given when "the iron is cold" will not be received with full emotional force. The analytic posture, the ambiguities created by the patient's lack of knowledge of the behind-the-couch analyst, and the interpretation at the time of active conflict, all increase the likelihood that an interpretation will be received with emotional force and not, for example, simply contribute to intellectualization. But in fragile patients (*some* of them, and at *times*), precisely the opposite is often required. An increase in control capacity and a decrease in emotional force are required if they are to be able to hold and perhaps make use of the difficult material offered interpretively. The danger is disorganization, not intellectualization, as in the case of neurotics; and flight is the outcome to be avoided. Once again, I have found that after repeated interventions of this sort, the patient becomes able to hear related interpretations even if the therapist later "strikes while the iron is hot." Familiarity with the contents itself permits the accrual of some coping capacity in that specific area.

3. *Increase the patient's relative degree of activity with regard to interpretive content.* In classical psychoanalysis, the patient's supine position on the couch, the position of the analyst outside his visual field, and the basic rule of free association work together to create a regressive tendency, a passivity in the patient as regards his own thought processes that facilitates the exploratory work. That the patient must be capable of shifts to psychological activity— that is, able to call upon the observing ego, to exercise judgment, and to think in an orderly fashion—is equally required and is not contradictory; these shifts between passivity and activity in relation to the emerging associations are central to the mode of analytic work.

For a patient who is more generally passive in the face of his inner experience and who cannot reliably regulate either the control or the expression (Rapaport, 1953) of what goes on within him, the assumption of still greater passivity (within the treatment) in relation to freely flowing mental content is too great a threat to control structures. Unless he is already slipping into psychosis and a relatively gross collapse of controls, a patient who is ordinarily in such a passive-helpless state in both control and discharge of inner impulse/fantasy/affect processes will not ordinarily be able to assume a passive (free associative) relation to his own inner life. He will regulate this (by massive blocking or by flight if necessary) himself.

But there is also another kind of passivity for the patient in the therapeutic situation—passivity in respect to interpretive content introduced by the therapist. Here the emergence of new content and its penetration into consciousness are entirely beyond any available "activity" of the patient's control processes. The therapist decides what to say and when; the patient can only react—perhaps with understanding and relief, but all too often in these fragile panic-near situations, with rigid and reflexive rejection of the content and/or flight and/or disorganization. It is the capacity for ego activity, for (for example) bringing the observer function into play, that allows the better functioning analytic patient to take these "intrusions" by the therapist and make something useful of them. Can anything be done, in work with more fragile individuals, to increase the patient's degree of activity with respect to content that the therapist introduces? I believe so, and it has to do once again with how the therapist presents the material. Greater activity in the patient can be induced either by arousing the patient's readiness, an anticipatory or orienting response that allows whatever defensive processes are available to be called into play, or by explicitly giving the patient more control over the fate of the interpretive content offered.

We define trauma in terms of a flood of stimulation too great for mastery at a given moment. The arousal of anticipation, the activation of small degrees of preparatory anxiety, increases the patient's readiness to cope with the stimulus influx, probably by calling his defensive repertoire into play. Young children today are introduced to surgery with advance information about it. This does not eliminate their anxiety but, to the contrary, activates it at low levels over considerable time; the effect appears to be a lessening of the traumatic, all-at-once, shock effect of unprepared-for surgery. The same can be done in preparation for the shock effect of the stimulus influx we call an "interpretation." Whereas with neurotic and well-controlled patients we would ordinarily not want to activate the control/defense repertoire prior to inter-pretation for fear of diluting its effect, with poorly controlled patients it may be precisely this activation of readiness/control and its effect of diluting the force of the interpretation that make it possible for the patient to receive it.

Thus, with some children who hold their ears, screech, run out of the office, or break into panicky rage when something difficult is verbalized to them, I have found it useful to increase their readiness (their degree of activity vis-à-vis what I have to say) by alerting them in various ways to the fact that something difficult for them to hear is about to be said and giving them some control over its timing. Using a technique illustrated in chapter 10, I might say: "Johnny, I want to tell you something that you're not going to like hearing. I'll wait until after you finish that drawing and then I'll tell you." Or: "Johnny, I have something important to say. Tell me when you're ready to hear it" (and then, after a while, since the child almost never tells one he's "ready":) "I'll wait five more minutes and then I'll tell you." (I might add, "You won't have to say anything, Johnny. I just want you to listen.") Or: "Johnny, I have something a little scary to say, but it will just take a minute. After the checker game I'm going to tell you." (And then, after the checkers, perhaps even giving the child my watch as a crutch to time the minute if he needs it, I'll say what I have to say.) To increase the child's control over the material, I may also tell him that he can stop me for a little while if it is too hard for him to listen and that we can continue a few minutes later. My experience with this has been excellent. The child more often than not *can* listen, can take in a bit of what I have to say; it gets easier over time, and, after some months, formerly untouchable content has become a regular part of our work.

These modes of alerting activity/readiness have felt right to me with young children. With adults I have given the patient control in other ways. For example: "I'm not sure about this; I'd like you to tell me what you think. It occurred to me that [and the interpretation is given]. Does this sound possible to you?" Or: "Look, I have a thought about what may be going on. I'm not sure of it, but I'd like to tell you so you can see what you think. Perhaps you can think it over and tell me your reaction next time we meet [and then the interpretation is given]." Clearly I am attempting to alert the patient to the fact that something is coming and (while I am saying my initial fore-warning words) allowing him to set himself in readiness. But especially, this mode of speaking aims to decrease the omniscience of the therapist and the certainty-of-truth quality of his words, and *explicitly to increase the patient's acceptance-rejection rights* over the content. My impression is that, whether accepted or rejected by the patient, the content *can* be heard when given in this way and gradually (if it fits) becomes more familiar so that it enters into the work less frighteningly.

4. *Increase the (psychological) "holding" (Winnicott, 1963a) aspects of the therapeutic environment.* The classical analysis of more or less intact patients is carried out under conditions of abstinence. Direct gratification of the patient's wishes is avoided; the analyst does not participate in word or deed as an actor in the patient's life. This condition increases the likelihood that derivatives of unconscious content will make their way into the patient's associations and fantasies where, both because of their presence and because of their not being acted upon, they can be analyzed.

But abstinence/deprivation is a relative matter. Some analysts are expe-rienced as distant, some as concerned; some are experienced as warm and kindly, some as cold and awesome. A substantial portion of this variation lies in the patient's perceptions but some of it lies in actualities of the analyst's person (cf. Stone, 1961). And further, even to say that abstinence/deprivation is a technical "ideal" to be approximated misses the point regarding the very real gratifications inherent in the analytic setting (chap. 10): the analyst's reliably being there for sessions, his giving full attention to the patient for the entire session, and his working consistently and nonjudgmentally to un-derstand what the patient brings.

As noted in the previous chapter, the analytic setting provides a context of safety in which the analysand's communication, developing insight, and trying out of change can take place. The analysis, like the child's growth, is enacted upon the solid stage of safety in a relationship. Without the stage, the action would not take place.

With the patients whose treatments I am discussing, the analytic stage of safety and reliability of relationship cannot be assumed. Nor can the capacity for successful internal regulation of psychological homeostasis. I believe that the work can proceed more successfully if the therapist allows such patients to "borrow" his control/defense capacity and highlights his consistent pres-ence for them by vocal tone, sentence phrasing, sheer extent of speech, and some explicit remarks. It is this that I refer to when I speak of explicitly increasing the "holding" aspects of the therapeutic environment.

Thus, the therapist may say: "I know this is going to be painful to you, and we can work on it together over time, but it seems clear to me that [and the interpretation is given]." Or: "Look, you've gone through this before and been just as frightened. Let's see if we can make some headway with it. I think you're feeling [and again the interpretation is given] and every time that happens you feel you're falling apart. Perhaps we can catch it this time and help you get it under control." The critical factor here is not the wording alone but a tone that is in itself reassuring. Still, the words, though supportive, and the tone, though reassuring, are the carriers of difficult interpretive content. This point is critical for the approaches I am advancing here.

The fact that these variations are always around *interpretation* is what, in my experience, prevents the work from becoming simply caretaking, in which patient pseudosafety and passivity are the outcome. The patient's hand is being held (figuratively, by the style of interpretive intervention) *only* and *always* so that he can take a difficult and threatening next step in the therapy. My experience is that patients dealt with in this way feel themselves *supported in hard work*, not "taken care of by a kindly doctor." I cannot stress this too strongly. The intent (and effect) of this work is to make it possible for the fragile patient to work with the interpretation of content that is active and frightening. He is given a lot of support, but he feels, in the end, quite challenged—stressed by the content. This stress, however, is at some optimal, workable level, achieved through one or another of the variants of intervention described above.

A NOTE ON INSIGHT AND SUPPORTIVE THERAPIES

The clinical procedures described blur the distinction between insight and supportive therapies in at least two ways. (1) Support, a style of intervention that attempts to keep the patient's defenses functioning at their best and provides a "holding" object-relational context in the patient-therapist relationship, is used to advance interpretations (i.e., to work toward insight). And (2) there is an underlying belief that insight is one of the best forms of support. This is true not only in the sense that helping the patient achieve self-understanding gives him increased capacity for self-control and diminishes his vague fear regarding things within but also in the sense that it is one of the major experiences that facilitates his ultimate use of the therapist as a supportive (structure-maintaining and growth-producing) object.

In the previous chapter, I noted that to a considerable degree insight therapy, far more than supportive therapy, draws upon—is oriented by—psychoanalytic *technique* (while both can be equally oriented by psychoanalytic *theory* more generally) (and see Blanck and Blanck, 1974, 1979). In this chapter, by contrast, I have drawn especially upon the psychoanalytic theory of *technique* in attempting to develop procedures for work with unanalyzable patients; but I have drawn upon it, first, by relying heavily on interpretation, as does classical psychoanalysis, and, second, by examining the psychology of the interpretive act in order to understand how that psychology can be *reversed* in significant ways and thus make it possible for these fragile patients to work with interpretations. Let me discuss each of these in turn.

The role of interpretation. When, in chapter 10, I discussed the question of what is supported in supportive therapy, I suggested that the presence of an interested therapist supports the brittle or severely ill patient's *ties to human objects* and capacities for the *maintenance of defense*. But to the question of how such support can become more permanent I could say only that the answer is not readily at hand. In the present chapter, I approach these issues in a very different fashion. Rather than see the support of the patient's object ties and defenses as somehow effecting therapeutic change, I propose that such support be utilized in the here and now of the patient-therapist interaction to make it possible for the patient to receive and work with interpretation and, through this, slowly to achieve some limited self-understanding.

Why interpretation? Is it sacred? Hardly. As I said at the outset, this work grew in a trial-and-error way. In retrospect, I understand the value of interpretive work with these fragile patients in at least three ways: (1) Interpretation is efficacious in itself provided that it is well timed and tactfully offered. The naming (Katan, 1961), the clarification, of inner experiences helps bring these experiences out of the shadows, permitting the patient to draw upon his cognitive powers for aid in adaptation. These possibilities, in the setting of the supportive and nonjudgmental relationship to the therapist, certainly exist for the more fragile patient just as they do for the more intact patient. (2) Interpretation is one of the unique things the therapist has to offer. The nonspecific supportive aspects of the relationship are inherent in the therapist's presence, benevolent concern, and consistent empathic listening. He need do nothing special to bring them about. But when the patient is in acute distress and the content is clear, the therapist is in a unique position to offer what no one else ordinarily can offer the patient: a new level of self-understanding. Done in the ways described here, I find that these patients can make use of it. And (3) whatever those developmental and therapeutic processes are that enable a person to "take in" another in such a way as to be able to use that internal object to foster better functioning and/or growth, those processes seem to me to be expedited between patient and therapist when the therapist has been able to help still some of the patient's anxieties by promoting self-understanding, thus being a "good object" in actuality. This is more hunch than certainty, and I offer it as having bearing on the question of how internalization of the supportive aspects of the relationship takes place.

Reversals of the psychology of the interpretive moment. In each of the clinical procedures described here, I have attempted to offer interpretive content while stimulating the patient's defenses to their highest possible level and while actively giving the patient a sense of the therapist's supportive presence. In strong contrast to the interpretive moment with a more analyzable patient, for whom one might want to heighten the affective impact of interpretation, here the reverse holds, and the effort is to soften that impact.

Analytic work requires some optimal level of tension in the patient. If a conflict is not active, or if the patient is too well defended or (on the other hand) if a patient is too flooded, or if his reality situation is too much in chaos and crisis, analytic work does not proceed as well as it might. Either too little or too much anxiety interferes with the ordinary ongoingness of an analysis. It is clear, however, that "optimal tension" is relative, varying from person to person. Individuals differ in the degree to which they can sustain adequate functioning in the face of anxiety, without its mounting to disruptive or incapacitating levels.

In the treatment of patients I have been discussing, the change possibilities that come from interpretation are inevitably accompanied by anxiety, guilt, rage, humiliation, or depression at a level far beyond what is optimal for the patient. How to work with the change potential of interpretation while keeping the level of the anxiety tolerable is a question that underlies the variations in interpretive style that I have been describing. Their intent, to increase the defense and object-relational support structure while increasing the anxiety level (through the interpretation), is to support the patient's tolerance for strain at a higher level of demand. In this way, as noted above, support of the patient in the here and now of the therapy relationship makes it possible to introduce interpretive work, and its potential benefits, into treatments that might not otherwise be amenable to it.

12

Developmental Perspectives on the Mutative Factors and the Languages of the Psychotherapies

My intent in this chapter is to address psychodynamic psychotherapy in its broadest aspect, inclusive of but not limited to psychoanalysis; to present a broad view of the mutative factors in the treatment process, linking it to the considerations regarding therapy with nonanalyzable patients that were presented in chapters 10 and 11; and to return to the several developmentally based theoretical languages of psychoanalysis (chap. 5)—the languages of drive, ego, object relations, and self—here adding a language of reality relations, and to expand on their clinical significance and use. I shall generally use the terms "therapy" and "therapist" in this chapter, but I mean to include "analysis" and "analyst" throughout. I intend the points I make to be applicable both to the broader category (therapy) and to the more specific one (analysis).

In the real world of the psychoanalytically oriented therapies and therapists, we have a large number of practitioners—varying widely in natural talent, training, and experience—working with an array of patients who evidence a wide range of psychopathology. Only a very small propotion of practitioners predominantly conducts psychoanalysis with patients who would have been classically considered appropriate for such treatment, organized around intrapsychic conflict in a well-structured personality and carried out in a setting of abstinence, technical neutrality, and relative anonymity of the analyst. For the rest, patient variation is far more the mode. I do not regard this as a problem—instead, as a challenge to utilize our knowledge, much of it gained through psychoanalysis, in the most flexible and exploratory ways. It should be expected that significant technical and conceptual variations characterize

First presented in May 1984 to the Canadian Association of Psychoanalytic Psychotherapists for Children, Toronto, Ontario, Canada.

the work with these varying individuals. Nor should it be surprising if psychoanalytic theory, as a broad and general developmental psychology, could speak constructively to these variations in both technique and conceptualization.

Although I believe that the most significant legacy Freud left us is his demonstration of the power of open-ended listening, that very open-endedness is a principal cause of malaise in therapists, especially when they are starting out. It produces feelings of ignorance, incompetence, and fraudulence, of being overwhelmed by the material. This is a basic "countertransference" position quite aside from the general characteristics that bring a person into the field or the specific anxieties aroused by the patient (Reich, 1951). A prominent way to cope with the anxieties produced by open-ended listening is to seek certainty—certainty regarding this particular session, this particular patient, or regarding human function, psychopathology, and therapeutic technique altogether. The path to such certainty comes from the therapist's own analysis or from influential teachers or from the pervasive intellectual atmosphere of the region in which he trains. And this certainty is used to resolve the inner anxieties of ignorance and fraudulence. To the degree that it also fits with one's professional surround, it ensures the good will of colleagues and even referrals and therefore financial stability.

I do not mean to caricature. The certainty need not be narrow. It can be as broad as, for example, a commitment to the centrality of oedipal pathology (recognizing the myriad ways in which that can reveal itself) but may still operate with only a small segment of the data of human experience and psychopathology. I argue for greater breadth, both of technique and of conceptualization; but I am well aware that my "breadth" is, from other standpoints, just an expanded narrowness. There are, for example, many potentially mutative procedures and many conceptualizations (e.g., behavioral and confrontative issues, analysis of family systems) that my framework more or less ignores.

Some writers, most notably Gedo (1979) and Gedo and Goldberg (1976), have attempted to systematize models of therapy and conceptualization for patients across a broad range. Others like Kohut (1971) and Kernberg (1975) have focused on specific variations in technique and conceptualization for particular subgroups of patients without explicitly developing the variations across the whole range—though Kohut (1977) certainly moved in that direction later on. I shall not here be that systematic. Like Peterfreund (1982), I shall be emphasizing pragmatic listening, but within a context of maximally possible abstinence, technical neutrality, and impersonality, with what is "maximally possible" varying in specific therapeutic instances. And I do work centrally with transference and resistance. Also, I stay with the broad range of formulations (I have called them languages) that psychoanalysis has produced over the years. My sense is that all these languages play a role in every treatment and that, while overarching formulations can be made in each individual case, this whole is less than the sum of its parts. That is, the real mutative effect is in the day-to-day work on small details, on differing aspects of the personality, whether these "fit" together, are tied together conceptually, or not; and the grand integrative formulations, while esthetically satisfying, are as much for ourselves as for the patient.

So, my aim is to counter the "certainties," the rigidities of technique or formulation, that flow from the inner need of therapists to find their way in the morass of associative content and that is inadvertently or intentionally engendered by the commanding position still held (I believe) by psychoanalysis in the domain of theory regarding inner life. I shall attempt to counter these certainties by discussing, first, a broad array of mutative factors operative in all therapies, including psychoanalysis, and second, a broad array of intellectual schema to encompass the data of lives.

In developing my arguments, I shall not be giving clinical examples, in part because most therapists have encountered and thought about these issues and can therefore test my arguments against their own experience. Further, I find that the more broad-ranging my technical and conceptual approach, the less I can illustrate it by vignettes. Relatively full presentations, however, would be unwieldy in content and would threaten confidentiality. Of equal importance is what I now believe to be the questionable nature of clinical reports as "evidence" (cf. Spence, 1982). We and our patients shape the material of their analyses; we shape a view of their history; we shape our two-person relationship. Schafer (1983b) describes the positive values in recognizing this subjectivity, seeing treatment as the development of various narrative "tellings" of lives; and Gill (1983) tries to use to technical advantage the fact that all analyses are two-person *interpersonal* situations. But the view that the "facts" are "out there" to be found and that we are just reporters of these facts in our papers is a simplification.

HOW DOES CHANGE OCCUR IN THERAPY?

In discussing this question, I shall start with the assumption that an understanding of change in the developing child bears on an understanding of change in psychotherapy. This assumption, I recognize, may not be correct, but I shall follow it to see where it leads. I am not suggesting an identity between developmental and therapeutic change; the formed and disturbed adult is hardly a developing child. While change in the course of development comes very significantly from the developmental process itself—from maturation of capacities, learning, phase-specific modification of major needs and wishes, reality-induced changes in the person's life situation—I shall focus on those changes that are linked to the relations between two people: parent and child, therapist and patient. This will permit the tapping of the developmental framework.

My way of proceeding here will be to note those things that experience has taught me contribute to patient change in psychotherapy, and then to link them to modes of developmental change. The actual process by which these views were developed, however, was much more intertwined than that—with observations regarding therapeutic change leading me to think about them developmentally *and* with hypotheses about developmental change leading me to think about therapy differently and, at times, to try out variations in technique.

Interpretation—the progressive clarification of that mix of conscious and unconscious inner life, of history, and of behavioral enactments in and out of the transference that make up the human mind—is a powerful tool for bringing about change, although it is clear from clinical experience that there is no one-to-one correspondence between insight and change. Interpretation is what we as analytically oriented therapists *do*. It is what we do that (ordinarily) no one else in the patient's life does, and for good reason: they neither have our technical knowledge of the working and contents of the human mind, nor do they establish the kind of relationship (listening, abstinent, transferential in a controlled environment) that allows the relevant material to emerge. Although I will say many things below about other mutative impacts of the "mere" relationship of patient to therapist, nothing is meant to diminish my conviction that what we can valuably *do* (while we are listening and while the patient may make use of us in his or her own way) is interpret.

Interpretation brings the power of the cognitive apparatus and the clarifications and differentiations of speech into the shadowy and conflictful areas of mental life. Not only is the patient thus enabled to think about what previously was "unthinkable"—was driving him without awareness or was unnerving him in the shadowy margins of the mind—but he learns, through the nonjudgmental, matter-of-fact verbalizations of the therapist, that such matters of mind are knowable to others and thus not uniquely, disturbingly one's own, and that they need not be cause of condemnation, horror, or personal rejection.

But interpretation in this sense draws on the role of speech as a socially shared act and cognition more broadly in the developmental process. As the child learns speech, he can begin to express in a "cooler" medium, in general, what before could be expressed only in action, image, or affectivity. Speech and cognition permit higher levels of learning, of social sharing, and new forms of displacement that assist in the developing control process. Katan (1961), among analytic writers, has most simply and elegantly described the role of verbalization as a source of control in early childhood. Within psychotherapy, interpretation, elevating inner phenomena to higher levels of cognitive clarity, capitalizes on this developmental progression, indeed repeats it in significant ways.

Nonetheless, I believe that the theory of analytic technique to some extent exaggerates interpretation in its central mutative role. Two features of analytic thinking contribute to this exaggeration. First, the theoretical view of the mutative centrality of interpretation is carrying an extra load; that view is multiply functional for us as therapists and theorists. Speech and the use of intellect are preferred modes for most persons who go into the field; it serves personal characterological countertransferential aims (Reich, 1951) to focus on *our* speech acts in the work. Also, historically, the role of interpretation protected us against the charge that analysis was merely "suggestion"; it was not (we said by our actions in treatment); it was intellectual work. Related to this, interpretation, the use of verbal concepts to describe inner "entities," (fantasies, wishes, defenses) brought us closer to "science." Science deals with things and their specifications; we would deal with the *things* of inner life, the reified, conceptualized flow of human experience. Though interpretation has great power and is indispensable in analytic work (and, I believe, in so-called supportive work as well), it carries an extra load of significance that limits our thinking in some ways—especially about the role of *other* mutative factors.

A second basis for the exaggerated role of interpretation comes from the central place given to oedipal-level pathology in the developmental history of psychoanalytic theory and its explanation of pathology. If one begins work with the study of hysteria and phobia, with some obsessive-compulsive neurosis added in, one can come out with an oedipal-level theory. But, and this is the point, the oedipal-level child is developmentally at a place where speech is central in his or her functioning; events thus coincident in time may put their stamp upon one another (Greenacre, 1958). In the oedipal-age child, articulated wishes and fantasies can be formed, flutter in and out of conscious life, and be subject to repression. Memories of events and experiences, too, are recorded to a significant degree in verbal terms (cf. Schachtel, 1947). Furthermore, neurotic patients in general (rather than more disturbed ones), in spite of focal and/or spreading conflict, presumably have made most or all of the normally expected developmental advances in ego and superego function: judgment, anticipation and planning, and, for my purposes, speech. To work with oedipal-level pathology in such patients is to work within a situation where speech, interpretation, has a natural fit, and so yields results that reinforce the claims regarding its own centrality.

But certainly there is enough of an expansion in our attempts to understand pathology—of borderline, narcissistic, and psychotic forms—that we have now moved beyond the centrality of oedipal pathology for significant portions of human psychopathology. At risk of seeming facetious, I can characterize what I believe our historical situation to have been by reference to an old joke. A drunken man is seen on all fours under a streetlight at night, searching the ground. A passerby asks what he is doing and is told that he is looking for a lost coin. Where did he drop it? Down the block. "Why are you looking for it here, then?" The reply: "Because the light is better here."

The light is better for oedipal-level pathology. The sicker, less well-structured patient, the experiences of the preverbal period, and the days of centrality of the one-person and two-person (rather than the oedipal triangular) relationships are "down the block," shrouded in darkness. The higher level pathology of the oedipal period, amenable to speech and memory, was easier to "find" and to make sense out of. But, as I mentioned at the very start of this book, for an observer of early childhood, it is unthinkable that the disturbances of the first two or three years of life do not have a primacy in the development of psychopathology. The core of boundary formation and self-feeling, the basic attitude toward one's own impulses and affects as well as their direction and degree of specification, basic attitudes toward, relationships with, and inner representations of others are all laid down in that early period. Indeed, I would turn the issue of oedipal pathology around and ask: If someone gets stuck at that level, can things have been adequately developed before? Or, if things are adequately developed before, will someone get stuck on the issues of the oedipal level? Barring specific, focused acting out of the parents during the child's oedipal age or specific trauma at that time, the answer I would give to both questions is: I doubt it very much. Naturally oedipal-level pathology is superimposed upon and even transforms the earlier pathology, as all later developments reshape to a degree what went before (cf. Blos, 1962, on the stage of late adolescence in this regard). Additionally, the greatly advanced scope of language and thought in the oedipal-aged child may, in a way that *fits* with the verbal work of analysis, give the most readily recognizable shape to earlier pathology. But, nonetheless, the whole (or the appearance of the whole as it is reshaped at the oedipal period) may be *less than* the sum of its parts—that is, causing us to see too little of what went before.

Thus, I believe that the central mutative role of interpretation is somewhat exaggerated in the theory of psychoanalytic technique because interpretation serves multiple functions for its practitioners and because a focus on oedipal-level pathology reinforces the received wisdom regarding its centrality. Nonetheless, I believe that interpretation *does* have a central mutative role, and in this it repeats the history of the development of the child, his mastery of cognition, and the mastery that cognition, in turn, makes available to him. But there are, I believe, other significant mutative agents in therapy, and my discussion until this point has had the intent of opening up a receptivity to a consideration of them.

The mutative role of *"support," when it provides the context for interpretive work* in so-called supportive therapy, warrants special discussion. I shall discuss the "supportive" features of even a classical psychoanalysis later on (and see chaps. 10 and 11), having to do with reliability and the atmosphere of safety; here I am referring to a more active support.

The term "supportive psychotherapy" is, I believe, a euphemism. All too often it means: "I don't know how to help this patient but perhaps if we just stay in contact with each other, something good will come of it." Or "I really prefer to work with someone who is better put together than this person and who can make better use of insight, so I'll see this person in (or refer this person for) supportive therapy." By and large it is a wastebasket term, often used to designate an intellectual wasteland. In chapter 10, I illustrated attempts to draw on developmental theory to generate hypotheses for modes of working in more rational ways (in the sense of having a *rationale*) in this area. In chapter 11, I took this further, giving centrality to interpretation in supportive work, but interpretation in significantly modified ways. I would like to continue the development of those ideas here.

I believe that the dichotomy between supportive therapy and interpretive (insight) therapy is a false one and has stultified the development of technique in the "supportive" domain. Interpretation can and must play a central role in both forms of treatment, across the full range of pathologies. The real dichotomy is in the *context* in which those interpretations are given. Interpretation can be given in the context of *abstinence* or in the context of *support*. "Abstinence" refers to all those aspects that characterize it in classical psychoanalysis: impersonality, objectivity, and neutrality of the analyst and, especially, nongratification of the patient's wishes. "Support" refers to those ways of speaking or relating that help the patient to cope with and bear the interpretation as it is given. The reason for giving such support may be that the patient is fragile (i.e., prone to disintegration of function under the press of strong negative affect), likely to flee treatment, or unaccustomed to reliance on speech for coping (whether on the basis of personality, education, or culture), so that, as in early childhood, he has to be eased into the developmental stage of reliance on speech and thought. For the child, the move into speech (and distal perception—sight and hearing—altogether) involves a partial renunciation of nonverbal (touch and affect) contact; but the well-developing child masters that loss for the trade-off of the gain that comes with speech. But for the fragile patient, nonverbally wishing for (and frightened of) care and fearing the fantasied destructiveness of contact, neither the move into the frightening clarity of speech nor the move to the renunciations that reliance on speech entails is made easily.

Generally we give our interpretations in the context of abstinence for healthier patients, those with reliable defenses and psychological structure. Why do we give such patients this frustrating "gift" of abstinence? I think developmental thinking helps clarify what goes on. Children develop under conditions of optimal strain, optimal demand, optimal frustration. Too much strain gets in their way, leading to anxiety or anger or frustration or helplessness at levels that are not constructive and too much to deal with; but too little strain, too much gratification, also stands in the way of development. Thus Winnicott (1963c) writes that the good-enough mother must "fail" the child, fail to meet all his needs; but by doing this in optimal doses she creates a situation where the child can manage the "failure" and grow a step in his functional capacity. Tolpin's (1971) excellent paper is also based on the child's taking in parental functions under what amounts to conditions of optimal strain and performing them himself through a "transmuting internalization." The better-functioning patient uses abstinence as the equivalent of "optimal strain." Gratification confirms fantasy, replays old conflict. Abstinence sets up a tension in which growth is possible.

But for the less well-functioning patient the "strain" that is "optimal" is at a lower level; he can bear less, having fewer reliable psychological tools to fall back on. We can lessen the strain by *not* introducing anything threatening; but then we are back to a know-nothing supportive therapy. Or we can, as described in chapter 11, actively increase therapist support so that the patient can bear the stress of interpretation more adequately. We decrease the strain not by decreasing the threatening inputs (interpretations) but by increasing their supportive context. In this way, "psychoanalytically oriented supportive psychotherapy" is psychoanalytically oriented in at least two ways: it draws heavily on interpretation for its mutative effects, and it draws on psychoanalytic developmental and clinical theory for its conceptualization of human functioning.

Another way to look at support versus abstinence as the dichotomous contexts in which interpretations may be given is by asking which context will help elicit the content in *workable* ways (that will not flood the patient or cause him to flee) and which will allow the patient to *take in* and use the interpretation. My experience is that the context of support works better on both counts with the less well-integrated and less well-defended patient.

Thus, to question what is mutative in the psychotherapy of certain fragile patients, I suggest that support and interpretation *in combination* are mutative. Support alone may go nowhere; interpretation alone is potentially overwhelming. Together they permit change to take place. This mutative potential of support and interpretation in combination again mirrors the developmental process with that other "fragile patient," the young child. The lovingly available parent who conveys painful or frightening information (the developmental equivalent of interpretation) to the child is in the position of the therapist of the ill patient. In the case of the child or of the patient, the supportively given, sometimes frightening facts have a better chance to be integrated and incorporated into a growth process.

In contrast to interpretation, which I believe is an activity more or less unique to the therapeutic relationship, the remaining mutative factors are all things that the ordinary sensitive parent provides for the growing child, whether by active doing or by providing a model that the child draws upon or incorporates. In this way, all these factors are part of the "corrective emotional experience" (Alexander, 1956) that therapy provides, not in the sense of active role playing of the kind of parenting that a specific patient may need, but because the therapist *is* different from the parent—reliable, reality oriented, and with the patient's benefit at the center of his attention. The humane and sensitive therapist is or does all these things in the ordinary course of his everyday work.

Restimulated by Kohut's (1959, 1971) writings on the topic, the subject of *empathy* has received considerable attention in the recent literature (T. Shapiro, 1974; Schwaber, 1981). The question of whether empathy is a special form of knowing, and of how and whether we can know the inner experience of another, has long been debated and with no clear-cut resolution. I shall make no attempt to resolve the question here. Rather, I will treat empathy as a technical rather than an epistemological problem. We make empathic statements to patients, but I doubt that we have special empathic "knowings" that are different from the "knowings" that form the bases for interpretation. We "know" by inferences from theory; we know by putting a patient's statements together and drawing a conclusion; we think we know by some inner sense of attunement to the subjective states of the patient (ordinarily thought of as "empathy"); and we think we know "intuitively" in other (not always known) ways. But I believe that all such "knowings" may underlie either an interpretation or an empathic statement.

What is the difference between them that I am proposing? An interpretation, I propose, is a statement of a form that links an item "A" to an item "B," with A and B each being an aspect of the patient's life. It has many varieties. Thus, in schematic form: "You are feeling A because of what happened (B) between us yesterday"; or "you are feeling A because you did B"; or "you are doing A in a changed form but it is just like what you always did in the past (B)"; or "you are doing A because you are thinking B"; or "whenever your thoughts go to A, you start speaking of B"; ad infinitum. A and B can be thoughts, fantasies, memories, affects, or behaviors; they can be in the past, the transference, or the extra-analytic present; they can be simple or complex, broad or narrow. But all interpretive statements *link* two (or more) features of the patient's life. As such, *implicit* in such linkage, and no matter what the *affective* power of the particular linking statement made, is an evocation of the patient's cognitive functioning. An interpretation is an offer of a piece of intellectual understanding. Again, whatever the affect that may be aroused (because of the content, or because of the way the interpretation is given), an interpretation is meant *in part* to call forth subtle and automatic processes of judgment, reasoning, and logical thinking. Lewin's (1954) discussion of how interpretations can, in effect, tell the patient to "wake up" into higher levels of thought organization recognizes this feature of interpretation.

By contrast, an empathic statement, I propose, is a statement of the form: "You are feeling A" (or, probably less powerfully, "you are thinking A" or "what you were trying to do was A"). There is no *linkage* of "A" to any other item. A is *described*, not connected in an effort to *explain* it. This too calls up the patient's cognitive processes, but they are processes of labeling and clarification of (ordinarily) subjective inner states. When it is done sensitively in terms of voice tone and inflection, I believe it promotes self-acceptance and a feeling of acceptance by the other (the therapist). As the interpretation promotes *understanding*, the empathic statement promotes a feeling of *being understood*.

Naturally there is no sharp line between these two. Understanding or being understood may come with either or neither. Some therapist statements are *partial* linkages, halfway between "A is linked to B" and "you feel A." Thus: "you are feeling A again, which you always do when B happens." Here a link is stated but the emphasis is on "you are feeling A." That the patient "always feels this when B happens" can be background.

What an empathic statement, thus defined, does is to provide a clarifying description of some inner state. As such, in Loewenstein's (1957) sense, this is in part preparatory work for certain larger interpretations. A more complex and substantial interpretation will best be made when the patient is familiar with the terms of the interpretive equations (the A's and the B's), and the patient can become familiar with some of them through such statements. But also, and here is the point I wish to emphasize in the present context, such statements can be mutative in themselves—potentially promoting a feeling of being understood, of self-acceptance, of greater affect tolerance in the region of what has been stated so that higher levels of function can be built around them. Again drawing on Katan's (1961) ideas regarding the role of verbalization in early childhood: the parent who labels feelings and inner states for the child brings them into the region of social communication—they are shared, the child is not unique and alone with them, they are capable of being understood, the power of words and the psychological achievements words facilitate can be applied to them. I believe that it is in the domain of feeling rather than thoughts or actions that such empathic statements have their greatest power, in part because of the inherently less articulated status of feelings and in part because of their potentially disruptive effect. Recent work by Stern (1983) demonstrates the affect attunements that mothers spontaneously make with their children starting in the second half year of life in order to "be with" their children—not to communicate something but to "be with" as an end in itself. There is no doubt in my mind that empathic statements of this sort between adults, when the patient feels the therapist is "with" him or her, are technically valuable and facilitate the treatment. (The caricatured "uh-huh" of the silent analyst may have this function.) But once again, what, if any, special form of "knowing" they are based upon, and whether such "knowings" do not underlie at least many interpretations as well, are bound to be the subject of endless and ultimately unresolvable dispute.

Under certain circumstances, the therapist's *confirmation of the patient's "objective" reality* is also of mutative significance in therapy. By "objective" reality, I refer to realities of the patient's current life or past history. We can never fully know that reality. But, as therapists, we do not work as total subjectivists. We form some conception of the realities even if approximate and in broad outline, of the patient's life. We may at times be speaking only of the patient's subjectively experienced objective reality; but it is his reality nonetheless. Whether the subjective experience of the actuality of present and past is veridical or not, the concept that it is has psychological importance.

A concern with the patient's reality is significant in therapy in at least three ways. First, when we begin to discover that the patient's "reality" is in significant part his own creation, we focus on *that* fact to help the patient assume responsibility for his own thoughts, to block his attempt to use the attribution of them to reality as a defense—and thus to continue to open up the patient's inner life for exploration. Second, we respect the significance of the patient's conscious experience—how things felt, how they seemed to be—without necessarily ever knowing what stemmed from inner life and what from external reality—recognizing that experience is the crossroads where the two meet in any event—and by the focus on experiencing, staying in touch with the patient and with what matters to him.

But it is the third consideration regarding reality, when we have a sense of what the reality is (was), that I wish to focus on here. Work in this area has the potential for helping the patient come to terms with the realities of his past—that it may not have been as good as he wished it to be, or that it was better than he had been able to take advantage of (for reasons of inner conflict)—and thus promoting the painful process of acceptance of one's family and of oneself as a product of history, which is surely one part of personal wisdom. If those who do not study history (here, reality) are condemned to repeat it, as the saying goes, the "study" of it is first and foremost the recognition and objectification of what it *was*. I have, with patients, again and again seen how a confirmation of aspects of their painful reality permits them to discard denial and/or hypocrisy (especially about the parents), to get in touch with affect and/or to increase their trust in their own judgment and reality sense.

Such statements do not come frequently in any treatment—rarely more than a few times over the years no matter how destructive the patient's "reality." The work turns back with profit to the patient's denial processes, efforts to repeat the reality, affective and/or fantasy responses, and the like. Nor do such confirmations of reality have to be given in extra-analytic ways, that is, with a radical shift in the therapist's way of working. They can, for example, be included in interpretations. Thus: "it is hard for you to let yourself believe that 'X' *really* happened"; or "the fact that 'X' really happened makes you expect the same from me"; or "you are showing me that 'X' really happened by making it happen again and again with your family and with me." Each of these confirms a reality, without any special educative or affective tone; they are, in effect, interpretations. But they need not be in that form.

Although such confirmations come up very infrequently, I believe that they have significant mutative effects and that they have them without impairing the overall tone of the work; in my experience they have principally involved major parentally denied seductions, abuses, and abandonments in the past. Such confirmations, too, are parallel to very significant inputs that the child receives from the well-functioning parent: straightforward statements of painful realities that can foster their assimilation into psychic functioning, that enable appropriate response (affective or behavioral), and that counteract denials or other evasions.

And then there are mutative effects of that set of things that the "good-enough therapist" simply is for the patient—*is* because of his way of functioning that itself permits growth and change to take place in ways similar to the ways in which the good-enough parent facilitates growth in the child. In treatment, these factors additionally enable the patient to make use of the special interpretive, empathic, and confirming initiatives that the therapist offers.

Among these is the fact that the therapist can speak of the patient's sexual, aggressive, and other impulses *without condemnation* (Strachey, 1934), leading to modification of conscience. Conscience, originally in part a precipitate and internalization of the parental critique, forever seems to be modifiable by example from the outside (e.g., the behaviors that are permissible at Mardi Gras time or when far from home; also see Freud, 1921) and in the therapeutic instance by the therapist's matter-of-fact acceptance of impulse life, even apart from the interpretively based modifications. Closely related to this is the example of the therapist's *persistent and tough-minded reality orientation,* with reality including all the "badness" within: the impulses and fantasies that the patient regards as unique, distressing, and to be disowned. In the course of interpretive work, the therapist's matter-of-fact acceptance of them as part of life's reality is a by-product that beats a path in which the patient may follow.

Beyond these, and still connected with the patient's impulses and fantasies, is the fact that the therapist continually *survives,* in the sense of not being drawn into reciprocal sexual fantasy or behavior and not retaliating with rage or rejection in the face of the patient's rage. In this sense, the situation closely parallels Winnicott's (1963b) proposal that the mother who repeatedly survives the infant's destructiveness teaches the infant that his destructiveness will not destroy, can be safely (gradually) "owned" (see chap. 9), and can be expressed even toward loved ones.

And then, though this is often slow in coming (because so much of the therapeutic dialogue pertains to the patient's self-perceived "badness") there is also the patient's slow realization that he is *valued* by the therapist—valued enough to be worked with in the face of perceived "badness" and valued enough for the therapist to be reliably there, attentive, and working in sessions day in and day out, year in and year out.

All of these together—noncondemnation, reality orientation, survival, and postive valuation—provide a *context of safety* in which growth can take place in therapy as in childhood, and in which ventures toward change can be risked (see chap. 10; also Sandler, 1960; Schafer, 1983b). Although there is no doubt that, in a well-formed adult, the most powerful and persistent incentives toward rigid reliance on established defenses and characterological modes come from the person himself, some of those incentives always come from perceived threats from the outside; and in children and in patients who are indeed living in environments destructive to life or to the self, these incentives are in fact initiated by threats from the outside. The slowly established context of safety in therapy reduces at least the threats seen as coming from the outside and tips the balance toward the possibility of risking change in the face of the internal threats.

And finally (as discussed in chap. 10), change comes about through the *use* the patient makes of the therapist, whether the therapist wills it or not— in parallel to the use the child makes of the parent. The patient uses the therapist as an object of *identification,* a source of *education,* and a source of *confirmation.* By "confirmation" here I am not referring to the therapist's active confirmation of the patient's external life reality, but rather to those confirmations of the patient's thoughts and feelings pervasively experienced in a treatment as the patient-therapist pair, through the interpretive exchange, develop a common language and a common understanding of the patient's psychic life. Because of the patient's trust in and awe of the therapist, these confirmations help him to believe in his thoughts and to reach inner conviction regarding the discoveries of the therapy. And by "education" I refer not to explicit and directed teachings by the therapist but to those guidelines that the patient "finds"—whether we wish and intend it or not—in the therapist's words and behavior, in those aspects of his manner of living that become known to the patient, and, not least, in his mode of therapeutic functioning itself—the use of words, the orientation toward reality, and the acceptance of impulse and fantasy without condemnation. And by "identi-fication" I mean what we usually mean, taking what is other and gradually making it self—which merges with "education" in part, as I have defined it above.

These mutative factors in psychotherapy are broad ranging and, through-out, have parallels to those factors that facilitate development in the child. Though interpretation may be the unique thing that therapists have to offer (even in so-called supportive psychotherapies as I have defined them), its effect is not only facilitated and made possible by all the rest, but all the rest themselves make significant additive contributions to the therapeutic effect. And no matter what we *think* we are doing when we do treatment, there is no way (short of controlled experimentation that would make a mockery of the therapeutic enterprise) of teasing out the proportional contributions of the many listed factors to the ultimate therapeutic outcome.

THE SUBSTANTIVE LANGUAGES OF INDIVIDUAL LIVES

In the previous section I discussed the question of how change occurs in treatment, alluding to the broader question of how developmental change takes place, in so doing attempting to enlarge our conception of the mutative factors in psychotherapy and psychoanalysis. In this section I should like to bring developmental considerations to bear on the question of how we con-ceptualize what goes on in our patient's lives. The developmental consider-ations that I shall draw upon are those discussed in part II, especially in chapters 4 and 5. Central to the discussion is the suggestion that significant aspects of development take place in affectively powerful formative moments, moments that have differing experiential "shape" in our lives. Psychoanalytic theory, I suggested in chapter 5, has attempted to capture these differential shapes of experience in its several psychologies: the psychology of drives, ego function, object relations, and self. In this section I shall refer to them as "languages," both because they are *our* linguistic attempts to capture the currents of the flow of experience and because, in treatment, they are indeed languages that we use in speaking to patients as a way of staying close to their experience.

In chapter 5, I suggested that the four psychologies unfolded in three great waves in the literature, partly as a result of clinical experience in classical analysis, partly from new modes of observation, partly from the special at-tunements of individual contributors, and partly through contact with a widening scope of patient pathologies. I shall review and expand upon these "four psychologies" here but, in the light of remarks in the previous section,

I shall add *reality* to these "languages" of therapeutic communication. The five overlap and are separable conceptually only to a degree.

As I have read and worked with varied clinical and theoretical contributions over the years, my general reaction (to an aspect of these ideas, not the totality) is: "that makes sense; there's a piece of the truth there." Though many of us have previously used languages of drive and ego in our clinical work and found them adequate to the task of conceptualizing the material and, at times therapeutically powerful, from an introspective, phenomenological point of view, the languages of object relations, self, and reality seem equally significant and powerful. For some patients, I find that these languages attain a commanding position. That is, the repetition of internalized object relations and overall the significance of the object, the problem of self-other boundaries, the centrality of feelings of self continuity and cohesion and of feelings of gradiosity and shame and deflation, and the powerful impact of personal reality and the continual task of its mastery—all these are certainly part of the ongoing anatomy of inner life. And although the experiences in the phenomenological domains of drive, ego, object relation, self, or reality can be readily translated into the theoretical language of any of the others, I am not sure that there is always a gain in doing so. Therefore my aim here is to take what I know to be true for myself, what I have been finding useful in my work with patients, and what I tried (in part II) to describe in terms of developmental theory and apply it more broadly to the clinical domain.

Though I shall, of necessity, describe these languages of lives and of therapy one by one, I have noted that they all overlap. Indeed I believe that they are all interrelated and hierarchically organized in any individual life and in each individual's treatment. I also believe that each appears in every life and in every treatment although the hierarchical arrangements vary and the particular language, the optimal way of phrasing interpretations, varies also—from person to person and, over time, in each person. In each of the subsections to follow, I shall discuss the phenomena to which the theoretical language refers, the "principles" that guide individual functioning in that domain, the task of the therapist in relation to these phenomena, and issues that are specific to each domain; I shall also give illustrative interventions that speak to the content discussed.

First then, the language of *drive*. From this standpoint, the psychology of the individual is seen in terms of lasting urges, forged in the crucible of early bodily and family experience, represented in conscious and unconscious fantasies, undergoing endless vicissitudes, repetitions, and displacements, and organized especially around conflict—conflict signified by anxiety, guilt, aspects of shame, symptom formation, and pathological character traits. Important aspects of the psychology of ego function are inseparably tied to the drive psychology. Rigid or failed defenses and their expression in everyday life and in the resistance within psychoanalysis, as well as adaptive, sublimatory, and smoothly functioning defenses of all kinds which may or may not enter the analytic work, are all aspects of what we call ego function that are inseparable from the development and psychoanalytic therapeutics of drive. Conceptually, the principles that guide human functioning in this area are those Freud (1911) wrote of: the *pleasure principle* as modified, under the press of frustration and anxiety, by the *reality principle*. The therapist's task is *interpretation*, with the aim of gradually producing modification of conflict, conscience, and inflexible modes of defense, all permitting reorganization to take place with greater success in the patient's acceptance of thoughts and urges, in conflict resolution, affect tolerance, displacement, and sublimation. Though interpretation is central in this work, variously expressed by Freud in topographic, structural, or genetic terms, as remarked earlier the analyst's nonjudgmental stance and tough-minded reality orientation probably contribute in and of themselves to the modification of conscience and to the acceptance of *inner* reality. Interpretations in the language of drive may, for example, take the form of: "I believe that you're angry not only at your mother but also at me"; or "each time you have a loving thought about me in one session, you have nothing to say in the next, and today seems to be no exception"; or "you'll remember that you first came to treatment because your mind would 'go blank,' and the fact that this just happened after your telling me that you couldn't help liking your friend who is homosexual tells us something about that"; or "how comforting it would be to believe that *I* am trying to stop you from masturbating against your wishes so that you don't have to see that you yourself want to stop but also feel you can't stop." Each of these makes a statement (or implies a formulation) about urge and/or defense and/or conflict.

Second, the language of *internalized object relations*. From this standpoint, the psychology of the individual is seen as an internal drama, derived from childhood, that each of us carries around within us and in which we enact one or more or all of the roles, and which is repeated perpetually in endless variations (cf. Sandler and Rosenblatt, 1962). Developmentally, this can be understood as coming about through the laying down as memories and fantasies of early interactions (or imagined interactions) between the person and significant caretakers, so that behavioral expectancies, longings for particular gratifications, knowings of behaviors that will produce expectable responses are recorded and can be repeated. What is laid down as memory need not be, and probably usually is not, veridical; it is the child's *experience* that is laid down, and that is forged out of the inner state that meets the external input. Kernberg's (1976) suggestion that the units of mental life to begin with are self-affect-object units (i.e., self-other interactions tied together by an affect experience, such as the feeding experience or the unanswered cry) is consonant with this point of view. These early laid-down memories and fantasies are perpetually repeated, in part because of the stress of those experiences—and here Kris's (1956b) concept of strain trauma (rather than shock trauma) and the repetition of trauma altogether (Freud, 1920b) are relevant explanatory concepts. The internalized object relations are thus repeated in an effort toward mastery, but they are also repeated because of the longings and gratifications the person associates with them—gratifications that may or may not be "objectively" gratifying to outside view, but *are* the form of gratification that that person had and built himself around. One is reminded here of Albee's play *The Zoo Story* (1960), in which a man, a loner, is describing the daily battle he goes through to avoid being bitten by a vicious dog as he enters the hallway of his tenement building; then, responding to the growing horror and confusion of his listener, he gradually makes it clear that for him the dog is a relationship, and that everyone has to have some relationship, with something, whether vicious, lifeless, or whatever. And, indeed, everyone has to have, and to repeat, his *primary* relationships—because they, no matter how bad, are what the attachment to the parent consisted of.

The guiding psychological principle in the area of internalized object relations is, then, *repetition* (see chap. 5), of the strain trauma and of the object attachment. The therapist's task is, again, *interpretation*, with the aim of freeing the patient to meet new experience as new, without absorbing it into the old drama of historically based object relations. But here too, and apart from interpretation, by his very being and without playacting or any special concern for providing a corrective emotional experience, the analyst does just that—because he *is* different from the significant others of the past. From the standpoint of internalized object relations, pathology can be defined as the degree to which current life is experienced according to the categories and interpersonal dramas laid down in the mind from the past; the more this is so, the more pathology; the less, the less. It is the aim of treatment to enable the patient to respond to the present free of the categories of experiencing laid down in the past.

There is no doubt that many of these internalized dramas came to have, and may even originally have had, an important drive and frustration/gratification component. And theorists may argue, as Freud did in *Beyond the Pleasure Principle* (1920b), whether repetition alone can power behavior "beyond the pleasure principle," i.e., separate from the issue of drive and its gratification or frustration. But at the clinical level—in terms of what is *said* to patients—my experience leaves me with no doubt that interventions oriented to the repetition of the object relation in and of itself have powerful impact. In this area, then, in the language of internalized object relations, interpretations may take the form of: "Yes, they were cruel to you, but they were the only parents you had and so you keep them with you through continued cruelty"; or "everybody, myself included, becomes your father in your mind's eye, and then you know just how to behave—as his naive and innocent little seductress"; or "the pain of the abandonment you felt was so great that you continually try to free yourself of it by inflicting it on others"; or "you were so enraged at your mother for so obviously being your father's only interest that there was no other way you could remember her but as retaliatory and herself enraged at you." Though some of these statements include implicit reference to wishes, they address primarily the repetitions of the internal dramas.

Third, the language of *self experience*. From this standpint, the psychology of the individual is seen in terms of the gradually solidifying differentiation of boundaries, self-concept, the "I" experience, out of an at least periodically merged self-other totality of experience (see chaps. 4 and 9). The birth and expansion of the self experience, the work toward achievement of continuity over time and cohesion of the multiple elements of that self experience, and the work toward achievement of generally positive, though realistically and responsively flexible, affective tone (self-esteem) associated with the self experience are also referred to here. The thrust given to positive self-experience by new achievements in mastery (whether regarding adaptation, sublimation, or successful defense) and, contrariwise, the deflation in the sense of self that can come with failures of mastery or built-in defects of function highlight the overlap of aspects of the language of ego function and the language of self experience. The work of Mahler et al. (1975) and of Kohut (1977), in quite different ways, has addressed issues in these areas.

Although each of the developmental tasks relevant to the self experience has quite different significance for the basic intactness of the person, they are not, I believe, worked with stepwise in development; rather, each has its origins in the earliest months and progresses from there (see chap. 9). Nonetheless, failure to achieve a basic awareness of self-other differentiation, ultimately related to core reality testing, probably has the most pathological implications—though residual longings for self-other merger, in the setting of attained differentiation, is quite different and much less pathological in its implication (see chap. 15). Issues of noncontinuity (including derealization and depersonalization), noncohesion (including splitting), and unrealistically aggrandized or devalued self-esteem are also representative of disturbances in this area. Merely to list those disturbances is to make clear that each has been addressed from the standpoint of drive psychology as well; but the fact that drive psychology got there first, so to speak, does not mean that it is the last word on the subject. It is precisely because of the ubiquity of overdetermination and multiple function that all major psychological concepts can be applied to every aspect of human functioning. Each of the several "psychologies" or "languages" of psychoanalysis has a fittedness to significant moments in the child's development (chap. 5) and, in parallel form, has a particular attunement to the hierarchical arrangement of disturbance in a given patient.

The psychological principle that governs in the area of self (boundaries, continuity, cohesion or esteem) is neither the pleasure principle nor the compulsion to repeat but the principle of *maintenance*: maintenance of boundaries under the threat of merger (or of merger under the threat of panic in the face of awareness of separateness), of continuity or cohesion in the face of the experience of fragmentation (or of discontinuity and noncohesion in defensive ways to keep experiences separate from one another), of self-esteem in the face of shame, narcissistic injury, and deficit in esteem itself. Other faces of "maintenance" are withdrawal, protection, enhancement, exaggeration—as the person or the psychological state may require.

The principal therapeutic task in this area is *facilitation*, carried out through interpretation and the provision of a corrective experience. Mahler's (1968;

Mahler and Furer, 1960) work on a corrective symbiotic experience is relevant here, as is Kohut's (1971) on the patient's establishment of an idealizing or mirroring transference. Both reflect the fact that intense emotional bonding to the analyst/therapist facilitates boundary formation and the development of continuity and cohesion. This is perhaps especially so in a setting where words can be used to give shape to the experience as it is happening, though words alone, without the experience, may be empty. As proposed earlier in this chapter, the analyst's noncondemning reliable availability, throughout the patient's work on his experienced "badness," also creates a core of experienced value—of self-esteem.

Interpretation is an integral part of work in this area and is easier to illustrate than the effect of the relationship over time in itself. Interpretation in this area may take the form of: "You got frightened when I used the word 'we' because it made you feel I was invading you just as it used to be with your mother;" or "your parents' failure to respond to you made you lose touch with who you were, and so when I don't greet you as you come in you can't believe that you and I are the same two people who worked together in yesterday's session"; or "you're showing me what your parents thought of themselves and of you by behaving in such a way as to advertise how worthless you are"; or "succeeding at school made you feel like a person, separate from others, and so you rushed back with failure to get your parents and me re-involved with you." Each of these has an educative aspect, an aspect that touches on the patient's reality, and an aspect that addresses the patient's inner dynamics.

Fourth, the language of *ego functioning*. From this standpoint, the psychology of the individual is seen in terms of the slow accretion, over the long course of development, of capacities for adaptation, reality testing, and intrapsychic defense. These larger achievements are mediated by innumerable subachievements: the organization of the perceptual world, the development of language and of cognition (judgment, anticipation, planning, and thought) more broadly, the enlargement and availability of a storehouse of memory, the growth of family-syntonic and culturally syntonic communication modes, the expansion of the affect array (F. Pine, 1979), the development of the signal function of affects, and the harnessing, delay, transformation, and redirection of primary urges. Developmental failures, distortions, or restrictions in any of these processes hinder the adaptive, defensive, and reality-testing aims of the person. Overall, in life, the guiding principle for the person in this area is practically co-terminus with all of *development*; but more specifically, in treatment, the patient's task is the *resumption* of or *compensation* for failed or distorted development. And the therapist's task involves both *facilitation* of ego development (to the degree that the interpretive work and the therapeutic context of safety simply allow development to go forward) and active "*construction*" (to the degree that specific interventions, or withheld interventions—which allow the patient space to function—can be created to aid in the developmental task).

Modes of working in the facilitative manner are no different from those characteristic of the full body of psychoanalytic psychotherapy, through which affects may be differentiated, repressions lifted to increase access to memory, rigid defenses loosened as urges are better tolerated, and adaptation and reality-testing improved as unconsciously driven scotomizations and distortions of all sorts are revised. Modes of working in the constructional manner, on the other hand, require considerable variation from classical technique. I have tried to approach such variations in chapters 10 and 11 and will not review that work in full here. Such attempts to aid the patient in overcoming deficits in ego function may include: actively forewarning the patient of difficult material to be presented in order to signal him and to make up from the outside for the signal function of anxiety that may be absent, actively helping him to bear intense affect by one's empathic, supportive presence (usually with accompanying verbalization), or actively helping him to increase his access to the full range of inner cognitive life by including supportive/educative and conscience-relieving statements as we clarify and interpret that inner life. Each of these, to varying degrees in varying individuals, can gradually become assimilated so that the person becomes enabled to function in like manner more fully on his own.

Fifth, the language of *reality experience*: From this standpoint the psychology of the individual is seen in terms of both a continual exchange with inputs from one's surround and the recognition and integration of one's own unique givens. The first refers to the shaping, stimulating, frustrating, educating, traumatizing inputs from caretakers or from the accidents of personal history and the integration, adaptation, mastery, or acquiescence with which the person meets them. Additionally it refers to the evocation of particular inputs through the person's own behavior and his interpretation of all inputs in terms of inner fantasy from early on, once the individual personality begins to take shape.

By the recognition and integration of one's own unique givens, I refer to the whole array of special limitations and abilities in cognition, perceptual sensitivity, and motor skills from which one can build unique talents and abilities or with which one has to come to terms and make one's peace. This aspect of "reality," the person's own resources, can be seen as an aspect of the ego apparatuses but it is to a degree "external" to the psyche, a fact with which he must cope. The person's external appearance and physical health, too, are parts of the reality givens with which he must come to terms.

Granted that we never come to know the objective realities of the past (Spence, 1982; Schimek, 1975), patient and therapist nonetheless form a working conception of that reality. To the degree that recall or reconstruction of the past enters into treatment, we are doing excavation (to use Freud's [1937b] metaphor) but *not* philosophy of science. The patient's *experience* is that he has a history in reality, and whether or not we believe we come to know it accurately is generally irrelevant to that experience.

The guiding psychological principle in the area of reality experience is *mastery* or its opposite, submission. This refers to the use, the mastery through repetition or transformation, the recognition and acceptance—or their opposites—that an individual makes of his history. And, though the degree to which comment on the patient's reality is required in treatment varies with the degree of his personal integration and the trauma of his history, engagement with ideas regarding the patient's reality is part of every treatment. The therapist's task involves both *objectification* and *confirmation*. By "objectification" I mean clarification of ways in which the patient's reality impinged upon and shaped him and, conversely, sorting out the patient's contribution to his "real" history, the ways in which his evocations and distortions have produced it. The aim is the production of a reasonably objective view of both the patient's reality and his inner dynamics. By "confirmation" I refer to the lending of the therapist's rational perception to what the patient feels and fears but has been unable to put into words, to an understanding of what parents have done but hypocritically deny, leaving the patient with a split (seen and denied) view of reality, and to those features of the history that help make rational sense of the lifecourse pathology on which the patient has embarked. Confirmation of these, I find, has an enormously freeing effect for the patient, permitting the thrusting aside of denials, the release of anger, and ultimately the leaving behind of the past.

Much of this work is accomplished in the context of interpretive statements, but I find that, on one or two occasions in the course of many a treatment, straightforward descriptive assertions can be highly significant for the progress of the treatment. (Gedo [1979], for example, gives considerable weight to the effect of his clarifying a cognitive deficit that created disorganized behavior and confirming for the patient that certain failures were unintended by-products of poor planning ability. The net effect of these interventions, according to Gedo, was crucial to the establishment of the therapeutic alliance.) Such assertions may take the form of: "Your mother *did* allow your father to abuse you; and you paid a heavy price for that"; or "your father *really* was 'crazy,' as you suspected, and the things he said often *did* make no rational sense"; or "you *were* left alone in ways that were more than a growing child could possibly deal with, and that connects to your rage and depression when I go on vacation." In the last statement reality is confirmed within the context of an interpretation.

So much, then, for the several languages in which a psychotherapy or psychoanalysis is conducted. To repeat, I believe that all of them are relevant to every treatment because experiences organized around drive, ego, object relations, self, and reality are inevitably part of the life of every developing person. As noted in chapter 5, the several intrapsychic psychologies become interrelated in such a way that all psychic acts eventually come to have multiple functions (Waelder, 1936). In the adult-as-patient, we see all of them, organized in varying hierarchical arrangements in different persons and at different times in each person's treatment. The several psychologies are formed in each of us developmentally and thus inevitably have a place in every treatment process.

To write of "classical psychoanalysis" for the sake of argument always runs the risk of creating a straw man. But for the moment I may need the straw man to enhance the sense of contrast to the point of view developed in this chapter. Thus I note that classical psychoanalysis has focused primarily on the drive/ego/superego structural and conflict theory, on psychosexual (especially oedipal) and aggressive roles in pathogenesis, and on interpretation as the central mutative agent in treatment. Naturally, it has also done far more than this. But in fact I suspect that truth lies on both sides of the polarity— my presentation of classical psychoanalysis both is and is not a straw man, depending on which article, analyst, or analysis one is looking at.

A developmental perspective and work with patients unsuited for classical psychoanalysis, added to experience in psychoanalysis as theory and treatment, can produce a perspective that is far more wide-ranging. I have tried to give such a perspective. While what I have presented in this chapter is theoretically organized, it is also in an important sense atheoretical, following experience where it leads and allowing formulations to arise from the data as perceived through one person's particular looking glass.

In this chapter, I have tried to develop two major areas of thought regarding treatment. First, I have tried to draw upon both clinical experience and developmental observation to articulate a wide range of interventions, and also of behaviors and events that are simply inherent in the therapist's role and in the therapeutic encounter, which are of mutative force in clinical work; and I have tried to give both a clinical and a developmental rationale for each of them. Second, I have tried to describe five "languages"—in parallel to significant and formative childhood experiences—in which the therapeutic dialogue takes place, for each also giving the "principles" that guide the patient's functioning, the aims that guide the therapist's functioning, and a discussion of diverse aspects of related clinical issues.

B. DEVELOPMENT AND THE ASSESSMENT OF PATHOLOGY

In her paper on the symptomatology of childhood, Anna Freud (1970) pointed out that the relation of "surface" and "depth," of clinical manifestation and underlying psychological issue, is not linear. Any underlying psychological disturbance can eventuate in a number of specific clinical manifestations. Conversely, any surface clinical phenomenon may be the outgrowth of several underlying difficulties.

A developmental perspective, including both a conception of developmental lines in various areas and a familiarity with the phenomena of infancy and childhood, can shed light on the anatomy of pathology. In the three chapters that follow I shall undertake to bring this perspective to bear. Chapters 13 and 14, on common disturbances of childhood, attempt to show how selected overall syndromes can be looked at in more differentiated ways by examining their underlying and varying developmental roots and the psychological matrices in which they exist. Chapter 15 is an examination of the multiple paths of expression of underlying pathology of the separation-individuation process.

13

Disturbances of Learning and Behavior in Childhood

In this chapter and the next, I shall describe some of the characteristic psychopathology of school-age children, in particular borderline disturbances (chap. 14), behavior disturbances, and disturbances of learning. This period is the one that Bornstein (1951) called the second period of latency, roughly the years from seven or eight to ten or eleven, following the early latency period, in which the child is still very much involved in residual oedipal issues.

By age seven or eight, the child is normally solidly involved in the world of school and peer relations. The contrast to the preschool years is striking (though, of course, not absolute). The preschooler is ordinarily in close proximity to the mother and other family members for much of his day; the sights, sounds, smells, feel of family members are at all times the background, and often the foreground, of life, and contribute percepts and memories to the thought processes from which fantasy and wish are formed. The learning that takes place is in considerable measure learning on and about his own body and the bodies of others. From early self-other bodily differentiation (Mahler et al., 1975), through the learning of self-feeding, bowel/bladder control, self-toileting, and self-dressing, critical learnings have an intimate relation to body and mother. Additionally, family members in general have no peer in their significance as external others in the life of the child.

But the entry into school brings major changes. While family members remain central figures in the psychic life of the child, teachers and peers begin to assume importance as representatives of a wider world, affectively a bit more neutral, less intimate, providing new avenues of identification and attachment. Learning, too, changes. While motor skills continue to develop, learning linked to the body itself is less intimate and less central. And non-

Based upon a portion of a paper first published under the auspices of the National Institute of Mental Health in volume 2 of *The Course of Life*, ed. S. I. Greenspan and G. H. Pollock, 1980.

bodily learning assumes enormous importance—reading, writing, arithmetic, social studies (the world of school), and chants, games, tricks, rules (the world of childhood) (Stone and Church, 1973). The learning process itself is less tied to the parents; not only are they not always the teacher but things may be learned (formally, from the teacher; informally, by observations of others) that the parents do not even know or do not do. And, importantly, the child's physical proximity to mother is less, as he spends time in school and has the skills and inner achievements to go out of the house after school without mother to play with peers.

The contrast to the subsequent adolescent period is equally sharp. In adolescence, intimate bodily learning (the new sexuality) once again becomes central; the old family relationships and infantile fantasy are reactivated and achieve renewed force (Freud, 1905; Spiegel, 1951; Blos, 1962), and the child's task of defining his position vis-à-vis learning and same-sex peers, ordinarily reasonably well accomplished (for good or ill) in the school years, gradually becomes secondary to the task of defining his position vis-à-vis sexual development, heterosexual relationships, and the anticipation of full independence from the parents and physical separation from their home. For the child whom we will be discussing, all of this still lies in the future.

The contrast of the school-age years to the preschool and adolescent periods helps bring out the internal features of that age period as well. It is a time of the child's entry into the wider, nonfamilial world typified by peer relations and school. The formation of new relationships (with the opportunities they provide for displacement and reworking of old familiar relationships) and the achievement of new learnings are major psychological tasks of the period. Character formation (the establishment of a reliable personal style of thought, relatedness, impulse expression, and defense), while inevitably beginning earlier, continues in this period; and its *external* accompaniment—socialization to the nonfamilial world—is of increased importance. Although many of the indicators of such socialization are quite visible (play, relationships, school behavior and attitude), the subtler ones (modes of thinking, feeling, and doing) are also being shaped. Certain kinds of disturbances in this age period (including the ones I shall be discussing) can be viewed against this age backdrop, descriptively, as failures successfully to accomplish the tasks of the age. From a more interior/clinical view, they will also be looked at in terms of their intrapsychic specificity and their developmental implications.

The three areas of psychopathology that I shall discuss—borderline disturbances, behavior disturbances, and disturbances of learning—are not really parallel with one another; nor is any one of them a unified entity. I select them because they are common, because they can be viewed as failures in the adaptational tasks of the school-age years, and because light can be shed upon them by taking a developmental, depth-oriented, interior view.

These three forms of disturbance do not begin in the school-age period, but they are often first identified as problematic in that period. Working clinically, one is deluged with complaints regarding learning or behavior and with diagnoses of "borderline" in this age group. Although these disturbances have earlier roots, they often are first identified, or at least first begin to clash with social expectations regarding the child, during the early school years; hence they come to the clinician's attention.

We might suspect that any referral complaint that we hear about with very great frequency is being overused, in overextended or vague ways. Such is indeed the case, I believe, with the three areas to be discussed. A depth-oriented view can lead to some clarification, however. The approach taken here will be consistent with the one espoused in Anna Freud's (1970) paper on the symptomatology of childhood: to specify common genetic and structural features that underlie divergent surface pathologies and to specify varying genetic and structural features that underlie superficially similar presenting pictures.

As varied as each area may be regarding appearance or cause, disturbances of behavior and of learning have in common at least the presence of a surface sign: a child is not learning or a child presents a behavior problem. The same cannot be said of borderline children. At best, the common surface sign is that these children are "peculiar" in some way—hardly an adequate clinical formulation. And, at that, it may be that they are peculiar only to those who have sufficient familiarity with the quality, the "feel," of normal children of this age.

The three areas are also not strictly parallel in their relatedness to failures in the adaptive tasks of the school-age years—and again the borderline disturbance is the conceptual oddball. The identification of behavior problems and learning problems is clearly connected to school entry and the requirements of school performance, and many a child is first referred at the initiative of the school for one or both of these complaints. Behavior problems are additionally linked to issues of the age because of their impact on peer relations and because of the increasing strength and opportunities for independent action in children of this age—making problems in the behavior domain that much more worrisome or dangerous. But borderline pathology is not as explicit in its linkage to school entry and school requirements. Yet I think there are important ways in which it is age linked, reasons why the "peculiarities" of the pathology are identified at this age. This has to do with the greater degree of character stability, socialization, and peer and/or teacher relatedness that is normally expectable at this age. The "peculiarities" of borderline children are often violations of these age-linked, normally fulfilled expectations. When the major relationships are solely within the family, peculiarities of object relation or of ego function may go unnoticed by equally peculiar family members or may be compensated for in the mix of habitual family interrelatedness. Teachers and peers may not be so generous.

So the three areas of disturbance are not truly parallel. Indeed I have elected to discuss them not because they are parallel but because they are common in clinical practice, characteristic of the age, and vague and therefore requiring specification. In addition, they profit from being looked at in terms of the adaptational expectations of the school-age child and, from an interior-developmental perspective, in terms of the child's progress along a number of developmental lines.

DISTURBANCES OF LEARNING

The broad area of learning disturbance in the school-age period is one in which concerns of parents, educators, child clinicians, and the children themselves often come together. It is not surprising that this should be so. One of the basic tasks of the age is the establishment of the learning process as sufficiently neutralized and automatic such that new learnings can be accumulated. As mentioned earlier, such learnings, especially in school, are ordinarily different from the earlier, preschool, learnings in that they are less intimately tied to the body and are received from more impersonal sources. Peer-group learning is also prominent, but it is principally the disturbances of school learning that lead parents to seek help for their children.

While is has often been said that failures in love and work are central in adults' seeking of treatment, we can also readily recognize how central learning is to the "work" of the school-age child. Love, in this case especially "self-love" (self-esteem), is also centrally involved with success or failure in learning, as is one's esteem in the eyes of peers, teachers, and parents. Problems of learning are important not only because of the disturbances they reflect and the suffering that may accompany them but because they obviously have real consequences for the paths open to a child as he grows into later life.

There is no question that a wide array of routes to learning disturbances exists and that this variation speaks to a *nonunified* set of pathological entities in the area of learning failure. But in various secondary though still highly important ways, these conditions have much in common. Descriptively, the presenting symptoms are of course learning difficulties; functionally, they all have major implications for school success; and as a consequence of their presence, they often have an impact on self-esteem. Additionally, they all reflect failures in one or more of the three broad developmental lines on which the child must have progressed in order for learning to take place.

For learning to take place, the *basic tools* for the process must be biologically and psychologically intact and must have developed in age-appropriate ways. First and foremost, it is obvious that learning capacity will vary with general intelligence; indeed, one definition of general intelligence is precisely the capacity to learn. Beyond that, specific tools are needed for one or another kind of learning, tools such as capacity for intake of information through visual, auditory, and tactile channels (and output through all channels as well), perceptual discrimination, visual organization, visual and auditory short- and long-term memory, sequencing of concepts, and sustained attention. The last-listed, sustained attention, should alert us especially to the psychological-developmental achievements underlying some of these basic tools. The capacity to attend and, even more, the emotional investment in learning (so that learning *matters* and/or gives pleasure) are achievements forged in the developmental mix of object relatedness, drive-defense arrangements, and inborn capacities and are core tools (capacities) for the learning process.

Additionally, for school learning to take place, the child must have developed to the point where there is a reasonable *inner harnessing* of those affect states and behavioral expressions that, when present in unharnessed form, would readily upset the delicate balance of receptivity, sustained attention, and interest outside oneself that is necessary for optimal learning. If the child is still subject to affect storms (for example, of panic anxiety, of needy longing) and developmental-defensive modulation of these has not taken place, learning will ordinarily suffer. Similarly, if impulses and affects readily spill over into gross motor activity, the state of receptivity for learning will have suffered. I recognize, of course, that much learning is enhanced by affective involvement and even motor behavior. This is no contradiction. The "harnessing" of affect and motor behavior in development does not refer to their elimination but rather to their coordination with other aims of the individual.

And third, for learning to take place, the learning process must have a reasonable degree of *autonomy* (Hartmann, 1939; Rapaport, 1957) from a person's major urges and the fantasies connnected with them. There are changing currents in the relation of fantasy to function in the course of development. Very early on, for example, eating (sucking) is clearly a biological, life-sustaining process. That it remains so goes without saying, but the presence in childhood of food fads, disgust reactions, and food avoidances reflects the intrusion of fantasy (anal, cannibalistic, and so forth) into the biologically based process. Still later, with the attainment of "rational eating" (A. Freud, 1965), these fantasies have been more or less tamed in relation to the act of eating. Again, this does not mean that they are eliminated. The *relativity* of autonomy from drives implies two things: (1) An ego function or a process (such as learning) is relatively autonomous from drives in that it can always be *reinvaded*, reinterfered with; it is not impervious; the autonomy is not absolute. And especially relevant right now, (2) is it relatively autonomous not in the sense that drive components are totally eliminated but in that they are *united* with the function or process in nonconflictual ways; thus learning can be enhanced by the fantasy of becoming "just like mommy or daddy" and not only interfered with by such an idea.

From the point of view of development, then, learning requires (1) the availability of basic tools, (2) the harnessing of potential interferences with the learning process, such as too-intense affect or too-impulsive behavior, that can disrupt attention and intake, and (3) the achievement and maintenance of a secondary autonomy from drives and their attendant fantasies. In addition, with reference to developmental lines, and though it is not as widespread in its relation to the normal range of the psychopathology of learning, I shall have to introduce issues in the development of self-other differentiation, object constancy, and object relations in order to clarify one particular area of learning disturbance.

Let us turn now to an examination of some clinical material to see how differentiations among the disturbances of learning can be made with these developmental lines as background. I shall include instances with problems of a built-in nature and of a psychogenic nature, as well as various distinctions within and mixes between the two. The illustrations are organized under eight headings: problems of general intelligence, specific cognitive disabilities, interrelation of cognitive deficits and broader psychological functioning, learning problems secondary to other psychological conditions, learning failure as a specific symptom, learning failure as part of a general character trait, learning failure as a reflection of disturbance in object relations, and family-based disinterest in learning. "Learning" is of course not a unity in itself; I shall be drawing upon interferences with various aspects of that process and with various areas of information intake that may be disturbed.

Problems of general intelligence. Obviously, sometimes a child's reported "problem" of learning reflects his having a lower level of general intelligence than parents or teachers realize. I mention this not only for the sake of completeness but because it comes up as a problem in clinical work. It may become a problem for the child, but it starts as a problem for the parents or educators in their role of goal setters.

Some children, because their eyes are bright and their facial expression winning, or because their social grace is captivating, or because they are very verbal, or because their parents are quite successful, or for none of these reasons but because of parental hopes, are taken to be brighter than they are. This can be at any level: children whose work is fair rather than excellent or poor rather than adequate. Were the clinician to accept the problem as defined by the parent, even find rationale in the perennial intelligence test conclusion that "this score does not represent his true optimal level of functioning" (an often accurate but often misused phrase), or find no need to make an adequate intellectual assessment at all and work with the child around his so-called learning failure, then the problem becomes compounded.

No need to beat a dead horse. Such problems exist. I have more than once encountered resistance to the conclusion "low intelligence" in clinic or private work. The diagnostic task is adequate assessment; the therapeutic one, work with parents and school toward a realistic view of the child to avoid creating secondary problems for him. Easily said, but not easily done. We well know that in some families and in most schools, intelligence is intensely, often irrationally, valued. To help parents to develop a realistic view without the consequence that the child is seen as deficient and without provoking irrational feelings of guilt or failure in the parents is a task of no small delicacy and magnitude.

Problems of specific cognitive disabilities. In a book on the theme of psychoanalytic contributions to an understanding of development and psychopathology, one may wonder why specific cognitive disabilities (and also problems of general intelligence) are included. They are included because there *has* been a psychoanalytic (or at least psychodynamic) contribution in this area, albeit a negative one. That is, it has been all too easy to find psychodynamic "reasons" for any learning failure, especially since fantasies are bound to be attached to any significant failure and the clinical method provides the clinician with no good basis for distinguishing fantasy as "cause" from fantasy as secondary consequence. Additionally, I list cognitive disabilities here for completeness, because the working clinician should have knowledge of his full range of options, and because these disabilities exist in people who "have psychodynamics," so to speak, and almost inevitably become interlaced with the individual's defense system, wishes, self-esteem, and object relations.

Two brief illustrations of the phenomenon of specific disabilities: Some years ago, I consulted with a father and his preadolescent daughter on her problems in learning to read. Tutoring had not helped; the school regularly threatened failure and urged therapy. The girl herself seemed by and large rather well-functioning, related, adequately expressive, adequately controlled. Numerous test findings suggested a deficit in the capacity for organization of the visual field; though the negative case cannot be proved, nothing in the test or consultation findings suggested a specific psychological "meaning" for this failing. The problem slowed her enormously in her comprehension of the printed page. Interestingly, just at the time of this consultation, the girl had become fascinated with photography as a hobby. That fact fit. My impression was that she inarticulately sensed her disability and that photography was a kind of mastery, a turning of passive to active—it organized the visual field for her. I had follow-up many years later. She never had therapy; her reading never did more than inch along; and she became a professional photographer.

A second child, presenting pervasive and crippling pseudoimbecility (chap. 14), gradually (and only partially) gave that up during a long period of intensive psychotherapy. His intelligence blossomed in social perceptivity and language use. Some areas of school learning slowly gained over time, but many gaps remained, especially in arithmetic skills. While, again, the negative case cannot be proved, my impression was that the arithmetic failure reflected specific disabilities in various aspects of number concepts and could not improve with the general freeing of intelligence. Thus, what we had after therapy had begun to have its impact was a residual specific cognitive deficit. Just as a depressed paraplegic who recovers from his depression will show livelier facial movement but still will not walk, so, too, work on psychological aspects of learning will not automatically aid certain specific disabilities.

The growing attention to minimal cerebral dysfunction calls attention to problems such as these but also obscures and overstates for the uninformed. For what I am describing here is not a single syndrome, not necessariy a syndrome (a connected set of signs) at all, not necessarily including hyperactivity or poor attention span, for example (neither of these two children showed hyperactivity or poor attention span), but specific failings in specific areas. As people vary in height and eye color, in visual acuity and general intelligence, so too can they vary (presumably for neurological reasons) in specific cognitive capacities. L. Benjamin (1968, 1969, 1971) has done considerable work in the assessment and tailor-made remediation of such disabilities in children who show a deficit of the basic tools for at least certain kinds of learning. Although work with these children may at times involve major dynamic therapeutic issues and may involve sensitive work with parents, much of the work is also remedial and supportive in relation to their real difficulties in the educational environment.

Interrelations of specific cognitive deficits and broader psychological functioning. Though the distinction is necessarily arbitrary, I discuss these phenomena separately from specific cognitive deficits for clarity of exposition. I am still focusing on specific deficits, presumably with a neurological basis, that affect learning; but here I shall focus on their secondary effects in interplay with the child's intrapsychic life. In particular, I am concerned with reactions to the deficit and with the deficit as a nodal point for further symptom formation.

A child was brought to me for psychological assessment. The symptom picture (failures in writing and drawing, among other things) and a previous assessment were highly suggestive of specific problems in visual-motor co-ordination; he could also spell well orally but not in writing. The father's instruction to me was, however, "Don't tell me he's brain-damaged, I've already been told that." Indeed, the data again suggested visual-motor co-ordination problems. One especially revealing moment was the boy's attempt to draw a rocket. He could not get his hand to turn the pencil to make the angles go in the direction he wished; yet his eye could easily see that his final drawing was grossly distorted in its angles. The capacity for visual-motor coordination was flawed, but the negative visual feedback was received. The boy, pervasively anxious and embarrassed with regard to his deficit, wishing to please his father, who refused to acknowledge the deficit, and trying to turn the passive (failure) into active (success), announced to me with feigned enthusiasm that he was going to be a blueprint designer when he grew up. To my response (after our work was nearly completed) that he had real skills but, that blueprint design was not among them, that I thought he knew that from his rocket drawing, and that he was intelligent and could, however, do many other things successfully, he responded with enormous relief and the touching exclamation: "This has been the best day of my life!" I believe that the failure (of which he was aware but could not understand) plus the paternal denial pushed the boy into a brittle denial of the reality that he experienced every day (his failures) and left him preoccupied, on the edge of humiliation, and vulnerable (in self-esteem and in reality testing) to each new failure.

Such secondary reactions to deficit are not rare. Although "secondary" in a causal sense, they can be of major impact for the child's functioning. (I think here, also, of children with depressed mood and low self-esteem secondary to reading problems or to neurologically based problems in the acquisition of other skills.) The therapeutic problem is not minor. These children, and their parents, have to be helped to understand the reality of the deficit, including understanding of its *specificity*—that is, that the child is not totally "damaged." But such information itself can (after the common response of "seeing the light," as many facts of the child's life fit into place) produce further depression or denial. My experience is that when these secondary reactions are reasonably well established, only a period of intensive psychotherapy will break into them, quite apart from the patient's specific remedial needs.

A different phenomenon in this domain: Like the views of "somatic compliance" in psychosomatic illness, which held that biologically weak organs would be the ones to show malfunction related to psychological conflict, so too specific cognitive disabilities can become nodal points for symptom formation. For example a child with a dyslexic syndrome experienced inordinate confusion in her struggle with the printed page. Subsequently, when strong aggressive or sexual impulses were aroused, they culminated in parallel states of confusion. An anlage for experience had been laid down. The two came together especially in school, where impulse arousal led to "confusion" and thus further learning failure in nondeficit areas. The latter learning failure (math, history) gave way with interpretation of intrapsychic conflict, but not so the dyslexia. Incidentally, it should be clear that without psychotherapy we are unlikely even to be aware of such subtle interconnections of functioning, let alone work toward resolving them.

Learning problems secondary to other psychological conditions. In discussing the positions on various developmental lines that a child must have attained for learning to take place I suggested that a child must be able to hold in abeyance those powerful affect states or behavioral impulses that, when present, can disrupt the attentiveness and receptivity requisite for learning. The absence of affect- or impulse-control reflects problems that, although not focal to learning, nonetheless affect learning. Some children who show failure to learn need help, not primarily in the area of learning, but in other areas that have a secondary impact on the learning process.

Examples are, unfortunately, not hard to find. Janey, an abused and neglected child, was "not doing any work at all" in school, and this, combined with severe behavior problems and absenteeism, led to her clinic referral. Extremely needy, preoccupied with wishes for, fears of, and in general thoughts about her mother, this child showed near-average intelligence and no specific cognitive disabilities upon close assessment. Emotions were her problem; nonlearning was a secondary effect, one of many areas affected by her extraordinarily painful home situation. Preoccupied with her mother and anxieties linked to that relationship, she was unable to focus on learning. Put in contact with a tutor, the child began to learn. No specialized (deficit linked) remediation techniques were needed. Rather, the one-to-one relationship itself toned down her neediness and permitted attention to learning; even more, the learning became the vehicle for the relationship to the tutor and was fostered (by the child herself) as a mode of contact.

Other disruptive states operate similarly. An eight-year-old boy would get depressed each time a favorite pet was given away; learning would cease at these times. While nonlearning had the secondary gain of an attack on his family, who gave the pets away, the depression was primary and affected many areas beyond learning. Another boy, with fragile ego structure, was preoccupied with wishes for and fears of the destruction of his mother and therefore stayed home with the fantasy of safeguarding her and could not learn even when he was in school. Similarly, chronic thought disorder or pervasive behavior problems (constant fighting and running in the classroom) will obviously have effects on learning.

Each of these children shows a specific area of difficulty (learning) that can be understood and worked with therapeutically only by taking into account the broader pathology of which it is probably a relatively minor part. This is by no means the case with all psychogenic learning problems. Let me turn now to some quite different clincial pictures where the learning failure is far more central.

Learning failure as specific symptom. I have described learning failures resulting from deficiencies in the tools of learning (general intelligence or specific deficits) and from the learning process being swamped by other disorders of affect, thought, or behavior. But the process of learning *in itself* can be invested with psychological meaning that leads to interferences. Here we come to more classical neurotic pictures with bound symptoms that eventuate from conflict between impulse and defense. We see interferences with the secondary autonomy of the learning process, an invasion of the *process* itself or of specific *content* areas by conflictual fantasies.

Thus, learning can come to be equated with knowing about sexual events or family secrets and in either case can succumb to an inhibition in school that parallels the repression of ideas connected with sex and/or secrets. Allen (1967) has described voyeuristic and exhibitionistic conflicts interfering with seeing/knowing or "showing" what one knows. And the group working out of the Judge Baker Child Guidance Center in the 1950s and early 1960s described other essentially neurotic interferences with learning—for example, where success stimulates castration anxiety (Sperry et al., 1958; Grunebaum et al., 1962). In these instances, learning (as a process) and knowledge (as potentially taboo content) are the central targets of the pathological formation, not secondary to anything else. Just how it becomes that way is something we know little about at the level of general clinical theory, but we learn much about it in the in-depth study of each individual when intensive treatment is undertaken.

Sometimes the interference is much more specific. For example, a child referred because his school grades were falling sharply turned out to have a specific interference with the writing process. He had begun to write so slowly, with such a burden of inhibition, that he never finished his tests and would therefore get low grades. The fantasy that writing was an aggressive act, more specifically that writing involved "signing a death warrant," turned out to be central, and had taken shape after the death of a relative. In other children, neurotic interference with specific content areas also occurs: difficulty learning about wars in history class in a child struggling with aggressive impulses; failure in English composition in a boy who was anxious about whether body parts were "long enough" and felt compelled to lengthen his sentences until they became grammatically incorrect and unintelligible. In each of these instances, the specific school failure has an intrapsychic "meaning"; something about learning process or content has become involved in intrapsychic fantasy and conflict, has lost its affective neutrality in the process, and has become subject to defensive avoidance or other interference.

Learning failure as part of a general character trait. I have just described psychological disturbances that have specific impact on particular aspects of learning process or content. I would like now to turn to interference somewhat less precisely directed at learning per se—that is, to maladaptive character traits that subsume aspects of the learning process. That learning is interfered with is no accidental secondary effect, but nor is learning itself the focal or original "target" of the psychopathological process. Thus, broad characteristic features of a child such as a generalized inhibition (linked to unconscious active impulses) or avoidance of success or achievement (having roots in oedipal fantasies) will affect modes of play, of movement, of relatedness—and of learning as well. The issues will be structurally similar regarding those other impairments and learning even though learning itself is not the central focus of the difficulty.

For example, an eleven-year-old girl was referred by her pediatrician, who could find no organic basis for her constant fatigue. Home reports were that she was "lazy," often "lethargic." A picture gradually emerged of a very ambitious-aggressive young girl caught in an (oedipal) rivalry with a bright and successful stepsister. She defended against her active wishes by a turn to passivity and "lethargy," which affected her schoolwork as well. Learning became impaired; work output slowed; grades went down. Success, activity, ambition in general were renounced; learning, one more form of activity and success, was drawn into the inhibition.

Learning failure as a reflection of disturbance in object relations. While the disturbances of learning that I am now going to describe are of psychogenic origin and can be said to have a "meaning" to the person, I distinguish them from those just described (specific symptom and character trait) because of what I believe is the greater severity of the diagnostic picture. Based on disturbances in earliest object relations, they show, as do other sequelae of such early disturbances, the profound developmentally distorting impact of failures and aberrations in the mother-child dyad.

In recent years, two female patients, one a middle-aged adult and one a college student, told me about school difficulties in similar terms. Each could not do well because she could not study or do homework. And each could not study because the process, the sustained engagement with inanimate words and books, produced profound and painful feelings of aloneness. The result: flight into sociability, talk, no work, poor grades. Although both patients were well beyond childhood, both dated the problem back to that time. Both patients were sensitive and articulate; I think perhaps it would be quite difficult for a child to verbalize this material. There was an important difference in the early childhood experiences of these two patients, a difference that was reflected in the further subtleties of the painful feeling of aloneness. One had had early, repeated experiences of object loss; the love object (mother) was experienced as a differentiated other but was periodically lost. While studying, this patient's experience was one of isolation and the need for contact. The other patient had had early experiences that interfered with self-other differentiation; her life showed cycles of panic over merging (loss of differentiation) and a heightened sense of individuality (differentiation) accompanied by feelings of loss of connectedness to her family. Studying produced that sense of individuality and was accompanied by feelings, not only of isolation, but of fear of merging as well. The wish underlying the fear, the wish to terminate the isolation through merging, ultimately became clear. Neither patient had developed that "capacity to be alone" (Winnicott, 1958b), here alone with work, that comes from carrying the sense of the mother's presence inside.

A related report, this time of work with young children, shows early disturbances of learning that are linked to pathological mother-child narcissism (Newman et al., 1973). The children, all bright and precociously verbal, were their mother's pride; their intellectual functioning, especially the precocious speech, came to be experienced as an extention of the mother's narcissism. When these children reached school, they did poorly. (Admission to this research project was by way of being a "gifted underachiever.") What had happened, broadly, was that intellect had become part of the connectedness to mother, not a tool for learning about the nonmother world; and, further, because of the narcissistic investment in intellectual precocity, failure could not be risked by making the effort to learn; self-esteem vulnerability was too great.

Family-based disinterest in learning. Another phenomenon of sociocultural and educational significance should be mentioned in passing, though it rarely comes to us as a clinical problem in its own right. It has to do with those children, often the ghetto poor, for whom there are no family models for the value of learning, little or no family support for their learning, and little in the economic-cultural surround holding promise for those who learn. Many (by no means all) of these children learn poorly. But to say there is "learning failure" is to presume that they share goals of the society at large and have failed to meet them. It is not at all clear that this is the case; I would think instead of motivational, identificatory, and, especially, socioeconomic problems in work in this area.

To sum up regarding disturbances of learning, I have suggested that learning requires the child's adequate movement along developmental lines associated with growth of the basic cognitive tools of the learning process; maintenance of the relative autonomy of the learning process such that it does not suffer repression, inhibition, or other malfunction because it has been invested with conflict-ridden symbolic meaning; the harnessing of affective and behavioral interference with the attentional-receptive processes requisite for learning to take place; and the development of adequate self-other differentiation, object constancy, and early object relations so that peremptory needs for object contact do not make work in isolation impossible. Along the way, I have attempted to specify both the particular aspect of the learning process or content that is impaired (i.e., the presenting problem and its variations) and the psychological or neuropsychological route to that impairment (i.e., the underlying genetic and structural sources of the problem and their variations). From a clincial-therapeutic point of view I have called attention to issues requiring (1) careful assessment of cognitive skills and capacities; (2) guidance and education for parent and/or child; (3) sensitive handling of the affective accompaniments to information regarding deficits; (4) work with children around their secondary reactions to deficits of which they have an inarticulate awareness; (5) recognition of the need at times for remediation, at times for therapy, and at times for both; (6) recognition also that some disturbances of learning are secondary consequences of major affect, thought, behavioral, or even sociocultural disturbances which require primary attention in their own right; and (7) the need for intensive treatment of some learning disturbances that reflect the development of bound and focal symptoms, of pathological character traits, or the end result of early disturbances in object relations.

BEHAVIOR DISTURBANCES

Although we accept behavior as an omnipresent part of life, we certainly cannot view behavior disorder with like equanimity, and pathology involving the behavioral sphere is of great significance for clinical management. At its worst destructive of self or others, even the milder forms of behavioral disturbance have impacts upon the interpersonal sphere, not only the intraphysic one. As such, they are highly visible and are often red-flag warnings evoking the concern of parents, teachers, the courts, and others in contact with the child.

In spite of their importance, and perhaps because of their omnipresence, disturbances of behavior do not have any very specific diagnostic significance. They spring from many developmental sources and are found in varying personality contexts. In this section I shall once again try to describe and clarify some of the internal features of the broad landscape of behavior disturbances.

First, let us imagine a child who engages in compulsive rituals that involve his walking around his room at bedtime to arrange its contents in particular ways, or a child with tics that involve flailing motions of the arms or posturing of the whole body, or a child who is a sleepwalker, wandering in his home at night. In each of these instances, motor behavior (large movements of the voluntary musculature) is enmeshed in some inner psychopathological system, but they are unlikely to be called "behavior disturbances" by working clinicians. Clinical custom reserves the term for those disturbed behaviors that have an antisocial or at least interpersonally disruptive component. They are troublesome or dangerous in some way. These are often called "behavior *disorders*," a term that remains imprecise diagnostically (i.e., it fails to indicate what may be going on under the descriptive behavioral surface) but that I shall try to specify further as we go along.

Behavior disorders are a characteristic form of pathology in the school-age child for at least three reasons, all having to do with the child's position in the developmental ladder. First, school makes a great demand for motor restraint. With the exception of a very few, quite atypical school programs that allow a great deal of free movement, the child is seated at a desk for several hours each day. Not only does this place a great demand upon his capacity for motor restraint, but violations of that restraint come to be perceived as socially disturbing acts reflecting individual disturbance. The traditional shouting and running of young children as the end-of-day school-bell rings attest to the coiled-spring quality of the motor apparatus as that spring tightens through the long school day. Second, if we see development (as I believe we can) as a more or less steady movement toward decreased need for motor activity, or an increased capacity for sedentary activity as cognitive potentials expand, it becomes clear that the school-age child is still at the very early end of that continuum. Starting from the seemingly unending and exuberant capacity for movement in the young toddler, just learning to crawl and then walk, and culminating in the sedentary lives of the aged a lifetime later, movement plays a declining role in human life. Mittelmann (1954) speaks of an early motor phase in the second year and Mahler (1972) discusses roughly the same time in terms of a normal motor "practicing" period of great activity. Motility serves expressive, adaptive, and defensive functions. It gives pleasure, releases tension, serves as communication, and is a basis for peer relationships through play. That the motor apparatus should be involved in disturbed behavior as well comes as no surprise in this context. And the third developmentally linked reason why motor behavior is an expectable area for disturbance in the school-age child, in contrast to the toddler, is that the school-age child not only is very active but has motor capacities for strength and independent action that make his behavior a potential source of concern for others when it goes awry. He can hurt himself or others; he can run away; he can steal or cause property damage; he can disrupt a classroom. So we have, in the school-age years, the setting for multiple disturbances in the motor domain: a child naturally motoric, with the capacity for motor behavior of wide injurious as well as constructive range, and often (in school) in a setting where motor restraint is emphasized and motor action is disruptive. (I do not mean to imply that these problems would go away if schools only would allow more activity. Would that problems were so simply resolved! I am only trying to describe the setting for the child's vulnerabilities.)

There is considerable diagnostic confusion in the area of behavior disorders. In 1966 a working committee of the Group for the Advancement of Psychiatry proposed a classification of childhood psychopathology in which they listed (though they did not endorse!) no fewer than eleven terms frequently used diagnostically. Their overall definition is compatible with the one I am using here: "Children in this category exhibit chronic behavioral patterns of emotional expression of aggressive and sexual impulses which conflict with society's norms" (p. 254). Among the listed terms are several that can be used to highlight some of the sources of confusion in this area.

Thus, "antisocial personality," "sociopathic personality," and "dyssocial personality" are all purely descriptive terms; such a "personality" could behave in nonsocialized ways out of allegiance to a deviant subculture, out of neurotic self-defeating urges, or out of defective development of conscience, among other reasons. However, such terms as "psychopathic personality" or "impulsive character" purport to have specific diagnostic significance (the former in relation to conscience development and the latter in relation to characteristic features of action/delay or drive/defense relationships). Even in these instances, however, there is far from complete agreement on the meaning of the terms. In any event, their applicability in any particular case requires a depth-oriented, interior view of the person and not simply a symptom-descriptive approach. Still other terms in the list of eleven, such as "affectionless character" and "acting-out personality," have little agreed-upon meaning at all.

The GAP report's very real contribution to clarification is embodied in its delineation of two subtypes: (1) impulse-ridden personality (characterized by poor impulse control and little anxiety, guilt, or attachment to others); and (2) neurotic personality disorders, whose "behavior often assumes a repetitive character, with unconscious symbolic significance to their acts, rather than the predominance of discharge phenomena" (p. 249). (A revealing contradiction in this formulation comes in grouping these two under the overall term "tension-discharge disorders" even though the second is said not to have a "predominance of discharge phenomena.")

Behavior is of course inherent at every point in the life cycle. In childhood it includes at least exploratory behavior in new situations (Berlyne, 1960; White, 1963); "functionlust" (Hendrick, 1942), or pleasure in and exercise of capacities for functioning such as the grasp or eye-hand coordination early on, and hopping, jumping, racing in the school years; fight/flight reactions in the face of danger (Bowlby, 1969), and what we would designate as "appropriate" behavioral expression in the service of need satisfaction or tension reduction (e.g., in eating, going to mother). All these reflect evolutionary continuity; they are sources of the impetus to action that are characteristic of all the higher animal species. There is another normal form of behavior that is characteristic of human beings, whether or not of any other animal species. Referred to by Freud in his writing on the repetition compulsion (1920b), it involves the general tendency to repeat actively what we experience passively; thus, a child is frightened of an operation and then plays doctor, or is frightened of too-fast a car ride and then zooms his toy cars around his room. *All* these (exploration, exercise of capacities, fight/flight, gratification-seeking or pain-avoiding, and active repetition of things experienced passively) are expressed in the motor domain (among others), yet *no one* of them reflects behavior disorder. If anything, their absence, their inhibition, may reflect disorder of another kind. Nonetheless, any one of them can shade over into pathology in ways that may or may not be clear from the outside. Let me give two examples. They are intended as arguments for the need for an inner view of any behavior in order to understand its specifics and to know how to approach it therapeutically. Such an inner view represents the specification I have in mind within the "behavior disorders."

A mother who had brought her twelve-year-old son for help said that he "always ran away." I immediately wondered (silently, to myself) about the solidity of his delay/defense capacities and the stability of his attachment to his mother. But when I learned, in response to my question about his running away, that this behavior began at about age fifteen to eighteen months, when he "would always run down the street and I would have to dash after him to get him," my inner formulation shifted rapidly. Here seemed to be a mother not only with no understanding of the normal mode of motor activity of the toddler but one, perhaps, who imposed her fantasy explanations on those behaviors when they occurred. When I next heard that he also ran away (this time more seriously, to various places in the neighborhood, but for short times only) several times at about age nine or ten, I had to entertain various explanatory notions in the light of the history. Was this a "behavior disorder"? What would that mean? Was he impulsive, insufficiently aware of the consequences of his acts, insufficiently attached to mother? As the case turned out, this was the *form* of his attachment to mother. He acted on her expectations of his "badness" (and in ways specific to her fantasies, such as the running away) and was then punished in the setting of a sadomasochistic mother-child bond. Misbehavior and punishment were essential to their relationship; as he later (age 13) said to me: "How would I know she loved me if she didn't punish me?" Interestingly, in his midteens a new symptomatic act emerged transiently, that of wandering through the streets to fixed locations in a semi-fugue-like, obligatory state. Our work revealed this to be a repetition of a forgotten traveling incident with his father, who had disappeared from his life many years before; so "wandering" (a form of running away) had yet another *object-related* connection in his life: now to his father as well as to his mother. What we see here is neurotic character pathology—structuralized, ego-syntonic, object-related, and characteristic—that expresses itself in seemingly unsocialized behavior as well as in other areas.

Let us look at a second instance, or rather set of instances, where normal behavior (as in the first child's "running away" at 15 months) shades into disturbed behavior: A young child came dangerously close to being hit by a passing truck as he crossed a street with an adult, the adult quickly picking him up out of harm's way as the truck raced past; in his home afterward, he went to play with his trucks, controlling their movements in his play. The passive experience is turned to an active one as a means to mastery. Constructive; hardly pathological. But take another child for whom the passive experience is one of being beaten and who then goes to school and beats up others. The inner situation is similar to that of the first child—mastery of a passive experience through active repetition—but the second child would present as a "behavior disorder." To proceed hypothetically for a moment, if the first child continued at his truck play for days on end, the play becoming more compulsive, repetitious, less pleasurable, we would begin to consider that a minipathological process was at work, that the movement toward mastery had gone awry. But, although the reflection of the disturbance is in motor play, we certainly would not call it a "behavior disorder" since it does not break social rules. Yet, to switch back now to another actual situation, parallel phenomena (from an intrapsychic viewpoint) would be considered indices of behavior disorder if they did violate social rules. Thus, a particular child who chronically felt weak and unmanly would regularly, in a driven way, climb to high places, race up and down stairs, and in general take risks as a means of compensatory reversal of those feelings. Such behavior at home or at school led to the complaint that he was "hyperactive." I adduce these examples to show how normal behavior can shade into disturbed behavior. But I also want to emphasize how much of our labeling of behavior disorders comes from external, social criteria, even though we know very little about the "disordered behavior" without an understanding of its interior features. With this in mind, I should like to describe a number of phenomena that satisfy the *external* definition (antisocial or interpersonally disruptive action) in order to show differentiations in the interior circumstances underlying them. Which of these should properly be called "behavior disorders" is essentially an optional matter, though one requiring definition by consensus based on a reasonable rationale. While I shall make a proposal regarding this later on, my major aim is to describe at least a sample of the array of interior circumstances associated with disruptive action because an understanding of that array is critical to both the diagnostic and the therapeutic processes.

We often speak of "*tension discharge*" through the motor apparatus. Precisely what is meant by "tension" or "discharge" is generally not clear; but "tension discharge" is a phenomenological language, on the model of a corked bottle where pressure builds up and the cork pops. And yet, corks and pressure interact in different ways. A well-corked bottle may indeed build up great pressure and pop the cork; but a cork may incompletely seal the bottle, having a slight air leak, and then pressure will be released in a slow leak; or, finally, the cork may be so loose as not to require any real pressure buildup before it comes off. Psychological parallels can be drawn to each of these three situations.

In its most vivid presentation, the "popped cork" version of "tension discharge" is an "outburst." A child (or an adult, for that matter), ordinarily reasonably self-controlled, "reaches his limit" or "blows his top." When he is deprived/frustrated, or insulted/humiliated, or provoked/injured, he lashes out—hitting, perhaps crying, perhaps cursing, perhaps all of these. In recognition of the atypicality of this response we say that "he wasn't himself." There need not be external provocation; the outburst may come once or regularly, as the outcome of inner experiences, conflicts, anger, longings. The point I wish to emphasize is that *very real and substantial controls* over behavioral expression exist in such instances, even though they give way episodically, allowing socially disruptive behavior to emerge. In partial contrast, though also with important parallels regarding the presence of inner controls, are those finger-tapping, knee-bouncing children whose motor restlessness is often evident but whose "contained" restlessness, a kind of overflow phenomenon, is also indicative of the presence and maintenance of great control. Like the infant who sucks or rocks, and in contrast to the infant who screams and thrashes around or the toddler who races everywhere, there is a *limited* motor outlet here that permits a great deal of control to be retained. The parallel is to the cork that holds under pressure but has an air leak. There is a kind of slow release valve in situations where major motor restraint is required (e.g., in school). Although the motor overflow may have nuisance qualities, it is rarely viewed as a "behavior disorder," having no major anti-social, interpersonally disruptive aspect.

There is another situation that looks superficially like "tension discharge" but where, in actuality, little tension is either built up or "discharged." The cork is not really on tight at all, and it takes no pressure to release it. I refer to children in whom an impulse (to hit, to steal, to grab food, to run out of the classroom) has ready access to action, to motor pathways, with little or no delay, little or no cognitive or defensive working over of the impulse as a mediating process. In D. Shapiro's (1965) work on impulse disorders he attributes this phenomenon to a defect in planning, in the capacity to envision consequences of action; and he reserves the term "impulse disorder" for just this phenomenon. While I believe that the planning/anticipatory defect may be only part of the picture (albeit a substantial part), I would also propose, following Shapiro, that the term "behavior disorder" is best reserved for this constellation of minimal control, of minimal cognitive mediation of impulse, ready access of impulse to motor pathways. In an internal diagnostic sense (rather than simply an external-social sense), this gives the term "behavior disorder" some specificity and diagnostic significance. Although this phe-nomenon is seen clearly in adolescents and adults, it can be identified in early and middle childhood when the normal developmental achievement of delay over automatic motor expression of impulse should have been attained.

Turning to quite different internal phenomena that may, however, still be called behavior disorders from an *exterior* view, I should like to describe neurotic character disorders or neurotic symptom disorders that culminate in disturbances in the behavioral realm. Freud first discussed such a phenom-enon (in adults) in his paper on some character types met with in psychoan-alytic work (1916), specifically *criminals from a sense of guilt*. There he describes a person whose criminality has the unconscious aim of justifying a preexisting sense of guilt; it creates a cause for an already present affect. By extension, the point I wish to make is that these behavioral disturbances have uncon-scious meanings in a context of impulse derivatives in fantasy, of guilt, and of compromise formation—just as other neurotic symptoms do. The boy I described earlier as always "running away" presents such a picture; his running away reflects neither a defect in delay nor a gap in superego but rather the expression in action of unconscious memories and the form of his attachment to both his mother and his father. In short, the action expresses a fantasy in compromise (disguised) form.

The phenomenon is not rare. Children whose constant fighting and prov-ocation are attempts to reverse feelings of weakness, damage, and passivity illustrate it. Similarly the phenomenon is seen in a child whose stealing reflects, not the needy desire for food of a deprived child whose longing is not subject to control and delay, but instead dramatizes an oedipal-level fantasy—say, of possessing the mother (taking her "valuables") or of reversing the loss (in fantasy) of a penis by the theft of a water pistol. In each of these instances, the disturbed behavior serves some unconscious aim. As such, the behavior is the end product of a complex cognitive process, reflecting delay, defense formation, and disguise, and is hardly a simple failure of control.

In his paper on ego disturbances, Redl (1951) emphasizes how critical it is for us to have a refined conception of the particular area of ego disturbance in individual instances. Relevant to our present concern, he refers to a psychotic child who attacks a child-care worker under the delusional idea that he (the worker) is the child's (hated) father. He differentiates this from other forms of attack by a child, although each culminates in disturbed behavior that may look the same. Thus, hypothetically in his paper, one child has no delay capacity in the face of some frustration of need and attacks the frustrating person. Another, with substantial delay capacity, expresses all that pent-up (delayed) rage against the father, but does so under the sway of the delusional idea and perceptual distortion that a nonfather *is* the father. If we consider, in addition, that it may be precisely such a distortion that permits the expression of rage, we see here again that considerable cognitive work has gone on between impulse and expression in this psychotic child.

Yet another phenomenon often subsumed under the term "behavior disorder" involves those expressions of "antisocial" behavior that themselves reflect socialized behavior within a particular deviant subculture. In the case of adolescent marijuana usage today, we can no longer even refer to a "deviant" subculture. Marijuana smoking is part and parcel of identification with a group, acceptance of its values, and connectedness in reliable patterns of relationship to others within it. Within *this* group, some—whose drug use is excessive or otherwise eccentric—may themselves be viewed as outsiders, or at least no longer governed by the shared guiding values of the group. Some instances of childhood theft or gang fighting similarly reflect socialized behavior within a particular family or group subculture. This does not imply that clinicians need not be concerned with such behavior or that it might not simultaneously reflect failures in delay, reactions against depression, or the acting out of an unconscious fantasy in a particular individual. Quite the reverse; it may reflect any of these, or others, which is precisely why the externally identifiable antisocial behavior has so little specific diagnostic value.

In the preceding material, I have taken the term "behavior disorder" loosely to refer to actions that have an asocial or interpersonally disruptive aspect. But then I have tried to demonstrate that a number of quite different interior circumstances may underly such action. Diagnosis, which I see precisely as the process of understanding external signs through understanding of their inner structure and genetic roots, and which then speaks to issues of treatment technique, is obviously enhanced by taking such an interior view. Since behavior is omnipresent in human functioning and is certainly a central aspect of the active lives of young children, its disturbances can appear in any pathological context; what I have given here can be regarded only as a sample of the range.

My aim has been to detail some of the wide array of phenomena subsumable under the term "behavior disorder." But my personal preference, as already noted, is to reserve that term for those children characterized by a failure of delay between impulse and action. I have emphasized *failure of delay*. The delay of automatic motor or affectomotor expression as need or affect mounts is a major achievement of development in the infancy to early childhood period, and its failure has important consequences. In the foregoing examples, I have tried to show that some reflect such failures of delay while others reflect a considerable amount of "cognitive working over." In these latter instances, delay, control, and disguise have taken place and the disordered behavior is embedded in memories, fantasies, cognitive/perceptual distortions, bound symptoms, and/or character traits.

Just how the failure of delay develops or, rather, why delay does not develop is another issue. I believe that delay normally develops from a number of interlocking circumstances. (1) The infant has sufficient experience of gratification and relief following upon need that he begins to trust that relief will come again, and so he can *sustain tension states* next time around in ancitipation of relief. (2) The child who is thus developing a "basic trust" in his caretakers can scan his environment expectantly and learn about its features (since he will not be in a desperate, panicky, tearful state), thus learning where need satisfaction/tension relief will come from. And (3), although substantially later, a marked additional force is added to the tendency toward control and delay through the internalization of parental standards, the formation of conscience, with its accompanying affect of guilt that tends to accentuate control processes. According to this reasoning, the *failure* to develop the capacity (or tendency) to delay impulse expression may be seen as the inverse of these normal developments: (1) insufficient attachment to, or empathy for, others—reflecting failures in early trusting object relations—can lead a child to express his impulse without regard to others; (2) insufficient cognitive elaboration of possibility, of alternatives, of plans (cf. D. Shapiro, 1965) may follow upon the infant's absorption in his (unsatisfied) inner state when the surround insufficiently brought relief and he has not learned to explore it expectantly for relief; and (3) failures in conscience development, the absence of guilt, will further permit a ready access to impulse expression when those earlier tendencies are already present.

Above, I suggested reserving the term "behavior disorder" for instances "characterized by failure of delay." I have discussed the failure of delay but would now like to say a word also on the phrase "characterized by." I have in mind here the point Fenichel (1945) makes in his distinction between the "neurosis" and the "neurotic conflict." In brief, the latter is a focal conflict between "the drives, that is the id, and the ego" (p. 129); we speak of a neurosis, however, only when that focal conflict has developed further, influencing a larger sphere of behavior, be this symptom or character trait. Similarly, I would suggest that the term "behavior disorder" might usefully be reserved for those instances of failure of delay between impulse and action, those absences of cognitive working over, that are *characteristic* of a particular child, are repeated, predictable modes of reaction to an array of impulses and an array of settings.

In this chapter I have tried to do several things. First, I have tried to describe some of the characteristic descriptive features and developmental issues of the age seven to ten period, the later period of latency (Bornstein, 1951), when the child is normally solidly involved in the world of school and peer relations. Second, I have selected two of the characteristic areas of pathology of that age group (learning disturbances and behavior disturbances) and tried to show their relationships to the developmental issues of the age. Emphasizing that those disturbances are characteristic of but not specific to this age period, I tried to show that they are frequent precisely because of their tie to the developmental issues of the age. And finally, I have attempted to give a highly differentiated picture of the variations within each of these domains of pathology, attempting to demonstrate that an interior view adds considerably to our appreciation of the specificity and complexity of particular presenting pictures (cf. A. Freud, 1970).

I have attempted to discuss the developmental failures underlying each pathological presentation (and the normal developmental pathways that these children have been unable to follow) and the many genetic and structural distinctions in varying presenting pictures within each area. A particular view of the therapeutic process underlies these choices: the choice of detailed discussion of development and of diagnostic specificity and lesser discussion of treatment technique per se. In this view the two detailed aspects of the discussion are in fact central to the issue of therapeutic technique.

Knowledge of development can be invaluable to the therapeutic enterprise. In chapter 10, I tried to show that therapy (even psychoanalytic therapy as it is traditionally carried out) can be viewed in part as a process of facilitation of normal development in addition to the more customary view of it as a process of correction of interruptions and aberrations of development. Certainly in childhood, with developmental change still proceeding rapidly, this view is useful. An understanding of the current developmental tasks of a child can help us to understand the continuing pathogenic consequences of particular presenting problems (e.g., learning failure and its implications for self-esteem regulation; or school refusal and its confirmation of attachment to home and mother, making displacement to school, peers, and learning impossible). An understanding of how relevant normal developments that did *not* take place *should* have taken place (e.g., delay of impulse expression, neutralization of the learning process, development of signal anxiety and reliable internal structure) can give us clues to the historical sources of the presenting pathology. And, though developmental failures can by no means always be reversed by a later reexperiencing of the relevant developmental opportunities, an awareness of those normal modes of development can provide cues for technical interventions in individual instances.

Finally, knowledge of specific pathological mechanisms is also invaluable to the therapeutic enterprise. When Freud (1912) spoke of the analyst's "evenly suspended attention" to the associative material of the patient, he did not mean that the analyst's mind was blank, unaware of all that he had learned previously. What is intended is that the analyst not be precommitted to any single idea in that session, thus permitting new and surprising (or perhaps old and familiar) themes to achieve centrality. Our general theory of human functioning, our past knowledge of all our patients, and our knowledge of all that has transpired and is now transpiring with the particular patient in our office are all parts of what the therapist's mind should be "evenly suspended" *over*. The same holds for diagnostic specificity. Only when we have the full array in mind, only when we have learned from the accumulation of clinical knowledge, can our evenly hovering (uncommitted) clinical minds recognize the central phenomena in any particular patient, or in any particular session. The technical attitude of the therapist has to be one of exploration and discovery; but he has to be a *prepared* explorer who will recognize relevant variations in the terrain when he sees them. Only then will he understand, and only then will he be able to speak to the patient in descriptive or interpretive words that will help the patient understand, the pathological processes at work. Precision in interpretation ultimately follows from precision in understanding. Hence, an informed view of development and of specific pathological mechanisms makes possible a refined therapeutic technique.

14

Borderline Pathology in Childhood

The diagnostic term "borderline" is a spatial metaphor. It is intended to convey something about the status of certain relatively severely disturbed children who lie "between" psychosis, on the one hand, and neurosis or milder forms of pathology, on the other. It is a hazy area, but a few things can be said about the nature of the borders surrounding this domain, and a good deal can be said about the internal borders within this domain, about distinctions among the children who can be characterized in this way.

This chapter sets out to pursue these two tasks: to discuss the attributes that differentiate borderline children from those with other forms of pathology and, in so doing, to define some aspects of the borders "between" these children and the less and more disturbed; and, second, to describe a variety of syndromes found in such children, thus delineating borders "within" the domain of the borderline. While both approaches are intended to lessen the vagueness in the discussion of borderline children, the second has the additional aim of arguing against the search for a unitary concept of "the" borderline child. Just as we aim for specification beyond the diagnostic term "neurosis," we can aim for specification within the borderline domain. Although I place no value on the creation of new labels per se, I believe that the kinds of children to be described here are recognizable to most clinicians who work with children and deserve to be identified by the attributes that distinguish them from one another; labels help in that task.

In recent clinical practice, the flow of children who are given the diagnosis "borderline" has reached flood proportions. Whence the flood? The classical symptom-psychoneuroses are seen with decreasing frequency in childhood as in adulthood, and clinicians are alert instead to issues of character pa-

This chapter is a blend and revision of a paper originally published under the title "On the concept 'borderline' in children" (*Psychoanalytic Study of the Child* [29:341–368, 1974], New Haven: Yale University Press) and a second paper published as a portion of a chapter in *The Course of Life*, vol. 2, ed. S. I. Greenspan and G. H. Pollock, and in *The Borderline Child*, ed. K. S. Robson (New York: McGraw Hill, 1983).

thology, a form of pathology that can be essentially neurotic in structure but shades into more serious conditions at its more disturbed extreme. The post World-War II growth of the child guidance movement, as well as of research utilizing direct child observation, has brought to clinicians an acute awareness of the flagrant "psychopathology of everyday childhood"; and the rapid extension of clinical services to poverty and ghetto populations, following upon the civil rights battles of the 1960s and represented in the spread of Community Mental Health Centers, brought us into greater contact with children whose lives are blighted by social pathology (crime, addiction, prostitution, violence, hunger, abandonment, and so forth) as well as psychopathology, and whose overall functioning shows the toll taken by such massive pathological intrusions upon development. Additionally, the writings of a number of individuals (to be noted below) who have tried to isolate and define key intrapsychic mechanisms and/or failures in what they called borderline children (or related entities) gave a sophisticated clinical-intellectual context for formulations in this area.

Whatever its source, the frequent and increasing labeling of children as "borderline," with an associated looseness in the key meanings attached to the term, is clear. A multitude of phenomena—including isolation from others or indiscriminate relationships, nonavailability of stable defenses or rigid reliance on pathological defenses, panic states or affectlessness, hollow pseudomaturity or infantile behavior, and an assortment of peculiarities of social behavior, thought and language, or motor style—are used to produce the umbrella diagnosis: borderline. Is there something real here that so many clinicians are grasping at? Can the morass be sorted out? I shall make an attempt to answer these questions, as have a number of other writers on child psychopathology (Ekstein and Wallerstein, 1954; A. Freud, 1956; Rosenfeld and Sprince, 1963, 1965; Weil, 1953, 1956).

Some years ago, a group of colleagues and I agreed to meet regularly to discuss issues in child psychopathology. Our ready consensus was to begin with a look at the borderline child. Influenced by the writers we studied, when we saw children who had been (or could easily be) diagnosed borderline we kept concepts in mind such as the absence of phase dominance and regression to primary identification (Rosenfeld and Sprince, 1963), the tendency toward panic anxiety (Weil, 1953), fluidity of psychic organization (Ekstein and Wallerstein, 1954), heavy reliance on splitting mechanisms (Kernberg, 1967, 1968), and, from the point of view of Mahler's concept of the separation-individuation process (Mahler et al., 1975), early failures in that process (Masterson, 1972). While our group creative imagination could press clinical and metaphyschological constructs into forms that would subsume most of the cases we examined, my own sense was that in so doing we were engaging in a forced exercise.

In contrast, shortly thereafter, an enormous freeing of thought took place with our abandonment of the word "the" in the phrase "the borderline child" and its replacement by the term "borderline children." That is, we gave up the self-imposed demand to find a single unifiying mechanism and considered instead that we were dealing with an array of phenomena, having some larger developmental and pathological commonalities perhaps, but also having specific variant forms. In this it would be parallel to psychoneurosis, with its commonalities and variant forms. Behind this change also was the idea that the term "borderline" is a *concept*—one that *we* can *decide* how to use—and that our job was to specify the phenomena to which we would apply it. The rephrasing of our key term also set another aspect of our task: to identify the larger developmental and pathological commonalities that make this a reasonable, even if not tight, conceptual grouping, and then to describe its specific variant forms.

In other words children described as borderline are first defined by a dual negation: they are not (merely) neurotic, and they are not (clearly) psychotic. What they *are* remains to be stated. Additionally, although we could manage to subsume many children who are called borderline under one or another clinical construct (e.g., fluidity), we came to see this, not as a *gain* in clinical generalization, but as a *loss* in clinical specificity. In short, we felt we could do better with the joint conceptual tools of *broadly defined commonalities* plus *specific variants* in these children than with any single concept, mechanism, or process. In what follows I shall first discuss the "border" between neurosis and the borderline group of children, then describe various subgroups of children within this domain, and end with a discussion of the (far vaguer) border between these children and the psychotic child. In discussing the border between neuroses and borderline conditions, I shall also describe some of the broad commonalities among borderline children. And in describing the subgroups within the borderline grouping, I shall, of course, be giving the variant forms of this pathology.

MAPPING THE BORDERS

BETWEEN NEUROSIS AND BORDERLINE

We usually think of the essence of neurosis as involving an unconscious conflict between drive and an opposing force that culminates in anxiety, unsuccessful defense, and symptom formation. Beyond this, diagnostic considerations stem from the "content" of the conflict: the drives involved and the extent of drive regression, and the defenses characteristically relied upon. Temporal considerations (transience or fixity), the "spread" of the neurotic conflict to wider areas of functioning or a range of character traits in addition to symptoms, as well as the ego syntonicity or dystonicity of the resultant behavioral signs (symptoms and character traits) are also relevant.

But this "essence," the unconscious drive conflict, clearly fails to define neurosis adequately. Take the following example:

A twelve-year-old schizophrenic girl, Francesca, who had a variety of visual and auditory hallucinations centering on monsters, a variety of symptomatic bodily phenomena centering on liquid flow (of tears, vomit, urine, blood), and an insatiable oral craving, evinced interest in bloodsucking vampires. In a session with her therapist, whose time and attention she had been craving, she became attracted to the therapist's neck—specifically to a necklace the therapist was wearing. The girl immediately became upset and reported the taste of blood in her mouth (gustatory hallucination). Soon thereafter she expressed fear that the therapist would turn into a monster if she left the room, and Francesca tried to block the door to keep her there.

Here we have an unconscious drive conflict and pathological defense. The essence of neurosis? Hardly. While the inner workings of the child in this clinical vignette cannot be fully explicated, they seem to include defense against the oral-incorporative drive first by displacement (to the necklace), then by hallucination formation in part disconnected from the (inferred) initial impulse ("I feel blood in my mouth"), and then by disguise (loss of specificity) of the content plus projection outward (the therapist will become a "monster")—a final turn that allows the child to hold onto the therapist after all, but in a new way (keeping her in the room). But these are psychotic, not neurotic, phenomena.

So the concept that the core conflict between drive and an opposing force defines neurosis is insufficient. Such conflict is present far more widely than in the neuroses alone. Waelder (1936), in his important paper on multiple function, makes it clear that drive and defense, including varying degrees of conflict or coordination between them, are components of all behavior. Earlier (chap. 7), I tried to show how multiple function comes into being developmentally and gives order and permanence to the behavior of the child. For example, when we hear that an eight-year-old boy asks permission to take an extra piece of cake and to watch an extra (late) TV program when his parents are out, we may not be overly impressed by the psychodynamics of the situation. But when we learn that this boy has had a stormy history of separation difficulties and has gradually become able to give up his longings for the absent parent via displacement to alternative gratifications (cake and late TV show) and also to give up his fear of abandonment via a compensatory feeling of being "big" (eating more, staying up late), we see that such everyday behaviors, too, are constructed out of the history of conflict and accommodation between drive and defense. And this in the context of essentially normal development.

The unsuccessfully resolved unconscious drive conflict, which clinical work shows to be a core problem in certain patients (whom we call "neurotic"), is a necessary but not sufficient defining attribute of the neuroses. We actually define the neuroses (often only implicitly) as involving such a conflict *in the context of more or less normal development of the several sides of the personality.* And the several aspects of the personality are critical here. We speak of neuroses where (in addition to the neurotic conflict and pathology) ego development has proceeded to the point where secondary process thinking and reality testing are well established (though Freud [1924] points out certain secondary losses of reality focal to the neurotic conflict) and where some capacity for delay and at least some well-structured defenses have been attained. In addition, object relations have developed more or less normally through the early autistic (objectless) and symbiotic (undifferentiated) stages (Mahler, 1968); some degree of libidinal object constancy (Hartmann, 1952; and see chap. 8) and of specificity of object attachment have been achieved; and object relations have been subjected to the shaping influences of the drives at each of the psychosexual stages of development (receiving and taking, giving and holding, intruding [Erikson, 1950]). Furthermore, the triadic relations of the oedipal period have been experienced and dealt with in some manner. Superego development has proceeded to the point of at least some degree of internalization of standards— that is, with some experience of guilt for transgression and some internally powered efforts at control and delay of impulses. Whether anything more is added by our saying that drive development has also proceeded more or less normally (in the person who, for other reasons, is termed "neurotic"), or whether that is implied in the normal development of ego, object relations, and superego, is an arguable point. In any event, we usually think of neurosis as a focal drive conflict in the setting of more or less normal development of ego and superego functioning and of object relationship, although, of course, secondary regression may also have taken place. Hence we think of neurosis, from the standpoints of development and psychic structure, as a relatively "healthy" state—even though there can be much suffering and impairment of function.

By contrast, children who are generally considered "borderline" or severely disturbed do not show normal development of ego functioning and object relationship. Ego malfunction in such children includes, in particular, disturbances in the sense of reality and at times in reality testing, as well as a failure in the development of signal anxiety, so that unpleasant affect readily escalates to panic. Object relations are characterized by their shifting levels, by too great a dependence of ego structure upon the object contact, and by regression to primary identification. While superego forerunners are also likely to be impaired, these are not readily separable in their impact from the failures of judgment and affectional attachment that are already implied by pointing to failures in ego function and object relationship. Final superego formation is likely to be secondarily interfered with by prior developmental failures. Taken together, these features reflect the *general commonalities* among children considered borderline.

One feature that is frequently mentioned in work on borderline children (Weil, 1953; Rosenfeld and Sprince, 1963) is their failure to achieve the signal function of anxiety (Freud, 1933). That is, even rather early in development, the normal young child begins to anticipate when an anxiety-inducing situation is imminent (on the basis of memory of previous experience). Such anticipation is accompanied by mild anxiety that sets defensive operations into motion, be these flight, a turn to mother, or (later) intrapsychic defense. But the capacity for this (both anticipation and the availability of modes of defense) is a developmental achievement of great moment. The infant cannot do this and is helpless in the face of anxiety (unless mother intervenes); the intensity of this anxiety can rise to traumatic proportions—well beyond the person's capacity to master or discharge. For certain children, failure to develop the capacity to use the anxiety signal to set a reliable array of defenses into operation is both an indicator of past developmental failure and a source of continuing inability to develop mastery. For, if anxiety rapidly escalates to panic, the kinds of new learning, new trials at mastery, that can come at moments of delay in the face of danger will not be able to take place.

Early failures in the process of separation and individuation (Mahler et al., 1975) also have consequences for the later stability of ego boundaries and object attachment under stress. Rosenfeld and Sprince (1963), acknowledging their debt to Anna Freud, find a regression to primary identification to be a characteristic phenomenon in the severely disturbed children they studied. That is, quite the reverse of those later identifications which are basic to the growth of individuality and are a prime form of "adding something" to ourselves, some severely ill children begin to lose their sense of self as they merge into an undifferentiated self-other duo. Masterson's (1972) work on borderline adolescents also draws heavily on concepts of failure in the process of separation and individuation.

Ekstein and Wallerstein (1954; see also Ekstein, 1966) describe the unstable, fluid ego organization characteristic of some severely disturbed children. In these children the developmental achievement of stable personality organization has not taken place; instead, personality organization varies with (has not achieved autonomy from) changes in affect level and object attachment. Weil (1953, 1956) describes their pervasive unevenness of development and the equally pervasive oddness that follows from it. And Kernberg (1967, 1968), working mostly with adult patients, focuses on the pathological consequences of excessive reliance on certain primitive defenses, notably "splitting"—that is, the developmental failure of, or the regressive interference with, the integration of representations of the good and bad self and other into more realistic whole images. As I have noted (chap. 8), such integration can be conceptualized as fostering a toning down of idealization (via the effect of the "bad" on the "good" images) and tempering of rage (via the effect of the "good" on the "bad").

All these mechanisms and others are found in borderline children. In many ways, the persons whose work most closely links to my own views are Knight (1953a, 1953b), writing on borderline adults, and Redl (1951), writing on ego disturbances in children. Knight emphasizes, not single mechanisms, but a general tendency to ego regression in borderline adults; in any particular instance, the specific nature of the regression would still have to be identified. With a shift in emphasis from regression to primary developmental failure, that approach is essentially my own as well. And an argument for the value of specificity of identification of pathology within any broad domain is given by Redl in his paper on ego disturbances, in which he indicates that generalized "support" for an ill-defined "weak ego" leaves us high and dry when it comes to choices regarding technique. Rather, careful specification of particular areas of ego pathology permits tailoring of technical interventions to those weaknesses. This clinical philosophy underlies my approach to the specification of particular psychopathological phenomena in the borderline domain as well.

SUBTYPES WITHIN THE BORDERLINE DOMAIN

No hard and fast distinctions are implied in the following discussion. Diagnostic entities are our creations, intended to give order to the phenomena we observe. In part, the phenomena have their own order, and our diagnostic terms are attempts to discover it. For example, in the case of anal impulses and obsessional neuroses, there may be certain features of bodily experience (the physical separation of "higher" and "lower" parts, the alternation of being messy and being clean), certain features of societal controls (Erikson, 1950), and certain features of the learnings that take place simultaneously with the acquisition of bowel control (Greenacre, 1958) that make for a co-occurrence of anal impulses and the defenses of isolation, undoing, and intellectualization in obsessional neuroses. But such patterning in the phenomena only partially underlies diagnosis. Often it seems that almost all variations are possible. Our diagnostic terms are discontinuous, whereas human phenomena are continuous. It is in this sense that the following diagnostic subentities are given; they may flow into one another, or one may replace another over time, in the severely disturbed child.

Indeed, it may be best to consider them not only as diagnostic entities but simultaneously as aspects of the pathological phenomena. The first term implies *types of children*, more or less different from one another, while the latter implies a variety of *characteristics*, more than one of which may be found in any particular severely disturbed child. The two approaches are not contradictory; a particular child may show one aspect of the phenomena so predominantly that he well represents that as an "ideal type." I have attempted to select illustrative cases where one feature is predominant, but considerable overlap would often be evident if the full case material were presented.

Some children show remarkable variation in the degree of pathology of their overall mode of functioning—what I call *shifting levels of ego organization*. At one moment sensitively, often painfully, in touch with their thoughts and feelings, expressed in the context of a stable alliance with a trusted therapist—or, alternatively, simply playing-thinking-behaving in age-appropriate ways in the context of that same alliance and sense of therapeutic presence—at another moment, often suddenly within the same session, these children may become peculiar, voice odd ideas, lose the more mature relatedness to the therapist and instead speak illogically, uncommunicatively, and affectively withdraw. But there is no apparent panic; instead, there is a sense of familiarity, of ego syntonicity, in the child's move into peculiar functioning.

Ekstein and Wallerstein (1954; Ekstein, 1966) have written on such children, emphasizing how critical are the loss of contact and return to contact with the therapist in setting off and terminating such states. The absence of panic in the "peculiar" state is, I believe, an important key to understanding what is going on. Such children have not simply "broken down"; rather, they have regressively moved to a more primitive level of ego organization (and object relation). In the face of some disturbing (inner or outer) stimulus, anxiety arises and culminates, not in the triggering of a set of more or less adaptive defenses, but in the onset of this single, massive, regressive, maladaptive defense. But maladaptive how? Only to the outside; only for social adaptation. Internally it is highly adaptive; that is, it terminates the anxiety; it truly "works" for the child (hence I refer to it as an ego organization), though it works at a substantial price.

My understanding is that such children have achieved two quite different levels of ego organization. But both are *organizations*; they include modes of thinking, relating, and handling anxiety. The "higher" level is vulnerable, however, and too easily slips away. In terms of mechanisms described by other writers (and reviewed earlier), these children show marked fluidity of functioning and a pervasive oddness in their more primitive mode of functioning; although they do not demonstrate panic anxiety, they avoid it at a major adaptive price by a massive ego regression.

June was first seen at age eleven. I knew from records covering years of prior professional contacts (as well as from my own observations) that she would periodically go off into what she called her "kooky" moods—states of primitive rage expressed in mock form, of remarkable access to normally unconscious material, of perceptual confusion about the office and outside, and of distorted and idiosyncratic fantasies about her body structure. These alternated with the functioning of a sensitive, though painfully suffering, young girl who was in good reality contact and formed a good therapeutic alliance. Only much later did the inner stimuli (feelings experienced as crazy, which were handled by enactment of a crazy self) that touched off these states become clear.

Francesca, the child with the vampire fantasies, showed similar phenomena—although her pathology had developed to the point of including highly differrentiated and persistent delusions and hallucinations. The variation between levels of overall ego organization was striking. She emerged from her fantasy world, which was peopled with monsters, to speak to her therapist in heartrending terms of the "monstrous" way she was treated by the people in her real world. And then, when her own monstrous feelings would arise (her rage and her gnawing neediness), she would again go back to her world of magic and unreality—a state in which, as she once said, "the world is dead."

In terms of treatment, it is critical to recognize the anxiety-binding functions of the more primitive ego organization. Hence, while the therapist who works with such children (and all severely disturbed children) must gently and nonobtrusively convey a sense of his or her benign qualities, a good deal of exploratory, interpretive work is also required. This is not simply a matter of making up for deficits, of supporting the child through panic, or fostering delayed growth, though these may all come into play at times. Work with such children includes exploration and insight into the source of the anxiety, the function of the regression, the secondary gains in it, and the historical basis for its use.

In contrast in many ways to the children just described are those who evidence *internal disorganization in response to external disorganizers*. These are children whose lower level functioning is not *their* achievement—it is not an "achievement" at all; it does not "work" for them. Instead it reflects a true incursion upon their functioning, the result of an invasion that disrupted it.

It is my impression that such children are most commonly the product of rearing environments with a high level of social pathology (addiction, criminality, prostitution, violence, and so forth). In the children's psychiatric ward of the municipal hospital where I have seen them, they are often from ghetto/poverty areas, though the same disorganizing results can be brought about in other settings of intense psychological barrage upon the child's functioning. In any event, observation of such children in the ward teaches something about the "clinical course" of the illness and in turn permits inferences about its structure. These children arrive in the emergency room, sometimes with reported hallucinations or delusions, often with confusion in speech and relatedness, and frequently with reports of recent suicidal or homocidal behavior. On the ward, they rapidly pull together and indeed often come to be seen as more or less normal children. What are we to make of this?

I believe that the rapid recovery in the benign setting of the ward (shielded from their disorganizing environment) suggests that the basic developmental tools of ego function (here reality testing, reliable intrapsychic defense, secondary process thinking) and of nondestructive, trusting object relationship had indeed been formed, but that they were fragile, unable to withstand the distintegrating effect of chaotic life circumstances. In a benign setting, integration can take place. From a purely descriptive point of view, these children can also be seen as fluid—that is, functioning at different levels at different times. But the "fluidity" is captured better, I believe, by words like "breakdown" or "collapse" than by a phrase like "shift to a different level of functional ego organization."

Jayne, a ten-year-old black girl, was hospitalized after she announced that she would leap out a window and made a move to do so. In the preceding days she had stayed out of school without her mother's knowledge, apparently spending the days crying in a hallway. At first there was some question about the intactness of her thought processes and her capacity for self-control. In the hospital she soon became a charming girl, who actively wooed the adults' attention. There seemed less and less reason to keep her in the hospital, except that any move toward discharge precipitated self-destructive behavior, again raising the threat of suicide. Ultimately, we learned that Jayne had been grossly neglected by her mother, who preferred her other children, in a pattern that repeated how the mother had been treated by her own mother. Shortly before Jayne's suicide threat, a neighbor's child had fallen from a low window, had been hospitalized, and had received the loving attention of Jayne's mother. Jayne looked on longingly, and in a confused state sought the same treatment for herself. Only after Jayne and her mother, along with a supportive maternal aunt who nurtured both of them, were seen together and these events discussed and worked through to some degree was Jayne able to leave the hospital, safely we felt.

The summary paragraph of the psychological test report states the issues succinctly:

> Jayne is a child of average intelligence who can function well, given a stable environment which supports her rather fragile defenses. However, *she is easily stimulated to episodes involving loss of reality testing*, primitive oral aggression, *bizarre fantasies, and loss of control* of primitive aggressive impulses. She is also a profoundly depressed child who feels both that she has been quite deprived and quite guilty about ensuing angry feelings. It seems quite likely that in a disruptive environment, further suicidal ideation and attempts will occur. In spite of the extent of the disturbance, Jayne feels the need for and is able to use relationships with others not only to provide nurturance, but to support her defenses and reality testing. The diagnostic impression is of a borderline child.

Douglas was just past his fourth birthday when he was admitted to the children's psychiatric ward. His mother told of recent infantile babbling and of uncontrollable tantrums lasting two to six hours. An earlier clinic report on this child (at age 3) included the notation "psychotic child." On the ward he was initially described as showing "rambiling speech, nonresponsiveness to verbal commands, and giving the appearance of being occasionally out of contact with his surroundings." In addition his disturbance showed itself in the relative absence of a number of behaviors that one expects in a normal four-year-old: playfulness, some degree of modulated affect expression, cognitive freedom in exploration, and relatedness to others with at least minimal depth. Instead, his preoccupation with making order of his environment seemed to have absorbed all his available energy.

Douglas's mother, nineteen when he was born, was a prostitute, his father a criminal with multiple offenses. His mother reported that Douglas had had normal speech at age two and then a regression to babbling "for no reason." But in his third year, there were five reported "kidnappings" by his father, by then separated from the mother. This is just a sample of his life of instability bordering on chaos.

On the ward, Douglas blossomed. In a few months he formed an attachment to his therapist, speech returned, the tantrums ceased, he showed positive feelings and playfulness. He soon became the barometer of normality for the ward staff, the measure of what a normal child is like. In spite of a history akin to that of some symbiotic psychotic children (Mahler, 1968), he reversed the regressive process, put back together the pieces of development, and progressed. He was subsequently placed in a residential facility.

I believe the first line of treatment of such children is rescue. Rescue is not a fantasy of the therapist in this instance but a need of the child. It is essentially the benign setting, including a caring adult, that fosters integration and the use of capacities that are present in seed form. But to believe that the work is done at this point would indeed be a rescue fantasy. First and most obvious of course is the issue of return to the offending environment; and either extensive family work (often impossible to accomplish) or placement or long-term help for the child in withstanding the barrage is required. But second, and more subtly, the child's tendency to repeat actively what he has experienced passively, as a form of mastery and as an expression of his continuing love/hate attachment to his parents, can be forestalled only through long-term treatment that both supports and interprets, as needed and as possible for the particular patient. Obviously such long-term treatment is often more an ideal than a possibility, and so the generational repetition remains with us.

The group of children who show what I call *chronic ego deviance* are not really a group at all, since there is no unifying underlying structural or developmental feature by which all can be characterized. So this is a loose array, perhaps waiting for distinctions within it to be described as our clinical knowledge advances. Described by Weil (1953, 1956) some time ago, these children show aberrations of logical thought, reality testing, defense or object relation. Panic anxiety, failure to achieve phase dominance in the course of psychosexual development, unreliability of object attachment, of self/object differentiation, of stable defense may be characteristic of any one child. I stress the word "chronic" in describing the ego deviance to emphasize that the impairment is part of the child, not reactive, as in the group who respond to disorganizing environments, and also to emphasize that the instability of functioning can be expected to continue to show up; the instability is stable.

I have discovered one phenomenon in treatment that differentiates these children sharply from the preceding group. Children who are disorganized in response to external disorganizers tend to heal rapidly in the setting of a benign environment and a trusting relationship to the therapist; soon, from the point of view of basic ego intactness at least, they appear more or less normal. But some of the chronically ego-deviant children show the opposite phenomenon. That is, as the trusting relationship to the therapist develops, they permit themselves to *reveal*, perhaps for the first time, isolated bits of bizarre thought or behavior that they have concealed until that time.

Alex, age eight, the youngest child of now divorced parents, grew up in a home where the mother felt overwhelmed and where the longed-for father was irresponsible and unavailable. He was an odd boy. Some minimal brain damage contributed to this (his body movement was peculiarly lacking in grace), but the oddness went beyond this. Although he made contact with adults, it was in a somewhat undifferentiated manner and too passively, like a puppy dog with its master. No thought disorder was evident at first, but unrealistic ideas (people came at night and cut open his stomach) were soon revealed. A history of dangerous behavior (firesetting, knife throwing, an attempt to cut his penis), which at first seemed reactive to inordinate stress in his environment, soon came to be regarded more as an internal characteristic, the result of faulty judgment and the absence of more adequate defenses. When Alex was questioned about such events, his affect was bland, his judgment was poor, and his sense of the reality of what he had done was minimal. In his fantasies he was Superman, invulnerable, powerful; he claimed to know that this was not real, yet much of the time he behaved as though it were (as by dangerous risk taking).

Kurt, age ten, in spite of his characteristic glassy stare and affective blandness, related to his therapist as a person whom he could trust and lean upon. Yet, especially early in treatment, the therapist frequently felt Kurt disappear from contact with her, much as Kurt's foster parents had reportedly felt when he first came to live with them. Frightening events, such as a severe illness of his father, would precipitate disorganization—mechanical body movement, word gibberish, and a sense of panic. The withdrawals and panics were short-lived, but even at his best, peculiarities of reasoning, a sense of "oddness," and a wide open vulnerability mixed with a defensive paranoid-like suspiciousness were characteristic of him. His thought content flowed too easily from sexual wishes and confusion to primitive hunger, despair, and fears of and wishes for destruction. Today, three years later, the panics and withdrawals are rare, but the oddness is immediately evident.

Treatment for these children must vary with the nature of the specific failure or aberration of ego development (set, of course, in the context of the patient's whole life). It was Redl (1951) who first argued compellingly that indiscriminate support for a vaguely defined weak ego would get us nowhere; instead we have to specify the area of deficit and tailor intervention techniques to this. Earlier (chap. 10) I tried to demonstrate some instances of such work in the context of the implicit parenting function served by the therapist for the ego-deviant patient. Indeed, this whole chapter and the previous one have that same intent: to specify pathological conditions more precisely so as to enable us to adapt an essentially psychoanalytically informed treatment approach to the particular patient.

Of the borderline children described thus far, two of the groups (shifting levels of ego organization and chronic ego deviance) carry their pathology within, the former as a pathological defense organization and the latter as the result of developmental failure of various sorts; the current *reactive* component in the pathology is relatively small. In contrast, the reactive component is more substantial in those children whose internal disorganization is responsive to external disorganizers and in the group characterized by *incomplete internalization of psychosis*. In the latter, however, the reactive component does not simply reflect a destructive intrusion upon the child's functioning but is a core part of the child's attachment to the primary love object, usually the mother (see Anthony, 1971).

These children are generally the offspring of a psychotic mother and assimilate parts of her psychosis as a way of being close to mother and having her within. It involves more than conscious mimicry; hence it is pathological. But the internalization of the mother's psychosis is still incomplete; hence I call these children borderline rather than psychotic. The incompleteness of the internalization is made clear by the relative speed with which some of the more obvious indicator-behaviors drop away when the children are separated from their mothers and other love objects become available (see Anthony, 1971). Descriptively, fluidity of functioning is again apparent; formulatively, since the child moves toward merging with the mother, failure in the separation-individuation process (Mahler et al., 1975) can be inferred, as can the child's reliance on regression to primitive forms of incorporation for defense.

A while ago, Patti, age ten, arrived in a hospital ward with the report (confirmed by her) that she had been hearing voices and destroying some of her mother's precious possessions. But within a short time she came to be seen by the professional staff as a lovely young girl, capable of empathy and insight, and showing no evident pathology. Yet, when her mother visited, she was again severely disturbed for a while thereafter.

After she had been in the hospital for a while, Patti revealed, with terror in her eyes after getting a pledge of secrecy, that she had not destroyed her mother's possessions; she thought perhaps her brother had; but she had "confessed" to it in fear of her mother and at her mother's insistence. The voices, she reported, sounded to her like her mother's voice calling her (she had reported them only at home); but when she would answer, her mother would say something like: "I'm not calling you, you must be hearing voices; I hear them too." Everything we learned in Patti's subsequent treatment and in our contact with her mother tended to confirm this new story.

Yet to say Patti had "lied" earlier misses the point. She had adopted her mother's point of view and presented it (with the accompanying "feel"— affectively and with confusion—of a psychotic child). And whenever her mother visited, Patti again adopted pieces of her mother's character for a while and showed considerable preoccupation with things that merge into one another (the two halves of her notebook that opened and then folded together, the two overlapping parts—skirt and jacket—of a woman's suit) and with the similarities and differences between therapist and mother and herself. Human love objects were not automatically experienced as distinct and separate.

Patti's mother, we rapidly came to see, was a grossly paranoid schizophrenic woman, for whom the hospital and one of our staff psychiatrists became the conspiring enemy in her delusional world. She was also a sensitive and intelligent woman who sent a love poem to her doctor, and there is little doubt that Patti's sensitivity reflects some aspect of her maternal care. But in her psychotic periods (of which there had been several, including hospitalization), the mother used Patti as a partner; it was Patti, of all the children, who mattered most to the mother and who was the recipient and object of the psychotic behavior and entanglements. (When Patti was in the hospital, the mother began to use the next younger sibling in the same way, so that we finally had to find a placement for him too.)

For children like Patti, the psychotic-like phenomena seem to be part of the *attachment* to the parent, whether in love, hatred, or both. In this way their pathology differs from that found in the children who react to gross and widespread pathology with collapse, panic, repetition, or a search for rescue. Patti is enmeshed in and pursuing a specific, partially symbiotic relationship that has grossly pathological features.

There is no question that treatment, in cases like this, is a long and complex process, notwithstanding the gains the child may make if separated from the mother (e.g., by the hospitalization of either one of them). For, as with the other reactive group of borderline children (internal disorganization in response to external disorganizers), a large residue remains even when the obvious "reaction" terminates. In these children, extended work is required to relive (in the transference), to understand (through exploration), and to work through the relation with the primary love object. Within the essentially analytic/exploratory content of the sessions, the benign presence of the therapist—a differentiated other, who allows individuality and who does not require sharing of pathology as a condition for relatedness—will (whatever his theoretical orientation) inevitably provide a corrective emotional experience (Alexander, 1956).

There are other children who, though they vary in the precise area and quality of their pathology of ego function and object relationship, show enough similarity in the developmental route to that pathology to warrant grouping them for purposes of conceptualization and discussion of treatment. I call them children with *ego limitation*. That term could be used to refer to inhibited children, dull children, culturally deprived children, and others. But let me describe the children for whom I intend to use it.

Sometimes, for inner and familial reasons, a child "happens upon" an early adaptive-defensive mode that markedly curtails large areas of subsequent development. If this happens, and if at the same time the defense is "successful" (in *inner* terms, i.e., lessening anxiety, allowing gratification, fitting with the family), it may be retained for a long time with ever-growing damage to the developmental process. Thus, a pseudoimbecilic child (Mahler, 1942; and see below) whose inner psychological requirements are *not* to learn will show effects of that learning stoppage in formal school learning, peer relations, social sense, and everywhere else. Or, to take another example, Youngerman (1979) reports on a child, electively mute fairly continuously since age three, the development of whose entire thought process was impaired as a consequence of the refusal to speak. Speech externalizes inner fantasies and permits their correction against the response of others; by verbalizing certain ideas and seeing that wishes do not always produce effects, the child learns to abandon ideas of the omnipotence of thought; and of course speech is the instrumentality of relationships at a distance—*permitting* distal connection and not *requiring* highly charged body contact and affect and gesture as the continuing modes of communication. Youngerman shows the destructive effect, for subsequent development, of this child's having "selected" the limiting defense of mutism very early on as his mode of adaptation.

William, age ten, the firstborn child of extremely anxious, middle-class, Latin-American parents, presented as a pseudoimbecilic child (Mahler, 1942). Especially when William's younger sibling was born, the parents noted a change in his behavior. William, unquestionably of average to bright-average intelligence, presented himself as a fool, making inane statements and grinning with "dumb pleasure" as he did so. He used neologisms, expressed grossly distorted ideas about the body alongside accurate ones—always untroubled by, indeed broadcasting, his inanity. But for him, the "dumbness" permitted him to remain close to his parents—tormenting them by his illness and yet gratifying himself by the continued infantile sexual pleasures (being seen, bathed, dressed) that the parents permitted this "limited" boy.

For whatever reasons (only some of which are known), the signs of William's ego limitation were apparent quite early, in the preschool years, and by age ten the loss to the ego by years of deficit in learning could not be reversed by dynamic interpretation alone; he clearly needed major relearning or, rather, first learning as well. In this he differs from a child who has a neurotic inhibition of learning. In such a child the major work of ego development has taken place; the learning inhibition he develops is focused and is based on a specific symbolic meaning. In contrast, William's "choice" of infantile thinking and ego organization as a major adaptive-defensive tool had the effect of distorting the whole of his subsequent development.

It is my experience that children showing this early and severe ego limitation bring a wide range of serious failings in ego function and object relation into their later treatment. It is also my impression, however, that a defensive-adaptive style of such long duration and such great intrapsychic "success" is not readily renounced. Not only does work with such a child require sustained and sophisticated interpretive work to penetrate the child's heavily relied upon defense organizations but, and this is critical, once it is penetrated we are still left with a child with substantial deficits; the years of nonlearning have taken their toll. Interpretation (of, for example, the basis for the pseudoimbecility or the mutism) may lead to lesser reliance on the defense but does not create what has been missed in development. For this, an extensive educative process is required, along with continuing therapeutic work. But two cautions are in order: First, the educative process cannot be undertaken until the defense barrier is more or less abandoned, until the child understands it and is trying to give it up; otherwise, the "education" will be greeted with that very same defense style and will be cast away. Second, optimism about making up for the lost development of years, even after the defense is penetrated and educational supplementation is begun (either within or outside the therapy), is hardly warranted in such cases, where, in my experience at least, the child remains with considerable deficit.

Schizoid personality in childhood, exactly parallel to its adult form, seems to me to warrant inclusion in the broader group of borderline children. Such personalities, characterized by a sharply constricted and undeveloped affective life with emotional distance in human relationships and preoccupation with their own (often rich but peculiar) fantasy life, can be seen clearly already in childhood. The peculiarities of thought and severe limitations of object relationship reflect the developmental abberations or failures of the general borderline domain.

Brian, age nine, one of several children in a large family, lost his mother four years earlier when she died rather suddenly. Although the family held together after that, both before *and* after there were little affection and care shown to or by anyone in this family.

Brian looked depressed. His facial muscles were always just about motionless, he spoke in a monotone, and he moved slowly. He made almost no affective and individualized response to people, although he did function in school and was easy to manage. On testing, however, a rich, idiosyncratic, and peculiar fantasy life was evidenced—and this is what most absorbed and occupied him. While he seemed bland and blank from the outside, his thought processes were full and complex. Once, at the mention of mother (in a story), he told of a panic with everyone running so hard that their banging feet split the world apart. The panic was in the story; *he* remained bland. Fantasy seemed to replace object relationship and was excessively relied upon to retain equilibrium.

Essie, age seven and a recent immigrant, had not made friends at home or in school. She liked to watch television alone or just sit around with her own thoughts. She rarely played with either of her sisters. Seen in consultation, she showed odd ideation around a most unusual imaginary companion, more an object than a person, and gave evidence of a prolific imagination that she was driven to express in her sessions with me. The content had to do largely with inanimate, outer-space, destructive images. She revealed it not as a communication but as a monologue, while drawing. Essie's parents, while concerned about her isolation, were aware of but unconcerned about her unusual and all-absorbing thought content. Indeed, they contributed to it at times in not so subtle ways. When pressed, they said they felt that she would outgrow it.

Both these children were preoccupied with peculiar thoughts and were emotionally distant from other persons. Yet other aspects of ego functioning were intact enough to permit passable functioning, for example, in school. They can be distinguished from the children previously described by a number of contrasts and comparisons: they carry the pathology within (unlike those responding to external chaos or maternal psychosis); they are more organized than the ego-deviant children; they do not appear retarded (like the ego-limited children); and, while relying heavily on fantasy, they are unlike the children with shifting ego organization in that they do not shift. They simultaneously function in the real world and hold themselves aloof from it emotionally while relating mainly to their odd (but not delusional) thought processes. I am impressed with one critical defining feature: the fantasying works so successfully as a defense against drive and object relationship that threat is not experienced in disorganizing ways. These children do not experience panic. Hence they can stabilize a character structure, though at the price of oddness and isolation. In both children the family style supported isolation and fantasying. Perhaps, therefore, they were not fully alone when they appeared to be isolated but were somehow still with the family and its way of being.

Like the children with shifting levels of ego organization whose shift to a more primitive organization successfully wards off anxiety (even at the price of often severe disturbance of function), the preoccupation with fantasy in the schizoid children also will often work well to avoid anxiety (or indeed *any* affect). Treatment is therefore difficult. Since fantasizing works well for the children, it will not easily be given up; relationships to others are quite cut off, and so the therapist cannot easily become important to the child. And since the child does not *shift* between in-touch and fantasizing states, but rather stays safely shielded from others by affective distance and fantasy preoccupation, the therapist does not see the variability that allows for even periodic contact or interpretive inroads. Once again a long, sustained treatment seems necessary, with all the patience, restraint, and interpretive skill that are part and parcel of any full treatment, and all of which can lead to the slow growth of a therapeutic alliance.

Alerted by Kernberg's (1967, 1968) writings on adult borderline patients, I became attuned to certain children who show omnipresent *splitting of good and bad images of self and other*. Such children, often "sweet" or "good" on the surface, will, in treatment, reveal an absorbing inner preoccupation with hate and violence, often with homicidal or world-destruction fantasies, equally often with scant and precarious control over them. The splitting is evidenced in the lack of connection between the "good" and the "bad" self and other. Hate, unmodified by affectionate images, becomes icy or fiery, devouring of the self or the other (in mental life), and frightening—to the patient, and to the therapist who learns about it.

I first became aware of this as a phenomenon in childhood from an adult patient suffering from irreconcilable love-hate images toward her adoptive parents. She was able to recall the phenomenon vividly from her childhood. The "teacher's pet" in school, the good girl, she nonetheless recalls sitting in class absorbed with violent and destructive fantasy. Hearing this, I was reminded of the recurrent newspaper stories of mass murderers who, as the history unfolds, were "good" children, generally quiet and not too well known to anyone, but well behaved, disciplined. And then I was reminded of the comment heard among educators, that troublesome (noisy, school-failing) children come to the attention of the school, but that quiet children who may also be in trouble may not be noticed. These quiet children may be "in trouble" not only as nonlearners but also as instances of the kind of child of whom I am now speaking. Not all of the them by any means, but some.

Such were my thoughts at the time, listening to my adult patient speak. Since then, more alert to the issue, I have come across the phenomenon three or four times through supervision of the work of others or in consultation or treatment. There is no question that the phenomenon exists in childhood. Its attendant disturbances in thought processes and object relations warrant its being considered another form of the borderline disturbance.

When I saw Dominick as part of a teaching conference, he appeared as an angelic, fair-haired ten-year-old boy. His slightly-off eye contact and blank gaze were disconcerting, but most of what he said was normally childlike, though sparse. Nothing he said seemed to link to reports that he would wake at home claiming that monsters came out of his walls at night. With one exception: when I asked something about anger, he stared blankly and said: "If I got angry there would be no one left." He fled this remark, denied saying it, and would say no more. But my sense was that he was conveying the idea, not that he would be abandoned if he were angry, but that he would destroy all the world. Two weeks later, before he had been assigned to a therapist, his mother called in a panic. Her "sweet" boy had unaccountably stabbed a knife into her kitchen countertop. When she asked why, he responded: "So I wouldn't stab my sister." I did not follow his subsequent therapy, but I know that his destructive rage eventually entered his sessions, terrified him, and led him to stay away at all costs.

Albert, whom I did work with, was the only child of elderly parents. His preoccupation with alligators and occasional, seemingly random aggressive attacks brought him to me at age seven-and-a-half. I cannot describe this child in detail, but suffice it to say that the work went extremely well. After an initial period of exceeding difficulty, when it appeared that the "split" would not be modified and that the primitive rage and violence would either erupt dangerously or succumb to repression without undergoing modification, it gradually became possible to weave together the hating side of him with the rest of his personality and relatedness and to produce a remarkably well-functioning boy, albeit with residual fears that he was able to understand and half-control.

In summary, I have advanced the idea that a loose, but defensible, conceptual category of "borderline children" can be defined in terms of central developmental failures or aberrations in ego development and object relationship. These disturbances are identifiable in the school-age period because by that age one ordinarily expects to see some degree of character stability and of socialization in the child; the "peculiarities" of the borderline child generally violate that expectation. Within the broad borderline domain, there is a distinct clinical gain from seeking, not a single unifying mechanism that is shared by all such patients, but individualized descriptions of subtypes of borderline phenomena, subtypes which *do* have essential commonalities and whose commonalities of etiology and/or structure can lead us to individualized implications for treatment. I wish to make clear, also, that the listing I have given is meant to be neither exhaustive nor mutually exclusive.

I have made a number of specific comments regarding treatment of each subgroup. I would like, in concluding this section, to make one final point. Recently, when I was discussing some of the ideas presented here with a group of beginning therapists, the question was raised: Should we or should we not make interpretations to borderline patients? Referring to Knight (1953b) in excessively simplistic form, one person concluded that we were not supposed to make interpretations. Another, referring to Kernberg (1968), equally simplistically concluded that indeed we were supposed to interpret. What, they asked, did I think we were "supposed" to do?

I assume that by now my answer to that question is clear. With fuller understanding of the range of pathology subsumed under the concept "borderline," one cannot avoid the responsibility of creating an answer, tailored not only to the events of the moment (as in all dynamic psychotherapy) but also to the specific form of the pathology. Sometimes we do one thing, sometimes another. Should we interpret? I can only say: it all depends. On what? That is what I have tried to spell out, at least in part.

I have so far described the border between the borderline domain and neurosis, and some of the internal borders within that domain. In now turning to the line between borderline and psychosis, I wish to question whether it is possible to draw a sharp distinction.

BETWEEN BORDERLINE AND PSYCHOSIS

In reading some of Ekstein's (1966) cases, or thinking about some of the severe cases described by Rosenfeld and Sprince (1963)—all discussed as "borderline" in those papers—I have often asked: "Why not consider these children psychotic?" And when I have spoken of some of the children described here—for example, some of the chronic ego-deviant or ego-limited children with peculiarities of thinking—I have in turn been asked: "Why not call them psychotic?" And indeed, why not?

Except in the case of some specific entities, such as infantile autism (Kanner, 1942, 1949) and symbiotic psychosis (Mahler, 1952), I believe that no sharp distinction, based on any recognizable principle, can be drawn between the borderline children described here and psychotic (or schizophrenic) children. This problem may be inherent in the phenomena in this realm: absence of structure or else structuralized and adaptive use of quite primitive ego mechanisms. In any event it seems to me appropriate that clinical wisdom follow what has been viewed as clinical uncertainty until now. That is, when a child seems "clearly" psychotic or "clearly" not psychotic (yet severely disturbed) by whatever principles of judgment the individual clinician used, there is no diagnostic problem; but once it is not so clear, it should be recognized that there are no absolute principles, and certainly no widely agreed-upon ones, by which to make a judgment.

This state of affairs can be formalized and given clinical-theoretical recognition by stating that there is a continuum from the "borderline" cases discussed here to childhood psychosis. Ekstein and Wallerstein (1954, p. 368), for example, refer to the *slight degree* of control that borderline children have as distinguishing them from psychotics; clearly, this is a relative matter. The more the thinking peculiarities of the ego-deviant or ego-limited child dominate his thinking, or the more the child with shifting ego organization is "in" the state of unreality, or the more the child with an incompletely internalized psychosis carries it around with him, the more prone we are to consider this a case of childhood psychosis. And that indeed reflects the state of affairs within the child, who himself is in developmental flux. Consider his developmental position vis-à-vis the flux of reality and fantasy, the normal regressive aspects of his object relations and drives, and the degree to which he is influenced by his surround. There is a continuum between borderline and psychosis colored in part by features of the ongoing development of the child.

Usually, to call a person psychotic we look for some degree of structur-alization of the psychosis, some degree of fixity and of impact on many psychic structures, before we can view the pathological phenomena as characteristic of him. But the child is developing and in general shows lesser charactero-logical fixity because of the flux of development. In addition, the child is more highly responsive to and influenced by his environment than is the adult. These two features, characteristic of childhood in general, are also part of what makes it difficult to assess whether a particular child "is" or "is not" psychotic. The problem is *intrinsic* to our diagnostic mode of thinking, not just pe-ripheral or based on lack of knowledge. Hence the continuum notion (from borderline to psychotic) with no clear demarcation sseems to me most appropriate.

I said a moment ago that the borderline syndromes and the psychoses of childhood should be regarded as a continuum "except in the case of some specific entities" of psychosis. Two such entities have been clearly described. "Infantile autism" applies to children who, from birth, have been unrespon-sive to the persons around them. The characteristics have been well described by Kanner in 1942; other work done since then is highly suggestive regarding organic contributions to the syndrome (see the reveiw by Rutter and Bartak, 1971). "Symbiotic psychosis" (Mahler, 1952, 1968) applies to children who show more or less adequate early development, with a reversal usually in the second or third year, usually but not always involving a clear precipitating event, often in the nature of a separation, followed by panic in the absence of mother and/or secondary regression to autistic mechanisms (see also Speers and Lansing [1965] for brief descriptions of several cases).

A less clearly defined entity that may stand as an independent form of childhood psychosis, not just as a severer form along a continuum from borderline, is childhood schizophrenia. The discussion of such cases—under the rubric "Is there such a thing as childhood schizophrenia?"—has not proceeded very far. The Group for the Advancement of Psychiatry publication refers to "schizophreniform" psychotic disorder (1966, p. 254) to distinguish it from the adult form of the disease.

Naturally it must be so distinguished. The one thing that is certainly true of childhood schizophrenia is that it occurs in children! It is obviously true of children that much development has not yet taken place. Thus, the reality-fantasy distinction has not been sharply etched. When one asks: "Is this really a hallucination or is it just the fantasying behavior of a child?" the question is meaningless. The particular mental product is the form hallucination takes in a psychic apparatus that, in any event, readily engages in fantasying be-havior. Furthermore, in view of the fact that much development still must take place in the child, the predictive test for whether childhood schizophrenia is "truly" schizophrenia is also meaningless. Will this childhood schizophrenia develop into adult schizophrenia? Naturally the answer can only be "maybe."

Similarly, an adult schizophrenic episode can remit, recur, or become chronic. That, quite often, is the best we can say.

For the sake of clarity, I propose separating out an entity of childhood schizophrenia that is heavily based on regression and that culminates in withdrawal and thought disorder (including hallucination or delusions). I say this because earlier I proposed that all the borderline syndromes involve primary developmental failures; in severer instances (on a continuum) they would be called childhood psychosis. A child who shows more or less normal development and then undergoes severe disorganization of a regressive sort (in the elementary school years) may then be considered a case of childhood schizophrenia—the word "schizophrenia" emphasizing the likeness to the adult syndrome, and the word "childhood" emphasizing its differences.

I am not familiar with such cases, *except where there is acute brain disorder or gross trauma that triggers the disorganization*. Perhaps this is just an "ideal type," a theoretical end point that helps us define a variable (in this case the continuum from developmental failure to minimal development followed by regression). For in the childhood period, at least in my experience, we are still close enough to the developmental history of the schizophrenic child to see the failures that have taken place, the continuity of the pathology, the early signs and signals, so that the idea of normal development (even only "more or less normal") followed by regression carries no real weight. The developmental failures and aberrations are ordinarily all too clear.

Having set apart the clear psychotic entities of childhood, I am proposing that what we call "borderline" shades into what we call psychosis, that there is no sharp distinction, and that each clinician will of necessity label as his leaning dictates. All the borderline children I have described show developmental failures and aberrations of a sort that, when severe enough, would warrant considering them psychotic. That no sharp line has been drawn, I suggest, reflects the fact that no sharp line exists.

I have been discussing a number of kinds of severely disturbed children who have been, or can be, considered borderline. As a vehicle for discussion, I have taken the spatial metaphor "borderline" seriously and discussed the borders between this domain and neurosis on the one hand and psychosis on the other, describing internal borders within the domain as well.

I have suggested that what unites these children is the presence of severe developmental failure or aberration in the realm of ego functioning and object relationship. This distinguishes them from the neurotic child characterized by unconscious drive-defense conflict and symptom formation in the setting of more or less normal development. At the lower (more pathological) extreme, I have suggested that in principle there is no real distinction between the borderline child and some forms of psychosis in childhood. The two blend into each other. I have thus tried to treat the general vagueness about the distinction between borderline and psychosis with respect—that is to say,

I view it as clinical wisdom, as an indication of the fact (if fact it is) that there *is* no sharp distinction. The exception to this is the case of certain specifiable entities of childhood psychosis that are discontinuous with the borderline syndromes. These separate entities include infantile autism, symbiotic psychosis, and a form of childhood schizophrenia that is heavily based on regressive processes rather than solely on developmental failures and aberrations.

Most important, however, I have tried to describe a number of different kinds of children who may be considered "borderline." I have spoken of differing "groups of children": those showing chronic ego deviance, shifting levels of ego organization, internal disorganization reactive to external disorganization, incompletely internalized psychosis, severe ego limitation, schizoid character, and heavy reliance on splitting mechanisms. But I have also suggested that it may be better to refer to these groupings as "aspects of the pathological phenomena." By this I mean that any severely disturbed child may show more than one of these features. They hardly constitute a typology but rather represent forms that severe pathology takes in children.

The principal aim of this chapter has been to counter both the vagueness in the way the term "borderline" is used and the search for "the" borderline child—a single syndrome based on a single mechanism or developmental failure. That seems to me too simplistic and would still leave us with whole groups of very sick children whom we have no adequate way to describe.

15

Pathology of the
Separation-Individuation Process
as Manifested in Later Clinical Work

The concept of separation-individuation, prominently associated with the work of Margaret Mahler (1963, 1965, 1968, 1972; Mahler et al., 1975), is in part endangered by two fates that endanger many new psychoanalytic concepts: overextension and underutilization. The overextension is obvious in the flood of usages of the terms. The underutilization is less obvious because those who do not incorporate the concept in their thinking simply do not use it. It is the aim of this chapter to provide several clinical examples of pathology of the separation-individuation process. By attempting to specify some distinctions within the phenomena, I hope to counter simultaneously the dangers that the concepts will be overextended in vague ways and that their relevance will go unnoticed.

I shall attempt to distinguish between pathology of the relation to the *differentiated* other and pathology of the relation to the *undifferentiated* other, the latter being the primary phenomena with roots in the separation-individuation process. Additionally, I shall try: to show that the confusion between these two comes from a focus on surface presentations and that an interior, in-depth view is needed to distinguish between them; to draw a further distinction, within the pathology of the relation to the *differentiated* other, showing that some of this pathology is in fact tied to the *differentiation process itself*, and is thus also linked to the separation-individuation process; to comment, through clinical examples, on the relevance of concepts regarding separation-individuation to other phenomena, notably, depersonalization and derealization, "as if" character, and folie à deux; and actually pervading all the others, to illustrate again and again pathological manifestations of disturbances in the early separation-individuation process.

Originally published in the *International Journal of Psychoanalysis* (60:225–242, 1979).

PRELIMINARY CONSIDERATIONS

The central question addressed in Mahler's work (Mahler et al., 1975) is how does the infant, originally unaware of self, other, and the distinction between them, come to achieve such awareness? We ask that question because we do not assume the existence at birth of preformed concepts. A further question is: How does the infant come to make an attachment to an "other," experienced as a specific and differentiated other? The first is a question of object *construction*; the second, of object *relation*. We find that the attachment is there before the other is yet experienced as other, a fact of enormous consequence. This period of attachment prior to the awareness of self-other differentiation is what Mahler refers to as the stage of normal symbiosis. "Attachment" here is vague, itself nonspecific. It exists for much of the first half of the first year and then only slowly alters during the separation-individuation phase.

The assumption of nonawareness of differentiation (in the first half year) rests on one prior assumption, one readily observable phenomenon, and one set of observations from our research. The prior assumption has already been stated: that the infant is not *born with* differentiated concepts of self and other. The readily observable phenomenon is equally clear: later on, children *have* such differentiated concepts. Hence, they must have developed sometime in between. Why do we assume they have not developed in the first half year? Because (and these are the observations from our research) we see behavioral phenomena in the five- to ten-month period which suggest that the awareness of differentiation is growing *then*. Hence it is more parsimonious to assume that the learning is occurring at this period (primarily) rather than earlier. The phenomena include peekaboo, stranger anxiety, inspection of the mother's face, and others that I shall not review here. To signify the developments of this period, Mahler refers to it as the *differentiation* subphase of the separation-individuation process.

I stated that the infant's attachment is there before the other is yet experienced as other and that this fact is of enormous developmental consequence. What are these consequences? First, the growing awareness of the mother as a differentiated, nonself being is experienced as a loss; while there may be an objective gain in cognitive comprehension, the emotional sense of loss follows the awareness that certain treasured sensations are not part of the self but can come and go. Second, the fact of prior (undifferentiated) attachment both facilitates and complicates the development of relationship to the differentiated other (that is, object relationship); it facilitates because the attachment is already there; it complicates because the experience of loss forever endows the relationship with the mother with painful undercurrents. And third, the growth from attachment to the *undifferentiated* other to attachment to the *differentiated* other sets up a developmental pathway that can be traversed in *both* directions, with halting steps forward and regressive moves backward, each at times of central clinical significance.

The differentiation period is followed by the so-called practicing period, a time of elated motor mastery during which the toddler seems relatively less concerned with the mother's comings and goings than he was earlier or will be (again) later; motor behavior appears to absorb his attention. Then the motor feats fall into place as functional tools of the child, and the still very young child "rediscovers" his mother. But his awareness of differentiation is now much further along, learning having taken place all through the practicing period. And so the toddler arrives at 18 months or so more aware of differentiation, not yet emotionally ready for it, and enters what Mahler refers to as the "rapprochement" period, a time of low mood (because of the sense of loss of the fusion with mother) and of efforts to deny that loss (by stubborn efforts to coerce mother to act as an extension of the child)—in all a critical developmental period for the resolution of issues of fusion and differentiation. The normal working through of these issues carries the child into the period of libidinal object constancy, a time when the child learns to hold the differentiated other close in mind, closer than she could be in actuality, in such a way that her internal representation itself can serve comforting functions (chap. 8)—all of this with no loss of the child's autonomy because he can move where he wishes, carrying the mother permanently within.

In overview, our study of *separation* is the study of the growth of awareness of separateness, not of actual separations such as Spitz (1945, 1946) or Bowlby (1969, 1973) has studied; it is an intrapsychic achievement serving reality testing but at the price of emotional pain. *Individuation* refers to the taking on of those characteristics that mark the person as a person in his own right; the conceptual irony (though the developmental commonplace) is that the child individuates largely by taking into himself characteristics of the significant others from whom he has differentiated; this route to individuation holds seeds of self-other confusion that I shall discuss later. *Symbiosis* refers, not really to the biological concept of absolute mutual dependence, wherein two organisms each require the other for life to continue (though it can come to mean that in fantasy later on), but refers to the absence of awareness in the child of differentiating boundaries in the highly invested mother-infant "dual-unit" (Mahler et al., 1975).

In what follows I shall attempt to highlight, through clinical examples, a number of issues and concepts regarding the later psychopathological manifestations of disturbances in the separation-individuation process. I shall draw on material from child, adolescent, and adult patients. As of now, I am more impressed by the commonality of the issues across ages than I am by any specific tie of certain phenomena to specific ages. Or, put otherwise, the phenomena vary, but I believe that the variation is determined by the core pathology rather than by the age of its carrier.

SOME ISSUES HIGHLIGHTED BY CLINICAL PHENOMENA

SOME NEGATIVE INSTANCES

Let me begin by describing a case that highlights ambiguities in the clinical application of concepts regarding the separation-individuation process. I believe that we are seeing, in this case, pathology primarily of well-differentiated object relationships even though the patient's language often makes it sound as though there are failures of differentiation and failures in the development of a basic sense of independent selfhood. Theoretical clarity as well as diagnostic and technical choices are affected by our comprehension of the patient's associations.

Mrs. A. was an attractive, poised, articulate twenty-two-year-old widow who was self-supporting. Though childless, she was close to children, living near her older sister, with whose two daughters she was very much involved. Her relationships had a large measure of control; she kept her distance. And yet she was clearly related, had shown herself capable of taking in from the therapist and of forming a strong attachment to more than one man at different times in her life.

Mrs. A. often spoke of feeling like "nobody"; there was "no one inside," she would say about herself. On the other hand, she also spoke of her fear of venturing into new relationships; they would be too painful. But a sense of self, a self to be protected from pain, was clearly implied here. In a series of six sessions over a three-month period, much material about self and nonself emerged.

In one session, more than a year into the therapy, she came in guilt-ridden, having left her two nieces with a substitute babysitter so she herself could go out. She began a long monologue: "I want you to give me an answer, but I know you won't. I want you to tell me my leaving was either right or wrong. I want everybody to tell me what to do; then I don't have to take responsibility for doing the wrong thing. I take credit for the girls' accomplishments, but I blame myself for their bad things. I feel in control of them. . . . It's as if they don't have minds of their own. I used to think I was them. Apart from them, there wasn't any me. I don't think I was ever separate from anyone I ever cared about or was emotionally involved with. When Alex [her former husband] died, I was annihilated because there was no me. That's why I don't want to care about anybody. I'll lose them and there will be nothing because I'm them." Asked about the word "annihilated," she said: "I feel so helpless and hurt as though I can be easily destroyed if I become myself. So I just throw myself in and become the other person. Then I feel in control and powerful. I don't know why but when you ask me to look at myself I want to cry. I hardly know that person." Some other material intervenes and then the session ends a bit more assertively: "On the one hand I don't want to give up struggling to be me, and on the other hand I still want to be down and disappear and be absorbed. The only problem is that— 'pop'—if the other person goes away, there is no me."

Much of the language (and this patient is thoroughly naive regarding psychological theory) is highly suggestive regarding symbiosis and separation-individuation. She begins with a desertion (by her, of her nieces) and quickly comes to her sense of lack of differentiation from them, indeed from everyone who ever mattered to her. There is "no me," no self, when she loses the other. She wants to be absorbed. And she feels "in control and powerful" when she "becomes" the other.

Yet some things do not fit. We hear the words, but the woman who is saying them is articulate, related, and—at this moment—insightful. Her bearing belies her words; she does not sound like someone who is "not there." Of course she may have distance now, may be talking about regressive processes from another time. But we have not seen the regression—not in the treatment now or previously, not in her reports of her life outside. And there is no panic. Yet, I believe we would expect regressive losses of self to be accompanied either by such panic or by quite disturbed behavior that is nonetheless ego-syntonic. She showed neither. And finally, real self feeling is continually implied in her words: I can be destroyed *if I become myself*; you ask me to look at myself and I *hardly know that person*; and, of course the session's ending, *"on the one hand, I don't want to give up struggling to be me"* (and on the other the wish to renounce self)—a complex, self-aware statement.

In the next session she began to speak of her former husband's irresponsibility. "I kept telling myself if he really cared about me he wouldn't do it again. I've just got to be more important than the way he treated me. I can't be as nothing as he acted." But then she shifts by degrees to *her* control of *him*: "I felt there was less of me. [Step 1; she is weak]. My own value and worth were measured by how well he did what I wanted him to do. If I were really valuable and he valued me he wouldn't do what I didn't want him to do and he would do what I wanted him to do. [Step 2; ambiguous; powerful wishes]." To the question whether this relationship was reminiscent of any other, the patient readily responded: "My father. He was choking me. He just wanted to own me. When you're strangled it looks one way, but when you're the owner it looks entirely different. In my marriage I quickly got to be the strangler. I didn't trust him. And I knew very well how to make demands and expectations and hold them by the neck until they agree. [Step 3; the tables have turned]."

The patient's father, a salesman frequently away from home, had kept a long-distance stranglehold on her through her growing-up years. Well into her teens, she could not go out with anyone without his permission or presence. She succumbed to his control, consciously angry, unconsciously attached.

In the next session, again after she expressed her wish to be passively attached to someone else, to be engulfed, she continued: "At the time there was no real caring about me as a person at all. My father never even knew me. I didn't want to be independent. I wanted them to soak me up. It sounds completely ridiculous to want something I can't stand—wishing for something I hated at the time." The therapist suggested: "Perhaps you didn't hate it; perhaps you got something from it." And the patient: "I had a sense of power; an ultimate weapon. I used to think to myself: you may have me by the throat, but I'll have the ultimate revenge." And then she described that revenge: the father's torment whenever any male paid attention to her, precisely because of his wish to "own" her, to control her completely.

What can we now say? The subtle shift from powerless selflessness to absolute control of the other, in the relation to both father and husband, reveals a complex object relationship, built on turning passive to active, and cloaked in words that bespeak selflessness. But the patient's experience is not all one of power; the passive experience, too, repeats. The emphasis on being "nothing" vis-à-vis a man is her way of continuing the object relation to the father; she was his special "nobody," with no wishes of her own; she wished passively to hold onto that relation, repeating it as the form of her connection to her father. And finally, her verbal wish to merge reflects, I believe, wishful fantasies of care, by way of making up for deficiencies in her actual experience of object relationship. In sum, in the context of the patient's solid functioning and absence of severe regression, and in the light of the absence of panic regarding the so-called losses of self, I view these aspects of her relationship to her father (holding onto the relationship as his "nobody," turning that into active control, and carrying a family-romance-like fantasy of absolute care) as indicating pathology of the relationship to the *differentiated* other, disguised by language that sounds as though there has been a failure of differentiation. But it is not the patient who is confused by this; she is just telling us about her experience and thoughts. *We* may get confused if, contrary to our usual set to look beyond surfaces to underlying meanings, we too rapidly assimilate surface language to new concepts that interest us.

Two months later, the patient returned to this material. Again she spoke of being left with nothing if people left her, of fearing to take the risk of entering relationships; instead, she "plays dead," shows no feelings, protects herself against "the ultimate abandonment." Then she remembered that she had been quite a fighter in the relationship with her father. She had held onto her feeling of self through it all. In subsequent sessions, this material led to clarification of two other aspects of her life, one having to do with her relationship with her mother and the other with *actual* separations.

In the next session, after her recall of being something of a fighter in the relationship with her father, she recalled how her mother had betrayed her in that fight. She began: "Mother used to say not to be angry at my father. It was one thing to be at odds with my father — I never knew any other way. But I felt so lost and empty when I realized my mother expected me to do something she was sure I didn't really feel. I had lost my ally. She actually expected me to be nice to him. That was the biggest hurt there was; it was a betrayal." And later: "When I was little, if she said something, I felt 'she's right.' I felt I was wrong to be me if she wanted me to be different. I felt I should not be a horrible angry person. . . . I wanted her to understand, and I felt I'd lost my only ally. I felt I could get her back by trying to be what she wanted, although I didn't *think* this at the time. I didn't think I was trying to get her back—only all the terrible hurt that I lost her. I'm sitting here remembering how strongly I felt that I'd lost her and didn't want to give up myself. But I gave up because I wanted to win her back. I laid down and died."

What has the patient told us now? Only that to be "nobody," a non-self, is the form of the object relationship not only to the father but to the mother as well. She will win mother back by giving up her feelings and being what mother wants. She will be *good*. The material with which I began this patient's presentation—her asking the therapist to tell her whether she was right or wrong to leave the babysitting responsibility; she "had to know, only others could judge" for her—demonstrates that these same issues are active in the transference.

And finally, after the patient's telling of how she wanted to win the mother back, the session ended with: "When I was in grade school, every stranger was somehow a threat because they would separate us. I'd stand frozen. I couldn't stand my mother talking to them because they would separate her from me." One has to know that this patient suffered separations and losses in her earliest years (though she was always in the care of loving relatives). Much of her talk of "annihilation" through abandonment is, I believe, reflective of the repetition of *actual* separation and loss—not of anxiety over awareness of self-other differentiation. The patient's panic some weeks later when the therapist was five minutes late for a session highlighted her fears of actual abandonment. And still later, when the patient erroneously showed up for a session on a holiday when the therapist was away, she had a saddened but reassuring feeling of her "self being there," as she was simultaneously able to acknowledge missing the therapist yet tolerate her absence.

In overview, the self-as-"nobody" was central to the differentiated object relationships of this patient. To be the father's "nobody" was to be his controlled, yet special, little girl. To become "nobody" for the mother by sacrificing her angry feelings and feigning good-girl behavior was her way of holding onto that relationship. Wishes to "be" the other as a source of strength thinly disguised her controlling the other through her neediness and through their need to control her; in this way she simultaneously turned the passive (controlled) experience into an active (controlling) one and held onto the "passive nobody" connection to the other. Although issues of the failure of separation-individuation were constantly suggested by her language, and indeed there is no reason to discount such material in its entirety, on balance I believe that more therapeutic power and developmental accuracy are attained in this case by interpretations centered on forms of differentiated object relationship.

I chose to begin the clinical part of this presentation with an extensive summary of work with this patient who does *not*, in my present opinion, reflect primarily pathology of separation-individuation, because she highlights so many of the conceptual slippages possible in a too loose application of these concepts. Whether a patient's pathology is primarily in the relation to the *differentiated other* or in the *failure of differentiation itself* is of great technical import. The former, as here, is responsive to work that is primarily interpretive in nature; the latter requires substantial reexperiencing of a primary object bond—though interpretive work will also have a very substantial place. These are not either-or issues developmentally, diagnostically, or technically; varying cases will reveal varying admixtures.

A second instance of a case *not* to be understood in terms of failures of the separation-individuation process can clarify some further points. The first case was intended to highlight the need for precision in our thinking about selfhood, merging, and differentiation; this one is intended to do the same regarding separation.

A girl in her early teens was referred by her parents because, among other things, she tended to spend most of her time alone, around the house. Though she had no siblings and both parents worked, she busied herself well at home alone. She had wide-ranging interests—reading, painting, cooking—and claimed to be entirely comfortable with at least that aspect of her life. A piece of history is of great importance: shortly before her birth an older child of the same parents was killed when she precipitously ran out in the street and was hit by a car. This incident was very much part of the family consciousness and hence of this patient's life. Not only was the girl frequently cautioned about the dangers of activity in her early years, but the periodic depressions of the mother, around anniversaries of the first child's death, led again and again to the experience of actual loss of mothering as this girl was growing up.

Not all this was known as the work began. What was known was that she claimed to be comfortable at home. It soon became clear that she wanted to be at home whenever mother was at home so that she would be near her. The mother's presence, and home as an extension of it, gave comfort. It was also soon learned that going out was experienced as a danger. The older sibling had died through activity; the patient might too. Gradually other aspects of the difficulty in separating from mother become clear. They included the *actual* experiences of object loss during the mother's periodic depressions and the child's uncertainty about when the mother would next become unavailable (through depression).

At no time in this long treatment was there any indication that the intense difficulty in separating and even the tie to the home itself had roots in anxiety over the *sense of separateness*. This was a well-differentiated young girl, with a firm sense of herself, a clear awareness of her mother as a separate, and depressed, person, and anxiety over separation, loss, and death. I bring in this brief case report, which seems to me so obviously *not* to be confused with problems of separation-individuation, because all too often people speak of any separation as though it can simply be renamed separation-individuation. Thus, the termination of analysis does not generally reactivate the separation-individuation process just because it represents a separation; the separation is ordinarily from the *differentiated* other (the analyst) and not from the undifferentiated mother-infant dyad (cf. Stone, 1961, on the basic psychoanalytic transference). And not every school entry or adolescent move toward independence reflects the separation-individuation process either. In individual instances, they may; but that has to be understood *intrapsychically* by inference to inner meanings and developmental status.

Let me turn to some cases, by contrast, where I believe the clinical material can best be understood in terms of failures in the separation-individuation process.

A thirty-year-old woman, an only child whose parents were both university professors, sought treatment for problems related to her "black sheep" existence. Close to alcoholism and promiscuity, she lived in other ways also at the edge of illegality. This behavior dropped away when she entered treatment, but the conditions for its periodic reemergence shed light on the psychodynamic constellations involved.

As the analysis progressed, the patient began to be more successful in her real life situation, even completing her degree at the college where one of her parents taught. At this point she began to experience extreme panic and confusional experiences of merging into her parents, a sense of loss of herself, even intensely frightening experiences of melting into the inanimate environment; and a rush back to alcohol and promiscuity followed. It became clear in the subsequent period of analysis that the black sheep self had been a pseudoindividuation, to emphasize her differentness from her parents; it returned in the face of her experience of loss of differentiation when she took on characteristics of her parents (success at learning).

The experience of loss of self is here accompanied by panic, in marked contrast to the first woman I described, who spoke about feeling like "nobody" but spoke in a well-integrated, in-control way. The experience of loss of self as an entity, harking back to the predifferentiated period, is ordinarily accompanied by panic or by pathological acceptance of the nonself position, which produces grossly peculiar behavior or psychotic thinking. Calmer talk of feeling like "nobody," of not knowing "who I am," is more often indicative of higher level problems of "identity," in Erikson's (1950) sense, of self-esteem in postdifferentiation phases of self-awareness, or of pathology of the relation to differentiated others, as in the first case report.

A second point has to do with this patient's sense of merging with the parents as she took on characteristics (i.e., academic success) of the parents. The developmental history of individuation is relevant here. As I said before, we view individuation as the process of the child's taking on characteristics that come to be experienced as the core of the "me." But the conceptual paradox (though the developmental commonplace) is that the child individuates, at least initially, by taking on characteristics of the principal "others" in his life—the very others from whom differentiation must take place. There are seeds of developmental difficulty sown by this process when the assimilation of parental characteristics is too much by osmosis, itself too undifferentiated. Sometimes the assumption of parental characteristics (even walking, food preferences, and voice tone) is not accompanied by a stable cognitive achievement of self-other differentiation, not organized into an experience of "me-ness," but instead confirms the illusion of undifferentiated mother-child unity.

Problems in this domain were present in this patient, based partly on developmental failure and partly on regressive phenomena. To be *like* the parents was insufficiently differentiated from *being* the parents—hence merging and panic. It would be dramatic to say that the normal mode of individuation, by taking on parental characteristics, creates a delicate tension so that the child (or adult) can all too readily fall from individuation into un-differentiated merging. But I do not believe that to be the case. The power of the *cognitive* differentiation of self and other—though contradicted by preverbal memory and by wish, yet anchored in perception of the real world—is indeed great and ordinarily provides a context in which likeness is safely distinguished from undifferentiated merging—though of course there are pathological exceptions to this and momentary exceptions for all of us.

After the rush back to alcohol and promiscuity that came to be understood as a pseudodifferentiation through being the black sheep, maximally different from the parents in external appearance, the patient restabilized and the work progressed—until the next episode. When the capacity to achieve external success and to feel worthwhile became more stable, the patient began ex-periencing acutely painful feelings of aloneness and isolation; again came the flight back to her former ways of living as well as flickerings of the sense of merging. This time it became clear that to be her own self in a successful way was to be *alone*, to lose the tie to her parents. The tie, at this point, was seen to have elements of undifferentiated connection ("I'm part of the home; they always think of me; they're always there") as well as connection to the parents as differentiated others. But to be the black sheep more forcefully preserved the tie to the parents; they were in fact "always thinking of" her when she was behaving in asocial and self-destructive ways.

I believe that the clinical material from this patient can profitably be conceptualized in terms of the pathology of the separation-individuation process. One measure of this was the successful progress of the treatment as those concepts were brought to bear, in the interpretive work, and in the sense that the analyst intentionally conveyed to this patient of "being there" for her, particularly at moments of her isolation and/or panic. In overview, problems of individuation were tied to unstable experiences of separateness (fear of merging) and unstable attachment (fear of loss of oneness and fear of loss of object relatedness). The black sheep behavior *simultaneously* pro-duced the feeling of being different from (separate, not merging) and tied to the parents.

Let me turn now to a second patient, a child whom we knew in our clinic from age eight-and-a-half through ten, when the parents withdrew her from treatment. Little is known of the history, but we do know that a twin sister of the mother's died during the mother's infancy (and this may have con-tributed to symbiotic, "twinning," problems in her) and that the mother went into a moderately severe depression when the patient was just two years of age. I shall focus only on the phenomenology of separateness and absence of differentiation. This is a child who does not panic when she "becomes" the mother but, rather, in an ego-syntonic way, lives out the oddness and unreality of that position.

Sara was referred by her school authorities, who described her as behaving like an "automaton," unrelated to others except in trying to please. She was

observed to copy work from other children's papers, even copying the other child's name onto her own paper.

In the initial evaluation, where a diagnosis of child psychosis was made, Sara tended to repeat her mother's words, reeling off "do's" and "don'ts" given to her by mother. In school she "needs to be told what to do" in order to perform, and at home she is told by mother when to go to the bathroom and the like. A number of "I-you" confusions were evident: For example, when someone else coughs, the child says "excuse me." In each of these ways Sara demonstrated self-other confusion, which seemed to us in this case to reflect a primary developmental failure.

Her behavior after therapy began equally suggested pathology of the failure of differentiation. Her opening statement as she entered the therapist's office for the first time was revealing: "Let's sit close to each other," she said, as she took a seat in the diagonally opposite corner of the room! Is this ambivalence? I think not, not in the drive sense at least. All of what we came to know supports a view that this was her expression of issues of close and distant, of merging and separateness. She then began to list the things that were similar about herself and the therapist—"our hair is the same," and so on—even including things that were obviously *dissimilar*. Later she did the same with birthdates and spelling of names; "we are the same" in obvious contradiction of reality.

But the outstanding aspect of her behavior, from the standpoint of both its function and its expressive poignancy, appeared in what became her regular behavior in session after session for some time. Sara would enter the session talking of how hard it was to get there ("It takes too many buses)"; she didn't think she could continue to come. We heard in this the mother's voice, which the child had assumed. This was not an inference; the child would say what we constantly *heard* the mother say, and in the same tone. The child thus became the mother as she entered the therapist's office. But as the session progressed, she dropped that behavior and began to be more herself. That self varied. At times she would be psychotic, unreal, distorting reality— certainly a part of herself, and perhaps itself a mode of differentiation. But at other times she would tell the therapist how unhappy she was, especially in school. At these times she came into an object relationship with the therapist as a differentiated other, one to whom she, an unhappy child, could tell her problems. Strikingly, as the session neared an end, Sara would again adopt her mother's voice. The suggestion was clear that the child carried the mother into the sessions by *becoming* the mother (rather than by holding onto the differentiated mental image of the mother); she gradually emerged from that imaginary union as the session proceeded and moved back into it as she prepared to return to mother; there is an ebb and flow of her merged and differentiated selves.

I will not detail the course of this therapy; but let me just mention that, after a winter vacation by the therapist and her subsequent return, the child moved into a more pleasure-filled, though infantile, relation with her. Peekaboo, "bye-bye" games, and singsong talk together became focal. With this, the mother started pulling the child out of treatment, away from the therapist, and eventually joint mother-child sessions had to be instituted. Although these were less useful to the child, they enabled the therapy to continue—at least until the (student) therapist left at year's end and the mother refused continuance with someone else.

Here we see an instance of severe pathology, organized largely around the failure of differentiation, with the child's frequent seeming acceptance of the undifferentiated state. Indeed, Sara often advertised that state by her peculiar behavior; yet was ready to begin to move beyond it with the therapist. Even if the mother had not been threatened by the child's relation with the therapist, and hence changed the therapeutic course, the work would have been slow and the outcome doubtful. In the treatment of related pathology Mahler and Furer (1960) have found it wise to work with mother-child pairs together.

These last two cases, in which I believe that pathology of the separation-individuation process can be inferred, can be contrasted with the first two, in which, despite (in one case) verbalization about loss of self and (in the other) major difficulties with separation, pathology of the early separation-individuation process, the pathology of the relation to the *un*differentiated other, was not convincingly clear as the clinical material unfolded. In concluding this section, let me bring in material suggestive of *postdifferentiation* pathology that is, nonetheless, *tied to* the early separation-individuation process.

The pathology of relations to undifferentiated others includes panic over merging and loss of self, ego-syntonic (but bizarre) living out of self-other unity, and grossly deviant development that scotomizes all awareness of self and other. Beyond this, we are familiar from our usual clinical work with disturbances in relations to *differentiated* others, including ambivalence, wish-taboo conflicts, and actualities of gratification/seduction/frustration. There are also certain disturbances in relations to the differentiated other that are *linked to the differentiation process itself*. Borrowing phrases that Kernberg (1966) uses in a different context, I characterize these as "higher level" pathology of the separation-individuation process and the disturbances in relation to the undifferentiated other as "lower level" pathology of that process. I shall refer to three cases to highlight, respectively, three phenomena: aloneness, coercion, and disturbances of libidinal object constancy—all tied to differentiation but involving a differentiated other.

Aloneness. I have already presented the material for aloneness as part of my discussion of the thirty-year-old black sheep. When that patient succeeded *like* her parents she had a sense of panic and of *becoming* her parents (merging); later, when she became more solidly individuated, having internalized the characteristics leading to success and having begun to define a sense of self around them, she felt intensely alone, had flickerings of the sense of merging, and rushed back into her alcoholic/promiscuous life, which reinvolved her with her parents in actuality.

Mahler (1972) has suggested that the rapprochement subphase is structured around the child's growing awareness of aloneness; no longer can the illusion of unity be maintained, and the child experiences himself as alone in a big world. In the normal course of events, object relation and object constancy functionally replace what had formerly been satisfied by the illusion of unity. Now, certainly not all problems over intense aloneness can be traced back to the aftermath of differentiation. Spiegel (1966), for example, has shown the relation of the affect of longing to the specific, loved (and differentiated) other. For most, intense aloneness does not lead to dedifferentiation of self and other; for some it leads to substitute object gratification (alcohol, food, drugs), displacement to other relationships, a turn back to the self-as-object, or successful maintenance of the painful alone state. But for *this* patient, it led back to merging and regressive behavior because the aloneness was related to the experience of the self-as-alone (i.e., differentiated) rather than to the longing for the differentiated other.

Coercion. In the work with seven-year-old Lawrence, his coercion of the mother emerged clearly. Like the form of aloneness in the previous patient, this can be seen as a postdifferentiation phenomenon that is tied to the process of self-other differentiation.

When Lawrence was brought to our clinic at age four, he was in an embattled relationship with his mother. Among their pathological interactions were the mother's constant threats to leave and the child's actual abandonment of her by refusing (for years) to eat with her, instead eating alone in his room. Later, at school, he did fairly well; the pathology was predominantly reserved for the home. In school, however, he had to hold onto the belief that his mother was sitting on a bench outside waiting for him (which she had done briefly), with a kind of splitting of the ego (Freud, 1927) in which he both knew and did not know that she was not really there. In the therapy sessions, leaving the mother and returning, locking out the therapist and then opening the door, and wandering around the building were prominent activities.

Lawrence seemed well differentiated from his mother; at least we saw none of the indications of the wish/fear/enactment of merging that I illustrated in some of the other cases. But the normal process of differentiation leaves the child with the internal representation of the mother to functionally replace the illusory symbiosis of the earlier period. This inner representation is what Winnicott (1958b) has in mind when he writes of the child's developing the "capacity to be alone" by being alone in the presence of the mother and subsequently internalizing the sense of her presence, and it is what is referred to by the concept of libidinal object constancy (Hartmann, 1952; chap. 8). In our research on normal development (Mahler et al., 1975), we saw that in children who have considerable awareness of differentiation from mother but have not come to terms with that awareness affectively and have not stably internalized the mother as a constant mental representation—that is, in children in the *rapprochement* subphase—a phenomenon of coercion emerges. The child is insistent that the mother do what the child wills. This was central in both Lawrence and his mother vis-à-vis the other. Such coercion, under the headings of negativism, stubbornness, or control, can be understood in libidinal and aggressive object-relation terms: in the second to third year, the child turns upon the mother that effort at control that she applies to him in the toileting battle, or that the child is engaged in with an internal "other," his own feces. But we felt we saw an additional determinant: the child, now aware of self-other differentiation and having primitive notions of causality that are sufficient to disrupt the infantile omnipotent notion that his wishes produce mother's actions, uses coercion to deny, reverse, and undo those new learnings. If coercion succeeds, the child is again in omnipotent control of mother; she is an extension of him; the consequences of differentiation have been undone. Although I do not believe that all coercion includes this among its primary determinants, I believe that this early root in the separation-individuation process is present to some degree in some patients. With coercion, there need be no loss of the sense of self, no loss of awareness of the existence of the other-as-other; but the affective consequences of differentiation (helplessness, aloneness) are undone.

Libidinal object constancy. Problems of object constancy are also suggested in Lawrence's case (witness the split of the ego regarding mother's presence on a bench outside school); but many of the phenomena can be understood in terms of feared (actual) loss of the differentiated other as well as in terms of difficulties in establishing a constant inner sense of the other. We do not have a full sense of the inner situation with which he is dealing. But problems of holding onto the inner image of the object are evident in clinical work of all kinds. Fleming (1975), for example, describes an adult who remembers, as a child, struggling to recall the face of the missing mother; the attainment of the capacity to hold onto the image of his analyst was crucial in his analysis. The inner representation of the object serves multiple functions, including the replacement of the infantile symbiosis *and* the relation to the differentiated other, and it is not possible to say that solely one or the other is disturbed. In any event, patients with defects in the development of libidinal object constancy can be thought of as retaining the basic sense of differentiation but as having difficulty with a next step in the separation-individuation process, that of holding in memory the well-differentiated concept of the other. At times, this difficulty is precisely because of the rage at the "lost" (i.e., differentiated) mother, rage that tends to destabilize the internal object representation (McDevitt, 1975).

Thus, for certain forms of aloneness, coercion, and instability of libidinal object constancy, a concept of higher order separation-individuation pathology is useful; it is pathology of the relation to the *differentiated* other that is *tied to the process of differentiation itself.* Each of these phenomena can be explained by reference to pathology of drive and object relation without reference to separation and individuation. At times I believe that this is an adequate, indeed a better, explanation; but at times it is not. Ultimately theoretical preference enters in. Theoretical preferences affect our work and therefore our patients; we ought to be maximally aware of the range of theoretical choices available to us, and of the varying choices required to understand the full range of patient pathology.

SOME ADDITIONAL ISSUES

In this section, I should like to bring in material from three more patients, each selected to raise further issues regarding the pathology of the separation-individuation process; secondarily, each case will serve as a bridge to a brief discussion of some other forms of pathology that have been linked by others to the separation-individuation process. These are depersonalization/derealization, "as if" character, and folie à deux.

Nadia is a late adolescent girl whose therapy highlighted a distinction between primary developmental failure of separation-individuation and secondary regression as a defense; she also showed qualities akin to (though not identical with) depersonalization and derealization. Nadia came to treatment as a twenty-year-old college sophomore because of bouts of tearfulness and depression and difficulty in making friends. She often daydreamed of the warmth of her childhood homeland, feeling that people here were "cold." Her vocal style contributed greatly to the sense of her disconnectedness, her not being "there"; she spoke softly, haltingly, often in half-sentences, puzzled in tone, unclear, yet with the sense that the listener would understand. The sense of absence in her speech cannot be overemphasized; it was often eerie to listen to her.

From the outset, differentiation problems were suggested in her wish that the therapist know her thoughts without being told, in her wanting the office lights off (at dusk) since the lights "create contrast; when they are off it seems warmer, closer," and in her feeling that "by myself something is lacking, missing; I need the other person in order to start." That the sense of indivisible unity of therapist and self was a background feeling became evident when she saw the therapist enter from outside for the first time (always before having seen her emerge from her office) and, puzzled, uttered the half-sentence: "I didn't...know...you were...," a half-sentence that turned out to express a complete idea: she didn't "know" the therapist *existed* outside of their contacts ("I didn't know you *were*"). Her feared loss of self was evidenced in her fear of being "influenced" or "brainwashed" by the therapist, in her fear of being "bereft" if she "gave" the therapist all her thoughts, in her need to disagree because "to agree is to lose myself," in her concern that the therapist could not tell her apart from all her other patients. In one striking piece of therapeutic work, the patient's disturbing feeling of being "selfish" because she was pursuing a certain pleasurable activity at someone else's expense yielded only to the interpretation that it made her feel "*self*-ish," that is, like a self, a person, functioning on her own.

This patient was not psychotic. She functioned at least reasonably well at school and on her job. To the best of my understanding we were seeing a phenomenon confined mainly to the transference, a failure of early development elicited by and relived in the relation to the therapist. The work proceeded reasonably well, and the patient began at times to speak in a more communicative fashion, speaking to an *other* who had to be helped to understand. She also began to date young men occasionally. On one occasion she came in and told the therapist about her date; she spoke like an adolescent—partly excited, partly worried. Then she got to the point where the young man wanted to kiss her goodnight and suddenly, in the session, she shifted totally. Her speech became uncommunicative, vague, as it had been earlier in the therapy. It was not hesitant because of her dealing with difficult content, something entirely expectable and ordinary, but seemed rather to reflect the loss of an "I" talking to a "you." The whole event—a new date, clear communication, and the sudden shift in style of communication—occurred again a few weeks later.

I believe that we are seeing here a regressive movement along a pathway that has already been traversed in the progressive direction—that is, a movement back to loss of self and loss of the sense of the other—with a focal defensive intent, to obliterate the difficult moment of differentiated self-other relatedness being described with the boyfriend on the date. Freud (1936) pointed out that experiences of depersonalization and derealization serve defensive purposes. They are certainly different from what this patient reveals. In depersonalization and derealization there is still ordinarily retention of the observer ego, an "I" that knows that something is wrong, out of kilter, in the sense of self and/or world. Nadia loses even the observer function; she becomes unreal and undifferentiated to the external observer (the therapist) but she does not seem to be a self-observer of the process.

In Arlow's (1966) paper on depersonalization and derealization he asks where these phenomena might come from developmentally and suggests (among other things) "the phase of the transitional object, the phase during which the limits of the self and the nonself are not yet clearly demarcated" (p. 475). In Mahler's work on the normal separation-individuation process (Mahler et al., 1975), she begins with a discussion of how a reality sense of self and world are *created* in that process. Arlow explicitly states that he does not see the phenomenon of early undifferentiation in his clinical material, but Stamm (1962) gives clinical material to support his conclusion that "the symptom of depersonalization involves a regression . . . to a primitive, undifferentiated oral state in which the individual yearns for symbiotic union with mother" (p. 764). The sudden loss of the sense of self and other in the patient I have described, *akin* to depersonalization and derealization, seems to move back to primitive undifferentiation.

This is not to suggest that all depersonalization and derealization experiences have genetic roots in the predifferentiated (normal symbiotic) phase. It is one of the faults in analytic writings to blur the distinction between the universal and the particular. I suggest that the universal here is the defensive function served by depersonalization. Early differentiation failures, which set the stage for momentary losses of the sense of self and of reality, are only one *route* to such phenomena.

In the past few years I have come across a number of children who seem highly "suggestible," at least in relation to the mother. An impulse of the mother's, not necessarily unconscious, or a peculiar idea of hers is picked up by the child in a way that seems somewhere between mimicry and identification. The behavior often does not last; it is here today, gone tomorrow, when another piece of the mother's behavior appears in the child. I have thought of this as a kind of permeability of ego boundaries and wondered about its relation to the early separation-individuation process.

In one ten-year-old child the phenomenon was a recurrent one. When the mother worried about his getting sick, he would break into sweats; when she worried about her eyes being sensitive to the sun, he would get headaches. She feared that he would steal (and planned for him to dress as a thief on Halloween); and shortly thereafter a stealing incident occurred in school. She became concerned about his preoccupation with a certain television character but was herself preoccupied with his preoccupation and lent fuel to it. Whenever she feared trouble from him, he would present her with it. Sometimes the mechanism of influence was clear (as in the Halloween costume incident), but not always.

Let me try to come to a formulation of the phenomenon by reference to a number of other clinical phenomena. Adelaide Johnson (1949) has described the way in which certain parents transmit something to a child so as to bring about his acting out of an unconscious parental impulse. The parent meanwhile maintains his or her own repression and experiences the child's action as both alien (consciously) and gratifying (unconsciously). In these instances a focal impulse is involved, active in the parent but defended against. In the cases I have in mind this is less true; the communication is more promiscuous, more random. It seems to be the *transmission process*, with its implication for mother-child connectedness, rather than the specific *content* that matters most.

From another reference point, we can look at this phenomenon by contrasting it with identification. After all, the child's identification with the parent is a mode of normal learning. But the phenomenon I am describing was different from identification in two distinct ways. First, the maternal behaviors did not become part of the child in any permanent way; they were not only random as to content but transient as to longevity—again, "promiscuous"—so they did not truly come to be part of the "I." And second, they did not foster individuation but intimate connection. Either there was an inner experience of connection in both mother and child or the disturbed behavior of the child would come to be a cause of concern to the mother, leading to an increase in her involvement with him.

I would formulate such phenomena in terms of residues of early differentiation problems. At the moment I can do little more than suggest this, not having adequate longitudinal-clinical data to be more sure of my ground. But I am struck by the fact that—in contrast to the Johnson (1949) "superego lacunae" phenomenon or the common phenomenon of identification, both of which can involve *either* parent—I have seen this boundary-permeability only between children and their *mothers*.

The way in which the child transiently becomes the mother, living out her thoughts, style, or impulses, is reminiscent of "as if" characters (Deutsch, 1942), for whom global, yet transient, "identification" has become a way of life. Reading the beautiful clinical descriptions in that 1942 paper today, and seeing Helene Deutsch's attempts to explain the phenomenon largely in terms of faulted libidinal relations to early objects, one is struck by the incompleteness of our understanding when we have only drive theory to work with. The panel on "as if" character (Weiss, 1966) updates this work. In it, Helen Tartakoff suggested that "as if" phenomena have their genesis in the separation-individuation phase, and Maurits Katan linked them to Freud's (1923) concept of primary identification, in which attachment and identification occur simultaneously rather than the attachment preceding the identification. Considering the extent of the pathology, both in the "permeable ego boundaries" I have described and in the more developed "as if" characters, and considering its specific nature, I would speculate that here we are seeing a phenomenon whose *universal* aspects have to do with separation-individuation pathology, although the particular patient histories will still vary widely.

And finally a case that stands midway between the suggestibility I have described and folie à deux. The process of "becoming" the other person—that is, the apparent loss of differentiation in exchange for merging—can have an object-seeking quality, object-seeking on the only terms available, and not only reflect a failure of independent functioning. Akin to this, Anna Freud (1960) once described how the child of a depressed mother could try to follow the mother into her depression, could find the depressed state from its own repertoire of behavior possibilities and cathect it, as a form of *attachment* to the (differentiated) mother. While the result is a pathological one, recognition of the wish underlying the process permits us to see the patient's achievement through the pathology.

The case of Patti, age ten, described in the previous chapter as a borderline child with incomplete internalization of the maternal psychosis, illustrates some of the features of folie à deux. Recall that Patti arrived in the hospital confirming her mother's reports that she heard voices and had been destroying her mother's clothing and other possessions. The confirmation had seemed genuine; Patti had the affective feel (to the observer) and the cognitive confusion of a psychotic child. Yet we later came to see that this child's schizophrenic mother was ensnaring Patti in her illness, promoting the idea of hearing voices, and had selected Patti as her principal partner among her several children. But Patti had adopted her mother's point of view, not simply as a pose, for she certainly lived it out at times. Indeed we saw the child's participation in the mother's psychosis come and go as the mother came and went on hospital visits.

For Patti, the psychotic-like phenomena seemed to be part of the *attachment* to the mother. To see them simply as developmental failures of differentiation misses the point. Patti was enmeshed in and pursuing a specific, partially symbiotic relationship that had grossly pathological features. Merging here is a disturbed form of attachment more than a failure of differentiation—though of course the *form* of object seeking follows an old available pathway. The ease with which she moved into much better integrated functioning when separated from the mother suggests that she had moved successfully through the separation-individuation process earlier.

Patti's sharing of her mother's ideas about her destructive behavior and her "hearing voices" has kinship to folie à deux, though shared delusions did not fully crystallize. Two quite different points can be made about folie à deux, each with validity in individual cases. Thus, Deutsch (1938) wrote that "in folie à deux in psychotics, the common delusion appears to be...an attempt to rescue the object through identification with it, or its delusional system," and "the person affected by the suggestion...attempts through identification to *come closer* to the object or to find again a lost object" (p. 317). Here the emphasis is on *object* finding through identification, as I believe was the case with Patti. Anthony (1971), on the other hand, in his work with child-mother twosomes in folie à deux, while not ruling out the object-related aspect of the pathology, also finds major early developmental failures in the separation-individuation process. Differentiation failure and object seeking are clearly not mutually exclusive, and it may be that we can best look at folie à deux in terms of the relative balance between failure of differentiation and object seeking of a differentiated other along a pathological pathway.

I have only touched upon issues regarding folie à deux, "as if" character, and depersonalization/derealization with the intent of raising further issues and providing further distinctions within the pathology of separation-individuation, suggesting as well that an understanding of the separation-individuation process may enrich our understanding of other phenomena as well.

In this chapter I have tried to give a sense of the phenomenology of pathological presentations that I take to be reflective of early failures in the movement out of symbiosis and through the separation-individuation process. By way of contrast, I have described two cases in which, in spite of a heavy emphasis on issues of nonself (in one) and separation (in the other), the pathology seemed to reflect not failures of separation-individuation but instead the relation to the differentiated other. These cases made clear that the distinctions between the pathological formations growing out of the relation to the *undifferentiated other* versus the *differentiated other* can be made only through access to intrapsychic content and not through surface presentations. Additionally, I have distinguished between low-level and high-level pathology of separation-individuation, the former having to do with the undifferentiated other, the latter with the differentiated other but *tied to the differentiation process itself.* Throughout, I have tried to use concepts derived from work on separation and individuation to enable us to think in depth rather than to categorize phenomena in either-or ways, to enhance flexibility of thinking rather than to claim or disown this or that phenomenon for this or that theoretical idea.

Having described and illustrated the phenomena, I can now, more briefly, refer to a few of the common misuses of the terms "symbiosis," "separation," and "individuation." Although *symbiosis* is perhaps not the most apt of terms, we use it to refer to the early state of illusory unity before the infant is aware of self-other differentiation. As such, any pathological (or even beneficial) *differentiated object relationship*, no matter how intertwined and mutually dependent, is not a symbiosis in these terms. Sadomasochistic relationships or shared passive/aggressive/dependent relationships are complexly intertwined, but the relationship is ordinarily to a well-differentiated other and is therefore not symbiotic in our terms. And as for *separation*, it should be clear by now that the term refers to the sense of one's separateness and not to physical separations. This inner sense holds whether one is with another or alone; conversely, in pathological cases, the denial of separateness can be maintained whether or not the significant other is present. Actual physical separations are of profound significance in human functioning; they are simply different in their import from the sense of separateness. To repeat an earlier example, the termination of analysis does not ordinarily arouse separation-individuation residues; far more often it is the loss of the differentiated other, the analyst-as-object, that is the central affective issue.

Finally, we use the term *individuation* to refer to the child's (or adult's) assumption of new characteristics that define his unique and stable self—a process that, paradoxically, often involves identification with the characteristics of those from whom differentiation is taking place. It involves becoming a differentiated self and not simply being *different from*. Thus, an adolescent can maximize his differences from his family as a form of struggle against (intrapsychic) merging, these differences having nothing to do with true individuation as we see it. On the other hand, an adolescent may stay close to his family, conforming and intimate; if this represents his identification with the dependent-conforming style of his family, having made that part of what is now *himself*, then it meets our definition of individuation even though he is still at home and in close object relation to the primary developmental love objects.

There are many threads to the developmental process, many developmental lines along which people move. I have been focusing on the move from lack of awareness of separateness to the growth of such awareness, or, complementary to that, the change from attachment to the undifferentiated other to attachment to the differentiated other. These two ways of stating the developmental line, one emphasizing the growth of *awareness* and the other of altered *attachment*, point up, respectively, the cognitive and the affective/gratificatory aspects of the process. These two aspects, naturally intertwined in any actual instance, help us understand something about the fate of these early events as they do or do not come to our attention in later clinical work.

Clinical content in the domain of separation and individuation does not come up significantly in a large number of cases. It certainly comes up with some frequency, but not with absolute regularity, as does drive-defense conflict. Why is this so? Because there is a major cognitive achievement in the person's movement through the separation-individuation process. The growth of *awareness* of separateness is anchored in perceptual reality, which leads to an organization of stimuli and of memories around the self-other distinction. As such, this cognitive achievement, this awareness anchored in perception, is not easily lost. In this sense the outcome of the separation-individuation process—the achievement of self-other differentiation—is like other achievements, say, reality testing, which we can ordinarily count on being stably present all through even a full analysis that includes important regressive features in the transference. The absence of self-other differentiation, like the absence of the achievement of reality testing (of which it is part), ordinarily signifies serious pathology.

On the other hand, to the degree that the separation-individuation process involves not only a new awareness but a new form of *attachment*, affective-gratificatory processes are involved. Here, where we deal with the loss of old forms of safety (in the illusory symbiotic unity), we are dealing with something that has more a dynamic than a structured character. Like other urges and accustomed forms of gratification, it does not fade away when it is replaced by other, "higher," forms of gratification and attachment. It remains and I believe helps to account for not only the merging wishes (and panics) in seriously disturbed patients but for the normal wishes for union that one sees in love, in certain Eastern religions, in certain drug experiences, and in various transient phenomena within an analysis.

This chapter has been an exercise in the application of clinical-developmental theory to clinical-pathological data. Its ultimate measure is how well it helps organize the clinical data and how well it contributes to the therapeutic power of the technical interventions that it informs. Though many ambiguities must always remain, it nonetheless seems to me that, when present in conjunction with the understanding of urges, affects, and object relations, refined understanding of the separation-individuation process and its sequelae enriches our understanding and, transformed into technique, adds to our therapeutic effectiveness.

PART FOUR

RETROSPECT

Retrospect

Psychoanalytic technique is radical at its core. When Freud urged open-ended listening upon us, he opened up a Pandora's box full of the contents of the human mind. And potentially, at least in terms of modes of understanding (though not of intervention), there are no rules—neither the commandments of religions nor the experimental controls of science. That radical open-mindedness can be applied to observations of development as well.

And yet there are strong conservative forces within psychoanalysis as well, which ultimately stem from the seriousness of purpose with which we approach our responsibilities in the clinical situation. We are not ordinarily free, with patients, to follow whim, to ignore the lessons and constraints of prior experience. And so, too, with observations of development, in one's own children and in formal research; experimental manipulation is necessarily put aside for concerned effort and consistent respect.

In retrospect, I hope that these chapters have conveyed my own brand of quiet radicalism and flexible conservatism. The lessons of psychoanalysis regarding technique, pathology, and human development are not to be ignored, but nor should they be a straitjacket. Close-up observations of development, like the close-up observations entailed in the psychoanalytic process, continue to provide refreshing new insights that are to be tried out in relation to available theory and ultimately integrated into our theories and techniques or allowed to fade away, as appropriate.

A number of overriding points developed and illustrated here are the major contributions I seek to make in this book. First is a view of development and of clinical experience that permits an integration of the psychologies of drive, ego, object relations, and self, as well as of the influences of the person's experienced reality, in our understanding of human functioning. In this integration, an emphasis on *moments* in which experience is differentially organized has been a necessary concept for me, originating in my clinical experience and personal analysis. Second, I present a blending of developmental theory with the theory of technique, which has implications for our understanding of the bases for the effectiveness of classical technique, for the development of modifications in technique in specific clinical situations, and for the extension of the range of our potential modes of conceptualizing and interpreting each individual's psychic life—both contemporaneously in the transference and retrospectively in the experienced life history. Within this, I have laid particular stress on early experience, on quiet background pleasure and support, and on inputs from reality—but only because these have not been as fully stressed in the classical literature as have certain other features. And third is a highly differentiated approach to the description of psychopathology, drawing on structural as well as developmental considerations, in an effort to increase our ability to work with greater specificity in both experience-near and theoretically grounded ways with each person who presents himself or herself to us for psychological treatment.

At the start of this book, I said that both development and the therapeutic enterprise are full of surprises whose processes invite thought and whose outcomes invite wonderment. I have tried to contribute something to that thought. There is still endless space for wonderment, and so the work goes on.

References

Abraham, K. (1921). Contributions to the theory of the anal character. In *Selected Papers*. New York: Basic Books, 1953, 370–392.

——— (1924). The influence of oral erotism on character formation. In *Selected Papers*. New York: Basis Books, 1953, 393–406.

Albee, E. (1960). *The Zoo Story*. New York: Coward.

Alexander, F. (1948). *Fundamentals of Psychoanalysis*. New York: Norton.

——— (1956). *Psychoanalysis and Psychotherapy*. New York: Norton.

Allen, D. W. (1967). Exhibitionistic and voyeuristic conflicts in learning and functioning. *Psychoanal. Q.* 36:546–570.

Anthony, E. J. (1971). Folie à deux: A developmental failure in the process of separation-individuation. In *Separation-Individuation*, ed. J. B. McDevitt and C. F. Settlage. New York: Int. Univ. Press, 253–273.

Arlow, J. A. (1953). Masturbation and symptom formation. *J. Amer. Psychoanal. Assn.* 1:45–58.

——— (1966). Depersonalization and derealization. In *Psychoanalysis: A General Psychology*, ed. R. M. Loewenstein, L. M. Newman, M. Schur, and A. J. Solnit. New York: Int. Univ. Press, 456–478.

Beebe, B., and Sloate, P. (1982). Assessment and treatment of difficulties in mother-infant attunement in the first three years of life: A case history. *Psychoanal. Inquiry* 1:601–623.

———, and Stern, D. N. (1977). Engagement-disengagement and early object experiences. In *Communicative Structures and Psychic Structures*, ed. N. Freedman and S. Grand. New York: Plenum Press, 35–55.

Bell, S. (1970). The development of a concept of object as related to infant-mother attachment. *Child Devel.* 41:291–311.

Benedek, T. (1938). Adaptation to reality in early infancy. *Psychoanal. Q.* 7:200–214.

Benjamin, J. D. (1959). Prediction and psychopathologic theory. In *Dynamic Psychopathology in Childhood*, ed. L. Jessner and E. Pavenstedt. New York: Grune & Stratton, 6–77.

Benjamin, L. (1971). Learning disorders in children. Report to the Fleischman Commission, New York State.

————, and Finkel, W. (1969). Time disorientation in mildly retarded children with sequencing disorder: Diagnosis and treatment. Paper read at Amer. Orthopsychiat. Assn.

————, and Green, B. E. (1968). Differential diagnosis and treatment of a childhood aphasic disorder: A case study. In *Learning Disorders*, ed. J. Hellmuth. Seattle: Special Child Publications 3:225–247.

Beres, D. (1965). Structure and function in psychoanalysis. *Int. J. Psychoanal.* 46:53–63.

Bergman, A. (1971). "I and you": The separation process in the treatment of a symbiotic child. In *Separation-Individuation*, ed. J. B. McDevitt and C. F. Settlage. New York: Int. Univ. Press, 325–355.

———— (1980). Ours, yours, mine. In *Rapprochement*, ed. R. F. Lax, S. Bach, and J. A. Burland. New York: Aronson, 199–216.

————, and Furer, M. (1974). Child psychosis: A review of Mahler's theory and some recent developments and thoughts. Presented at Amer. Orthopsychiat. Assn., San Francisco.

Berlyne, D. E. (1960). *Conflict, Arousal, and Curiosity.* New York: McGraw-Hill.

Bernfeld, S. (1938). Types of adolescence. *Psychoanal. Q.* 7:243–253.

———— (1944). Freud's earliest theories and the school of Helmholtz. *Psychoanal. Q.* 13:341–362.

Blanck, G., and Blanck, R. (1974). *Ego Psychology: Theory and Practice.* New York: Columbia Univ. Press.

————, and ———— (1979). *Ego Psychology II: Psychoanalytic Developmental Psychology.* New York: Columbia Univ. Press.

Blos, P. (1962). *On Adolescence: A Psychoanalytic Interpretation.* New York: Free Press.

Bornstein, B. (1951). On latency. *Psychoanal. Study Child* 6:279–285.

Bowlby, J. (1944). Forty-four juvenile thieves: Their characters and home life. *Int. J. Psychoanal.* 25:19–52, 107–127.

———— (1969). *Attachment and Loss. Vol. I. Attachment.* New York, Basic Books.

———— (1973). *Attachment and Loss. Vol. II. Separation: Anxiety and Anger.* New York: Basic Books.

———— (1980). *Attachment and Loss. Vol. III. Sadness and Depression.* New York: Basic Books.

Brazelton, T. B. (1976). Mother-infant reciprocity. Presented at Albert Einstein College of Medicine, New York.

————, Tronick, E., Adamson, L., Als, A., and Wise, S. (1975). Early mother-infant reciprocity. In *Parent-Infant Interaction*, CIBA Foundation, Symposium 33. Amsterdam: Elsevier, 137–154.

Breuer, J., and Freud, S. (1893). Studies on hysteria. *S.E.* 2.

Broucek, F. (1977). The sense of self. *Bull. Menninger Clinic* 41:85–90.

———— (1979). Efficacy in infancy. *Int. J. Psychoanal.* 60:311–316.

Brunswick, R. M. (1940). The preoedipal phase of the libido development. *Psychoanal. Q.* 9:293–319.

Čapek, K. (1922). *R.U.R. and Other Plays.* New York: Oxford Univ. Press, 1961.

Caplan, G. (1960). Patterns of parental response to the crisis of premature birth. *Psychiatry* 23:365–374.

Décarie, T. G. (1965). *Intelligence and Affectivity in Early Childhood.* New York: Int. Univ. Press.

Deutsch, H. (1938). Folie à deux. *Psychoanal. Q.* 7:307–318.

———— (1942). Some forms of emotional disturbance and their relation to schizophrenia. *Psychoanal. Q.* 11:301–331.

Drucker, J. (1975). Toddler play: Some comments on its functions in the developmental process. *Psychoanal. Contemp. Science* 4:479–527.

Eissler, K. (1953). The effect of the structure of the ego on psychoanalytic technique. *J. Amer. Psychoanal. Assn.* 1:104–143.

Ekstein, R. (1966). *Children of Time and Space, of Action and Impulse.* New York: Appleton-Century-Crofts.

———, and Wallerstein, J. (1954). Observations on the psychology of borderline and psychotic children. *Psychoanal. Study Child* 9:344–369.

Emde, R. N., Gaensbauer, T. J., and Harmon, R. J. (1976). *Emotional Expression in Infancy.* New York: Int. Univ. Press.

Erikson, E. H. (1950). *Childhood and Society.* New York: Norton.

Escalona, S. (1953). Emotional development in the first year of life. In *Problems of Infancy and Childhood,* Transactions of the 6th Josiah Macy Foundation Conference, ed. M. Senn. Packawack Lake, N.J.: Foundation Press, 11–92.

——— (1968). *The Roots of Individuality.* Chicago: Aldine.

———, and Heider, G. M. (1959). *Prediction and Outcome: A Study in Child Development.* New York: Basic Books.

Fairbairn, W. R. D. (1941). A revised psychopathology of the psychoses and psychoneuroses. *Int. J. Psychoanal.* 22:250–279.

Fantz, R. L. (1961). The origin of form perception. *Scientific American* 204:66–72.

Fenichel, O. (1945). *The Psychoanalytic Theory of Neurosis.* New York: Norton.

Ferenczi, S. (1913). Stages in the development of the sense of reality. In *Sex and Psychoanalysis: The Selected Papers of Sandor Ferenczi, Vol. I.* New York: Int. Univ. Press, 1950, 213–239.

Fleming, J. (1975). Some observations on object constancy in the psychoanalysis of adults. *J. Amer. Psychoanal. Assn.* 23:743–759.

Fraiberg, S. (1969). Libidinal object constancy and mental representation. *Psychoanal. Study Child* 24:9–47.

Freud, A. (1926). Introduction to the technique of the analysis of children. In A. Freud, *The Psychoanalytical Treatment of Children.* New York: Int. Univ. Press, 1946, 3–52.

——— (1936). The ego and the mechanisms of defense. *The Writings of Anna Freud (W)* New York: Int. Univ. Press, 2.

——— (1951). Observations on child development. *Psychoanal. Study Child* 6:18–30.

——— (1956). The assessment of borderline cases. *W.* 5:301–314.

——— (1960). Four lectures on the psychoanalytic study of the child. Papers read to the New York Psychoanalytic Society.

——— (1963). The concept of developmental lines. *Psychoanal. Study Child* 18:245–265.

——— (1965). *Normality and Pathology in Childhood.* New York: Int. Univ. Press.

——— (1970). The symptomatology of childhood. *Psychoanal. Study Child* 25:19–41.

Freud, S. (1897). *The Origins of Psychoanalysis.* (Letter 69). New York: Basic Books, 1954.

——— (1900). The interpretation of dreams. *The Complete Psychological Works: Standard Edition (S.E.)* New York: Norton. 4, 5.

——— (1905). Three essays on the theory of sexuality. *S.E.* 7:135–243.

——— (1908). Character and anal eroticism. *S.E.* 9:169–175.

——— (1911). Formulations on the two principles of mental functioning. *S.E.* 12:218–226.

—— (1912). Recommendations to physicians practicing psychoanalysis. *S.E.* 12:111–120.

—— (1913a). Totem and taboo. *S.E.* 13:1–161.

—— (1913b). On beginning the treatment. *S.E.* 12:123–144.

—— (1914a). On narcissism: An introduction. *S.E.* 14:73–102.

—— (1914b). Remembering, repeating, and working through. *S.E.* 12:147–156.

—— (1914c). On the history of the psychoanalytic movement. *S.E.* 14:7–66.

—— (1915). Instincts and their vicissitudes. *S.E.* 14:117–140.

—— (1916). Some character types met with in psychoanalytic work. *S.E.* 14:311–333.

—— (1919). Lines of advance in psychoanalytic therapy. *S.E.* 18:159–168.

—— (1920a). The psychogenesis of a case of homosexuality in a woman. *S.E.* 18:147–172.

—— (1920b). Beyond the pleasure principle. *S.E.* 18:7–64.

—— (1921). Group psychology and the analysis of the ego. *S.E.* 18:69–143.

—— (1923). The ego and the id. *S.E.* 19:12–66.

—— (1924). The loss of reality in neurosis and psychosis. *S.E.* 19:183–187.

—— (1926). Inhibitions, symptoms, and anxiety. *S.E.* 20:87–172.

—— (1927). Fetishism. *S.E.* 21:152–157.

—— (1930). Civilization and its discontents. *S.E.* 21:64–145.

—— (1933). New introductory lectures on psychoanalysis. *S.E.* 22:5–182.

—— (1936). A disturbance of memory on the Acropolis. *S.E.* 22:239–248.

—— (1937a). Analysis terminable and interminable. *S.E.* 23:216–253.

—— (1937b). Constructions in analysis. *S.E.* 23:257–269.

Fromm-Reichmann, F. (1950). *Principles of Intensive Psychotherapy.* Chicago: Univ. of Chicago Press.

—— (1959). *Psychoanalysis and Psychotherapy.* Chicago: Univ. of Chicago Press.

Gedo, J. E. (1979). *Beyond Interpretation.* New York: Int. Univ. Press.

——, and Goldberg, A. (1976). *Models of the Mind: A Psychoanalytic Theory.* Chicago: Univ. of Chicago Press.

Gill, M. M. (1963). Topography and systems in psychoanalytic theory. *Psychol. Issues,* Monogr. 10. New York: Int. Univ. Press.

—— (1965). Personal communication.

—— (1979). The analysis of the transference. *J. Amer. Psychoanal. Assn.* 27 (Suppl.):263–288.

—— (1983). The interpersonal paradigm and the degree of the therapist's involvement. *Contemp. Psychoanal.* 19:200–237.

Glover, E. (1931). The therapeutic effect of inexact interpretation. *Int. J. Psychoanal.* 12:397–412.

Greenacre, P. (1941). The predisposition to anxiety. *Psychoanal. Q.* 10:66–94.

—— (1958). Toward an understanding of the physical nuclei of some defence reactions. *Int. J. Psychoanal.* 39:69–76.

Greenson, R. R. (1967). *The Technique and Practice of Psychoanalysis,* vol. 1. New York: Int. Univ. Press.

Group for the Advancement of Psychiatry (1966). *Psychopathological Disorders in Children.* New York: G.A.P. Publications.

Grunebaum, M. G., Hurwitz, I., Prentice, N. M., and Sperry, B. M. (1962). Fathers of sons with primary neurotic learning inhibitions. *Amer. J. Orthopsychiat.* 32:462–472.

Harrison, S. I., and McDermott, J. F., eds. (1972). *Childhood Psychopathology.* New York: Int. Univ. Press.

Hartmann, H. (1939). *Ego Psychology and the Problem of Adaptation*. New York: Int. Univ. Press, 1958.

—— (1950). Comments on the psychoanalytic theory of the ego. *Psychoanal. Study Child* 5:74–96.

—— (1952). The mutual influences in the development of ego and id. *Psychoanal. Study Child* 7:9–30.

—— (1955). Notes on the theory of sublimation. *Psychoanal. Study Child* 10:9–29.

—— (1964). *Essays on Ego Psychology* New York: Int. Univ. Press.

Hendrick, I. (1942). Instinct and the ego during infancy. *Psychoanal. Q.* 11:33–58.

Holt, R. R. (1963). Two influences on Freud's scientific thought: A fragment of intellectual biography. In *The Study of Lives*, ed. R. W. White. New York: Atherton, 364–387.

—— (1967). The development of the primary process: A structural view. In *Motives and Thought, Psychol. Issues*, Monogr. 18/19. New York: Int. Univ. Press, 344–376.

—— (1972). Freud's mechanistic and humanistic images of man. *Psychoanal. Contemp. Science* 1:3–24.

Jacobson, E. (1964). *The Self and the Object World*. New York: Int. Univ. Press.

Johnson, A. M. (1949). Sanctions for superego lacunae of adolescents. In *Searchlights on Delinquency*, ed. K. R. Eissler. New York: Int. Univ. Press, 225–245.

Jones, E. (1953). *The Life and Work of Sigmund Freud*, vol. 1. New York: Basic Books.

Kanner, L. (1942). Autistic disturbances of affective contact. *Nerv. Child* 2:217–250.

—— (1949). Problems of nosology and psychodynamics of early infantile autism. *Amer. J. Orthopsychiat.* 19:416–426.

——, and Lesser, L. I. (1958). Early infantile autism. *Pediatric Clinics North Amer.* 5:711–730.

Kaplan, L. (1972). Object constancy in the light of Piaget's "vertical décalage." *Bull. Menninger Clinic* 36:322–334.

Katan, A. (1961). Some thoughts about the role of verbalization in early childhood. *Psychoanal. Study Child* 16:184–188.

Kernberg, O. (1966). Structural derivations of object relationships. *Int. J. Psychoanal.* 47:236–253.

—— (1967). Borderline personality organization. *J. Amer. Psychoanal. Assn.* 15:641–685.

—— (1968). The treatment of patients with borderline personality organization. *Int. J. Psychoanal.* 49:600–619.

—— (1975). *Borderline Conditions and Pathological Narcissism*. New York: Aronson.

—— (1976). *Object Relations Theory and Clinical Psychoanalysis*. New York: Aronson.

Klaus, M. H., Jerrauld, R., Kreger, N. C., McAlpine, W., Steffa, M., and Kennell, J. H. (1972). Maternal attachment: Importance of the first post-partum days. *New England J. Med.* 286:460–463.

——, and Kennell, J. H. (1976). *Maternal-Infant Bonding*. St. Louis: Mosby.

Klein, G. S. (1962). Blindness and isolation. *Psychoanal. Study Child* 17:82–93.

—— (1976). *Psychoanalytic Theory: An Exploration of Essentials*. New York: Int. Univ. Press.

Klein, M. (1921–1945). *Contributions to Psychoanalysis*. London: Hogarth, 1948.

Knight, R. (1953a). Borderline states. *Bull. Menninger Clinic* 17:1–12.

—— (1953b). Management and psychotherapy of the borderline schizophrenic patient. *Bull. Menninger Clinic* 17:139–150.

Kohut, H. (1959). Introspection, empathy, and psychoanalysis. *J. Amer. Psychoanal. Assn.* 7:459–483.

—— (1971). *The Analysis of the Self.* New York: Int. Univ. Press.

—— (1977). *The Restoration of the Self.* New York: Int. Univ. Press.

Kris, E. (1955). Neutralization and sublimation: Notes on young children. *Psychoanal. Study Child* 10:36–47.

—— (1956a). On some vicissitudes of insight in psychoanalysis. In *Selected Papers.* New Haven: Yale Univ. Press, 1975, 252–271.

—— (1956b). The recovery of childhood memories in psychoanalysis. *Psychoanal. Study Child* 11:54–88.

Lester, E. (1977). Discussion of "The Psychological Birth of the Human Infant," Amer. Psychoanal. Assn., Quebec.

Lewin, B. D. (1946). Sleep, the mouth, and the dream screen. *Psychoanal. Q.* 15:419–434.

—— (1954). Sleep, the narcissistic neuroses, and the analytic situation. *Psychoanal. Q.* 23:487–510.

Lichtenstein, H. (1965). Towards a metapsychological definition of the concept of self. *Int. J. Psychoanal.* 46:117–128.

Lindemann, E. (1956). The meaning of crisis in individuals and family living. *Teachers College Record* 57:310–315.

Loevinger, J. (1966). Three principles for a psychoanalytic psychology. *J. Abnorm. Psychol.* 71:432–443.

Loewald, H. W. (1960). On the therapeutic action of psychoanalysis. *Int. J. Psychoanal.* 41:16–33.

—— (1971). Some considerations on repetition and repetition compulsion. *Int. J. Psychoanal.* 52:59–66.

Loewenstein, R. M. (1956). Some remarks on the role of speech in psychoanalytic technique. *Int. J. Psychoanal.* 37:460–468.

—— (1957). Some thoughts on interpretation in the theory and practice of psychoanalysis. *Psychoanal. Study Child* 12:127–150.

Mahler, M. S. (1942). Pseudoimbecility. *Psychoanal. Q.* 11:149–164.

—— (1952). On child psychosis and schizophrenia: Autistic and symbiotic infantile psychoses. *Psychoanal. Study Child* 7:286–305.

—— (1958). Autism and symbiosis: Two extreme disturbances of identity. *Int. J. Psychoanal.* 39:77–83.

—— (1963). Thoughts about development and individuation. *Psychoanal. Study Child* 18:307–324.

—— (1965). On the significance of the normal separation-individuation phase. In *Drives, Affects, and Behavior, 2,* ed. M. Schur. New York: Int. Univ. Press, 161–169.

—— (1966). Notes on the development of basic moods: The depressive affect. In *Psychoanalysis: A General Psychology,* ed. R. M. Loewenstein, L. M. Newman, M. Schur, and A. J. Solnit. New York: Int. Univ. Press, 152–168.

—— (1968). *On Human Symbiosis and the Vicissitudes of Individuation.* New York: Int. Univ. Press.

—— (1972). On the first three subphases of the separation-individuation process. *Int. J. Psychoanal.* 53:333–338.

——, and Furer, M. (1960). Observations on research regarding the symbiotic syndrome of infantile psychosis. *Psychoanal. Q.* 29:317–327.

——, and —— (1972). Child psychosis: A theoretical statement and its implications. *J. Aut. Childhood Schiz.* 2:213–218.

————, Pine, F., and Bergman, A. (1975). *The Psychological Birth of the Human Infant*. New York: Basic Books.

Malone, C. (1966). Some observations on children of disorganized families and problems of acting out. *J. Amer. Acad. Child Psychiat.*, Monogr. 1, 22–41.

Massie, H. N. (1975). The early natural history of childhood psychosis. *J. Amer. Acad. Child Psychiat.* 14:683–707.

Masterson, J. F. (1972). *Treatment of the Borderline Adolescent: A Developmental Approach*. New York: Wiley.

McDevitt, J. B. (1975). Separation-individuation and object constancy. *J. Amer. Psychoanal. Assn.* 23:713–742.

———— (1980). Separation-individuation and aggression. A. A. Brill Memorial Lecture, New York Psychoanalytic Society.

Mittelmann, B. (1954). Motility in infants, children, and adults: Patterning and psychodynamics. *Psychoanal. Study Child* 9:142–177.

Money, J., and Ehrhardt, A. A. (1972). *Man and Woman, Boy and Girl: The Differentiation and Dimorphism of Gender Identity from Conception to Maturity*. Baltimore: Johns Hopkins Univ. Press.

Nagera, H. (1967). The concepts of structure and structuralization. *Psychoanal. Study Child* 22:77–102.

Newman, C. J., Dember, C. F., and Krug, O. (1973). "He can but he won't": A psychodynamic study of so-called "gifted underachievers." *Psychoanal. Study Child* 28:83–130.

Omwacke, E. B., and Solnit, A. J. (1961). "It isn't fair": The treatment of a blind child. *Psychoanal. Study Child* 16:352–404.

Peterfreund, E. (1978). Some critical comments on psychoanalytic conceptualizations of infancy. *Int. J. Psychoanal.* 59:427–441.

———— (1982). *The Process of Psychoanalytic Therapy*. Hillsdale, N.J.: Analytic Press.

Piaget, J. (1930). *The Child's Conception of Physical Causality*. London: Kegan, Paul.

———— (1937). *The Construction of Reality in the Child*. New York: Basic Books, 1954.

———— (1952a). *The Origins of Intelligence in Children*. New York: Int. Univ. Press.

———— (1952b). *The Child's Conception of Number*. New York: Humanities Press.

Pine, F. (1971). On the separation process: Universal trends and individual differences. In *Separation-Individuation*, ed. J. B. McDevitt and C. F. Settlage. New York: Int. Univ. Press, 113–130.

———— (1979). On the expansion of the affect array: A developmental description. *Bull. Menninger Clinic* 43:79–95.

Pine, R. (1978). The First Child. Undergraduate honors thesis, Wesleyan Univ., Middletown, Conn.

Proust, M. (1918). *Remembrance of Things Past: Swann's Way*. New York: Modern Library, 1928.

Provence, S., and Lipton, R. (1962). *Infants in Institutions*. New York: Int. Univ. Press.

Rapaport, D. (1951). Toward a theory of thinking. In *Organization and Pathology of Thought*, ed. D. Rapaport. New York: Columbia Univ. Press, 689–730.

———— (1953). Some metapsychological considerations regarding activity and passivity. In *The Collected Papers of David Rapaport*, ed. M. M. Gill. New York: Basic Books, 1967, 530–568.

———— (1957). The theory of ego autonomy: A generalization. In *The Collected Papers of David Rapaport*, ed. M. M. Gill. New York: Basic Books, 1967, 722–744.

———— (1960a). On the psychoanalytic theory of motivation. In *Nebraska Symposium on Motivation*, ed. M. R. Jones. Lincoln: Univ. of Nebraska Press, 173–247.

——— (1960b). The structure of psychoanalytic theory. *Psychol. Issues*, Monogr. 6. New York: Int. Univ. Press.

———, and Gill, M. M. (1959). The points of view and assumptions of metapsychology. *Int. J. Psychoanal.* 40:153–162.

Redl, F. (1951). Ego disturbances. In *Childhood Psychopathology*, ed. S. I. Harrison and J. F. McDermott. New York: Int. Univ. Press, 1972, 532–539.

Reich, A. (1951). On countertransference. In *Psychoanalytic Contributions*. New York: Int. Univ. Press, 1973, 136–154.

Roiphe, H., and Galenson, E. (1982). *Infantile Origins of Sexual Identity*. New York: Int. Univ. Press.

Rosenfeld, S., and Sprince, M. P. (1963). An attempt to formulate the meaning of the concept "borderline." *Psychoanal. Study Child* 18:603–635.

———, and ——— (1965). Some thoughts on the technical handling of borderline children. *Psychoanal. Study Child* 20:495–517.

Rubinstein, B. (1974). On the role of classificatory processes in mental functioning: Aspects of a psychoanalytic theoretical model. *Psychoanal. Contemp. Science* 4:101–185.

Rutter, M., and Bartak, L. (1971). Causes of infantile autism. *J. Autism. Child Schiz.* 1:20–32.

Sander, L. W. (1977). Regulation of exchange in the infant-caretaker system: A viewpoint on the ontogeny of "structures." In *Communicative Structures and Psychic Structures*, ed. N. Freedman and S. Grand. New York: Plenum Press, 13–34.

Sandler, J. (1960). The background of safety. *Int. J. Psychoanal.* 41:352–356.

———, and Rosenblatt, B. (1962). The concept of the representational world. *Psychoanal. Study Child* 17:128–145.

Schachtel, E. (1947). On memory and childhood amnesia. In *Metamorphoses*. New York: Basic Books, 1959, 279–322.

Schafer, R. (1968). *Aspects of Internalization*. New York: Int. Univ. Press.

——— (1976). *A New Language for Psychoanalysis*. New Haven: Yale Univ. Press.

——— (1978). *Language and Insight*. New Haven: Yale Univ. Press.

——— (1983a). Personal communication.

——— (1983b). *The Analytic Attitude*. New York: Basic Books.

Schecter, D. (1968). Identification and individuation. *J. Amer. Psychoanal. Assn.* 16:48–80.

Schimek, J. (1975). The interpretations of the past: Childhood trauma, psychical reality, and historical truth. *J. Amer. Psychoanal. Assn.* 23:845–865.

Schmale, A. H. (1964). A genetic view of affects: With special reference to the genesis of hopelessness and helplessness. *Psychoanal. Study Child* 19:287–310.

Schur, M. (1966). *The Id and the Regulatory Principles of Mental Functioning*. New York: Int. Univ. Press.

Schwaber, E. (1981). Empathy: A mode of analytic listening. *Psychoanal. Inq.* 1:357–392.

——— (1983). A particular perspective on analytic listening. *Psychoanal. Study Child* 38:519–546.

Settlage, C. F. (1980). Psychoanalytic developmental thinking in current and historical perspective. *Psychoanal. Contemp. Thought* 3:139–170.

Shapiro, D. (1965). *Neurotic Styles*. New York: Basic Books.

Shapiro, T. (1970). Interpretation and naming. *J. Amer. Psychoanal. Assn.* 18:399–421.

—— (1974). The development and distortions of empathy. *Psychoanal. Q.* 43:4–25.

Silverman, L. (1978). Unconscious symbiotic fantasy: A ubiquitous therapeutic agent. *Int. J. Psychoanal. Psychother.* 7:562–585.

Speers, R. W., and Lansing, C. (1965). *Group Therapy in Child Psychosis.* Chapel Hill: Univ. of N. Carolina Press.

Spence, D. P. (1982). *Narrative Truth and Historical Truth: Meaning and Interpretation in Psychoanalysis.* New York: Norton.

Sperry, B. M., Ulrich, D. N., and Stauer, N. (1958). The relation of motility to boys' learning problems. *Amer. J. Orthopsychiat.* 28:640–646.

Spiegel, L. A. (1951). A review of contributions to a psychoanalytic theory of adolescence: Individual aspects. *Psychoanal. Study Child* 6:375–393.

—— (1959). The self, the sense of self, and perception. *Psychoanal. Study Child* 14:81–109.

—— (1966). Affects in relation to self and object: A model for the derivation of desire, longing, pain, anxiety, humiliation, and shame. *Psychoanal. Study Child* 21:69–92.

—— (1979). Moral masochism, unconscious guilt, and punishment dreams examined in relation to ego adaptation and success: Implications for the concept of the superego. Presented to the New York Psychoanalytic Society.

Spitz, R. (1945). Hospitalism: An inquiry into the genesis of psychiatric conditions in early childhood. *Psychoanal. Study Child* 1:53–72.

—— (1946). Anaclitic depression. *Psychoanal. Study Child* 2:313–342.

—— (1957). *No and Yes.* New York: Int. Univ. Press.

—— (1959). *A Genetic Field Theory of Ego Formation.* New York: Int. Univ. Press.

Stamm, J. L. (1962). Altered ego states allied to depersonalization. *J. Amer. Psychoanal. Assn.* 10:762–783.

Stein, M. H. (1967). The analysis of character. Presented to the New York Psychoanalytic Society.

Stern, D. N. (1971). A micro-analysis of mother-infant interaction. *J. Amer. Acad. Child Psychiat.* 10:501–517.

—— (1977). *The First Relationship.* Cambridge, Mass.: Harvard Univ. Press.

—— (1983). Infancy research and its relation to clinical theory. Presented at New York University Postdoctoral Program, October.

Stewart, W. (1963). An inquiry into the concept of working through. *J. Amer. Psychoanal. Assn.* 11:474–499.

Stoller, R. J. (1968). *Sex and Gender: On the Development of Masculinity and Feminity.* New York: Science House.

Stone, J., and Church, J. (1973). *Childhood and Adolescence.* New York: Random House.

Stone, L. (1954). The widening scope of indications for psychoanalysis. *J. Amer. Psychoanal. Assn.* 2:567–594.

—— (1961). *The Psychoanalytic Situation.* New York: Int. Univ. Press.

Stone, L. J., Smith, H. T., and Murphy, L. B. (1973). *The Competent Infant: Research and Commentary.* New York: Basic Books.

Strachey, J. (1934). The nature of the therapeutic action of psychoanalysis. *Int. J. Psychoanal.* 15:127–159.

Strupp, H. H. (1973). Toward a reformulation of the psychotherapeutic influence. *Int. J. Psychiat.* 11:263–327.

Sullivan, H. S. (1940). *Conceptions of Modern Psychiatry.* New York: Norton.

———— (1953). *The Interpersonal Theory of Psychiatry*. New York: Norton.

Tolpin, M. (1971). On the beginnings of a cohesive self: An application of the concept of transmuting internalization to the study of the transitional object and signal anxiety. *Psychoanal. Study Child* 26:316–352.

Waelder, R. (1936). The principle of multiple function: Observations on overdetermination. *Psychoanal. Q.* 5:45–62.

———— (1960). *Basic Theory of Psychoanalysis*. New York: Int. Univ. Press.

Wallerstein, R. S. (1973). Psychoanalytic perspectives on the problem of reality. *J. Amer. Psychoanal. Assn.* 21:5–33.

———— (1981). The bipolar self: Discussion of alternative perspectives. *J. Amer. Psychoanal. Assn.* 29:377–394.

———— (1983a). Reality and its attributes as psychoanalytic concepts: An historical overview. *Int. Rev. Psychoanal.* 10:125–144.

———— (1983b). Self psychology and "classical" psychoanalytic psychology: The nature of their relationship. *Psychoanal. Contemp. Thought* 6:553–595.

Webster's New Collegiate Dictionary (1971). Springfield, Mass: G. & C. Merriam.

Weil, A. (1953). Certain severe disturbances of ego development in childhood. *Psychoanal. Study Child* 8:271–287.

———— (1956). Certain evidences of deviational development in infancy and early childhood. *Psychoanal. Study Child* 11:292–299.

Weiss, J. (1966). Clinical and theoretical aspects of "as if" character. *J. Amer. Psychoanal. Assn.* 14:569–590.

White, R. W. (1963). Ego and reality in psychoanalytic theory: A proposal regarding independent ego energies. *Psychol. Issues*, Monogr. 11. New York: Int. Univ. Press.

Winnicott, D. W. (1955). Metapsychological and clinical aspects of regression within the psychoanalytic set-up. In *Collected Papers*, New York: Basic Books, 1958, 278–294.

———— (1956). Primary maternal preoccupation. In *Collected Papers*. New York: Basic Books, 1958, 300–305.

———— (1958a). *Collected Papers*. New York: Basic Books.

———— (1958b). The capacity to be alone. In *The Maturational Processes and the Facilitating Environment*. New York: Int. Univ. Press, 1965, 29–36.

———— (1960a). Ego distortion in terms of true and false self. In *The Maturational Processes and the Facilitating Environment*. New York: Int. Univ. Press, 1965, 140–152.

———— (1960b). The theory of the parent-infant relationship. In *The Maturational Processes and the Facilitating Environment*. New York: Int. Univ. Press, 1965, 37–55.

———— (1963a). Psychiatric disorders in terms of infantile mental processes. In *The Maturational Processes and the Facilitating Environment*. New York: Int. Univ. Press, 1965, 230–241.

———— (1963b). The development of the capacity for concern. In *The Maturational Processes and the Facilitating Environment*. New York: Int. Univ. Press, 1965, 73–82.

———— (1963c). From dependence towards independence in the development of the individual. In *The Maturational Processes and the Facilitating Environment*. New York: Int. Univ. Press, 1965, 83–92.

———— (1965). *The Maturational Processes and the Facilitating Environment*. New York: Int. Univ. Press.

———— (1971a). *Playing and Reality*. New York: Basic Books.

———— (1971b). *Therapeutic Consultations in Child Psychiatry*. New York: Basic Books.

Wolfenstein, M. (1966). How is mourning possible? *Psychoanal. Study Child* 21:93–123.

———— (1969). Loss, rage, and repetition. *Psychoanal. Study Child* 24:432–460.

Wolff, P. H. (1959). Observations on newborn infants. *Psychosomatic Med.* 21:110–118.

Youngerman, J. K. (1979). The syntax of silence: Electively mute therapy. *Int. Rev. Psychoanal.* 6:283–295.

Index